RUBY R. LEAVITT

NOMADS AND EMPIRE BUILDERS

Native Peoples and Cultures of
South America

By Carleton Beals

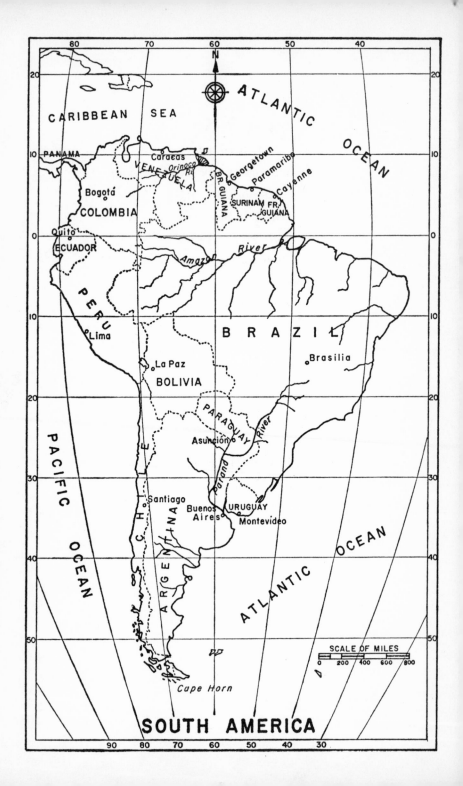

NOMADS AND EMPIRE BUILDERS

Native Peoples and Cultures of South America

CARLETON BEALS

THE CITADEL PRESS
NEW YORK

FIRST PAPERBOUND EDITION, 1965

Copyright © 1961 by Carleton Beals. All rights reserved.
Library of Congress Catalog Card Number 61-13158. Manufactured
in the United States of America. Designed by William E. Lickfield.
Published by The Citadel Press, 222 Park Avenue South, New York 3, N. Y.

Foreword

A PREFACE is always a postscript, written after the arduous effort of research and writing has been completed and the manuscript is on the way to the printer's. But the basic ideas set forth in a Preface almost invariably were imbedded in the mind of the author before he started, or the work would likely never have been undertaken.

In the case of this volume, some of those ideas represent a lifetime of thought, experience, and research, an abiding interest that has endured over many years. When this interest was actually generated, I cannot say. Perhaps when as a young man I lived among the Maya and Tarahumara of northern Mexico. Later on I spent much time with the Mixteca and Zapoteca of southeast Mexico. These multiple experiences and others have been touched upon in half a dozen of my books and miscellaneous writings. One result was the preparation of a comprehensive account of Aztec myths on which I have been working off and on for thirty years.

My interest in this field goes far deeper than the material itself. Over the years increasingly I have felt a great vacuum in the concepts and presentation of American history. The effort to link our cultural origins almost wholly to Europe, however inevitable and important that may be, has had the curious result of somehow preventing us from really becoming integrated with the American earth that nourishes us, for in slighting other important cultural origins from Africa, Asia, the Americas themselves, we sever many important roots; we deny ourselves a true knowledge of our past and hence a due understanding of the present, and we also deprive ourselves of proper enjoyment of the vast and intricate richness of our heritage. All this, though it would take a whole volume to explain, has more to do with our ability to survive in the storm of this atomic age than is readily apparent.

Quite apart from the fascination of the peoples of the New World prior to the European conquest, we owe more to them than is customarily appreciated; they are part of our own history and origins, and awareness of this is essential for our proper integration with the continent in which we live.

In North America, the historical hiatus between the two worlds was greater than in South America, where the break was not so brutal or profound, where the native cultures have had far greater influence on present-day customs, food, legal practices, land tenure, dress, marriage, art, and philosophy and where many millions of people still speak the ancient tongues and live the ancient ways little changed after so many centuries of alien rule. Knowledge of some of these things should be part of our intellectual heritage, and even though they may be unknown to the politicians who shape our destinies, they have sufficient bearing on present-day events to be a considerable factor in the success or failure of any good-neighbor efforts.

But quite apart from any such highfalutin notions which writers like to set forth as reasons for writing a given book, the simple truth is, I'm deeply interested in the early peoples of the Americas, their origins and their mode of living—from the most primitive on up to those remarkable peoples who built the Inca and Maya and Aztec empires. All told, their history represents a heroic, noble, and dramatic aspect of man's long struggle out of the mist of his troglodyte past toward the mastery of his environment, his endless sorrowful and also joyous struggle for material and spiritual greatness. And for me the Indians, past and present, are among the more creative and lovable of God's creatures.

Much has been written about the early peoples of South America, particularly about the Inca empire, but there has been no satisfactory account of the peoples of the entire continent. I began this book in order to fill in many of the gaps in my own knowledge, and then went on with the hope that it might prove helpful and exciting to others as well. That I have succeeded in my major purpose is most likely doubtful, but perhaps it contains enough to provide knowledge and enjoyment, perhaps also to stimulate others to go on to penetrate further into that fantastic and splendid world out of which has emerged so much of what we call America.

CARLETON BEALS

Mexico City
(En route to the Amazon and the jungles of
northern Brazil and the Guianas)

Contents

NOMADS AND EMPIRE BUILDERS

Native Peoples and Cultures of
South America

1

"God, Gold, and Glory"

THE first written account of New World peoples, so far as is known, was provided by Columbus—Cristóbal Colón—in his *Relaciones* of his perilous voyage of discovery in 1492. Very likely, crossings had been made before the "Admiral" scribbled the first record of American history via the Atlantic, the Pacific, the Bering Straits, the Polynesian Islands, and Antarctica. In more modern times, certainly Irishmen, Norsemen, and others had traversed the north Atlantic from A.D. 900 on, and Portuguese mariners may have been venturing across the south Atlantic since the early fifteenth century. But Columbus was the first vocal discoverer.

For seventy days out of Palos, Spain, the Admiral and his men peered anxiously through the long watches of day and night across the unknown western sea. At last, land birds, floating branches, and flowers—finally a light through the night and the glad cry of *"Tierra! Tierra!"*

He pulled his three small vessels—*Santa María, Pinta,* and *Niña*—to anchor off Guanahani Island (perhaps San Salvador or Watling Island in the Bahamas), and at dawn on October 12 with his two captains, he landed, richly attired, and planted the red and yellow Spanish standard and the two Green-Cross banners of their Most Catholic Majesties. Thereby two mighty continents previously in the darkness of isolation were forever linked together.

The naked folk he found were Tainos, a branch of the great Arawak family of peoples that stretched through the Amazons, northern South America, and much of the West Indies, perhaps lower Florida, too. He gave them "red caps and strings of glass beads and many other things of little value, which pleased them greatly." Swimming out to the vessels, they brought gifts in return: "parrots, balls of cotton thread, javelins and many things too tedious to mention. They were well built with handsome bodies and fine faces and large beautiful eyes . . . straight even legs and flat well-formed stomachs." Their coarse hair, "like silken horses' tails," hung in bangs to their eyebrows, "and was cut short behind, though a few wore it long and free-flowing." Some were as light skinned as any people in Spain, but nearly all painted their bodies "the same dark color as the Canary Islanders; some white or red or whatever color they found; others painted only their faces and noses."

The Tainos carried no weapons and knew nothing about iron. Their wooden javelins were "pointed with a fish-tooth or other similar things."

He marveled particularly at their well-made carved boats—canoes they called them, an Arawak word—the first "American" word ever to be recorded in print.

Each was hollowed from a tree trunk, small ones for a single paddler, others large enough to carry forty-five persons, propelled with great speed "by a baker's style paddle." If overturned, they were easily righted and bailed out with hollow gourds.

The Tainos' friendliness made the Admiral believe they could more easily be converted "to our Holy Faith, by love rather than by force." For he was an extremely devout man who kept all the fasts and confessed frequently. Throughout his *Relaciones,* his pious phrases have the flavor of the religious nationalistic crusade which had driven the Moors out of the Peninsula and which was now launched on the conquest of the greatest empire yet known to man— much of Europe and the larger part of the New World.

The Admiral was chiefly interested in the gold nose pendants he saw. By signs he learned that the gold came from a large island to the south where a king had "whole vessels of gold, and much gold," likely from Cipangu (perhaps Japan) off the Asiatic Coast, described by Marco Polo as being rich in spices and gold.

"I must reach there quickly," Columbus wrote, "this San Salvador seems 'poor in everything' "—and he promptly sailed toward the golden horizon.

A man greedy for gold is ill-equipped to understand alien peoples.

The Admiral's over-pious missionary approach also made him partly blind to the spiritual wealth of the new lands. God, gold, and glory were the moving forces of the Spanish drive of discovery and conquest. And the third element—glory—the chief integrants of which are power and fame—is scarcely a tool of truth or scientific anthropology.

But the Admiral, a man of extraordinary vision and rectitude, believed strongly in truth, and if his observations were superficial, and his provincial conclusions often erroneous, his descriptions are vivid and mostly accurate. He had considerable knowledge of botany and was deeply impressed by the lush beauty of the vegetation. They stopped at island after island, glowing with color, rampant with flowers and fruits, the shores lined with snow-white palms above calm purple waters. On the first islands he found no animals except parrots, lizards, and one big snake, but presently came upon what must have been an iguana, a Taino-Arawak word, later used by Amerigo Vespucci, the skin of which Columbus ordered cured to show their Majesties. Elsewhere the explorers found large mastiff dogs and, toward the end of the month, small barkless dogs—that was after they sailed into beautiful Nipe Bay in eastern Cuba (Cipangu) and began exploring the coast.

Here the Admiral was entranced by the scenery, "the most beautiful ever seen," dense with trees, flowers, fruits, singing birds, many palms, "the huge leaves of which were used to roof their houses." The grass was "as high as in Andalusia in the spring time"; there were purslanes, amaranths, thistles, sugar beets, yams, rhubarb, pokeweeds. On the islands were many *linaloas,* from which essential oils and perfumes could be extracted. "I'm having ten quintales brought aboard," wrote Columbus, "for they tell me it is very valuable."

Explorers sent ashore found many wonders; cotton growing on trees, which was carded and woven. In one house they saw "more than five hundred *arrobas,*" or more than six tons, and estimated that the yearly turnover in this one dwelling was possibly nearly a quarter million tons. They found *mamés* or yams, tasting like chestnuts, many kinds of beans, and balsam or aromatic resin.

Above all, they marveled at the cleanliness of the houses, the clay statuettes of women and the elaborate fiesta masks, the finely made fish nets and spears, but especially at the beds (*hamacas,* another Arawak word), cotton nets, "made with a kind of slip-knot, the cords

3

not criss-cross but loosely joined a hand-thickness apart along their lengths . . . the ends . . . looped . . . for attaching them to house-posts, so they hang freely . . . and swing in the air. . . . One can sleep peacefully in them." And so the hammock, invented by the Arawaks, most likely in Brazil, became standard shipboard equipment down through the centuries, and, like "canoe," the word became part of mankind's universal vocabulary. Later explorers in the Guianas came upon hammocks so finely made they could be rolled up and pulled through a signet ring—something only modern techniques could rival.

Except for a few nose and ear ornaments, no gold was visible. "*Nucay* . . . *Nucay* . . . *Nucay?*—Gold, gold, gold?" the Admiral kept asking everywhere up and down the coast. A ruler three days inland was said to have much *nucay;* Columbus took him to be the Grand Khan of Cathay and sent Rodrigo de Jerez and the Jew Luís de Torres (since he spoke Hebrew, Chaldean, and Arabic and perhaps could communicate better) and two shanghaied Taino Indians, to interview him.

Others continued to explore closer at hand. The *Pinta's* captain, Martín Alonzo Pínzón, found cinnamon, pepper, and red objects like nuts, heard many tales of gold and pearls, how on Babeque Island gold was sieved off the beach at night and melted into bars or objects.

The Admiral went ashore to confirm all this. The Indians told him about one-eyed men and dog-snout men in the interior, who cut human throats, drank human blood, castrated them and ate their flesh. The Admiral promptly went back on board to wait for his messengers to return.

These ferocious mystery men were very likely Canibs or Caribs (an Arawak word meaning "brave")—cannibals who had followed on the heels of the Arawaks out of the great Amazon mishmash of peoples, had started to overrun the whole of the Greater Antilles, and were already in southern Cuba. In Española he heard other terrible stories about them. One man lacking pieces of flesh said the Caribs had chewed them out. The Admiral was skeptical, commendably so, since no Caribs had yet reached Española. As he went along, he heard other strange legends, the "island of women" not a single man—perhaps Martinique—where there was "an infinite amount of gold."

The messengers returned, unsuccessful in finding the Grand Khan; but some forty miles inland, they had come on a large town of fifty houses (perhaps Bayamo in southwest Oriente Province) with a thousand inhabitants, for many families lived in each large dwelling. The people were very hospitable, gave liberally of their food, and both men and women kissed the Spaniards' hands and feet, "to see if they were really flesh and blood." Five hundred men and women followed them back to the boats, believing they were divine emissaries returning to heaven.

Columbus noted that the women wore "a cotton thing just large enough to cover their 'nature' and no bigger." Their chief, his son, and two attendants came aboard the *Santa María* to talk to the Admiral. But by morning all had vanished, perhaps on second thought preferring Cuba to a trip to heaven.

The messengers' most interesting report was about a dried aromatic herb, "which was rolled up in a certain leaf, also dried, like a musket made of paper, such as children make for Easter or Holy Saints' Day; lit at one end, the other is sucked, the smoke imbibed or inhaled, so their flesh is numbed and they become almost drunk, and in this way they feel no tiredness"—a complicated way of describing a cigar and its effects. Columbus wanted only gold and spices, yet here was a product that over the centuries would provide more profit than all the gold of the Indies, and the best *Tobaco* (a Tupi-Taino word) in all the world was in Cuba.

The Indians here and in Española brought them bread, made of yucca, yams, and various tubers; the flesh of big rats (the famed succulent *hutias* of Cuba), huge crabs, shrimps, and turtles. There were whales and many kinds of fish: some like multicolored roosters, "painted with designs in a thousand ways"; one like a pig was hard shelled, soft only at the ends, and the Admiral salted one to take to their Majesties. The snails were enormous but tasteless. He cut specimens of shiny mica from under water in the Teja River, and in Oriente marveled at the well-tilled fields and the great Moa mountains with forests of oak, madroño, and pines.

Here people spoke a different dialect and some wore elaborate headdresses. They had unusually beautiful boats, with palm-leaf ramadas for shade, and grew calabashes that were "a glory to see."

In one village he found human heads in covered baskets, hung from the posts in each big house, ancestor worship he judged, the

5

families in each menage probably of the same lineage. A big house with two doors and "hung with snail-shells and other things," he took to be a temple.

Tortuga (Turtle) Island and Española were densely populated, everywhere cultivated so they looked "like the wheat fields of Córdoba in May," the air was "like that of April in Castilla" and, as the nightingale there, the mocking birds sang here—"the sweetest sound there is." There were large, well-kept towns and houses, and the people had gold in noses and ears, which they gave him with good will. He traded for hammered gold and gold dust and lumps of gold and golden crowns and gold masks, one with big ears, tongues, and nose of hammered gold.

People came running to him with lumps of gold and asking for *chuq chuq*, imitating the sound of bells, "which they were crazy to have." One gold mask was brought in by the chief himself, for he wanted a wash basin and pitcher he had seen. Gold hereabouts was called *"tuob,"* farther along the coast *"caoana,"* words constantly on the Admiral's tongue. In Española, the chiefs hung gold about his neck and put gold upon his head, and told about gold mines and other lands with vast quantities of gold.

There were no better, kinder people on earth, and "in all Spain there was no land that compared with this in beauty and goodness."

The more gold he obtained anywhere, the more lyrical he became about the goodness and comeliness of the people and the splendor of the landscape. And each time he obtained gold by trading or as a gift, the Admiral turned away from the hundreds of canoes following the boats, and the hosts of people swimming in the sea sometimes eight miles out, and went into his chapel and knelt, bidding those with him to do likewise, and gave thanks to God "for making me worthy of receiving this great wealth."

So was the curtain first raised for Europe on New World marvels and New World peoples.

2

On Columbus' later trip to the mainland, his third, he sailed off Venezuela through turbulent Boca del Serpiente—Serpent's Mouth —in the Gulf of Paria, beyond Trinidad, which he described "as beautiful and green as the orchards of Valencia." In August, 1498, he saw deer with "a hoof like a goat's"; at one point a canoe with 24 men ventured out, well armed with bows, arrows, and small wooden shield—"whiter skinned" than others he had seen in the Indies, of "very fine appearance, with handsome bodies, long smooth hair, cut in Castilian fashion, on their heads cotton kerchiefs of colors and designs," which he believed to be a religious headdress. The Indians were cautious, and, to attract them, he held aloft "basins and other shiny things" and set sailors dancing to pounded drums on the deck, "in the hopes the natives would be glad to see the fiesta." To the Indians, however, this meant one thing—a war dance—and they shot arrows and withdrew.

The Admiral still believed that Cuba and these shores were part of the Asiatic mainland. But as other explorers—Spanish and Portuguese in the south, Dutch, French and English explorers to the north —traced the actual dimensions, the truth became known. Soon maps became out of date almost as soon as they were published. Duarte Pacheco Pereira (1498), Alonso de Ojeda and Juan de la Cosa (1499), Vicente Yañez Pinzón, Diego de Lepe, Rodrigo de Galván Bastidas, Vélez de Mendoza (all three 1500), crept along the coasts of Central or South America. Cristóbal Guerra, his four ships and crews, were lost. Yañez raised the cross of possession at Rostro Hermoso (Beautiful Face), 8° south. Lepe went up the Amazon nearly 300 miles. Others discovered the Orinoco and Magdalena Rivers. Also, in 1500, Pedro Alvarez Cabral, driven off his African course, landed in Brazil. In 1501–1502, Gonçalo Coelho reached 23° south, or—according to "Astronomer" Vespucci, who claimed to have gone on this voyage— 52° south. They also discovered the "giants" of Curaçao. Manuel Nuño saw South America in 1502 and may have put in at the Plata River.

Juan de la Cosa (who had been with Bastidas), voyaged again in 1504 to Cartagena, Colombia. Juan Díaz de Solís followed in 1508, was killed in Argentina seven years later. Alejo García sailed in 1525; Sebastián Caboto in 1526.

By then Vasco Nuñez de Balboa had crossed the Isthmus of Panama and gazed upon the Pacific from a peak in Darién. Presently Jiménez de Quesada climbed up into the Chibcha realm on the lofty Andean plateau. Francisco Pizarro toppled the Inca empire; Diego Almagro and Sebastian Benalcazar fought their way up to Quito, Ecuador. Almagro and, later, the audacious Pedro de Valdivia, struggled down over the Andes and fought the mighty Mapuches and Auraucanians of Chile. As early as 1520, Fernando Magellan (Magalhães) sailed along Patagonia and through the Straits of Magellan, discovering the giant Big Feet people, the Patagones.

Turn back to Amerigo Vespucci. It was Emerson who lamented that "broad *America* must wear the name of a thief," for Vespucci, some authorities believe, did not take part in several voyages he wrote about, and likely did not see some parts of South America he claimed to have seen. Often the dispute about this waxes as hot as that over the authorship of Shakespeare's plays. In any event it is fortunate his first name was chosen to designate the New World; it is hard to conceive that otherwise we might be calling ourselves "Vespuccians" and keeping our courage up by singing "Vespuccia, the beautiful."

Certainly various passages in his accounts are cribbed from Columbus and other explorers, and his story of cannibalism in Brazil is almost identical with an incident described by Cabral. His tales are obscure, contradictory, pedantic, and frequently more concerned with the stars than land or people, yet his astronomical findings and distances are frequently inaccurate. He rarely put down when or where he saw things.

Some years ago, Stefan Zweig sought to rule out Amerigo's discrepancies by branding several accounts as forgeries—something which Zweig cribbed from the 1926 writer Magnaghi, already roundly refuted, and even more extensively by Argentinean Roberto Levellier in 1951, who introduced new pipe-dreams into the picture.

Vespucci had quick access to all the latest reports and to the New World plants, animals, and people brought to Spain and Portugal. A Florentine banker of a distinguished but bankrupt family, employed by Lorenzo de Medici, he was sent to a powerful commercial house in Sevilla (later to Lisbon), which financed numbers of New World expeditions, including Columbus' third voyage.

By the time of Vespucci's more detailed and gaudy 1504 *Letrera,* which contradicted many things he had said earlier, the world he described had been covered by many other navigators. It was contributory to Amerigo's fame that a German map maker put his name on the New World land maps in his latest publication, and this was repeated in a map drawn by Leonardo da Vinci in 1514. But whether Amerigo did all the things he claimed to have done or not—nowhere does his name appear in either the Sevilla or Lisbon archives—his accounts came from authentic sources.

In his vague way of never identifying place or time, he writes in his *Fragmento:* "When I went on discovery for the King of Castilla, we found ourselves in a land [probably Venezuela] where we got 119 marks of pearls valued at 15,000 ducats in Castilla, and do not imagine they cost us the value of ten. And I myself, for a sheep-bell I gave an Indian, got 157 pearls, which were worth a thousand ducats, and do not think he considered it a bad bargain because the minute he had the bell, he put it in his mouth and went off through the forest . . . afraid I might regret the sale." (This is reminiscent of an episode in the *Cid*.)

Strangely, though he claims he rowed up the Amazon for seventy miles (later he reported that the Brazilian coast was more densely populated than Europe), he saw no living person, except for some fishermen downstream on his return. His account, written July 1500, follows the *Capitulación* of Pinzón, who described the river and the fresh water surging many leagues out to sea. Lepe's account may also have been at hand. Many other tales were available by the time Vespucci recapitulated his adventures extensively in 1504.

His accounts of the natives on his alleged third expedition probably refer to the coastal Indians, the Tupinamba (recent conquerors of that area), and correspond to the prior impressions of Cabral. Despite their meagerness, Amerigo's descriptions are largely borne out by the remarkable observations a few years later by the German, Hans Staden, who lived among the tribes.

"First then as to the people," writes Amerigo, "such a multitude that it would be impossible for anybody to count them, as is told about in the Apocalypse, people, dignified, gentle and amenable." All went stark naked, men and women. He fails to mention their elaborate feather headdresses, their girdles, their capes, or the elaborate painting of their bodies as described by Staden. "They had large strong physiques, well-formed and proportioned, their color verging on red, abundant black hair; were agile when walking or at play, and had beautiful faces which they themselves mutilated. For they perforate the cheeks and lips and noses and ears; and do not imagine those openings are small or that they have only one; for I have seen many who have seven perforations in the face alone, each the size of a plum; and they fill up those holes with blue stones; beautiful crystalline and alabaster marble, snow-white bones and other elaborately fabricated things according to their customs." It was "monstrous" to see a man with seven stones in his cheeks and lips, "many of them four inches wide" and weighing perhaps 16 ounces, "without counting the stones hanging from three rings from as many openings in each ear."

"Their weapons," reported Vespucci, "are the bow and arrow; and when they meet in battle they do not cover any part of the body to defend themselves, so that even in this they are like animals. . . ."

Actually they used also an oval-blade club with sharp edges and tapir-hide shields, and they built excellent palisade trenches.

"They love to fish, and the sea there is very fine for fishing, for every species of fish is superabundant. They are not hunters, for there are many kinds of wild animals, especially lions and bears and innumerable serpents and horrible and malformed beasts, also enormous forests and trees of vast girth, so they do not venture to expose themselves naked, without defense or arms to so many dangers." Later accounts reveal that they did a great deal of hunting.

He described their cannibalism. "A father has been known to have eaten his children and wife; and one man I talked with was said to have eaten three hundred human bodies. I even stayed 27 days in a certain city where I saw in the houses, salted human flesh hung up from the rafters, just as we string up bacon and pork." (Or were they the bodies of monkeys, which the natives also ate and still do?)

On his third trip, five degrees below the equator, the men went ashore and left gifts for the people who would not approach. (This is the Cabral story.) "The following morning from the ships we saw the people on shore making many smoke signals. Believing they were calling us, we went on land, where a great multitude had gathered. They would not come near, and two men were outfitted with supplies for five days and objects of barter to go among them."

On the seventh day, when they had not returned, the Spaniards "jumped ashore," and the natives "sent their women to talk to us, and seeing they were suspicious, we sent one of our men, a strong agile youth, to the women, while we went back on board the small boats . . . The women made a big circle around him, touching him and looking at him in astonishment. Then we saw a mountain of a woman with a big club in her hand, coming up behind the youth. She stretched him out on the ground dead with a fearful blow. At once the women seized him by the feet and dragged him toward the hill, while the men ran toward shore shooting their arrows at us and creating such panic . . . that none [of us] was able to use his arms. However we did discharge several mortar shots, not hitting anybody . . . and all ran off toward the hill, where the women were cutting the Christian to pieces and roasting him over a big fire before our eyes . . . showing us the pieces and eating them. The men made signs that they had already killed and eaten the other two Christians, which grieved us exceedingly."

He proceeds to mistaken conclusions, disproved by later observers, about their lack of government, law, religion, and marriage. "They have no personal goods but have everything in common. They live together without a king, without authority, and each is his own master. They take as many women as they wish, and the son cohabits with the mother, and the brother with the sister, the cousin with the cousin and any man with the first woman he meets. Marriages are broken at will . . . they have no church, and do not have any law and are not even idolatrous. . . ."

The women were "tall, clean, and attractive, and not one had drooping breasts; and in those who have had children the shapes of their bellies and the size of their openings are no different from those of virgins, and the other body parts, which out of decency we won't mention, remain the same." They had "no more shame of their shameful parts than we do showing our nose or mouth." They were eager to copulate with Christians, and when they did, "their excessive lust caused them to lose all shame."

Another "atrocious custom among them, quite beyond human credulity: the women, being very lascivious, by means of a certain device of theirs and the bites of certain poisonous animals, caused their husbands' members to swell up so that they looked deformed and brutal as a result of which many lose their organ and become eunuchs."

They were a very prolific people . . . "when their children, that is their daughters, are old enough to procreate, they must be corrupted first by their nearest relative, the father excepted; then they are married. Unlike our women, theirs made no fuss about childbirth; they eat everything, go the same day into the fields, wash themselves and scarcely feel anything from their parturition." Frequently, especially when angry with their husbands, they committed abortion.

The people "live to be 150 and rarely get sick, and if a bad illness overtakes them, they cure themselves with certain roots and herbs."

They were so healthy, he remarked—perhaps with a trace of humor —"Physicians would have a bad time in such a place."

3

Caballero Antonio Pigafetta, Knight of Rhodes, who sailed with Magellan when his five ships left Santa Lucar at the mouth of the Guadalquivir on September 20, 1519, told of these or other coastal South American people at 24½° south—where Amerigo allegedly landed on his third voyage—"a country larger than France, Spain and Italy together" and "very abundant in all good things."

The Indians here "imagined that the small ships' boats were children of the ships, and that the said ships gave birth to them when the boats were hoisted out to send the men hither and yon; and when the boats were alongside the ship, they thought that the ships were giving them suck."

Both men and women were "well built," not "very black but rather brown," though they "paint their bodies all over with red, also their faces." Naked except for a girdle made of large parrot feathers, they "openly show their shame," for they "cover only their posterior parts, which is a cause of much laughter and mockery." They have "no hair on the whole of their bodies," nor on their faces, "because they pluck it out." Nearly all "except the women and children, have three holes in the lower lip from which hang three round stones about a finger in length. . . ."

"Some live 100 or 120 or 140 years and more."

"Their king is called Cacich" (Cacique). They "are not Christians and worship nothing," [not true] but "live according to the usage of nature, rather bestially than otherwise."

"Their dwellings called *boy* [*bohio*, as in Cuba?] are longish; they sleep upon cotton nets, called in their language *amaché* [hammocks] . . . fastened to large timbers from end to end of their houses. They make fire to warm themselves right under their bed. In each house there dwells a family of a hundred persons, who make a great racket. . . . They have boats, made of a tree all in one piece, which they call *canoo*. These are not made with iron instruments, they have none, but with stones like pebbles, with which they plane and dig out the boats . . . large enough for thirty or forty men . . . Their oars are made like iron shovels; and those who man these oars are black people, quite naked and shaved and look like enemies of hell."

They gave the Spaniards "refreshments of victuals, such as fowls and *anta* [tapir] flesh like that of a cow, also a variety of fruits, called *batate* [sweet potato] pineapples, sweet and of singular goodness, and many other things . . .

"The people . . . make bread, round in shape, and they use the marrow of certain trees, between the bark and the tree, not at all good, resembling fresh cheese.

"The people of said place give, in order to have a knife or fish-hook, five or six fowls, and for a comb they gave two geese, and for a small mirror or a pair of scissors they gave so many fish that ten men could eat of it. And for a hawk's bell, they gave a basketful of fruit and *batate:* this has a chestnut taste and is the length of a shuttle. For a king of cards, like those used to play in Italy, they gave me five fowls and thought they had cheated me."

"There are an infinite number of parrots of which they give eight or ten for a looking glass." He observed "small cat-monkeys, resembling a lion: yellow and handsome and agreeable to look at (the lion marmoset) . . . There are also pigs that have their navel on the back, and large birds with spoon-shaped beaks and no tongues."

The Indians ate "the flesh of their enemies, not as good meat, but because they had adopted the custom . . . This custom arose when the son of an old woman was killed by his enemies . . . The friends of the woman captured one of said enemies . . . and brought him to her . . . immediately said old woman . . . rushed upon him like a mad dog and bit him on the shoulder . . . He managed to run away and told how they had wished to eat him, showing them the bite . . . After that those captured on one side or the other were eaten . . . But they did not eat up the whole body of the man taken prisoner, but bit by bit. For fear that he should spoil, they cut him up into pieces, which they set to dry in the chimney, and every day they cut off a small piece and ate it with their regular victuals in memory of their enemies. . . .

"For a hatchet or for a knife they used to give us one of their daughters . . . but their wives they would not give us for anything in the world. . . . According to what they say, the women of this place never service their husbands except at night. When attending to business out of doors, they carry all required for their husband's victuals in small baskets on their heads . . . and their children in a cotton net fastened about the neck."

"The husbands carried a Brazil wood or black palm wood with

a handful of cane arrows. They do so because they are very jealous of their wives."

"One day a beautiful girl came aboard our captain's ship . . . saw a nail of finger's length in the master's cabin and hid it in her hair, since being stark naked she could not conceal it otherwise, and bending forwards went away. The captain and I saw this mystery."

At 34⅓° (the Rio Plata) they encountered "cannibals." "One of these men, huge as a giant, came to the captain's ship to find out if others could come. This man had a voice like a bull, and while he was on board, out of fear of us, his companions carried off all their goods to a castle. . . . We landed a hundred men . . . and . . . tried to catch some of them; however, they gained in running away. These people did more with one step than we could do at a bound. . . ."

At 49 degrees south—present-day San Julián—where they put up for two months for the winter they "saw a giant, who was on the sea shore, quite naked, dancing and leaping and singing, and while singing he put sand and dust on his head. Our captain sent one of his men towards him, with orders to sing and leap like the other so as to reassure him and show him friendship . . . At once this sailor led this giant to the small island where the captain was waiting. . . . Astonished, beginning to be afraid, the giant raised one finger on high, believing we came from heaven. He was so tall that the tallest of us came only to his waist; however he was well built . . . had a large face, painted red all over, and his eyes also were painted with yellow around them, and he had two hearts painted on his cheeks. He had little hair on his head and it was painted white." He wore a cape of "the skin of a certain beast, skillfully sewed," and on his feet "the skin of the same animal shaped like shoes."

"There is a great quantity of these animals in the same place . . . This beast has its head and ears the size of a mule, and the neck and body of a camel, legs of a deer, and tail like that of a horse, and it neighs like a horse." (The guanaco of course, related to the llama.)

The giant "carried . . . a short thick bow, with a thick cord made of the gut of the said beast, a bundle of short cane arrows, feathered like ours, though with no iron at the tip, instead small white and black cut stones . . . The captain caused food and drink to be given to this giant, then showed him various things, among others a steel mirror. When the giant saw his likeness in it, he was greatly terrified and jumped back, knocking down three or four of our men . . . The captain sent him off with two bells, a mirror, a comb and a chaplet of beads. . . ."

More giants "came one after the other, all naked, and began to leap and sing, raising one finger to heaven, and showing us a white powder made of the roots of herbs which they kept in earthen pots. . . . They had nothing else to eat except this powder. Therefore our people made signs for them to come aboard ship and offered to help carry their bundles. The men came with only their bows and arrows, but their wives came after them, laden like donkeys, carrying their goods. They brought along four of those little beasts out of which they make their clothing, leading them by a cord like dogs coupled together. . . ."

"These women are not as tall as the men, but are large enough . . . We were all amazed and astonished, for they had breasts as long as an arm, their faces were painted, and they were clad like the men, except they wore a small skin before them to cover themselves."

The Spaniards went on a hunting party with the giants, eighteen men and women, in two groups. These people had "their hair cut short, and clipped like monks with a tonsure." They "wear a cotton cord about the head, to which they hang their arrows when they go hunting . . . [and] wrap up their penises because of the intense cold."

"They have no houses, only huts made of animal skins . . . and go hither and yon with these huts as gipsies do; they live on raw meat and eat a sweet root, called *capac*. The two giants we had in the ship ate a large basketful of biscuits and rats without skinning them, and drank half a bucket of water each time."

"The captain named these people Patagóns [because of their big feet]."

"When these giants have a stomach-ache . . . they put an arrow down their throats, about two feet long; they then vomit a green bile mixed with blood: the reason they throw up this green matter is they sometimes eat thistles. When they have a headache they make cuts across the forehead and also the arms and legs, to draw blood from several parts of their body. . . .

"When one dies ten or twelve devils dance around the dead

men . . . These are painted, and the enemy is taller than the others and makes a great noise and more mirth than the others. . . . The greatest of these devils is called Setebos and the others Cheleule. . . ." One man said "he had seen devils with two horns on their heads and hair down to their feet, who threw fire from their mouths and anuses."

Six days later, going to cut wood, "our people saw another giant, his face painted and dressed like the others. . . . Approaching our people, he touched his head then his body, then did the same to our people, then raised both hands to heaven . . .

"He was brought to a small island where the ships were and where we had built a shed to store things . . . This giant was of even better disposition than the others, a gracious and amiable person who liked to sing and jump. When he leapt he caused the earth to sink in a palm's depth . . . He was a long time with us, and we finally baptised him as 'John.' This giant learned to pronounce the name of Jesus, say the Pater Noster, the Ave Maria and repeat his name as clearly as we did, but he had a terribly strong loud voice. The captain gave him a shirt and cloth tunic and seamen's breeches, a cap, a comb, some bells and other things and sent him back . . . He went off very happy and satisfied. The next day . . . he brought one of the large animals before mentioned, and the captain gave him more things. . . ."

4

One of the world's greatest exploits! Francisco de Orellana toward the end of February 1541, left Quito in Ecuador to look for "the lands of cinnamon," and with fifty-seven men sailed down from the Andes on the Napo to the Amazon and on to the Atlantic Ocean, a trip of nearly 4,000 miles.

The great epic is related by the friar, Gaspar de Carvajal, one of two men of God accompanying the expedition. Carvajal was wounded several times, and received an arrow in one eye which penetrated his skull so that the point projected out behind his ear. Yet he lived for more than forty years afterward—one of the most distinguished careers in the entire Spanish New World empire. Like Bartolomé de las Casas, he often fought to abolish abuses against the Indians.

Often the expeditionaries had almost nothing to eat; at other times they gorged on food given them by friendly natives or by raiding shore villages. At one time, they reached "a privation so great" that they were eating nothing but "leather, belts and shoe-soles cooked with certain herbs." Some ate herbs they did not know and turned temporarily insane.

Very early on the trip, from friendly Indians they heard of a great kingdom of gold, ruled by an overlord named Icú and of the "Coniupuyará" (grand mistresses), dreaded female warriors—the Amazons—who would surely kill them.

On the lower Napo they traded with peoples who brought them food, turtles, parrots "large as a leather shield," and partridges "larger than those of Spain," manatees and many kinds of fish, roasted cats and monkeys, biscuits of maize and yucca. Four giant "white" Indians, a span taller than the tallest Spaniard with hair to their waists and decked out in gold and splendid dress, called to see them.

On February 12, 1542, they sailed into the Amazon, at that juncture called the Marañón; "it seemed as though we were launched on a great sea"—though they were still 3,000 miles from the mouth.

For two weeks they drifted on. Canoes came out with presents, and they were well received by the Great Chief Aparia when they went ashore. Here they decided to build a second brigantine, for the first one was already badly rotted.

It took them a week to cut the timber, they forged thousands of nails; cotton served for oakum, and the Indians provided them with resin in lieu of tar. It took forty-one days, in all a lay-up of fifty-seven days. They pulled out on April 24.

They came eventually to the land of the great Lord Machipero, who had 50,000 fighting men and whose glimmering white villages stretched along the river for two hundred and fifty miles, in places solid for twenty miles. A swarm of gaily colored canoes came up the river, bearing warriors, accoutered in full-length shields, "made of the shell-like skins of lizards and the hides of manatees and tapirs." All were yelling, beating drums, blowing wooden trumpets.

The Spaniards, whose powder was wet, had to fight back often hand to hand, from their boats, in the water, on shore, in the villages. While the fray was going on, some of the Spaniards collected more than a thousand turtles which the Indians raised in pens.

The dreadful struggle lasted nine hours. Eighteen Spaniards were seriously wounded before they were able to escape downstream. The fight was soon resumed and lasted all through the night till noon the next day. Fresh Indians kept moving in on their vessels from each large village, "countless Indians" . . . encouraged by "white-daubed sorcerers," and the battle went on for forty-eight hours more without letup.

In the land of Chief Oniquague, which extended for three hundred miles, and was also hostile, they captured a fortified village after a fierce fight and rested there for three days. In the realm of the Omanas they were attacked constantly, but finally captured a small village high on the bank. Here they found yucca and maize biscuits and much pottery, plates, bowls and ollas, some with a capacity of a hundred gallons. The porcelain candelabra were "the finest ever seen in this world, better than the work of Málaga, glazed and with astonishing bright colors and accurate drawings and paintings." In the back country, they were told, there were "as many objects of gold and silver as of clay in this place." There were also frightening feather-woven idols, big as giants with distended perforated ears and disks on their arms and calves like candlestick sockets. The inland roads widened out to fine royal highways, leading apparently to populated areas the Spaniards dared not investigate.

They found friendly people again in the land of Chief Paguano, where one village was eight miles long. The interior overlord had llamas, as in Peru. Here were much silver and much food; fruit, pineapples, pears, *aguacates,* plums and custard apples.

They moved on through bellicose villages where the people, "of medium stature and very highly developed manners and customs, defended themselves in a very manly fashion."

By then—June 3—they were well down the Amazon at what is modern Manáos—halfway on their long trip. Here the Rio Negro came in with a great tide that blackened the mainstream for eight miles. They captured a wooden palisaded village where they found much food.

Many settlements were too large to be attacked, but finally they entered a village with a big public square. "In the center . . . was a hewn tree trunk ten feet in girth, on which was carved in relief a walled city, with a gate having two tall windowed towers and columns flanking facing doors."

The whole structure rested between the claws of two very fierce lions, "looking backwards as if suspicious of each other. In the middle of the tower there was a round space with a hole through which they poured chicha wine for the Sun. In a house nearby were kept feather clothes and headdresses for fiestas. The people said they were subjects of the female Amazons to whom they paid tribute of parrot and macaw plumes for the temples. They worshiped this miniature temple as the emblem of their 'mistress.' "

On down the river, at other villages, 5,000 warriors lined the shore. In a kingdom stretching for 210 miles, they saw heads nailed to seven gibbets—the "Place of the Gibbets," they called it. At another village, the people fought in their houses "like wounded dogs" until the Spaniards finally set fire to the place, burning several women and children to death. Here they seized many turtles, turkeys, parrots and much corn bread. A girl told them that many Christians lived in the interior, including two white women—probably survivors of an ill-fated 1531 expedition led by Diego Ordaz.

In another village from which the Indians fled, the Spaniards found "a wine dispensary," and "our companions were not a little delighted." They also found a good quantity of cotton goods. A temple contained war adornments, including "two woven mitres of many colors, neither of cotton nor wool, like those bishops wear."

The climax came when they neared the lands of the Amazons. Indians jeered and told them that they would be seized and the female warriors would finish them. It was below here that Carvajal was first wounded, by an arrow which went in "as far as the hollow region." In this engagement, the Spaniards had to fight in the water up to their chests. The enemy was led by many women warriors who clubbed down any Indian male who faltered.

"These women are very white and tall and have long hair, braided and wound about their heads. They are very robust and go naked, their privy parts covered with bows and arrows. One drove an arrow a span deep into one brigantine, and this kept up until both vessels looked like porcupines." Seven or eight Amazons were killed, whereupon the Indians lost heart and fled. But many more warriors came from other villages by land and others "in a great fleet of canoes." The Spaniards hurriedly embarked and slipped down stream. Near here Carvajal lost his eye in a shore ambush.

A captive told more about the Amazons, for he claimed he had carried tribute to them. (His tales partly sound like distorted rumors of the far-off Inca Empire, the splendors of Cuzco and the Ñustas, or Virgins of the Sun. The headmistress was Conori. They dressed in wool because they had many llamas as in Peru. Their dress, which reached to their feet, consisted of a blanket girded about the body from the breast down, or worn as a loose cape over the shoulders, or clasped together in front by a pair of cords. Mistresses of rank and distinction ate from gold or silver vessels; plebeian women ate from wooden or clay vessels.

They dwelt in seventy villages, connected by fine roads, with guards at various arches to collect tolls and duties. Their capital had fine buildings and temples dedicated to the Sun, with many gold vessels for the services, brightly painted walls and ceilings, and these were lined with gold and silver female idols.

The women were unmarried, and no man was permitted to remain in their dominion after sundown. They did bear children. "When the desire came to them, they assembled a horde of warriors and made war on a great overlord, in colder country with much firewood and rich in gold." Captives were brought back to their own land—white men of great stature—and the women kept them as long as their caprice lasted or until pregnant; then they sent them back to their country. If the women gave birth to a male child, they killed him and sent the body to the father; if a female child they raised her with great solemnity and instructed her in the arts of war.

The Spaniards drifted on through temperate lands, "where much wheat could be harvested and all sorts of fruit trees grown; besides, the high rolling savannas were suitable for breeding all sorts of livestock, because . . . there are many kinds of knee-deep grass as in our Spain, also wild marjoram and colored thistles . . . and there were many very good trees . . . groves of evergreen oaks and plantations of oaks bearing acorns (for we ourselves saw them) and groves of hard oaks, and there is a great deal of game of all sorts."

In the Kingdom of Chief Quenyuco, the Spaniards were met among the islands by two hundred pirogues, colorfully decorated with various emblems, each carrying up to fifty men, shouting and playing on trumpets, drums, pipes, and stringed rebecs. On shore were many battalions, playing and dancing about with palm leaves —joyous that the vessels passed by without pausing to attack them.

In the Kingdom of Arripurí, which took eight days to pass, men were "taller than very tall men," gaily decked, with clipped hair dyed black, and the Spaniards called it "The Province of Black Men." These people ate human flesh, had no gold, only silver, and used poisoned darts.

The Spaniards drifted on through the realm of Nurandalugua-burabara and at long last reached the islands at the mouth of the river. Here after incredible hardships, near starvation, they managed to repair their vessels. "Rigging for the sails was made out of vines, as well as the cordage for the sea [voyage] and sails out of the blankets in which we had been sleeping." They had no food left "except what could be picked up at the water's edge . . . a few small snails and reddish crabs of the size of frogs."

"We passed out of the mouth of this river between two islands . . . on the 26th of the month of August on St. Louis's Day. . . . At the end of nine days . . . our sins drove us into the Gulf of Paria," where the powerful currents trapped them for seven days, "during which [time] our companions never dropped the oars from their hands." For food only some *hogos* or plums were left. But they escaped, and two days later, more dead than alive, reached the settlement of Nueva Cadiz on Cubagua.

5

In Peru the Spaniards came upon a great civilized people, in some respects more advanced than those of Spain. The Quechua, Aimara, Coya, and others were ruled by the Incas, a blood-related nobility. The Emperor (Sapa Inca) was allegedly descended from the Sun, the Supreme Being.

From their great, stone, gold-adorned capital, Cuzco—Navel of the Universe—imperial power reached to Colombia, through Peru and Ecuador, to Bolivia, deep into Argentina and Chile. Laterally it extended well into the upper Amazon region and possibly to the distant Ecuadorian islands, the Galápagos. It was a larger land empire than that of Rome, and the Incas were better road builders than the Romans, better engineers also. Their astonishing suspension bridges over great chasms are still used in remote places.

Intensive irrigated agriculture, utilizing artificial fertilizers, made use not only of the rich valley lands but the precipitous slopes of the barren Andes, by means of irrigation and stone terraces. More land was used, better and more intensively, for the most part, than in modern Peru. Enormous royal herds of llamas and alpacas provided carriers, wool for the cold uplands, and meat. Llama dung was often used to plaster houses and for fuel.

The mining of tin, copper, silver, and gold was well advanced. Among many specialized trades and professions were: artists, musicians, engineers, architects, poets, silver- and goldsmiths, jewelers, weavers, stonemasons, carpenters, traders, medicine men, teachers, wise men, soothsayers, and priests.

The Spaniards landed in Túmbez on the northern Peruvian desert, and Francisco Pizarro's little force climbed up through the wild barren Cordillera Maritima of the Andes, heading for Cajamarca, "The Place of Frost," where Emperor Atahualpa was taking his baths at his summer palace. Well informed by spies and couriers of the movements of the Spaniards and their small number, he waited there tranquilly with 40,000 warriors. On the final lap (after manning intermediary garrisons) the Spaniards had but 177 men —67 horsemen, only three arquebusiers, and not more than twenty crossbowmen.

They reached the lofty crest under circling condors—great birds of prey—passed royal gold mines, and camped in the thin cold air, huddling miserably around their fires. Seven days later they looked down on Cajamarca Valley, carpeted green with meadows and corn fields separated by hedgerows, and upon the shining white houses of a city of ten thousand people. On the outskirts, a league distant, were the steaming baths, frequented by Atahualpa and his nobles, the Incas, and their retainers. A cloud of tents stretched for miles.

Such wealth and power caused the Spaniards to quake. But they "coolly surveyed the ground" and, "with as bold a countenance" as they could muster, wrote Pedro Pizarro, they prepared to advance to the city. Commander Francisco Pizarro—an illegitimate swineherd from Extremadura who could not read or write—divided his force into three columns and, with banners flying, they entered the metropolis in the late afternoon of November 15, 1532. The place was deserted—not a living soul, not a sound except the tread of the marchers and their horses.

The city was built of plastered adobe, with thatched or wooden roofs, a few buildings of quarried stone. In an outer grove stood a large Sun Temple and a convent of Ñustas, or Sun Virgins.

The Spaniards clattered into the large triangular plaza, surrounded by spacious halls, maintained as communal rooms for assemblages or visitors. At one end of the plaza was a stone fortress; another stood just outside the city, formidable with its triple walls.

Though rain and hail had begun to fall, Pizarro dispatched Hernando de Soto with twenty horse to interview the emperor, and, hard on his heels, his own brother, Hernando Pizarro, with fifteen horse. The riders galloped across the plain and whirled past the outposts, with clanging armor and shrilling trumpets.

On the other side of a small stream, more warriors were drawn up, shields and weapons ready. The Spaniards ignored the frail bridge and splashed through the water at full tilt. The warriors politely directed them on to the emperor's lodgings.

These were in a large galleried pavilion, plastered white and with many tints, a garden behind, in front a courtyard and a covered swimming pool, carved out of living rock, with hot and cold water faucets—"The Inca's Bath," reserved under penalty of death for the Emperor and his wives. The courtyard was filled with brightly dressed nobles and chiefs and their wives.

Atahualpa sat beside the pool on a low cushioned stool under a canopy, several favorites standing beside him. Two women on either side held a gauze curtain before his face, for he rarely showed his countenance to his followers. Hernando de Soto and several horsemen rode up to him and, without dismounting, made a "respectful obeisance" and addressed him through an Indian interpreter, Felipillo (or Martinillo?).

The emperor ordered the women to lower the gauze curtain and looked at the Spaniards without change of facial expression. He was stout, with a handsome grave countenance and fierce, slightly bloodshot eyes. Though more plainly dressed than his followers, he wore a fringed woolen cap or crown, the *llautu*. The strands, about "a half-finger thick" encased in gold tubes, covered his forehead, and the free ends hung in tassels to his eyebrows.

De Soto explained that they were subjects of a powerful monarch across the sea and had come to offer their services and instruct the emperor in the True Faith. They brought an invitation for him to visit their commander in his present quarters.

The emperor sternly upbraided the Spaniards, accusing them, while on their march to Cajamarca, of having desecrated the mats in the room where his father, the Inca Huayna Capac, had slept, and he ordered that recompense be made for the food and objects they had appropriated en route.

Another version has it that Atahualpa did not speak at all; then, as the silence grew embarrassing, an attendant said, "It is well."

De Soto then asked the emperor himself to speak. Atahualpa smiled faintly and said he was observing a fast but would call on Francisco Pizarro the following day. He commanded the Spanish captain and his men to occupy the communal buildings but no others; on his arrival, he would give him "instructions as to what he was to do."

Hearing this, De Soto put his horsemen through skillful maneuvers, almost riding down the nobles and bringing his own horse rearing before the emperor, so close that foam from its flanks flecked the royal garments.

Atahualpa sat unmoved without change of expression, but several nobles shrank back in fright. According to the Spaniards, the timorous ones were put to death that very night.

De Soto told Pizarro everything that had happened. The commander concocted a scheme to ambush and seize the emperor on his entry into the plaza, thus depriving the great army of its head. But all that night the Spaniards scarcely slept, keeping constant anxious vigil. Atahualpa's spies reported to him that the invaders were huddled in the large halls, in utter panic, for they "urinated repeatedly and senselessly out of pure fear."

The Spaniards were alerted at dawn. Francisco Pizarro divided his horsemen into two squadrons under his brother Hernando and De Soto; put one body of foot soldiers in charge of his brother Juan, and led another force himself. Pedro de Candia and several soldiers were sent with trumpets to mount two small cannon (falconets) on top of the fortress. When all the Indians and Atahualpa had entered the place, they were to fire off the cannon and sound the trumpets, and the horsemen would gallop out, followed by the foot soldiers. Bells were put on all the reins in order to help frighten the Indians.

Atahualpa made no haste. About nine o'clock he ate a leisurely breakfast and ordered food served to everybody. Toward noon he set forth in the royal litter, followed by the Lord of Chincha in another litter, and several more notables in hammocks, and flanked by thousands of troops, with others before and behind. The imperial guards had gold and silver helmets and gold and silver plaques on their shields and attire. Three large squadrons of dancing, singing Indians preceded the entourage. Two thousand servitors, clad in colored livery and looking for all the world "like animated chesscastles," swept the road ahead and laid down red rugs.

Atahualpa's litter was carried by tall Indians in shining gold attire. His palanquin was lined inside and out with multicolored parrot feathers, "so well attached that each feather seemed to have grown there," and the whole was decorated with gold and silver plaques and gems. All his force marched in perfect rhythm.

Finally through the main plaza gate came a captain, richly accoutered. He strode across the quadrangle, heeled around, and raised his long lance twice, whereupon the advance guard entered the plaza, singing in unison, parting toward the sides in perfect formation to permit those behind to advance.

Observing that Atahualpa had halted outside, Pizarro sent Friar Vicente Valverde and Diego Aldana, "a good soldier," with an interpreter to talk to him and require him in the name of God and the king to subject himself to the law of Our Lord Jesus Christ and His Sovereign Majesty. The Spanish commander would then consider the emperor a brother and would not permit anybody to molest him or injure his dominions.

The friar arrived at Atahualpa's splendiferous litter with uplifted cross and stated what he had been instructed to say, then predicated "matters of our Holy Faith," reading from the breviary he carried.

Atahualpa asked to see the book. As it was clasped shut, and he did not find the way to open it, he threw it on the ground disdainfully. He ordered Aldana to hand him his sword. The soldier drew it from its scabbard but did not hand it over. Enraged, Atahualpa told them they were all thieving pigs, that he would kill them all. Father Valverde scampered back to Pizarro to denounce the Inca Emperor's desecration of the Holy Word.

Atahualpa was carried on into the plaza erect on the throne in his litter, the Lord of Chincha behind him. Seeing no Spaniards, the emperor asked where the Christians were. "They are hiding in fear," a captain told him.

Pizarro signalled Candia, who fired the cannon, the trumpets sounded, and the mounted soldiers came out in a wild rush, riding into the assembled troops, slashing with their swords. The noise of the cannon, the trumpets, the hoofbeats and bells, the unexpected attack, threw the Indian force back in confusion.

Juan and his men launched themselves on the litter of the Lord of Chincha and killed him. Francisco advanced on Atahualpa's golden litter. But here the guards defended his majesty's person fiercely, and more rallied around. "For a long time we were killing Indians." At last a Spanish soldier "tired of fighting" got close enough to draw his knife to kill Atahualpa in spite of Pizarro's previous orders that he be taken alive.

Again the Commander cried out, "Let no one injure the Indian [king] on pain of death."

In the ensuing melee, a rush which carried half a dozen or so Spaniards to the litter, Pizarro was wounded by one of his own men. But they managed to break one of the carrying bars, and the emperor was tumbled out. Pizarro and several others caught him in their arms, saving him from injury. Soldier-chronicler Miguel de Estete snatched off the imperial fringe or *llautu* as a personal trophy.

Dismayed by this disaster, deprived of their leader, the entire imperial force broke. The Spaniards hacked them to pieces, and as the carnage continued, the dead were piled up at the gate. In panic, the survivors tore down one whole wall of the plaza, and fled across the plain. The Spaniards pursued them as far as the royal baths where many more were cut down, and the slaughter would have been even greater had not night fallen.

The last Inca emperor was a prisoner. The great empire was without an acting head.

Pizarro held him for ransom. The emperor promised to fill an enormous room with gold, a smaller one with silver, and the orders were sent out to all the land.

From Cuzco came the finely wrought replicas of birds and animals stripped from the royal gardens, with life-size reproductions of all the creatures of the empire. Even most important plants had been copied in metal. All these beautiful artifacts were tossed into the ransom room to be melted down.

Spanish emissaries scoured the land to hasten the shipments. Hernando Pizarro took a force along the magnificent imperial stone-walled highway, superior to anything in Christendom, and on down to the coast—over enormous suspension bridges, through towns and cities. The Spaniards marveled at the wide terraced fields, the vast herds of llamas, the signs of husbandry and civilization. They rode through snow and ice, down stone carved steps for thousands of feet, finally through the heat of the lower desert to Pachacamac to seize the treasures harbored in the great coastal city and temple. They impounded what gold was there, tore down the great idol, and smashed the holy edifice. Coming back, they passed through the

26

city of Xauxa, with its great market, "attended daily by 100,000 people."

Soon enough the gold was gathered—$15,000,000 worth according to Prescott; $50,000,000 according to Frank Shay. Atahualpa was murdered after a rigged court-martial, and the march on the great golden city of Cuzco, capital of the empire, center of the universe, began.

2

"Mad Geography"

THE South American world of the the pre-Columbian peoples was, and is, vast and varied. Except for a tiny coastal strip in the north Peruvian bulge, the entire continent lay east of what is today the United States—stretching toward Africa, most of it closer to Spain and Portugal than to present-day New York.

South America is shaped like a headless man with an enormous paunch (Brazil); while the Chile–Peru coast is the lean meat along the great spinal column, the Andes. The big toe sticks into icy waters: Cape Horn is a blunt cliff, 56° south on a small antipodean island of the archipelago of Tierra del Fuego.

Thus, from the Panama Isthmus neck at the tenth parallel north, the land mass widens out, slightly southwest to Peru, and southeast for three thousand miles to the Brazilian shoulder, 7° below the equator, which passes through the mouth of the Amazon and present-day Quito in Ecuador. From the widest points of the continent, the Pacific and Atlantic coastlines reconverge, so that the land tapers toward Antarctica.

It was not always thus. With what Huxley calls "retrospective prophecy," geologists and paleontologists have deduced that the pre-Cambrian land mass of Goyaz province, Brazil, is probably the oldest in the world.

Of the same era are the highlands that loop about Mato Grosso near Bolivia; the high Serra de Parecís scarp, a vast domain of sandstone, conglomerates and shale, and the Brazilian coastal plateau with its lordly sea-range Serra de Mar—from the northeast equatorial shoulder to Rio Grande do Sul and, with a narrow break, running into eastern Uruguay almost to the Plata Estuary, low enough there to be part of the flat Pampa.

These developments occurred when life consisted only of Proterozoic marine invertebrates—a few worms and sponges.

To the north, across a considerable sea channel from the Brazilian land masses, emerged the enormous Guiana–Venezuela plateau flanked by southern scarps from which, in the Sierra de Acuary, rises 8,000 flat-topped Roraima—"Mother of Rivers"—the setting for Conan Doyle's fantastic *Lost World* of prehistoric horrors.

Such was the beginning of the continent, before the islands were joined, or the coast lines filled in.

Hundreds of millions years later, the Goyaz mountains were joined up with the plateaus of Mato Grosso, Minas Gerais and São Paulo, when the Caldas volcano still glowed in riotous activity. This was during the Triassic period, the start of the Age of Reptiles. Rivers here in southern Brazil, since the coast was higher, were shunted south-southwest, almost as if rising from the sea, and later curling back to it at the Plata outlet. The eastern highlands from here to Bolivia, came slowly into being and, a million years later, near the beginning of the Tertiary age, perhaps in the Pliocene period, the Andes were thrust up, in places with volcanic violence.

The Orinoco and Magdalena Rivers were born, and the Goyaz–Guiana sea channel was converted into the greatest of all rivers, the Amazon. To this day the bed is nearly at sea level, only 300 feet at Iquitos, three-thousand miles inland.

This was the beginning of the Age of Mammals, and the day came when their twisted vertebrae and enormous femurs would be piled up in many rain caverns, like primitive Caesar's Columns of slaughter, as in inland Baía, where the creatures must have fought ferociously and agonizingly for the last water in one of the periodic droughts of that strange rugged region.

For, as the coastal masses in and around northern Baía, Piauí, Maráñha arose, there was created a great enclosed basin (the Chapada Diamantina), the weird setting of the master classic of Brazilian literature, *Os Sertões* (*The Backlands*), by Euclides da Cunha—shapeless mountain ruins, soon badly eroded by wind and storms to stupendous sculptural relics, a bewildering variety of multicolored quartzites and mica-glistening itacolumites. The vertical dark blue talc, emitting a metallic gleam, and the vermilion clay were periodically peeled away from glittering crystalline igneous rocks—a phenomenon also visible in northern Chaco, and in similar depressed basins in Minas Gerais and in back of Rio and São Paulo.

2

Three dominant regions cover most of Latin America: the highlands, the Amazon, and the Argentine Pampa. The altitude, climate, rainfall, rivers, and soil in each of these and in half a dozen minor areas have determined the flora and fauna and the life and society of man. The backbone of the continent, the Andean range, starts in the north—four arms run south, from the Isthmus, from west of Maracaibo and from Trinidad island off Venezuela—and one runs to the Straits of Magellan and Tierra del Fuego. The three northern arms enclose wide páramos or savannas including the Antioquía plateau, and much of the broad basin of the Magdalena River. In Ecuador the Andes become one intricate knotted mountain range, but in Peru widen out again to three ranges. They throw a wide arm about the vast windswept treeless uplands of Bolivia, with their red soil, white saline beds, and harsh rock mountains. There are to be found big Lake Poopó, site of ancient cultures, and Titicaca, the world's loftiest navigable lake.

In northern Chile and Argentina, the Andes make a wild tangle. There is found the 14,000-foot Atacama Puna, barren and bitterly cold, with only a few shepherd huts. Nearly all ranges are eternally snow-clad, for often they rise to majestic heights, second only to the Himalayas: Chimborazo (Ecuador, 20,702 feet), Huascarán (Peru, 22,302 feet), Sorata (Bolivia, 21,286 feet), and Aconcagua (Chile, Argentina, 23,000 feet). Chile alone has 515 mountains higher than any in the United States outside of one in Alaska. No spectacles are more superb than the vast forms of Aconcagua, Tupangato, Piuqüenes, Manolejo (all above 20,000 feet), and other giants rising in white majesty above Santiago, Chile. Indeed, the whole length of Chile is walled with white, with sparkling glaciers and ice. The great snow chain beyond La Paz, Bolivia (although that city is 12,000 feet above sea level), is as breath-taking as the Swiss Alps, but starker, more unruly—"mountains in rebellion," the Bolivian writer Arturo Vilela calls them. Deeply glaciated, with enormous moraine dams, the southern reaches, below 39°, are dotted, both in

Argentina and Chile, with beautiful lakes—some large enough for overnight steamers—cupped in soaring snow walls.

The heavy rains and Andean snows feed great navigable rivers: Magdalena (Colombia, 1,000 miles), the Orinoco (Venezuela, 1,700 miles), the Amazon (Brazil and half a dozen other countries, 4,000 miles), the Uruguay (Argentina, Uruguay, Brazil, 980 miles), the Paraná (Argentina, Bolivia, Paraguay, Brazil, 2,450 miles). Even the Tocantíns, an easterly tributary of the Amazon, is 1,750 miles long; and the Madeira–Mamoré tributary, reaching back into Bolivia and Peru, more than 2,000 miles.

Of them all, the Amazon River is the mightiest—with one-fifth of all the moving waters on the globe. Three thousand miles up from its Atlantic outlet, it already has as much water as the Mississippi River at its mouth—this before some of its major tributaries have added their flow. The Amazon is a colossal dragon with the green scales of trillions of leaves. Its red mouth is in the Atlantic, choked like a stuttering Demosthenes with a whole archipelago of islands, the largest of which, Marajo, a rich cattle kingdom, is the size of Switzerland. The river is a dragon with 11,000 tails or tributaries which fan out over a territory almost as large as the United States and into nearly all bordering countries, hooking into the lofty Andean snows, curling about the border mountains of Guiana and Venezuela, reaching far up into Bolivia, Colombia, and Ecuador. Even the Peruvian Montaro River, not even mentioned in Webster, a tributary thrice-removed (which flows into the Apurimac which flows into the Urubamba which flows into the mighty Ucayali which flows into the Marañón), already at 12,000 feet in the Andes, is as large as the Hudson River near its mouth. Ocean-going vessels steam for 2,000 miles up the Amazon to Manãos, and at high water smaller steamboats go a thousand miles further, well beyond Iquitos. Large power launches penetrate many hundreds of miles more up various tributaries.

At the river's widest point, any one of thirty-eight American States, if put in the center of the stream, would still leave room on either side for the waters to flow past; and a number of states, such as Connecticut, could not be seen from either shore. From its 200-mile-wide mouth at the Equator, the river shoots forth a powerful current 600 miles into the Atlantic, nearly a third of the distance to Africa, and for a hundred miles out the water is so fresh that passing ocean vessels let down their buckets for drinking water.

The ocean tide roars back in upon the river fast as a train, spear-headed by a fifteen-foot crest in a 500-mile inland backwash. The flood sweeps under stilted houses, tosses trees into the air like match-sticks, carries away piers and boats and sometimes fishermen. Sharks, swordfish, and tarpon ride in with the tide and explore for 2,000 miles upstream. Twice every day this mighty battle between ocean and river goes on.

The Andes, and only the Andes, provided the conditions for the rise of great early civilizations—those of Chavín, the Inca, and the Chibcha, among others.

The flourishing **Amazon basin,** however, was the great incubator of peoples. There were to be found 20,000 species of trees, some not yet scientifically classified, a rampant vegetation; in one province, more species of moths and butterflies and beetles than in all the rest of the world together; and myriad kinds of animals, reptiles, amphibians, sea and river creatures. Man was equally prolific—eighty languages and thousands of sublanguages, not all of them ever successfully classified.

The Pampa: An endless sea of grass, changing color with the wind from green to silver; a plain, except for a short season wholly flower-less, largely treeless except for the widespreading round *ombú* tree, it often stretches for hundreds of miles without a permanent water-course—or a stone. Only in the west is there some barrenness, and near the sea in places are great salt mud marshes infested with gigantic crabs, dangerous to horses and cattle.

In pre-Columbian days, since it provided no minerals, building materials, or ready source of food, the Pampa was inhabited mostly by restless nomad hunters. The early peoples had no animals to ride across it, no proper techniques to subdue this vast rich domain; the highland Inca empire reached to the foot of the mountains, but ventured little beyond. Only near the great rivers traversing the Pampa was the land seriously cultivated. Not until modern times did it begin to be populated—after the introduction of the horse opened it up for bands of roving plainsmen—the Gauchos—and for millions of semiwild cattle, which provided an easy food source.

Peruvian writer Manuel Seone vividly describes these latter deni-zens, mostly inbred with pre-Columbians: "Round, without psycho-analytical angles, is his face, with thick ruddy cheeks. Round is his sombrero, flat-crowned like the Pampas . . . Round is the traveling lasso, a dancing acrobatic halo. Everything seems influenced by the curve of the landscape, enslaved by the soft distortion of the landscape."

3

Lesser regions have harbored notable peoples and cultures. Magellan was the first European to behold the great Indian headland fires and the fires of snow-clad volcanoes along the channels and on the huge island south of the Straits of Magellan, which he named Fireland—Tierra del Fuego—larger than Ireland and twenty-five times the size of Rhode Island. A weird beautiful spectacle: fire amid ice and snow and glaciers towering above flowering meadows, cascades leaping down among pine and oak forests and joining the rushing purplish waters where white dolphins playfully led his vessels deeper into this strange region. "Trying to leap up to their mother, the Moon," the Indians said of the dolphins, and the Alakaluf on the Pacific Chilean Islands and Patagonian coast considered themselves also children of the Moon, orphaned when she went off seeking the Sun.

The Chilean islands make up a fourth of the modern country's land area and, with Fireland and Patagonia, in Chile and Argentina, comprised a region that had a certain ethnic unity: for the Araucanians and their cousins, the Pehuenche, had infiltrated both sides of the Andes. Islands south and east were shared with "canoe people," the Yahgan; on Fireland and north were the "foot peoples," the Ona, and the Tehuelche, the giant Patagones—Big Feet, Magellan called them.

The Straits of Magellan, the Beagle Canal, the intricate web of island channels with their myriad marine plants, marine life, and birds, were later threaded by Charles Darwin in the *Beagle,* and he and the Argentine writers José S. Alvarez and Roberto J. Payró have left us notable descriptions of the island world and its teeming life: the deep dark fiords under snow ranges and violet glaciers, the rich flowering meadows and the mighty forests, but no source has ever fully uncovered the mystery of the human giants roaming over the bleaker wind-swept Patagonian plateau of Argentina, with its small gnarled trees, scrub growth, and bunch-grass.

Unique also was the upper Pacific coast under the Andes—another subregion—though it had some characteristics similar to the coast from dreary lower California to the forests of Vancouver. The

South American shore stretched from the Auraucanian forested rainland, through the Mapuche or Auraucanian Vales of Paradise, with fruits and grains, through the endless Chilean–Peruvian desert and finally Ecuadorian jungle and swamp. High above the northern Chilean desert, lived plateau peoples—the Atacama and Diaguita. Then on the coast came the Peruvian Nazca, a memorable people, the Ica, Chicha, Lambayeque, the Mochica (later, the Chimú), who produced one of the world's great art forms—in all some thirty-six "cultures" all finally smoothed over by Inca conquest. In Ecuador, the Esmeralda, Manta, Huancavilca, Caraque and Puna, among others, roamed the jungles, hunting and fishing.

A third subregion was the desolate Chaco, a vast empire east of the Andes, north of the Pampa, taking in large parts of Argentina, Paraguay, and Bolivia, partly dominated by the Guaraní, a powerful resourceful "nation," whose language still prevails in Paraguay —even newspapers are printed in it. The Guaraní were linguistic cousins of the Tupí—among the most widely distributed of all South American peoples.

Nothing in the Chaco is more memorable to the chance traveler than those vast spider-webs six feet across, spun from dark to dawn, spanning roads and trails and glistening in the early sun with diamond dewdrops like a dancer's veil. Though mostly so parched and empty, the region sustained a considerable and varied population, chiefly because of the numerous stone water caverns and pits and the enormous rivers traversing it through bands of lush vegetation.

It is one piece in aridity and climate with the Mato Grosso plateau of inner Brazil, another vast empire northeast, where rise the headquarters of the great Paraguay River and a dozen mighty Amazon tributaries.

The Brazilian coast highlands, a fifth subregion, hold some of the oldest secrets of man's life on the continent. A temperate region, with much in common with the Pampa, it becomes hotter as it decreases in elevation in the north, so that northeast Brazil, especially mountain-locked basins in Baía, and Minas Gerais, constitute a separate region with wide variations in fauna and flora.

The far northern equatorial seaboard—of Colombia, Venezuela, and the Guianas—is a tremendous empire with coast swamps, vast llanos, plateaus, mountains. Of all South American countries, Colombia, a third of it in the true Andean area, half of it inner Amazon jungle, has the most varied resources and living conditions.

The Guianas were strangely apart. From the ocean, pink with the detritus of big rivers, swamps extend far inland (some have since been drained and sea-walled as in Holland), showing patches of assai and trulli palms, until the rain forest—another ocean, but dark green. Abruptly then the land rises—becomes the land of 500 million years ago—a lofty sandstone shelf cut by gigantic gorges, enormous roaring rivers. At points along this shelf are the great falls, a score of them, and one the highest in the world. Presently foothills run to the flat-topped mountains—curious pillboxes, "monstrosities out of the sea of jungle and savanna and desert," with steep precipices to their fantastically eroded edges. Beyond are the Rupunini savannas, a small portion of the vast Brazilian grassland area north of the Amazon.

Man in these various major and lesser areas adapted his life to the climate, the altitude, the animals, the sea and river creatures, the vegetation resources, so that the continent harbored myriad languages, cultures, civilizations—from the most primitive to several that were the peer of fifteenth-century European civilizations: from savage nomad hunters and fisherfolk, to intricately organized states, with highly developed agriculture and industry, trade and religion.

4

Climate, as already indicated, ranged from blazing equatorial sun to the deep freeze of Antarctica. But in earlier periods, as during the ice ages, when man probably first reached the continent, it was far different. The petrified forests of Patagonia, the paleontological remains there of enormous prehistoric creatures, some utterly different from elsewhere on earth, record that the bottom of the world once had a tropical climate with dense rain forests.

How long ago even geologists cannot tell, though Dr. Edward J. Zeller of the University of Kansas is perfecting an electronic and thermal method to determine when rocks were first plunged into permanent subzero temperature—in short, a thermal calendar covering millions of years.

The Tropic of Capricorn, 23° s, a little below Goyaz—a latitude, in our era, agreeable to the beginning of life, runs through Rio de Janeiro, Paraguay, northern Argentina, and Antofagasta, Chile, so that more than two-thirds of South America is today within the torrid zone. But climate-wise, except for the vast Amazon basin, the Chaco, and many coast lands, it is mostly a temperate region because of altitude. A single mountain, such as Huascarán in Peru, from base to summit, provides every known climate on the globe. Quito on the equator, 9,236 feet high, has a beautiful, all-spring-flowering climate. The coastal desert area of Peru and northern Chile would be hot teeming jungle country were it not for the icy Humboldt current sweeping out of Antarctic to cool the shores of the Pacific as far north as Ecuador.

Hence much of Latin America has long had a more equitable all-year temperature than almost any place in the United States. Though often shrouded in clouds or mist, the inner eastern slopes of the Andes above 5,000 feet—as yet largely inaccessible—have the most superb twelve-month spring to be found anywhere—the so-called *Ceja de la Montaña*—"Eyebrow of the Mountain"—and the deep-cut, ever-smiling Yungas, the inner valleys of Bolivia, are paradises, sung about by so many Bolivian writers and poets.

Even Punta Arenas (Magellanes) on the Straits of Magellan, has a milder climate than the New England shore, rarely getting below freezing in winter, though summers are cool, ranging from 44 to 63 degrees. Today it is an all-year golfing, tennis, race-track and yachting center, with summer skiing only five miles away on an adjacent snow mountain. In contrast, the adjacent Atlantic Patagonia, though more equitable most of the year than Southern Texas, sometimes has killing frosts.

Montevideo, Buenos Aires, and Santiago in the Vale of Paradise correspond to Los Angeles or Norfolk, Virginia and have similar climates, though the seasons are reversed. The Pampa and the southern Brazilian plateau, also much of the mountain coast area farther north, are delightful, and were there any validity to the Ameghino theory that all human life originated in this general region, the New World Adam and Eve would not have suffered greatly wearing only fig leaves.

The northern Chaco, though occasionally it has killing frosts, registers the hottest summer temperatures on the continent, similar to those of Nebraska and Iowa, but not as bad as Yuma, Arizona. Farther north in the tumbled Brazilian coastal mountains reaching toward the equator, especially in summer drought, as in Baía and Piauí, the temperature was and is a violent daily shuttle, ranging from almost freezing at night to 95° in the shade at midday. Those rocky areas quickly store up the heat oven-fashion and release it even more rapidly.

As Euclides da Cunha describes it: "Over the tops of the hills down the furrowed slopes, the broken silica chips seem to take fire and gleam vibrantly, like sparks; the quivering atmosphere near the earth is like that at the mouth of a furnace . . . The day, incomparably bright, blasts the silent landscape, and the leafless branches of heat-stricken vegetation shrink back into the bosom of agonizing nature, in a long-drawn-out spasm of immobility and peace . . not a breath of air stirring in the luminous placidity of the blistering hours."

Even the Amazon basin, though hot the year round, is no furnace, for it rarely gets as broiling as our Midwest in summer, and there are pleasant places where the night temperature drops to forty degrees Fahrenheit, making blankets necessary.

5

Most of the Amazon basin, a land of monsoons, has fairly heavy rainfall, from 72 to 120 inches. Since the soil of much of this region, except for flood areas, is thin—not more than 10 per cent of the 2,000,000 square miles is alluvial according to C. F. Marbut—the vast jungle is nourished chiefly by the rain and by its own rot: a "constant cycle"—as Louis Bromfield described a similar South Pacific forest—"of birth, growth, death, decay and rebirth."

The Guiana rain forest and the Orinoco savanna have similar conditions, though in the lower Orinoco rainfall reaches 156 inches. Caracas, not far distant, but 3,400 feet high, has a mean annual precipitation of only 32 inches. Thus, throughout the continent rainfall varies widely.

The deserts of northern Chile, the nitrate region, and most of the Peruvian coast see rain only once about every twenty-five or fifty years, then rarely as much as an inch, though the winter *garúa,* or mist of Peru, is often thick and dripping. But the dryness is so great that sands are almost powder, and tawny or pinkish dunes— the *médanos*—engulf mountains thousands of feet high. Nothing is more fantastic than the ten-thousand-foot red plateau of Peru, strewn with gigantic white haystack dunes, concave at the back (for the wind blows only in one direction) and bellied in front with exquisite lace-like markings like the hoop-skirts of two centuries ago. Ollagüe, 12,000 feet up on the Chilean-Bolivian frontier, sits in drifting waste, and farther south the Atacama desert, rising far up into the Andes, shrouds elevations of 8,000 feet and more in white powder.

Enormous stretches of the Maritime Range are utterly barren, showing only brilliantly tinted rock surfaces in vast canyons like our own Grand Canyon. The Lima-Arequipa highway goes through enormous lofty stretches where there is not even microscopic evidence of vegetation, devoid also of bird, insect, or animal life—as forlorn as the moon. Flora Tristán, the grandmother of Paul Gauguin, traversed those dreadful stretches on mule-back more than a century ago and handed down an anguished story of her tribulations.

Only along streams hurrying down to the sea, such as the wide valleys of Chiclayo, Moche, Chiara, and a few patches of alluvial pampa, are seen winding ribbons of green, though in Inca times, by means of colossal irrigation systems, more of the mountains and coast were cultivated than today. But from Copiapó to Pisagua in Chile not a single permanent stream relieves the landscape.

In contrast, in many places in south Chile there are 400 inches of rain annually, and dense forests of pine, cypress, gigantic evergreen oaks and beeches flourish. The rain lessens to 120 inches further south in Chilean Patagonia, and of course Argentine Patagonia on the other side of the Andes enjoys little rain.

Although from May to September in years of over-heavy rainfall, parts of the Pampa turn into temporary shallow lakes, in normal years the rainfall is so well adjusted to soil absorbency that there is no run-off, yet no stagnant water. Only places in the west have near-desert conditions; and in dust storms, sometimes a rider cannot see the head of his horse. Toward the north, precipitation also decreases until the arid Chaco, in the upper extremes, is a smooth billiard-table plain, alternately flooded or baked bone-dry. A similar condition prevails in much of the vast interior Mato Grosso plateau, often cooler than the Chaco. There are to be found also the swamps of the upper Paraguay River. El Pantanel, the largest in South America, in flood time devours thousands of horses and cattle.

In all six Brazilian northeastern coastal provinces, from Piauí (particularly in Ceará) to Sergipe, rainfall is capricious, with complete droughts every decade or so, which since time immemorial have driven the people forth into the Amazon basin in order to survive. The drought is even more persistent in the *sertões*, the immediate tableland of the interior of Baía and Piauí, though tempestuous rains sometimes bring raging rivers to life in dry beds to run into blind swamps and blotterlike sands and die—such as the Vasa-Barris,

38

the Self-Emptying River, renamed by the natives, because of its clay sediment, the Irapiranga, or "Vermilion-Colored Honey."

As Euclides da Cunha describes those hills and plains, "At the height of the droughts they are positively a desert; but when the rainlessness is not prolonged to the point where it causes a painful exodus, man may be observed struggling like the trees, with the aid of the reserves he has stored up in days of plenty; and in this fierce, unsung, terribly obscure combat . . . in the solitude of the uplands, Nature does not wholly abandon him (even) . . . in those last hours of desperation when he had drawn the last drop of water from the last of his water pits." Certain growths provide emergency stores of water.

6

"Neotropica," as South America is labeled, is the most unique of the seven distinct zoogeographic regions of the world. It covers the largest area in latitude—78°—and has the highest percentage of endemic animal and plant life found anywhere. Partly this is because during the Tertiary geologic period, the Panama Isthmus resubmerged, leaving the continent isolated. Also it has the most extreme altitudes, the highest livable areas, the most absolute deserts, the greatest rivers, and the most tropical forests of the western hemisphere, plus antarctic conditions. South America still has many surviving creatures which, if they ever existed elsewhere, have become extinct.

The fauna was even richer in the Pleistocene when man probably first appeared on the continent—enormous megatheria, the ground sloths, mighty glyptodonts, armadillo-like brutes, the *pyrotheria* (hippids: various-toed horse-shaped creatures, possibly extant at the time of the European conquest), and huge bulky herbivores, including the great *toxodonts*—enormous beds of their bones have been found in Patagonia—great mastodonts (primitive elephants) and strange ungulates, as well as carnivorous *borhyaenids*, rodent-like opossums and other marsupials; grotesque *macrauchenia* (which looked like a combined camel, horse, and elephant) appeared; so did huge turtles and huge porcupines, which later moved north and decreased in size.

Such creatures, so different in morphology from those of the rest of the world, caused a recent authority, William Berryman Scott, to brand them as "outrageously absurd," a most subjective criterion. Later, from the north, came bears, canids such as foxes, and deer. Many of the previously named creatures and later arrivals were companions of the first man on the continent. Some monstrous splendor must be imbedded deep in the race memory.

Here we are chiefly interested in the fauna and flora, the animals and plants, which provided food, medicines, dyestuffs, clothing, shelter and weapons to early man up until the time of Columbus. The "mad geography" (a phrase perhaps coined by Picón-Salas) which produced such heterogeneous and unusual biological expressions, inevitably had a tremendous effect on human beings: their lives, their bodies, minds and health, their evolution and societies. During centuries of adaptation, the highlanders of Peru came to have a 25 per cent larger lung capacity than the rest of the human race. A man who eats corn smells and may think differently than one who eats wheat or manioc.

3

"Where the Sabiá Sings"

THE "canoe people" of the far south made vessels out of reeds, hollow trunks, bark, and the skins of seals, and sea lions, even intestines, which they inflated like modern lifeboats. They lived on the fruits of the sea: leopard, crab, and monk seals, sea lions, sea elephants; on turtles, whales, and fish: crustaceans, delicious pale rose sea spiders, sea urchins, huge barnacles, oysters, mussels, mollusks, and shellfish in general. Here, and north as far as Peru, people enjoyed that prize delicacy of all shellfish —later called "Damas del Sur" by the Spaniards—with its white, pink, and gray flesh. Shells were used as cutting instruments and ornaments, and the shells of the giant concha and razor mussel were used as containers, horns or trumpets, or to bail out boats.

On Tierra del Fuego and elsewhere they used dogs to help them drive mullet and smelt into nets. The Chono first caught a female crab, a long-legged lithoid, then let her back into the water on a noose, whereupon half a dozen males would attach themselves, and the whole batch would be hauled in. She was used many times. Fiddler-crab juice was used to alleviate earache.

It has been claimed that the Fuegians stabled ground sloths in caves on Last Hope Island. The rich meadows flanking the Straits of Magellan and the peat-moss of Fireland provided fine grazing for guanaco, a small wild llama, valued for food, clothing, shoes. Its skin even provided portable *toldas* or tent-houses. Small plains rodents, the viscacha, were found in Chilean Patagonia, and pumas were caught on the mainland and islands everywhere, as were species of deer.

In southern Chile people ate the large fungus found on giant evergreen beech trees (still considered a delicacy), seaweed, and mosses.

Emilio B. Morales in his *Canales Fuegeños* describes "the exotic flora," the green, yellow, and red algae, the many climbing vines, the large yellow violets, the raspberries and gooseberries, "white and yellow marguerites, white mariposas, red *sanguimanes, chilcos* and fuchsias, Antarctic *alenas,* and other growths that provide a vigorous color note to the dark green of the landscape." Chilean lilies (allied to the cucumber) were like red bells. There were miles of flowering heather.

On the mainland, the Tehuelche and other "foot people" preyed on rats and foxes (these were eaten all over the continent), on the *mara,* a large Patagonian harelike rodent, and especially on *tuco tucos,* a sort of gopher so tame it could be caught by hand; guanacos, of course; "ostriches" (the rhea), met with from the bottom of the continent up into the Amazon and inner Peru. From these birds, besides food, they procured charms and medicines, and used the feathers for capes, curtains, and bed coverings; head plumage for war and religious rites, often dyeing them beautiful colors. These soft "ostrich" robes can still be bought in the Punta Arenas market.

Innumerable birds and their eggs contributed to their diet, especially among the islands: to mention only a few, striped geese and pigeons, marine crows, caracara hawks, stormy petrels (Mother Carey's chickens, early English navigators called them). There were probably 3 species of penguins, Johnny, Jackass, and Tufted Rock-Hopper. Kelp ducks, more like geese, were hunted on kelp beds. Long-spurred screamer birds were penned up for fighting contests. On Estrado Island, and only there, were great assemblages of long legged *avutards, bandirrias* (ibises) and other unusual birds with thick plumage.

Farther north on the Pampa, the guanaco disappears; foxes, wolf-like canids, deer, and other temperate-zone animals provided sustenance. The Querendí were such fleet runners they could easily run down any animal on foot.

Uruguayan Indians fed owl flesh to convalescents to whet appetite. The Huarpe in northwest Argentina would leave large gourds floating on the lake waters, then would put other gourds over their heads, swim out, and grab unsuspecting ducks by the legs. A well-known bird of northwest Argentina, the Chaco, and Mato Grosso, and one often tamed was the large stalking seriema, famed for its loud ringing call.

In drier regions, in lieu of water, people often drank the blood of animals or the root juices of the enormous thistle—described so vividly by W. H. Hudson in his *Far Away and Long Ago.*

In the desolate Chaco (a Quechua word meaning "hunting ground") the rivers and pools were so thick with fish that often they could be scooped out by hand or by hollowed gourds (just as Captain John Smith's men used to scoop fish out of the Chesapeake with their frying pans). The Chacoans, among others, also used nets, fishermen often dived in with scissor nets which they opened up under schools of fish. Fish were clubbed, speared, even killed with bows and arrows. Other groups used stupefying drugs to poison the water. Fish not eaten at once were smoked, or dried and powdered.

Among other animals they hunted peccaries, deer (they wore red hats or blankets to entice them), jaguars, anteaters, caymans and crocodiles, armadillos, *capunches,* iguanas, tapirs, and boas, turtles, and lizards. In bad seasons clouds of locusts provided an important source of food—at all times considered a delicacy. They also ate beetle grubs and tasty bamboo worms, which were said to have induced visions.

A rich bird life helped them survive: ducks, geese, rheas, buzzards and particularly, talkative black and white cuckoos, which were housebroken to keep mice and insects away.

The Abipón avid for honey, plucked their eyebrows out, claiming it enabled them to see bee and wasp nests more easily.

Palm trees, particularly *mbocayás,* and coconuts (*yatai-quazú*) along the rivers served greatly: the tender top shoots—"palm cabbage"—were roasted; the seeds and pith (of scant nourishment) were eaten and provided starch and flour for mush; the sap was made into beer; grubs in decayed trunks were a delicacy. The leaves provided thatch for houses and lean-tos, and were shredded into fibers to make ropes, cords, and baskets, even clothes.

The Chaco and Mato Grosso people ate algarroba pods, *chañar,* nustal, and tuna fruits, mountain oranges (*sachalima*), *sachacandia, cucurbitaca,* and bromelias. In many places wild rice was plentiful. Gourds (used for food, decorations, and fiesta rattles) and peanuts were often cultivated; so were beans, *tasi,* corn, pumpkins, squash, and melons.

In such a dry land tubers—there were dozens of edible species—

were most important; and tree roots, such as the *ombú*, were boiled.

The Paraná River basin and the Chaco seem to have been the incubating ground for centuries of peoples who later spread across the continent, and some of whom reached North America.

2

The Inca highlands had many unique animals and plants. Garcilaso de la Vega, son of a Spanish captain and a Ñusta, or Sun Virgin, tells of the wonders of totemic and sacred animals:

"On the principal animal festivals, especially the greatest, honoring the Sun, called Raymí . . . the Curacas (chiefs) presented the Incas menageries with many wild animals, such as jaguars, lions (pumas), bears, monkeys, wild cats, macaws, vultures . . . and condors . . . also large and small serpents . . . great toads and lizards." The seacoast Curacas presented seals, crocodiles, boas, and anacondas, the latter said to be thirty feet long—quite a feat to haul such a creature over the mountains. Birds were kept a league south in Surihualla—"Plain of Ostriches." Often creatures were kept in Cuzco zoos; pumas, jaguars, and bears in Puma Curú and Puma-Chipana. These fierce animals were used to punish criminals. Ocelots —beautiful creatures—were kept as pets; a figurine in the Chiclán museum shows an ocelot at the foot of a throned official.

Sometimes gold replicas were presented at court—llamas, lizards, toads, serpents, foxes, pumas, jaguars, and many birds—all to become part of Pizarro's later loot.

The highlands also traded for fur seals, sea lions, and dolphins. The paca, a rodent, was domesticated and eaten as a great delicacy, was also placed as a food-offering in the temples.

The furs of the much-valued chinchilla were reserved for the royal family; it was often hunted with tamed *hurones,* a sort of ferret, "the best-trained on earth," remarked Chronicler Cieza de León. Viscachas, burrowing rodents, were used for food, furs, and wool. The fur robes had a high price, according to both Garcilaso de la Vega and Cieza. Every year a little wild relative, the vicuña, was rounded up above the 15,000-foot level, sheared for the Inca's sole benefit, and released.

Vast herds of llamas and alpacas—mostly state-owned—were maintained, and the meat, hide, and fur periodically distributed. The animals also provided medicines and charms. The foetus of a llama, especially in Bolivia, was commonly buried under the doorstep of a new house. The dung was used for fuel and for plastering houses.

44

In the Bolivian and Chilean uplands the most palatable flesh and soft furs of the large *abracoma* rodent were much sought. They were domesticated, and their remains are found in Machu Picchu tombs. Small short-legged deer were encountered in the higher punas; pigmy deer roamed eastern Andean forests. George Eaton found their bones also in Machu Picchu graves.

Other animals were beloved—and utilized—for they are shown on pottery, gourd, and textile designs: howler, cebus, spider, and other monkeys; nine-banded armadillos; corn-eating rats and mice; spotted cats (tamed as pets), black and white jaguars, pumas, dogs, foxes, and deer; opossums and bats. Bat skins, softer than any cloth, were made into robes for the Incas.

Spotted snakes and other reptiles, lizards, iguanas, turtles and tortoises were common; also amphibians such as frogs and toads. Many small fresh-water fish were caught in lake and streams, such as the *ipi, vuilluncho, carache,* and small catfishes in Lake Titicaca. Shellfish were brought up from the coast.

Grasshoppers, locusts, spiders, ants, fresh-water shrimp, lobsters, crabs, scorpions, starfish, octopus and squid, conches, clams and snails were known, and many provided items of diet.

Among birds were spotted and barred owls, partridges, parrots, macaws, toucans, crested hawks, condors, wild pigeons, Muscovy and other ducks, broad-billed herons, geese, kingfishers, humming-birds, curassows, flamingos, and others difficult now to identify.

"Besides the red-fringed *llautu* headdress," wrote Garcilaso de la Vega, "the sovereign wore two wing feathers of a bird called *cora-quenca* [the *maya*, probably a fork-tailed nighthawk]. . . . The feathers, white with a black patch, were taken one from . . . [each] wing . . . so as to match. I myself saw them worn by Inca Sayri Tupac. The birds . . . dwell in the wilds of Villacanota, thirty-two leagues from . . . Cuzco, in a small lake at the foot of those inaccessible snowy mountains. . . .

"The Inca wore these feathers because no others . . . had ever been seen or heard of in the world, and all others, even the heir to the throne, were forbidden to wear them. For . . . these birds being alone, resemble the first Incas, who were no more than two, man and wife, come down from heaven. The feathers of these birds were looked upon as a memory of that time."

The flora, like the fauna, of the highlands was limited, but the Quechua had access to the warmer mountain valleys, and in the latter centuries of the empire to coast and jungle products. They also traded far and wide. Nearly all timber had to be imported: hard and soft palm woods, ironwood, *jaracandá*, red *guarabú, jurema,* and mahogany.

But the Peru tree or *molle* (the false pepper) was widely distributed. The red berries were used for making *chicha* beer: as condiments, resin, dyes, and for medicine (the bark and leaves too), for liver and kidney ailments, rheumatism, toothache, and in suppositories to cure worms.

Other trees provided bark cloth and bark paper; and many fruits, apples, plums (*capulí*), prunes, were cultivated. Papayas were obtained from warmer valleys, and they traded for tropical nuts, fruits, and condiments: sassafras, sarsaparilla, *sapotes, guayavas,* and *chirimoyas.* Chirimoya seeds were ground up and used to kill lice.

The *palta* (Quechua) or avocado (Aztec *avocatl*) was found by Inca Tupac Yupanqui, on subduing the Cañarís or the Ecuadorean frontier; he took seeds back to Cuzco and, according to Garcilaso, "from there disseminated the tree over the entire empire." The Inca appreciated this fruit so greatly "that in December when the *paltas* began to ripen he decreed a fiesta, the Acatay Mita, which lasted six days and six nights."

Its food value was great—all the vitamins. If mashed for an iced drink, it was "very healthful and useful for newlyweds." Dried and mixed with rose-petal syrup, it served to alleviate chest hemorrhages; it was good for diabetes; as an astringent (sometimes taken with toast and burnt sugar), for dysentery and diarrhea; and was applied on poisonous insect and snake bites. The bark was used to cure abscesses.

The Peruvians (jungle, highlands, and coast) cultivated popcorn (*fasán calla*), *yuca* (manioc), *acullo, achera, yacón,* sweet potatoes; barley, oats, *quina-quina,* goosefoot, squashes, amaranths, chiles, coca, cacao, tobacco, and cotton. Many beans were grown: white, absinth, *taihui,* kidney, navy, string, snap, scarlet runner, *pallar,* and lima beans. "Lima bean warriors" adorned Moche pottery. Wendell C. Bennett lists nine root crops besides potatoes.

The *massúa* (mashúa), a food tuber, was eaten guardedly for, allegedly, it diminished sexual appetite, but this was offset if the eater at the same time held his penis (or a symbolic stick) in his hand. According to Cobo, the Inca sent *massúa* to his armies so the soldiers would forget their women.

The important *oca* (a wood sorrel) with enormous edible tubers, was described by Father Bernabé Cobo: "The temperament of the *'Oca'* is cold and damp. The leaves and branches . . . cooked and eaten in time of pests or typhoid epidemics, are preventative of all contagion, especially if cooked with the roots of the *escorzonera.* The juice is useful against all inflammations and acute gout, against deafness if a few drops are put in the ear. Mixed with scorpion acid, it reduces kidney pains and earache; the leaves, cooked with sugar or syrup, and taken after fasting, moderate high blood pressure and burning urine, work against every inflammation, against burning fevers and fright, against sore throat and stomach pains due to over-eating."

However, the three major cultivated highland food staples were: maize, *quinóa,* and potatoes.

Quinóa, a grass grain, was used in dozens of dishes, in salads, as mush, for making biscuits (*ppiri tacta*), was boiled, fried, ground, and toasted (*cañaguá ocú*).

Even more important was the potato: innumerable species of varied chromosomes, of every shape, size, and color. Potatoes adapted to the low country, to middle altitudes and also the cold regions, up to 15,000 feet. The white potato, considered inferior then and today, was fed only to animals. The prize was a fine-grained mealy yellow potato with a nutlike taste. Potatoes were frozen (*chuño*), dehydrated, made into flour, bread, gruel, mush; they were boiled, roasted, and fried; also used for many medicinal and magic purposes.

Quinine (*quina-quina,* or Myroxylon Peruiferum, to mention only one variety) with its perfumed nectarlike leaves, was a beloved plant. As the poet Pedro de Peralta wrote in 1732:

> Not like the suave perfumes of the Orient
> Whose fumes are pretended incenses,
> Nor like those from the precious sweat
> Of chosen animals, excretions for the senses,
> Your resins, Peru, are without parallel,
> Giving health rather than mere scent,
> So much so, that the aromatic spell
> Of their emanations more than others, is refulgent.

Hundreds of wild plants were collected, especially in warmer valleys, for food and medical purposes, of which Cobo early in the seventeenth century scientifically identified 144. Among useful plants (using their vulgar names) were *pingo-pingo, jataca, sano-sano,* horsetail, tortora, *caruzo, arreacha,* pimpernel, *pihuayo, incucha roots, maguey (chuchau), mogo-mogo,* willows, breadfruit, nettles, paper trees (bougainvillaea), camphor, cinnamon, and thistles.

Not least was the sacred bright red Flower of the Incas (*Ñucchu*), a salvia, which had magical and curative powers, and was strewn thick as a red blanket in the path of the Inca when he traveled— as described by Alejandro Coello and others. The flowers were thrown over prisoners condemned to death "as an act of pity and piety." Hung on a bamboo pole, they advertised a chicha shop.

3

On the Brazilian plateau, the Caingang cultivated white beans and three kinds of corn: red, white, and violet. They hunted for pine nuts, honey, and wild tubers. Here were many *jabotica* fruits, pineapples, papayas. *Caraguatás* provided fibers. Along the northwest Brazilian coast were great forests of *babassú* palms, bananas, coconuts, fruit trees too. But inland the vegetation shrank to dwarf trees and scrub forest land (*caatinga*): spiny growths, twigs sharp as glass splinters, twining like green vipers through the low trees; and epiphytic sea-green cactuses, sinking tentacles into the *urucurú.*

Often corn fields withered, and water pits gave out, but if people did not flee the area, they survived by using edible roots and tubers that stored up sap underground. The slender roots of the dwarf cashew nut (*cajuys*) get larger with depth, finally unite into a vigorous stock far underground, like an enormous underground tree. In the *macambia,* the stored-up sap is above ground, protected by spathes, and a single stalk, cut and held over a cup, will fill it to the brim with crystalline water. No growth was more useful than the *carudo,* the tube-reed hollow-stemmed heliotropes streaked with white and having spiked flower clusters.

Important food animals were rabbits, opossums, sloths, anteaters from pigmy to giant size; hairy, soft-tailed and tiny armadillos. Their hard shells were used for containers, ladles, musical instruments. Porcupines provided tender meat, and the quills were used for adornment and other purposes. The white-fleshed paca and the large running agouti, another huge rodent, were delicacies and important food sources. The early peoples also trapped foxes, pumas, and *mocos,* a species of rock cavy or guinea pig, an endemic creature, skeletons of which have been found in the early Lagoa Santa caves in the Brazilian highlands. Raccoons, coatis, and kinkajous were tamed, also eaten; so were the large-maned foxes and the smaller "bush-dog." Wild "pigs" were of great value: the small collared peccaries (*caeteti, sairó*) and the white-lipped peccary (*quexado, cafushe*) that ran in herds of 200 or more—noisy teeth-grinding animals.

Deer came to water holes, and here, as elsewhere, the huge tapir survived down to modern times and still crashes through the *caatinga*, breaking down small trees like matchsticks.

For some Amazon peoples, the tapir, a creature often weighing over a quarter of a ton, was taboo, but others made full use of its meat and hide (especially for war shields). Monkeys (cebidae) of which there are eleven genera and innumerable species, were kept as pets and hunted with bow and arrow, blowgun, and poisoned dart for food. The howler monkey's voice is truly hair-raising.

The Caypabara, largest of rodents, sometimes weighing up to a hundred and fifty pounds, was a very important food source, but its flesh was taboo on the Madre de Díos river, as was also that of deer.

The jaguar, puma, and the beautifully striped ocelot were considered great hunting trophies and played a great role in legend, magic, medicine, reincarnation, and heroism.

If rain-forest biological nature was riotous and overpowering, actually mammals were not present in great numbers. But aquatic and arboreal animals abounded.

Sharp-toothed bloodsucking vampire bats provided many early gruesome legends, and are disease carriers (murrina, rabies, and others) even today.

Three-foot iguanas were caught and tethered. Their eggs were also eaten.

Deadly are the fer-de-lance and *jararaca* snakes, still more so the ten-foot bushmaster (*surucucucú*), but the flesh of many snakes was eaten. Snake skins had many uses, and tongues were used as love charms. Vast medical lore, magic, and cultism were involved with serpents. The boas, beautifully colored and patterned, sometimes reported as fifteen feet long, mostly fed on rodents and were often made house pets to eliminate pests. Their skins were treasured trophies and adornments.

4

The great river anaconda (*sucurri, yacumamá*), a powerful constrictor often twenty-five feet long, was worshiped or feared as an evil spirit. The Jívaro, whenever a baby was born, posted an old man at the river bank all night to blow smoke across the water to prevent the anaconda from eating the child. But anaconda oil facilitated childbirth.

Dangerous were the seven-foot electric eels that generated 500 volts in two thousandths of a second, for they could stun, even kill a man, horse, or cow. Their flesh was eaten for rheumatism, and weakened specimens were used for shock therapy. As defense, a giant toad, sometimes weighing five pounds, expelled a toxic fluid from its skin. Small bright-colored frogs were even more toxic, and their venom was used to poison blowgun darts. Frog broth had numerous medicinal uses. The *huampalli* toad was a symbol of female fertility and women kept them in their homes. A toad secretion or other animal and vegetable products were used to change the growing colors of feathers of parrots (*tapirage*) and perhaps other birds—for using them in feathered capes.

A giant six-foot otter (*sauro or ariranha*) abounded on the Orinoco, Amazon, Paraguay, and Paraná rivers.

Small black and pink river dolphins also provided food (taboo for some tribes), oil, medicines, magic, and folklore. The eyes were love charms; the teeth were symbols of a cure for toothache. Some Indians believed the dolphins were transformed into singing Loreleis to wreck boats.

The sea cow or manatee (*peixi-poi*), attaining the weight of 600 pounds or more, was important for its food, hide, and fat, products important in trade, particularly between the Ucayáli Indians and the Quechua. Its fins were hung about the neck, and feet-filings were put in drinks to cure heart ailments.

Nothing was more important and festive than the great communal turtle harvesting. "The cattle of America" were sought every September to November, when the river was low and the females appeared by tens of thousands on islands and sand beaches. They labored at night, digging three-foot holes and depositing 100 to 150 eggs each, which they covered over and tamped down. The eggs hatched out in about a month, and the baby turtles scrambled straight to the water. Turtles and their young were avidly preyed upon by birds, jaguars, reptiles, and man.

Adults were flipped over on their back, killed and dried or kept in palisaded pools and fed with *mandioca* and legumes for long periods. Orellana and his men on their trip down the Amazon frequently raided such turtle pens.

Hundreds of thousands of eggs were dug up every season, eaten fresh or crushed with bare feet in canoes to obtain oil, conserved in copper or clay receptacles used for illumination. The shells served for many artifacts. Today, these river turtles are in danger of extinction.

Stinging rays (*tapaderas*) and cannibal fishes (*serrasalmus,* sp., the *piranha* or *piri*), were a menace. Sting-ray spines, able to cause severe wounds, were used for weapon points and for tattooing. *Piranha* were, and are, greatly feared, for they could snip off a finger, but the flesh was good, and the sharp teeth were used for cutting instruments. Another fish, minute in size, the *cañero,* or *candiru,* hooks itself into the vagina or the penis aperture of a bather. Protective devices were often used.

Among fish, the most valuable for food were the leather catfishes, the *dorado* and *sábalo* and the scaly *pirarucú,* sometimes thirteen feet long and weighing eight hundred pounds. The flesh was processed and often traded. A smaller species was the slim, transparent *pintado* of eastern Brazil.

The *dorado* or *pirajá,* a yard long and weighing 100 pounds, was tasty, and had a large edible roe, but the *sábalo,* half that size, were a superior eating fish. Delicious was the very oily and prolific sea fish, the *lisa,* the *tainca* mullet, sometimes a yard long.

5

Insects, locusts, termites, the larvae of beetles, particularly a rhinoceros beetle, of moths and butterflies, were eaten. Hank and Dot Kelly in *Dancing Diplomats* tell how their Jívaro friends gleefully popped winged ants into their mouths "like gum-drops."

A luminous beetle was tied to the toe to help in night hunting, used as an adornment, and even eaten. Cochineal or cactus scale provided valuable red dye (*macnú*).

Fire ants and black *tucandero* ants causing frightful pain were used in initiation rites. The large *Formica Cephalotes* was used, because of its powerful mandibles, to bite together and hold fast the lips of bad wounds, or in ritual puberty ceremonies.

6

The Amazon has more orders and families of birds than any other of the world's zoogeographic regions, and 36 per cent of them are endemic, found originally nowhere else. Food, pest, and feather-ornament birds abound. Various ducks (including the black, white-faced *ireré* tree duck), *curassows, guans* and *chachalacas,* parrots, parakeets, macaws, trumpeters, rheas, orioles, thrushes, etc., were tamed or domesticated. Grouse and quail were hunted, often tamed by traps, decoys, snares, sticks and stones. Cranes, long-legged herons (hunting for frogs and fish), bent-billed scarlet flamingos ("goose of the north"), were common aquatic birds. The flamingo's legs were used for flutes and pipes.

The six-foot *jabirú* stork (white feathers, naked jet black head, and scarlet lappets) was a semisacred fowl.

The toucan (*Dios-te-dé*, or "God-gives-you") was beloved and much utilized. Its cry presaged rain; the broth of its tongue ("the coral drop") was used for heart trouble. Parrot tongues were eaten by mutes, and ash of the beak was dissolved in chicha to cure garrulousness.

The harpy eagle, with powerful talons and a "stoop" as swift and lethal as lightning, lived on sloths, monkeys, and rodents. On occasion, small pigs and babies were said not to be immune. Often these birds were caught young and raised in captivity, for their feathers were valued as trophies, for arrow shafts and headbands, and were prominent items of early trade. The meat, fat, and excrement had special medicinal values for the Tupí tribes of the Xingú and Araguaya rivers.

Important for food and oil was the red-brown, white-spotted oil-bird, or *Guacharo,* which inhabits caves.

All over Brazil sang that most beautiful of songbirds, the *Sabiá*. Antonio Gonçalves Días wrote in his sad "Song of Exile," *Canção do Exodo:*

> Minha terra tem palmeiras
> Onde canta o Sabiá.

> My homeland has palm trees
> Where the Sabiá sings.

And Henriqueta Chamberlain entitled her charming autobiography of childhood in Brazil, *Where the Sabiá Sings.*

7

At hand in the Amazon was the most varied plant life on the globe—products obtainable by wild-fruit collection, semicultivation, or domestic cultivation. The Xingú tribes transplanted wild *piqui* trees, whose fruit was 95 per cent oil, close to their settlements and irrigated them. The Tupí-Cawahib of the upper Madeira tied the stems of wild grass together so the ripe seeds would fall in small heaps. Tribes, when clearing ground for huts or farming, usually left useful wild trees growing, especially palm trees.

Often more knowledge and skill were required to process wild products than for cultivating plants. By intricate methods certain fibers and fruits were processed to produce a brown or gray powder used in lieu of salt. Eliminating poison from bitter manioc was a hard chore. From that plant (also cultivated in gardens) they also got rubber sap, food tapioca from the grated roots and its oily non-poisonous seeds, and a much-liked beer, *masato*.

Manioc had great importance in puberty, marriage, fertility, childbearing, and other rites.

One tribe tells of a girl, pregnant out of wedlock, who was to be killed, but a stranger appeared, advising them she had been impregnated by a plant not a man. When she died after her child was born, the shoot of a never-seen plant sprang from her remains. So was manioc discovered and thereafter considered sacred. It resembles our Ojibway Hiawatha tale.

From various forest products, the people obtained resin for preparing blowguns, arrows, glazing pottery; various lacs and varnishes, balsams, and rubber. Locust tree (*algarroba*) and *sibú* resin were used for lamps. Most useful were various copifera varnishes, such as *copayiba*, etc. The strong-scented resin of these and other plants was used to attract deer. On the Rio Negro calabashes and gourds were lacquered with *canayurú*, a product of assava and begonia leaves. Plastic adornments from resins and saps were made with wooden molds. Natural plastics were also used for glazing ceramics. The resinous bark of the mimosa served to waterproof pottery. Other gums and resins served as glue for affixing feathers to arrows, waxing threads, calking canoes (as Orellana learned), fixing stone and glass blades and axes to handles.

Rubber from trees and plants such as the *Castilloa elástica* were used by the Omagua, Nambicuara, Witoto, and others for balls, rings, syringes, shoes, skin covering against rain, sun, and bites.

Balsams were used for flatulence, or to heal wounds, and was burned to provide smoke to be inhaled for headaches, colds, and lung complaints.

Macundú people extracted oil from *maquema* bark for dysentery.

Other oils served for food, unguents, or for lamp fuels. Carab wool oil (*carabá*) was used as a hair dressing, lotion, and for face and body paint. The leaves of a sort of aromatic myrtle, *arrayán*, were used to clean teeth and eliminate bad breath.

Many trees and plants (such as *choloque*) provided shampoos. Concerning the *Fevillea trilobata* of the sapindaceous trees, Nicolás Monardes, a colonial medical historian, wrote in 1565, "two or three of these fruits with hot water, to soap and wash clothing, do more than a pound of soap." Sapindaceous fruit was delicious; mashed up, they were used to heal bone fractures, and the bark and root were used as astringents and tonics.

Pigments were important. Nearly all had medicinal applications. Others were used to keep off parasites, for sun protection, or permanent tattooing. Orange to purple dyes were provided by the bignonia *chicha;* black or blue from the genipa of the *jaguá* tree and from the *inga;* yellow from the *tataibá* and other plants; blue from varieties of anil. The bright red seeds of the *urucurí* or achiote —the *bixa orellana*—were washed and mashed and the residue pigment dried, mixed with oil or gum, and kneaded into balls. It was employed for cosmetics, body painting; for ceramics and art work; for coloring cloth, baskets, furniture, wood. According to Father Cobo it was used for coloring chocolate and other drinks. The peoples were well versed in herb cures, drugs, aphrodisiacs, and abortives; insecticides, poisons, antidotes for poisons and for snake, scorpion, and insect bites—such concoctions as *níssola, guaco,* and *tolmuz. Barbasco* was used to stupefy fishes. Curare, or arrow poison, was prepared in many ways with different ingredients, though apparently it always included strychnine from the *ramú,* as well as boiled ants and spiders.

The narcotic datura (*chamico,* "Devil's Box") had many uses. Father Cobo told of an acquaintance who, knowing his traveling companion intended to rob him, dosed him with *chamico*. The man lost his senses completely, tore off his clothes, and tried to drown himself.

Datura had many medical applications: for pneumonia, a sedative, to heal skin diseases, tumors, ulcers, and gumboils. Cigarettes made from its dried leaves were smoked for asthma.

Another narcotic, *aya-huasca* (spruce), induced dreams and prophecy. *Parica,* an intoxicating powder compounded of a number of vegetables and the seeds of the acacia and *argico* and leaves of the *abuta* or *cocculis*—was snuffed through a royal eagle quill. For about five minutes it produced bulging eyes, contracted mouth, and body shakes, after that great gayety. Granadillas (supposed to prevent and also cure, yellow fever, malaria, and other fevers), chirimoyas, *acayas,* were gathered. When the *Mbayá* palm fruit ripened, tribes came from vast distances to gather it. The large brick-red mameys (Taino) were delicious; often the large seed was dropped into chocolate to flavor it.

The cashew nut grew far and wide, but the Tupí considered the *auraucana* nut the supreme food. Brazil nuts (*tocarú*), much traded, were important from the coast to the inner Beni, Madre de Díos, and Ucayali rivers. They were sometimes cooked, as were other nuts, with casava or corn flour. The dark red *ayecoc* or *curita-bimbi* (*caryocar amygdaliferum*), also known as the "almond of Chachapayas," was a huge tree. According to Spanish historian Antonio de Herrera, its spiny chestnuts were "larger than those of Castillo, tender to eat, soft and butter-like. . . ." "No other nut can compare to them," wrote José Acosta in 1590; "it is the most delicate and delightful, and the most healthful of all I have seen in the Indies . . . no 'almond' of Spain is so excellent, tender and juicy, substantial, full of oil and very smooth." "Three times the size of any others," said Padre Cobo. They were much sought after, even in the markets of far-off Cuzco, where they were called *tampa* or *tampa rurú*—i.e., axe-fruit—and they have been found in the ancient tombs of Chimbote.

Merely to name all the woods used in house-building and industry would require a thousand-page volume. Among the most useful were species of striped *aroeira,* cedar, *acarembá,* red *cordurú,* iron wood (*ubireta*), *baracuna, jurema,* ivory-white, red *guarabú,* black *jaracandá,* yellow-red *vinhatico, piquihi. Macanas* or war clubs were made of purple heart, snake-wood, *amará, ibiritanga.* Musical instruments, drums, trumpets, sounding languettes, rattles, etc., were made from appropriate woods.

8

U.S. Navy explorers Lewis Herndon and Lardner Gibbon wrote in 1853 about the Rio Branco area: "Of trees fitted for nautical construction, there are twenty-two kinds; for the construction of houses and boats, thirty-three; for cabinet work, twelve (some of which—such as the *jaracandá,* the *muirapinima,* or tortoise-shell wood, and the *macacauba*—are very beautiful), and for making charcoal, even." They reported twelve trees that exuded milk from the bark: that of the *aroeira* and assai being poisonous, but having "extraordinary virtue" for curing syphilis. "A young American, dreadfully afflicted with the effects of mercury, and despairing of cure, had come to Pará to linger out what was left of his life . . . in a tropical climate. A few doses of the *mururé* sent him home a well man." They also mentioned *manacá,* an amber plant, being used for syphilis, which the German Von Martius labeled "vegetable mercury."

Perfumed woods such as *carunje,* vanilla, cinnamon, rosewood, and *pau santo* were used for containers, beads, and necklaces.

Ceiba, ficus, ubigarrá, umbauberra, uasá aperba, paraparaiba, provided lighter woods: for ear and lip plugs, paddles, rafts, and canoes. *Tatabá* and cashew bark was also used to make canoes; fig wood and others for dugouts. The most usable wood for bows—flexible and strong—was the *tecoma conspicua,* a begonia tree.

Of all trees, the palms were probably the richest gift to man. Some twenty genera of palms with innumerable species and subspecies were exploited for oil, fruits rich in vitamins, beverages, mushes, gruels. Herndon and Gibbon found "twenty-three well-known varieties of palms, all more or less useful," on the Rio Branco. "From the bark of the *piassaba* (called by Humboldt the *chiquichiqui*) was obtained cordage . . . equal in quality to the coir of India. From the leaves of the *tucúm* were obtained the fibers of which all the hammocks of the country are made. Roofs of houses thatched with the gigantic leaves of the *bussú* (babassú) will last more than ten years. The seed of the *urucuri* and *inaga* . . . make the best fire for smoking Indian rubber; and most of the palms give fruit, which is edible in some shape or other."

The Huarrau Indians utilized the *murichú* palm for house timber, fences, posts, turtle pens, traps, receptacles, bows, clubs, blowguns, and manioc grinders; thatch for roofs; fiber for clothes, hammocks, baskets, fire-fans, mats, fishing tackle. From it they obtained starch for bread, sap for wine, other drinks from the fruits, baskets from the leaves, and edible larvae from its trunk.

Most important palms were the *assaí, mancol, bacabá* or *turí,* the *lú,* the *patúa, avará* and *marajá.* Throughout the Amazon, the palms provided indispensable starchy foods, fresh greens, and wine. Palm oil served for cooking, illuminating, medicine, soap-making and, mixed with dyes, cosmetics and body paint that kept off insects and provided insulation.

The gigantic trumpets of the Uapes River were made of sections of the large prop root of the *paxiuba palm,* which seems to stand on stilts. The carnauba palm provided one of the finest waxes known, now used by American housewives. From it beads, polished shell earrings, and adornments were made, also carved statues.

In places agriculture reached high levels: maize was grown, beans, eleven varieties of sweet potatoes; yellow, white, red, or blue yams; squashes, pumpkins, gourds, *guacos;* peanuts, manioc and mandioca (*cari carahú*), yucca, cassow, arrowroot (*maranta*), tobacco (Barba tobacco later became famous around the world); cotton (the *Huimba* cotton, also wild, was delicate and glossy and used for mattresses); coca, cacao; morning glories; reeds, many grasses, *arracacha,* castor bean (upper Xingú), *urucú* berries and *genipa* fruit (for dyes), *huatusas Mangaberra* on the upper Xingú provided latex for coating balls, used in games.

Among cultivated fruits were *mamona* (upper Xingú), papayas, plantains, pineapples, *lucumos* and *sapotes,* Surinam cherries (*capulí*) *guayavas, ingas,* and *sicamas.* Many species of capsicum (chilies and peppers) were grown. The *mioto-uchú,* and *aguyi,* were malarial preventatives.

The Amazon peoples, though most tribes subsisted on a relatively few items, had more extensively varied animal and vegetable products than any people who have ever lived, a range of foods, woods, and fruits far greater than today in the United States.

9

"Mad Geography" and its biological manifestations helped create a confused linguistic pattern—phonetical, morphological and lexical —for South America has the greatest language diversity of any continent on earth. Dr. J. Alden Mason sets the number of dialects at about 5,000. Of distinct language groups, Dr. Paul Rivet, the great French ethnologist, lists 83. For merely the relatively unimportant Timote family of Venezuela, he names thirteen sublanguages. In 1913, Alexander Francis Chamberlain also estimated 83 separate language stocks of families; in 1936, Pericoty García put the figure at 94, with a total of 558 major languages and, of course, thousands of dialects.

Merely to list all these families and languages, their geographic boundaries, their characteristics would be impossible in a modest-sized volume. But major "race-culture" groups can be indicated.

The outstanding societies in the modern sense, subsequent to the early Chavín empire, and at the time of the Spanish invasion, were the three Andes coast "nations": the Incan, Chibchan, and Araucanian.

1. *The Inca state.* "Inca" was merely the caste designation for the brother-sister sovereigns and their blood relatives (a few notable outsiders were admitted), constituting the ruling nobility. Quechua, the lingua franca, was the language imposed on many peoples from Colombia to Chile and Argentina, who, if not entirely relinquishing their mother tongue, became bilingual.

The most important allied tongues, older perhaps, were the Aimara and Colla, around and beyond Lake Titicaca, and these may have been the basic languages of the great pre-Incan Tiahuanaco culture. The core of Quechua-speaking peoples included different dialects in many instances, viz., the Ancash, Cajamarca, and Chalcapoya peoples. Quechua was dominant in the Puno and, at a lower level, in Arequipa.

2. *The Chibcha* built up one of the major New World cultural centers, though often downgraded in literary, historical, and cultural studies because of its lack, except for a few early stone temples, of architectural remains. But their superb metalwork, ceramics, and art handicrafts indicate they were not far below the level of the important Mayan, Aztec, and Inca civilizations. Their power, centered in Bogotá, Colombia, stretched southward into parts of Ecuador.

The most outstanding scholars of their culture have been Jacinto Jijón Caamaño, under whom the great Max Uhle worked, Pío Jaramillo Alvarado, the Frenchman Paul Rivet, and the Mexican, Moisés Saenz, who have left us studies of Ecuadorian Indian life. Three outstanding American archaeologists and anthropologists in this area have been Donald Collier, John Murra, and Edwin N. Ferndon, Jr.

3. *The Araucanian* language groups, related to the Puelche, Het, and Tehuelche, occupied central areas in Chile and Argentina. The more northern Mapuche and Picunche were perhaps mixtures of Araucanian with other peoples, such as the Diaguita and Atacameño. The Araucanians were a great musical people, the only ones in the western hemisphere to develop more than a pentatonic scale,

and they invented many original instruments found nowhere else. Fiercely independent and mighty warriors they wiped out numerous Inca and Spanish expeditions trying to subdue them.

Also on the Pacific Coast, imbedded in later Inca culture, were two brilliant groups, one in south Peru and the other around present-day Trujillo: the Nazca and Moche (the last changing into the Chimú). Both peoples were well advanced in agriculture, used fish and guano fertilizers, and had extensive artificial irrigation. They made magnificent pottery and were good builders though mostly in adobe, using cuneiform bricks. The Moche, who flourished about the time of Christ, produced one of the world's great art forms, chiefly expressed—at least what has survived—in ceramics and carving.

The mysterious southern peoples near Antarctica need not be rediscussed at this point. Three other major groups occupied much of the rest of the continent; the Tupí-Guaraní, the Arawak, and the Carib.

1. The *Tupi-Guaraní* originally centered probably along the great Paraguay and Paraná rivers and spread along the watercourses south to Uruguay and along the entire Atlantic seaboard as far as the Amazon River, driving out the numerous Gé peoples, so that the Tupí-Guaraní languages came to be spoken from easternmost Brazil to the foot of the Andes, from Guiana to Uruguay.

Guaraní survives as the living language of Paraguay. Five major Tupí language groups existed in the Paraná area. Seven Guaraní groups, with many sublanguages, were located in eastern Bolivia; two others, the Tapirapé and Canoeiro, along the Araguay River in Brazil. In the South Amazon area, three linguistic families controlled the Xingú valley, and ten, the Tapajoz. In the upper Amazon region, the Cocana and the Aguaré were Tupí. Along the Brazilian coast, Nycengatú Tupí (with scores of languages), Tupiná and Tupinamba were the major groups. In all, some hundred major Guaraní-Tupí tongues have been identified. Possibly related to them are the amazing Witoto people north of the Amazon, with five major language families, of which the Borón and Orejón were the most important.

2. Even greater in numbers and more widely distributed geographically were the *Arawak,* extending from Uruguay, the Gran Chaco, and upper Xingú to Cuba and the Bahamas; from the mouth of the Amazon well up into the Andes in Bolivia, Peru, Ecuador,

and Colombia. The Chayo on the Pacific coast may also have been Arawak. Originally the Arawak were supposed to have spread out of the Orinoco and Rio Negro regions.

3. The great *Carib* family extended from the greater Antilles to central Mato Grosso, from Peru to Pará. The bulk of them lived north of the Amazon, in the Guianas, Venezuela, and lowland Colombia. Their original diaspora was apparently out of the region between the upper Xingú and the Tapajoz. In the Guiana-Venezuela area alone there were 110 Carib languages, grouped under eleven family languages. There were three more linguistic families in the Mount Roraima highland area.

Finally, special mention needs to be made of the Jívaro, the famous—or notorious—headshrinkers of inner Peru and Ecuador. They have occupied a considerable territory for a thousand years or more. Though generally classed among the more primitive indigenes, they were among the most intelligently organized in sex, family, social, and "national" relationships and highly skilled in practical arts and handicrafts. Fiercely independent, they inculcated patriotism from earliest childhood to adulthood. Their headshrinking operation was merely part of a victory rite, something indulged in by all peoples, ancient and modern.

They add their own curious uniqueness to the hodgepodge of pre-Columbian peoples. How are we to explain this fantastic South American pattern of divergent peoples? Whence did they come? How? When? What records have they left?

4

Out of the Caves of the Past

DID man originate in the New World? So believed the great Argentine paleontologist, Florentino Ameghino, whose first discoveries were made in 1870. No one now takes his thesis seriously, for it rests on the most dubious evidence. A few South American archaeologists and anthropologists, however, such as Joaquín Frenguelli, do admit the possibility of autochthonous development of man in the western hemisphere, though not on the Ameghino basis and at a considerably later date. No proof of this is at hand, however.

But if the two "fossil" human teeth found by Melcíades Alejo Vignati in 1941 in the Chalmalal strata at Miramar on the Argentine coast are, as Theodore D. McCown admits, from the early Pleistocene or even the Pliocene—the latter Tertiary Age of Mammals (in recent years renamed the Villafranchian era)—they could represent the earliest known evidence of hominids from any part of the New World. On the other hand, McCown also points out they could have been there as the result of later burial, not necessarily incorporated in the deposit by the natural process of stratum formation.

Otherwise, only comparable in antiquity are the prehuman hominids called Australopithecinae and their split pebble tools discovered in 1956 in the African Transvaal and the somewhat later Pithecanthropus bones of Java and China (1891, 1929, 1936, 1941).

As elsewhere in the world, prehistoric man must be traced by fossils, bones, teeth and skulls, tools and artifacts, kitchen middens, wood and stone carvings, cave and wall paintings. The dating of such finds rests on paleontological evidence, strata formations, cultural level identification, coexistence with prehistoric botanical and zoological forms, relation to glacial epochs, etc., in short, "stratification and association."

Today more precise dating of organic material (provided no contamination has occurred) as far back as 37,000 years (possibly perfectible to 50,000 years) may be obtained by carbon testing, i.e., measuring the degree of Carbon-14 radiation. During life, it is believed, all organisms store up an equal percentage of Carbon 14 (cosmic radiation acting on nitrogen), and, after death, this disintegrates at the rate of one-half every 5,568 years (i.e., "Carbon-14 half-life"), half the remainder in the next 5,568 years, and so on. Results are not always reliable. Wet conditions may introduce fresh carbon after "death" and thus make material "younger." Atomic fall-out may destroy all hope for this method, except for deeply buried specimens; in labs, materials not properly protected have been ruined. Fluorine testing is also an important tool, and other chemical tests may be developed. Scientists are also working on electronic devices, so as to date more closely—back hundreds of thousands of years—stones, shells, and other materials, but thus far no viable process has been perfected.

The task of unraveling the story of early man therefore devolves not merely upon anthropologists, archaeologists, and ethnologists, whose techniques are better suited to later periods, but upon paleontologists, geologists, ecologists, botanists, climatologists, experts on glaciers (the first to force anthropologists to retreat from arbitrary doctrines about man's time span in the New World), geneticists, behaviorists, sociologists, electronic experts, chemists, and physicists —all the specialized fields of modern science.

Some limitations to possible knowledge about early man have been pointed out by Ralph Beals and Harry Hoijer in *An Introduction to Anthropology:* The archaeologist, when his field work has been done, "usually can define the type of geographic environment in which people live, and so . . . something about their adaptation to it . . . often what weapons and tools were used, but not what containers or clothing [exceptions in desert regions or caves] . . . what animals were eaten but not what berries [yet hackberry seeds were found in the 37,000-year-old Texas Lewisville site; popcorn and true corn were found in 6,000-year-old Bat Cave in western

New Mexico]. . . . From burials, cult objects . . . shrines or temples, he may infer something of the systems of religious beliefs, but
not the organization or training of religious specialists. . . . He
may establish the size and pattern of settlements and infer the general character of the social organization but not such specific features as the presence or absence of clans . . . [and this often merely]
because of the ethnologist's knowledge of the cultures of peoples
still existing who led a similar life." However, through the anthropologist "we gain a humbling perception of the enormous time it
took man to accumulate . . . the basic controls over nature that
made our recent extraordinary advances possible. . . . He shows
how in all times and places man has faced similar problems. . . .
He has helped us identify . . . the preconditions for a number of
the great expansions of human knowledge and culture."

Yet, Western man long suffered from astigmatism in these matters—prejudices born of racial, cultural, and national snobberies,
particularly toward non-European areas. Even scientists have been
sadly bemused by the Biblical legends, mainly the concept that man
originated in the Near East—which today seems unlikely. The larger
part of funds available for archaeological research over the years
has been expended in this limited area, with steadily diminishing
returns, at the expense of richer, more important, explorations on
other continents. Only lately has much been done in Africa; still less
in Asia, and only the surface scratched in South America. Even in
Europe, only lately, new discoveries in Italy and elsewhere have
forced a reassessment of man's life on that continent.

Thus Western scientists, hypnotized by the unilateral descent of
man from the Middle East—Caucasian man—have concentrated on
the single cultural chain that apparently accounts for the rise of the
dominant political groups who lately have ruled the earth for a few
brief centuries—a mere dot in man's million-year time span on this
planet—a rule now slipping away in confusion. This eye-blinder
attitude has fed Western man's vanity if not his intelligence, has
given rise to such absurd race chauvinisms as "Aryanism," etc.
"White Councils" have ruled not merely pithecoid elements in the
South of the United States, but often have held sway in the nobler
kingdom of so-called science.

This has led westerners—such as Max Schmidt—until lately, to
attempt to make New World culture almost entirely derivative of
and dependent chronologically on Old World cultural develop-

ments, denying American peoples any independent evolution and inventive capacity. This, few American anthropologists, working more realistically on local details, have ever believed. As Julian H. Steward has pointed out—a most obvious example—llama-raising is in no way comparable to Old World cattle-raising, hence cannot account for Andean patrilineal tendencies. And how, then, explain these?

Few anthropologists on this side of the water doubt "the possibility of transoceanic influences," but "most of them repudiate the theories that bring whole cultures from overseas."

Only by close examination and empirical treatment, not so much of cultures as a whole, but of the history of "each element, element-complex and pattern," can a start be made at learning man's early story. This, if less dramatic than world schemes, such as those of Paul Rivet, eventually may pay off better.

But Rivet at least sees problems whole, sees interrelations, sees the need for more far-flung investigation—before even his own theories can be properly verified. It is probable, he remarked sagely, "that when all the continents have been explored to the degree that western Europe has been, the 'Western looking-glass illusion' will disappear. . . . Western Europe is really a secondary population zone."

Nationalism and national vanity, he adds (and Ameghino's theory, for instance, is far more patriotic than basically sound), have no proper place in science, even though everywhere, militarists and politicians try to chain them to the gun carriages of aggression, war, and death. It is always difficult to obtain a truthful image of alien peoples and cultures, even today, let alone in early epochs.

Peruvian writer Luís Alberto Sánchez attacks the difficulty more philosophically. Concerning prehistoric facts, he remarks, "The West has suffered from an excess of subjectizing the world. When it does not know something, it denies its existence. . . . That which is not seen has never existed. This represents Cartesianism, the Western rationalization of blindness. . . . The tactic of suppressing that which is not known, is ancient indeed in the scientific petulance of the West." Of course, accepting the unknown as fact rather than as a possibility is equally invalid.

Localism is important, specific minor culture examinations are imperative, but on the other hand, many Western scientists have been inadequately concerned with man as a whole, with the globe as a whole, and have not insisted that these same intensive examinations must be promoted everywhere on earth. In the first place, the epic of South American man (hence that of North American man) cannot be unraveled without due study, never achieved of the under continent itself.

2

Scientists have also been bemused by "the prejudice of modernity," partly induced by the strange idea that this is the perfect unsurpassable age—at least in the United States. Really ours is merely an arrested stage of barbarism, as future man—not necessarily Caucasian—will appreciate, provided man survives as a species, something we suicidal Caucasians, among others, are striving mightily to prevent.

Until rather recently, United States anthropologists were ruled by the hard and fast dogmatism that man came to this continent only 2,000 years or so ago. Any scholar who sought to overturn this belief found it difficult to get his ideas published or to secure academic advancement. Clearly such a short span was insufficient to account for the evolution of new species of the potato, corn, beans, and the hundred other domesticated food products that nurtured the great civilizations of the Quechua, Maya, Nahuatl, etc.; or to account for the rise of magnificent cities and the highly developed property, religious, political, and military systems; the knowledge of mathematics (zero, the decimal system) and astronomy, which predated and was often superior to that of western Europe of Columbus' day; or of engineering and architectural skills! The Incas built better roads than did Rome or contemporary Europe of their period. Inca agriculture was advanced: fertilizers, irrigation, terracing, soil conservation often went far beyond the knowledge and practices in Europe. Their resettlement policies—organized, scientific and effective—make Mr. Rex Tugwell's late depression efforts seem like a childish puttering of political hypocrisy.

Our own history, the phenomenal rise of the United States, was the product, not of the few brief years of the industrial revolution, but of tens of thousands of years of technological evolution elsewhere.

Also, in the million years of man's existence on this earth, he must have circled the globe many times in many ways. If the great mammals could do it, if botanical species could do it, surely man was not their inferior. As brilliant Joaquín Frenguelli of the National La Plata University has put it, speaking of paleolithic Pampas finds (and reinforcing José Imbelloni's theories of Melanesian and proto-Indonesian invasions), "It would seem strange that so vast and favorable a continent as America had remained closed to the Paleolithic Ecumene while an enormous interchange of mammals was going on between America and Asia and vice versa."

Naturally, the further back one seeks, the scantier, less reliable the evidence, and until recently instruments for appraising much of that evidence have been lacking, just as those of today will soon seem inadequate. But it is precisely science's task to attempt to pierce the unknown, not merely shut mysteries away as a child draws curtains to shut out the dark.

Similarly, United States scientists long clung, even more dogmatically, to the one-race derivation of New World man. Any deviation from this monoracial, mono-route, monogeographical, monoculture theory (though so out of keeping with everything known about man's energy and proliferating curiosity) was as dreadful as a Victorian lady showing her legs, or as the doubting of the story of Eve and the apple by Bible cultists. Students who ventured afield, could not get their conclusions published in scientific journals. Not all the Hitlers and McCarthys are found in politics.

Only recently, even in Europe, have the bars been let down to admit proofs that man there is of multiple race and cultural origins (from Africa and Asia as well)—most discouraging for all white chauvinists. But in the New World the set doctrine still followed the dictum that "all Chinamen look alike." All New World "Indians" were adjudged to be Mongoloid, to have been latecomers across the Bering Straits. Only in the last decade or so has effort been made even to identify this northern immigration with varied cultural and linguistic developments in Asia—from Tibet to Mongolia. Either the newcomers had already become a mixed race in Asia before coming to America, particularly Caucasoid and Mongolian peoples (the theory of W. W. Howells and others), or the original long-headed archaic peoples, known as Amurian Caucasoids first came and were later intruded upon, by Mongolian and other migrations. But even this covers only a few aspects of the racial enigma of the Americas.

Though research has been slowed down because of the world's present primitive dedication to military rivalry, recent New World discoveries (plus the gradual long-span accumulation of data on cranial and skeletal measurements, blood types, linguistic affinities, artifacts here and in Asia and Africa, etc.) have raised new doubts. Numerous pet doctrines, long held with religious fervor, have had to be interred, and new problems now contribute excitingly to the mystery of man's origin here.

The only possible scientific approach, other than that of persistent digging, must be one of freely admitted ignorance, a flexible handling of all old and new evidence. A huge X must still be written over the whole question, while the search for the meaning of smaller $x's$ goes on. There is now considerable evidence of New World countermigrations to Asia and Polynesia, perhaps also to Africa and elsewhere.

In the western hemisphere itself, some important known migrations have been from south to north, not vice versa; there is even considerable evidence that the plains moundbuilders and others along the Gulf Shore, perhaps even farther north, came from an early diaspora out of Mexico.

Many authorities have urged that a combined investigation, stratigraphic, petrographic, and climatic, be undertaken to forward knowledge about early man in South America. But the "paleonthropological literature concerned with ancient man in South America," remarks Theodore D. McCown, University of California anthropologist, "gives no evidence that either anthropologists or geologists have systematically undertaken such studies." The gap is wide, and so conjecture wallows in muddy emptiness.

3

Three major theories have been set forth:

1. The New World man was autochthonous. (This does not rule out later migrations or countermigrations: blood and culture mingling from outside the continent.) This theory insists that Homo sapiens (at least the Indian race, if a multiple origin of man is admitted) originated in the Americas. The archedifice of this idea was first erected by Florentino Ameghino, though hints are found among earlier studies.

2. Most United States anthropologists have insisted that pre-Columbian Americans were all a Mongoloid homotype, a people who drifted across the Bering Straits some thousands of years ago, then filtered into South America. American anthropologist Aleš

Hrdlička, the fanatic tzar holding to this theory, smote down anybody suggesting other possibilities. A stern disciple is Junius Bird of the New York Museum of Natural History.

3. Man in the New World had multiple origins. Many fanciful ideas have been advanced, such as the Lost Tribes of Israel (believed by many New England settlers about North American Indians); an ancient Atlantis (about which the Populist fanatic, Ignatius Donnelly of Minnesota, wrote a best-seller back in the eighties); an early lost Pacific continent, the fabulous "Mu"; that early invaders were Chaldeans, Phoenicians, Babylonians, etc.; that they were derived from Egypt. Lord Kingsborough spent his life, health, and fortune trying to prove this last about the Aztecs and went insane, but fortunately salvaged for us some of the finest materials of the Empire of Anahuac. William James Perry (1926) and Elliot Smith (1929) put forth the idea that a heliolithic Egyptian civilization crossed all Asia, then the Pacific from island to island, and spread as far as Antarctica.

More reasoned suggestions, some presented with considerable supporting evidence are: Early American man is derived from Mongoloids and from Amurian Caucasoids; from Celts, Norse, Tibetans, Melanesians, Polynesians, Australoids, Africans, Oceanic Negroes, and Mediterranean peoples. Some, or all of these peoples, it has been suggested, were fused into what has become known as the Indian race.

Paul Rivet remarks: "It is curious that the historic period of American evolution is merely a repetition of the ethnic events which conditioned the original population. Ever since it was 'discovered' America has continued to be a focus of attraction for the most varied races and peoples, just as it was during the long period of pre-Columbian formation. . . . Thus Indian America, at the same time that it was gathering in the inheritance of the peoples and races which contributed to its formation, was able to develop its own civilization on this general base, by means of a series of inventions and creations which rivaled the inventions and creations of the Old Continent."

The Pacific, prior to Columbus, he contended, had long been a busy two-way street, and not merely at the antipodes. How could that be, insist most United States authorities, when proper seagoing vessels were not in existence and early man was not likely to venture to any island unless he could see it, as Steward argues? During the

68

late war, shipwrecked persons survived by collecting rainwater and killing fish and birds, through thousands of miles and many months of drifting in tiny boats. H. H. Bancroft in his Pacific Coast history supplies statistics in a footnote of several nineteenth-century years, of an amazing number of Chinese junks—some of which are fine seagoing vessels—from across the entire Pacific. Prehistoric man certainly reached islands thousands of miles apart in the vast open stretches of the ocean. Adequate investigation of far southern climatology and the antarctic steppingstone islands reaching toward New Zealand and Australia may someday provide startling information.

4

What actually has been discovered about paleolithic man in the Americas? Most discoveries have been made in North America, but this has great bearing on South America, where even carbon-dating has as yet been little utilized.

The Trenton, New Jersey stone instruments found in 1875, apparently date back to the end of the Quaternary clay; similarly those near the Colorado River in Texas (1924) and near Folsom, New Mexico (1926–28). Since those dates, new discoveries have been made by the score in many parts of the two continents.

Near Clovis, New Mexico, stone implements at least 8,000 years old have been found. Similar remains in Nebraska and Colorado are estimated by Kirk Bryan and Luis L. Ray to be not less than 10,000 or more than 25,000 years old. Bone tools have been found, which Rivet believes preceded stone art, in a pre-Wisconsin glacial period. The Nevada Tule Springs site yielded artifacts, associated with camels, early bison, and horse bones. Finds in Florida at Vero Beach (F. H. Sellards, 1916) and Melbourne (J. W. Gridley, and Frederick Brooms, 1923, 1926), came from deposits also containing such extinct forms as *Elephas colombii*.

The "desert" culture of the Great Basin has been tentatively set at about 11,000 years, but some carbon readings go back much earlier. There, grinding stones for seeds were utilized as early as 8,000 years ago. The world's oldest known basketry containers were found in dry caves of this region. Sage-brush sandals, dated 9,000 years ago, were found at Fort Rock Cave in Oregon. From the Pleistocene at Malakoff, Texas, come carved stone heads, weighing up to 120 pounds, with bore holes to represent teeth.

In 1932 at Pelican Rapids, Minnesota, a young female skull with abnormally large teeth—"Minnesota Man"—was found in an ancient glacial lake and was estimated to date back 20,000 years. Since then great controversy has raged. The re-dating by carbon testing of the Mankato Age, would put the find at less than 11,000 years ago, provided the skull was not intrusive.

Bone and artifact finds at Brown Valley, Minnesota, were re-dated as between 12,000 to 8,000 years ago. Similar parallel flaked stone points found in Wyoming have been dated at nearly 8,000 years.

Mark R. Harrington, Fenley Hunter, and Ruth D. Simpson, in various excavations at Tule Springs, Nevada, found camel, bison, mammoth, and horse bones split and end-burned to extract the marrow; fire pits for roasting a camel; stone choppers, scrapers, awls, and bone tools. Charcoal, apparently but not necessarily of human origin, dates back 23,800 years. On Santa Rosa Island off the California coast, men hunted dwarf mammoths, perhaps 30,000 years ago. A large cemetery there, 7,000 years old, has yielded bone tools, shell beads, and ornaments.

Midland man (Texas), with distinctive artifacts found with numerous extinct animals, was thought to date back about 12,500 years, but subsequent shell-testing has given readings of 20,000 years. John N. Rosholt, with his new, extremely dangerous process, utilizing daughter products of uranium, has established dates of 15,000, 17,000, and 19,000 years ago. Charcoal from hearth sites, containing artifacts and Clovis points, encountered recently near Lewisville, Texas, have been dated (correctly?) at more than 37,000 years.

Man was definitely on the North American continent during the last Wisconsin glaciation, probably earlier.

Recent carbon-dating in the Valley of Mexico takes the story back to a possible 16,000 years in that area. Human and other bones, going back 11,000 years, found in an ancient marsh, indicate that the individual had been hunting a mammoth.

"Tepexpán Man" there was moderately round-headed. It has been generally believed that the earliest migrants were dolichocephalic.

Kitchen middens at nearby Tequixquac, tentatively dated 7,000 to 9,000 years ago, suggest settled agriculture. They have yielded ceramics, exquisite clay figurines, a dancing girl, the sacrum of an extinct llama, recarved, with bored nostril holes, to represent perhaps a coyote.

Radiation datings from the southern tip of South America have

70

enabled Bird to back-date previous estimates of 5,000 years, to at least 8,700, which also predates Rivet's suggested 6,000 years for possible Australoid migration. Man's companions there were an early horse, mylodon (a ground sloth), and other great mammals. In Ecuador, Max Uhle, not always reliable in stratigraphic matters, found mastodon skeletons apparently squatting on human remains and artifacts.

The important South American discoverer, consumptive Peter Lund, a Dane, in 1835–44 found 18 human skulls (he explored 800 caves) near Lagoa Santa in Minas Gerâis, Brazil, all decidedly dolichocephalic or long-headed, in association with prehistoric animal bones. In 1835–43 D'Orbigny—not a reliable witness—dated the Pampas layers, where fossils had been encountered, as identical in age with the Lagoa Santa deposits. The Argentine F. Seguín (1863), found human remains with Arctotherium bones on the Carcaraña River, again a doubtful scientific decision. In 1881 Santiago Roth found a skull under a gigantic glyptodont (armadillo-like mammal) shell on the banks of the Arrecifes—probably of the upper Pleistocene. Was this very ancient or did it merely represent later use of the shell as a dwelling? Three more early skulls were found on the Arrecifes in 1888. In 1919, thirty miles north of Santa Fé on the Pampa, human bones were found dating from the upper Pleistocene, and an arrowhead in the horn of a long-extinct deer. Many amazing discoveries over a period of forty years or so were made by the indefatigable Florentino Ameghino and his brother Carlos.

Many of these discoveries, made over a hundred years, mostly exclusively by European and South American scientists, have been considered unreliable by United States scholars, though they themselves have done little in that area to add to basic information. "Neither anthropologists or geologists have systematically undertaken studies comparable to those made in East Africa a quarter of a century ago," McCown remarks. Mention should be made, however, of George Gaylord Simpson, who at least made a start in that direction. His work, *Patagonian Journal,* was published in 1934, and later he investigated the mammal-bearing Tertiary of South America—as set forth in the *Proceedings* of the American Philosophical Society in 1940. In 1943 he gave us a brief paper on the origin of Latin American fauna. But in general, as McCown insists, progress can be described "only in a negative sense."

More recent finds have been made. "Lerma points," discovered first in Tamaulipas, Mexico, have been unearthed at El Jobo, Venezuela and in Central Argentina, dating back 8,000 years.

As Ralph L. Beals expresses it, "The study of the earliest cultures in the Americas is still in its infancy. . . . Man lived on this continent in association with a considerable number of now extinct animals, including . . . the mammoth, mastodon, horse, camel, giant sloth, an extinct species of bison. . . . He arrived before the end of the last or Wisconsin glaciation and probably was here before the next-to-last or Mankato advance of the ice, which is generally dated about 11,000 years ago [some . . . date it 20,000 years ago]. It is possible that man's antiquity in North America may be substantially greater than this, and a pre-Wisconsin Age is possible." However, as yet, no *assured* evidence of earlier dating is available.

Julian H. Steward writes: "Man indisputably was present in the New World during the last phases of the glacial period, which was certainly 15,000 and possibly 35,000 years ago."

5

Ameghino—his conclusions have been almost wholly disproved—believed that mammal life in Patagonia (fossils exist) in the Eocene (lower Tertiary) evolved from the first Pitheculitus (ape-type) into the Homonunculus (small man-type: the Santa Cruz skull), then into the upper Anthropops; that the first Hominidae (ape-man genus) appeared in the south Pampas during the Miocene (other geologists, such as A. Mochi, say the lower Pleistocene) as the *Tetraprothomo argentinus*.

Enter here, Ameghino's own direct paleontological discoveries. The Tetraprothomo was represented by a femur and an atlas (upper vertebrae) and part of skull (now in the Paris Museum) which he found at Monte Hermoso. Most scientists now doubt that the femur was human, and they contend that few soft Pampa clays (in which Tetraprothomo was found) belonged to the Tertiary.

The next link in Ameghino's design, a purely hypothetical one which he called *Triprothomo platensis,* midway toward the *Diprothomo argentinus* (a pre-man type), has never been found. Of Diprothomo, he found skulls near Buenos Aires; and, from later Pliocene strata, crania from Miramar, Chapaldmalal, Necochea, Baradero, Fontezuela, Arrecifes, Ovejero, etc.—all quite human.

Evolving from them, Homo sapiens, or *Prothomo pampensus,* he contended, reached full physical development at the dawn of the

72

Quaternary, i.e., a million years ago, in the Buenos Aires area, then spread over the earth, via Bering Straits, Greenland, and Asia or to Africa, as simian types had even earlier. Thus a small ape emigrating to Africa, before the era of man, he declared, had evolved into the man-like apes of Africa and Asia (skeletons of which were later found), not progenitors of man but parallel forms. Later man re-emigrated to the New World.

Similar origins have been claimed for camels—from cat-size species embalmed in Patagonia up to four more modern fossilized species; and for the horse (fifty species from five- to three-toed), for elephants, mammoths, mastodons (from certain purely South American mammals with prehensile nose extensions; almost certainly a case of parallelism); and for all anthropoid apes, Ameghino contended. Some of these creatures (such as the glyptodon) got only as far as North America, never reaching other continents. The capybara, still widespread in Paraná jungles, reached Florida before perishing. The marsupials, like the opossum, according to this thesis, crossed over to Australia, where they evolved into the kangaroo; also, South America, notes one commentator, "had all the ungulates that ever lived or are yet living in the other continents." Unfortunately, this statement is untrue, viz., antelopes.

Various of the theories about animal origins, of course, contradict prevalent North American claims that most prehistoric creatures migrated from the Arctic into South America, but that, too, is admitted in part by Ameghino, on the basis that they represented countermigrations of new species, evolved from Pampean ancestors, in Asia and Africa. Considerable clarification is required by all parties, to say the least.

The Ameghino autochthonous theory has been hotly combated on paleontological and geological grounds, by imputations of the unreliability of the discoveries, and by failure to find any link between the Patagonian mammals and higher primate evolution. Actually no cebid ancestral type has been discovered in the western hemisphere, only lemurs and tarsoids.

But he stirred much interest, controversy, and investigation, unfortunately much of it merely negative—an effort to prove him wrong. As previously mentioned, Frenguelli, among others, still believes that an "American man," if not of such remote ancestry as Ameghino claims, "could have evolved during the Pampas Age, totally or wholly Quaternary, along with the characteristic mammals." Apart from that, various South American and European authorities believe that Ameghino's work, regardless of his theories, contains much material that sooner or later must be taken into account in determining the true history of man in the Americas.

6

So too has the monotype monogeographical Mongoloid explanation been cast aside by most, though it still has stubborn defenders, chiefly in the United States. Partly the argument rests on the exact definition given to "Mongoloid." Hrdlička did admit possible migrations of four "yellow" race subtypes: (1) Long-headed—Algonquins, Iroquois, Sioux, Shoshones, Pimas, Aztecs, certain Venezuelan, Brazilian coast, and Tierra del Fuegian tribes; (2) Round- or short-headed—Northeastern Indians, moundbuilders of the center and east of the United States and the Gulf of Mexico (including Yucatán), Central America, the Peruvian coast; (3) A second brachycephalic subtype: the Athapascans of Alaska and northwest Canada; here and there in California (Hupa), Arizona, New Mexico, Texas, and northern Mexico (Lipán, Apache); (4) The Eskimos.

Rivet says this easy homogeneous classification is based on superficial external characteristics, which at first glance seem Asiatic: pigmentation of skin and eyes, paucity of face hair, the Mongolian eye, high cheek bones. Yet many New World peoples had few or none of these features. When one leaves off looking at these external characteristics, divergencies begin to appear. Between a Guajiro and a Patagón, or between a Maya and a Botocudo, there exists with regard to height, facial and cranial structure as great differences, if not greater, than between a Swede and an Italian, or an Avignonese and an Englishman, so to speak of the unity of the American race is as absurd as to speak of the unity of the white race. To link up in this same ethnic trunk, super-brachycephalics such as the Maya and super-dolichocephalics such as the Pericoa; very tall Patagón and people of very short stature, such as the Motilone, would be to consider anatomical characteristics, on which anthropology rests, of no value whatever; as Mendes Corrêa points out, this would put an end to all ethnic anthropology.

But even in external characteristics, the unity is far less than Hrdlička fanatically insisted; for instance, that the "fundamental color" is brown-yellow. "Actually," says Corrêa, "there are American peoples who uniformly possess a pale yellow skin while others are almost black." The early Spanish and Portuguese explorers frequently observed that many people in the Caribbean were lighter skinned than their own people. The Auraucanians of Chile are considerably lighter skinned than most North American Indians, who have a decided copper tinge. Hrdlička's conclusions, Corrêa insists (most charitably), are clearly "geographic prejudice." Such peoples if scattered elsewhere here and there on earth would not be recognized as belonging to the same anthropological type at all.

Hrdlička also insisted that all New World languages—in spite of wide phonetic, lexical, and morphological differences—were polysynthetic with agglutinative tendencies. Thus in English "manly," "humanly," "manliness." This is not true at all, says J. Alden Mason of the University Museum of Philadelphia. Many tongues show tendencies toward inflection. According to Hrdlička the New World languages had the same formation for the names of numerals, methods of expressing the plural, use of prefixes, suffixes, different vocabularies for each sex, the same relative value of nouns and pronouns, the incorporation of the pronoun of nominal object. Actually these characteristics are often missing. Hrdlička's conclusions were not based on sound linguistic knowledge of a continent having a hundred race stocks and thousands of sublanguages. Franz Boas, the great pioneer in American linguistics, noted that the designation of all American languages as polysynthetic and compounding is absurd. "The phonetic systems of the languages vary considerably. . . . It is impossible to characterize them generally with regard to sound groupings. . . . An equally great variation is found in grammatical procedures." Some languages used not merely prefixes and suffixes but inflexes; some used only prefixes or only suffixes, especially the latter, and he concludes (*Handbook of American Indian Languages,* 1911): "There is no common character to these languages." The fact is, so Mason pointed out: "As regards the aboriginal languages of South America . . . comparatively little data are available," and much of that unsatisfactory, based on the early work of priests, friars, and others who knew nothing about linguistics.

Hrdlička is "equally imprudent," says Rivet, when he speaks of a common civilization, as manifested in stone, clay, wood, bone, weaving, basketry, fire-making, clothing, limited house furnishings, agriculture, games, medicine, religion, concepts of nature, folklore, social organization, war-making. "This," he remarks wryly, "rather than proving the one race theory would prove the identity of all the peoples of the universe." Precise examination reveals differences as great as those among physical and linguistic characteristics.

Even if Hrdlička's conclusions are absurd, this, per se, does not exclude Bering Straits Mongoloid migrations; Rivet himself believes they took place; that of the Eskimo is indubitable. However, from 1926 to 1938, Smithsonian Institution carried on a systematic exploration over the routes that Bering Straits immigrants would have had to traverse, but found no paleolithic evidence, only some Eskimo-type neolithic artifacts in Alaska and the Aleutians. Brief summaries of the work of A. P. Okladnikov published in English, indicate that similarly no early sites have been found on the Siberian side prior to the Neolithic.

However, in 1948, J. L. Giddings, Jr., digging deeper, came upon artifacts of great delicacy and skill from the Upper Paleolithic and Neolithic Ages, that were faintly similar to other Paleo-Indian forms. To these finds he gave the name "Denbigh Complex," from their location on the west side of Norton Sound. There is a possibility, other authorities have pointed out, that the Denbigh Complex may be a spread northwest from more southernly cultures. Others believe it represents a mingling of elements from north and south.

D. M. Hopkins (1953) favored the idea that the deposits were made between 5,000 and 9,000 years ago during the post-Mankato period. Giddings then treated them by the carbon method, and the dates ranged only from 3,500 to 4,500 years, though a bit older when the specimens were acid-washed.

In 1934 on the Alaska University campus, Froelich Rainey unearthed several apparent stone cores and a flake, but these appear to have been fortuitous. In 1950 Helge Larsen found four periods of human occupation in two caves on Seward Peninsula. Carbon-testing of willow twigs on the bottom of the cave, but not directly connected with the materials, gave 6,000 years.

Thus far nothing has been discovered to indicate human presence on or near the Bering Straits prior to 5,000 years ago. Even this may represent northward migration. New evidence, of course, may be forthcoming at any time.

The anthropometrical measurements of Mongols, compared with Buriats of Siberia, for instance, are similar, though the Eskimos have small cranial capacity, are not so long-headed, have a considerably larger vertical face index and a much smaller nasal index.

In blood composition the Eskimos are remote indeed from traditional Asiatic peoples, having over 80 per cent O-type blood; whereas Koreans, Japanese, Mongolians, Manchurians, Northern Chinese, Buriats, all have 30 per cent or less. Only the Blackfeet Indians (23.5 per cent) and the Karadza (39 per cent), have an O-count as low as Orientals. However, later examination by William C. Blood put the Blackfeet O percentage at 45.5, but correspondingly reduced the Greenland Eskimos to 54.2 per cent. Even so both are far from the blood types of the Ainus of Sakhalin (25.7) or the Buriat of Siberia (32.4). Only among some Japanese, the African Pygmies, the South African Hottentots, and in India are similar low percentages of O blood found. Some of this data could as easily point to New World emigration to the Old World, not the reverse.

With regard to language similarities, Aurelien Sauvageot believes that the Eskimo tongue is allied to the Finno-Ugrian language phylum. In 1925, Edward Sapir presented American similarities between the Sino-Tibetan tongue and Na-Dêne and other New World language groups extending from inner Alaska to Hudson Bay, also with fragments of peoples in California, Lower California, and just north of the Rio Grande down to its mouth.

Unfortunately (for this is the most definite evidence we have of the theory of Bering Straits migration), he died before giving a full report. But the Na-Dêne tongue (if that) in the United States is but one of five North American phyla, and is but one of the hundreds of New World language stocks.

H. M. Wormington, Curator of Archaeology of the Denver Museum of Natural History, in her admirable *Ancient Man in North America*, remarks: "The later American Indians were Mongoloids, but this is not necessarily the racial type of the first comers to the New World." In fact it is not likely that the Mongoloid type, which came to the New World, had even evolved at the time of the Paleo-Indian, i.e., prior to 6,000 years ago.

7

The theory of multiple race origins has a much longer history, and is now largely accepted by many authorities, but with much bickering over possible ethnic ingredients and chronology. One of the headaches for the monorace theory is precisely the data on New World and Old World blood types.

Investigation of the blood is a relatively new science, more complicated than appears at first glance. L. H. Snyder in 1955 declared that it was possible to isolate 43,200 blood types. But roughly speaking the prevalent European blood types are O and A, with little B; the Asiatic blood types are predominantly O and B, except in Polynesia and Micronesia, where O is high. B, in short, is a pronounced Asiatic ingredient. But native Australians have a very high O percentage (Queensland, 60.3 per cent), with considerable A blood, perhaps a later admixture, and very little B blood.

In the New World, with the exception of one small group deep in the Amazon, the O percentage is well in excess of 70, in many instances is 100 per cent—almost universally so when unmixed Indians can be isolated and tested. Pure-blooded North American Indians average 91.3 per cent O blood; the Seri of Tiburón Island, 99.3.

New World peoples had (and have) two types of blood found in few other peoples: M, N, and MN. N is highest in Australia, M in the Americas. The N type is highest at the southern end of South America. Among somewhat mixed Mapuche, 57 out of 100 individuals had M blood, 9 had N blood, and 34 had MN blood.

Another factor, apparently wholly Indian, except for some traces among Chinese and Japanese, is the Diego factor, named from the Venezuelan in whom it was first discovered. Like Rh blood, it can have pernicious results if mixed with some other blood types. In some Indians, Diego-type blood adds up to 100 per cent.

Thus, except for the Carajá in the Amazon (with only 39 per cent O blood), most of the peoples in South America (often post-Conquest mixing may have taken place) have from 90 to 100 per cent O blood. Those with markedly less are the Mataco of Argentina, 78.8 per cent (15 per cent A blood), the Chilean Mapuche (75.6 per cent) A blood, 17.2 per cent, the Sibundoy and Santiago of Pasto, Colombia (70.6). The Colla of Peru, also have a low O percentage, but they have been tremendously mestizocized, because of the mining industry; actually pure-blooded Colla have been found by Mazza and other investigators to have 100 per cent O blood. On the other hand (except for the Carajá), few Indians of South America have even 1 per cent of B blood, and most have none at all—though this is the most important and characteristic non-O ingredient of Asia. The exceptions, and these show but little B content, are those previously noted as mixed groups, of which the Pato have as much as 10 per cent B blood, and one group of Colla as much as 13 per cent. (Eskimos have 4.8 per cent; Blackfeet, 2.1 per cent.) Even in these groups, the content is low indeed compared with Mongoloids. Here is a mystery that requires much pondering and investigation.

And how much of the pre-Columbian A content in some North American Indians might be due to the early Norse and Irish migrations?

8

Theories of multiple origin go back to early last century and subsequent studies by Griffith Taylor, Roland B. Dixon, Egon von Eickstedt, E. W. Count, and others. Paul Rivet, José Imbelloni, Martin Gusinde, Viktor Lebzelter, and various other German anthropologists have been strong proponents. In 1924, Dr. R. Verneau found what was to him proof in a Tunebo skull and other materials, that aboriginal Colombians had a Papuan or Oceanic Negroid strain. Walter Lehman has claimed evidence for pre-Columbian Negroes in Darién, Peru, and lower Bolivia.

Rivet's findings on various overseas migrations have been set forth sketchily but lucidly in his *Origins of American Man*. He eliminates various possibilities. No New World people knew the wheel, or glass-making, or wheat, oats, or rye; had no writing except for Mayan, Central American (and Chavín) hieroglyphics, none of which had the slightest relation to Old World forms. This automatically eliminates any derivation from peoples having such techniques at an early period; viz., Semites such as Tyrians, Phoenicians, Canaanites, Tartars, Egyptians, Babylonians, etc. Similarly it eliminates recent contact with the civilized Asiatics, such as the Chinese and Japanese —for one or all of these discoveries would have been brought over.

Rivet argued strongly for Australoid intrusion into the southern end of the continent, a thesis reiterated by Eickstedt in 1934. Lebzelter and Gusinde (1925–34), the two greatest authorities on Patagonia and Tierra del Fuego have also inclined toward belief in Australoid physical traits among Fuegians. E. W. Count (1939, 1941) and José Imbelloni (1937) are other adherents. Imbelloni has classified modern inhabitants of one of the Lake Titicaca islands (a penetration farther north than Rivet claimed) as, in his view, indubitably of Australoid descent.

American anthropologists mostly shrug off the theory by saying that the Australoids were not seafaring people (not entirely borne out by paleolithic indications of their one-time presence in Java, India, Burma and Indo-China), but no North American has really looked into the matter or added any new information. Rivet, along with Mendes Corrêa, believes the evidence for Australoid migration to the southern end of South America is much stronger than for very early Mongoloid migration to the north—with the exception of Eskimos.

The French anthropologist and others have built up considerable evidence based on cranial and skeletal measurements, blood tests, language, and culture—the presence or absence of given techniques and artifacts. Rivet presented cranial evidence from Patagonia and the early Ona (with the maximum head-length of any Americans) and the Australians, which were almost identical: the widest variations were in cranial capacity (larger than the modern average) and in the upper face index. However, since then, new tests by Martin Gusinde among the Ona in 1927, brought the face indices to near identity.

Like the Australians, the Fuegians did not know pottery-making or the hammock, both used skins for capes, had hive-type houses, similar coiffeurs, used boats made of bark sewed together, used a double-forked handle for axes, etc. The Alakaluf, however, have the blue "Mongoloid spot" at the base of their spines.

On the linguistic level, Rivet identified in the Tsôn (Con) language (Patagóns and Ona, Tehuelche, Teue, etc.), 93 parallel words designating parts of the body and natural phenomena, having phonetical as well as lexical correlations with certain Australian languages, e.g.:

English	Australian	Tsôn
Water	kallan	karra
Sea	kuno	kono
Hair	yal	aal
Kangaroo	kure	koori (marine wolf)
Tooth	yorra	orr
Excrement	ganiy	
	guna	ganun
Fire	makka	maka
Moon	mana	manea (night) amania (moon)
Hand	mar, mara	marr, mar
Foot	o-kal	kel
Blood	guara, gwaro	wuar, huarr

These conclusions have been flatly rejected by North American scholars, though McCown invariably remarks that the matter has never been sufficiently investigated. (To reject for lack of evidence is as ignorant as to accept without evidence.) North Americans, except for a few who have worked with specific South American tribes, have very little knowledge of linguistics, whereas Rivet and Erland Nordenskiöld are the towering scholars in the field. Rather than tight negation, an investigation should be made of possible morphological resemblances, which Rivet wished to do but had no opportunity.

These Australoids, Rivet maintained, remained largely in the far south. To believe—considering the proved northern limit of their antique expansion in Asia—that they must have traveled far north to the Bering Straits, then back to the far south, yet without leaving traces of passage, is patently absurd.

On the other hand, antipodean passage poses serious difficulties which Rivet recognizes. Though the Australoids were able to get to East Indian islands and the Asiatic mainland at least 6,000 years ago, they do appear to have been mediocre sailors. Nor has any trace of their passage been found on steppingstone islands, viz.: Tasmania, Auckland Islands, Campbell, Macquarie, Esmeralda, Wilkes Land, Edward VII Land, Graham Land. However, these have never been investigated by trained ethnologists. Rivet believes further proofs may be found, that the Australoids must have reached the New World during an Arctic glacial recession about 6,000 years ago. A. A. Mendes Corrêa believes this route was quite practicable then and at other periods. The islands had superabundant bird life and sea mammal populations for plentiful food.

9

Melanesian invasion has been far more extensive according to many authorities. This idea stemmed chiefly from G. d'Eichtal's "predominance of Oceanic races" in America. His theory, states Frenguelli, has been "verified by well-known ethnographers and corroborated by his own investigations in fields of anthropology, ethnography (archaeology) and linguistics."

Rivet claimed that America was chiefly peopled via Pacific water routes from southeast Asia and the Indo-Malayan Archipelago, the first coming in not later than the end of the Quaternary. Melanese descendants, of whom Rivet considers the Lagoa Santa cave dwellers as prototypes, were dolichocephalic or long-headed, with a pyramid-shaped skull, a very wide palatal arch, and notable prognathism (jaw-jutting). Besides Lagoa Santans, Rivet (from examination of skulls) identifies post-Melanesians as also residing in Lower California, Colorado, New Mexico, and Arizona, and especially in Colombia, Ecuador, Peru, and Brazil, as far south as Argentina.

He is chided by United States scholars on the grounds that some fifty Patalco (Ecuador) and Lagoa Santa skulls and 18 Baja California skulls he examined, did not provide a sufficient basis for such conclusions. This is likely true, though some of these same scholars have woven magnificent theories from a single skull, which they have never even seen, found hither or yon on the earth's surface. Sullivan and Hellman (1925) found Punín (Ecuador) skulls of the Pleistocene to indicate probable Australoid-Melanesian racial connections. E. Nordenskiöld has also written extensively on Melanesian influence in Colombia.

Melanesian migrations, Rivet believes, first began twenty to twenty-five centuries ago, a continuous process. However, Julian H. Steward of the Smithsonian Institution, discards any idea of great antiquity, saying that all Polynesian migration "occurred after 1,000 A.D.," that even if a few earlier comers did arrive on the scene," they could have made no great impact. Yet if no more than a hundred immigrants arrived, within three hundred years they could have totalled more than a million people!

Rivet assembles anthropometric data from New Caledonia and New Guinea and finds them almost identical with those of New World types. Incidentally, he notes, O-blood percentage is higher among Melanesians and certain Philippine peoples than among other Asians.

Also he finds these common cultural elements, most of which, of course, could have been independently invented:

Weapons: Blowtube, dart thrower, blackjacks, bow and arrows, slings, lassos.

Tools: Scrapers.

Transportation: Pole-balance for burdens.

Engineering: Fiber bridges.

Sailing: Similar type *muleta* oars, reed vessels, balsa wood, double canoes, side-balance canoes, eye-paintings on the prow.

Domestic utensils: Wooden mortars, wooden seats and pillows, hammock, mosquito nets, hairbrushes, combs.

Clothes and adornments: Fiber raincoats, bark cloth and bark pulp mashers, nets without knots, weaving, use of *cestain* and *plangi* penis sheath, nasal adornments, breastplates, tapirage or artificial coloring of growing feathers.

Calculators and recording: The quipú, or knotted strings. (Not merely Quechuan.)

Musical instruments: Shell trumpets, wooden drums, hide drums, musical strong bows, time-beaters, Pan flutes.

Games: Dice-boards, stilts, noise-makers, swings or voladors, *tika.*

Food preparation: Making of alcoholic drinks by masticating of tubers, roots, or grains with lime or other ingredients.

Agriculture: Terracing, artificial irrigation.

Fishing: Use of poisons.

Money: Shells, etc.

Religion: Shells as offerings, dancing with masks, head trophies, potlatch (feasting and dancing), sob greetings.

Mutilations: Leg deformations by tight bands, finger amputations for mourning, trepanning, gems incrusted in teeth, teeth-blackening, bloodletting.

George Fisher has also listed a large number of sociological similarities.

Rivet also points out:

1. All the common cultural traits listed are found also in Melanesia or Polynesia.

2. They are found chiefly in South America, not in North America.

3. They are most observable in *northeastern* United States, the Amazon Basin, and Colombia.

4. Melanesian elements are more pronounced among the early Lagoa Santa people.

5. Curiously—seemingly in contradiction—the Hoka language, scattered from South Oregon to the Isthmus of Tehuantepec and here and there in Nicaragua and Salvador, may be of Melanesian origin.

Without theorizing, Steward notes that the pre-Columbian occurrence in America of botanical species found on other continents, viz.: sweet potatoes (Maori varieties); the edible root, *pachyrhizus;* calabashes (*legenaua*); north Peruvian cotton (*gossypium*); plantains (*musa paradisiaca mormales*), and perhaps peanuts and coconuts, "indicate a diffusion from one hemisphere to another."

Melanesians, it has been argued, brought certain diseases to the New World which are found nowhere else. Eczematoid typhus of

Mexico and Guatemala, according to Charles Nicolle, is identical with that of Oceanic typhus, and is spread by rats—not lice, the only carrier for European and most Asiatic typhus. Other disease parallels, with race and geographic limitations, have been pointed out by various scholars.

There is, of course, the recent theory, propounded by Thor Heyerdahl, the intrepid adventurer and breaker of idols, with respect to Easter Island and Polynesian islands, that a countermigration westward perhaps carried fragments of Tiahuanaco or Inca peoples from South America, and established new island ruling groups, distinct from earlier Polynesians.

It is necessary, at this point, also to mention the general theories of José Imbelloni, a careful scholar and a bold thinker. The first comers to the New World, he argues, were short dolichocephaloids, Tasmanian in appearance, a primitive Australoid prototype, which dominated the Asia-Pacific world and crossed the Bering Straits in the Pleistocene, then were steadily pushed south so that their vestiges today are chiefly the Fuegians and Láguidos. Next arrived tall dolichocephaloids, also Australoids, from whom the Planido and Pampido tribes developed. Third came Melanesian hunters and gatherers, short ultra-dolichocephaloids, also proto-Indonesians, weavers and farmers, not so pronouncedly long-headed, predecessors of most Amazonians; finally, round-headed (brachycephaloid) Mongoloids arrived, bringing higher forms of agriculture and patrilineal institutions. They peopled the Andes, among other places. Still later, ultra-brachycephalics, endowed with artistic sensibilities, creators of political states, were progenitors of the Isthmian peoples. The latest arrivals, he avers, were the Eskimos.

Racially this theory may have germs of truth, but to be tenable it would require evidence of crossings other than via the Bering Straits; and, by placing too much emphasis on imported culture, it ignores many possibilities of autochthonous evolution.

10

In South America are discerned two broad divisions of peoples, as reflected in early artifacts and later cultural manifestations: the patrilineal versus the matrilineal cultures, for instance. The highland peoples were decidedly different (though the Chavín upland culture with its exuberant art may have been created by emigrating Amazonian river complexes): the Guaraní-Tupinamba, Arawak, and

84

Carib. Most decidedly is the division manifest among Atlantic seaboard peoples, the first to be seen by Europeans. As the prehistoric population *putsch* went on into the Caribbean, apparently cultural crisscrossing occurred; Mayan, possibly Incan influences, are discernible.

The earliest peoples, as indicated by the most ancient Fuegian kitchen middens—as also far north, as at the New Mexican Sandía caves—knew the use of fire, pressure stone flaking, and the processing of bones, the working of skins with stone scrapers and bone awls.

For a period of 10,000 to 15,000 years, peoples mostly lacked domesticated crops, used no salt, had no food-processing tools, no pottery, loom-weaving, basketry (?), skin-tanning, metallurgy; and they lacked musical instruments, did not use narcotics or stimulants. But these conclusions may be based on lack of evidence rather than a true picture. The earliest folk did not practice cannibalism or go in for war trophies, though Amazon forest gatherers soon resorted to cannibalism. There was no organized religion in the form of temples, priests, or idols; human sacrifices and ritual cycles were absent, though likely they had beliefs on the existence of the soul and life hereafter. They believed in witchcraft, omens, and magic. Most probably they had healers or shamans.

Some of these conclusions are derived less from physical evidence than from inferences from surviving primitive peoples, whose most ancient kitchen middens reveal that their mode of life, their equipment for life, has changed very slightly over thousands of years. The Ona of Tierra del Fuego, for instance, apparently gathered in patrilineal bands, without class divisions or any pronounced chieftain rule (except family elders) of 60 to 100 persons, all probably related, that exercised hunting rights in a given area into which no outsider could intrude except by invitation or permission. On the other hand, the Chaco peoples of the central diaspora were wholly matrilineal.

But 8,000 years ago, perhaps earlier, the peoples of the Great Basin in the United States and on into Mexico had developed a variety of processing tools and weapons, some very specialized for handling given seeds.

Other early peoples, those of the Chilean archipelago and Patagonia, came to have spear-throwers, bolas (three stones held in cords and thrown to circle the legs of wild animals or birds, a valuable instrument still used by Argentine gauchos), harpoons, and in a few instances fish-hooks. They practiced earth burial, though a few in more forested areas hung the dead from trees, and in northern forest areas, when the head of a household passed on, his body was preserved in the house and the dwellers cleared new land and put up a new dwelling. This was practiced from time immemorial by the Jívaro, the headshrinkers.

Thus we cannot convert our mysterious X for the origins of New World Man into a conclusive X-ray of fact; but gradually as we ascend through the centuries, we can discern more clearly the kind of people they were, how they lived, evolving from primitive nomad hunters and gatherers (though not all of them) into more settled agrarian communities, gradually developing pronounced political institutions, finally empires that permitted the accumulation of a greater body of knowledge.

The mighty and beautiful Chavín culture, with its dominant tropical forest motifs, which spread over most of the highlands as far or farther than the much later Inca empire—apparently a religious-cultural, not a warlike expansion—was one of the most tremendous elevations of human aspirations in all history, a sudden flowering of an almost universal mystic, aesthetic, and creative complex over a vast area. It is reminiscent of the meta-political spread of the great Oriental religions and of Christianity at a much later time, for the Chavín uplift may have occurred 4,500 years ago, according to Peruvian archaeologists Julio C. Tello and Rebecca Carrión Cachot, although American authorities believe it occurred soon before, or even after, the Christian era, for otherwise they would have to set aside existing arbitrary timetables laid out on glossy pages for the Nazca, Moche, Chimú, Tiahuanaco, and Inca cultures.

Coming closer to the Columbian intrusion into the later empires and peoples, we know a great deal more concerning their languages, philosophies, religions, their science, medicine, and art.

5

The Golden Ear

Agriculture was a decisive turning point that altered man's life and the organization of his society; it provided sedentary fixed residence that stimulated thought, invention, religion, and art.

The Incan Quechua, of course, had scores of cultivated plants, but a few crops gained early widespread distribution over the entire continent and spread to distant reaches of North America, viz.: beans, squash, maize, etc., and, in a vast South American area, the potato, which was to reach North America only many thousands of years later, via Ireland, and then only species which the South Americans considered and still consider inferior, though the three main kinds in the United States have since been tremendously improved.

It was originally believed that maize had been domesticated by the Mexican highland Nahuatl (pre-Aztecs) or even earlier peoples there, chiefly because of a wild semi-grass, a possible progenitor, known as *Teosintle,* and because, more than with many other New World peoples, corn was the basic Aztec staple. But the *Teosintle* could as easily represent a degeneration of a domesticated species.

One accepted ecological theory is that the origin of a species is approximated where the greatest number of varieties are encountered; that relatively few kinds have the hardihood and adaptability to migrate far afield. Though Mexico has many varieties of corn of many colors: white, black, yellow, brown, red, blue, and green,

Central America has more, and there are still more in Colombia. Russian scientists working there a few years ago, made intensive studies and arrived at the conclusion that the Andean Chibcha valleys were the motherland of corn's original domestication. However, it may even turn out, as some investigators now believe, that the diaspora point was in the springlike *yungas* of eastern Bolivia.

In any event, maize soon spread to nearly all New World peoples; it was the great staple of New England when the English colonists finally showed up there. Kernels have been found in archaeological remains dating back at least six thousand years. Curiously, many American authorities still place the development of settled agriculture in the Anahuac Valley of Mexico well into the Christian era. (Steward, for instance, says A.D. 500.) But the original domestication of maize must have occurred not less than 7,000 years ago.

The potato has an even more romantic history. It was cultivated from early times in Chile, Peru, Bolivia, Ecuador, and Colombia. To this day a Uruguayan species differs from all others in the world. Here again the original focus may have been the Bolivian *yungas* around Lake Titicaca (for there are found hundreds of species and varieties) or Chiloé Island off the Chilean coast.

Botanists have classified more than fifty varieties in the single Bolivian Chucuito Valley. One potato, commonly cultivated at altitudes over 12,000 feet is sterile, being a cross between a lower altitude cultivated variety and a highland weed potato.

The Spaniards found Arraucanian Indians on Chiloé, the rain-drenched island off lower Chile, cultivating a hundred different kinds of potatoes of a species entirely different from those in the highlands, and some authorities believe the first domestication occurred there. On the Chilean mainland about thirty kinds were cultivated. The great three-volume classical work on primitive medicine in Peru by Valdizán and Maldonado lists fifty-two major varieties in and around Cuzco, former seat of the Inca empire. In all, in the valleys near there are found ten round varieties, fifty long varieties, seven "flat kinds," two curly types, eight miscellaneous, and three wild varieties. The chief kinds of cultivated potatoes were white, golden yellow, black, blue, lead-gray, brown, and red. The jet-black *chapina* potato was used more for dyeing than for food.

Long before the Spaniards came, the potato had spread south to Uruguay and Patagonia and north as far as Mexico. In the southwest of the United States were various wild potatoes of a wholly different species from our "Irish potato."

Already by the time of the Conquest, some South American species had become adapted to fairly low warm country; others to cool rain areas of southern Chile; others to the freezing heights. There, three sturdy frost-resistant species, generally known as "bitter potatoes," are grown. The most widespread are known as *Luqui*. The best potato region of South America, except possibly Chiloé, is the highland country from nine to thirteen thousand feet where, as the first chronicler of the potato, Pedro de Cieza noted in 1538, "it freezes a little every month."

In Spanish the major varieties are called "races," for their characteristics have become so defined over centuries of domestication that they rarely show variations and some cannot even be crossed with each other. One leading French plant authority has asserted that this development and stabilization could have come about only after thousands of years of domestication—at least five thousand years before Christ, probably earlier.

The potato, on being brought to Europe, was never honored with its true original name, which in Aimara was "Cchoque." The Incas called it "Acshu," and Chilean Indians *"Chaucha,"* particularly the prized yellow species. (Today "Chaucha" is Chilean slang for a penny or centavo.)

When the sweet potato, which is really a morning-glory, was taken to Europe soon after the Conquest, it carried along its Taino name *batata,* which was soon corrupted to "potato." When the actual potato was introduced into Europe half a century later, it was given the same name as the sweet potato, and this corruption then returned to Latin America as "patata." But from Mexico south mostly it goes by the early vulgar Quechua word "papa," roughly the equivalent of our "spuds."

The scientific generic name for the family including the potato is *Solanum,* some 1,200 species included, which takes in also the eggplant, tomato, chilies, and peppers, the Jerusalem cherry, the deadly nightshade and the pernicious horse nettle. The numerous species of potatoes are mostly classified according to the number of chromosomes, using 12 as a base. Diploid potatoes, the simpler more ancestral types, have 24 chromosomes. Ten species of cultivated diploid potatoes have been identified. Among these are the black potato and the cherished Peruvian golden-yellow potato. Most diploid species are found at lower, warmer elevations, but several are frost-resistant and grow only at lofty altitudes.

The triploid species have 36 chromosomes. Of these the most

widespread is the *Luqui,* best of all frost-resisters. Another high-altitude potato widely grown is the only known cultivated penta-ploid, with 60 chromosomes.

The tetraploid potatoes (48 chromosomes), the most universal, are known as *Solanum tuberosum,* to which belongs our common white "Irish potato." In South America there are three great geographic subspecies: the Andean, Chilean, and Uruguayan potato.

Just as most of us are more likely to speak of "spuds" rather than *Solanum tuberosum,* so the South Americans have many picturesque nicknames for different potatoes, largely derived from pre-Conquest expressions. "Knife-breaker" is a potato so hard it can't be cut with a knife but is perfectly edible when cooked. Other nicknames are Gray-Feather, Bird-Egg, Red-Mother, Human-Head. One kind with reddish flesh is called, "Weeps Blood for the Inca."

The highlanders had many methods of storing and processing potatoes, in vogue for thousands of years and still used today. Eating potatoes were kept in large striped llama-wool sacks. Seed potatoes were stored in stone bins with straw and *muna,* an herb that prevented rot and sprouting, something U.S. growers could well investigate. As far back as the earliest known records, many potatoes, particularly high-altitude frost-resistant "bitter" potatoes, have been frozen or dehydrated or both. Frozen potatoes were known as *chuño,* an Aimara word meaning "frozen." Other words designate various refinements of freezing and dehydration.

In parts of Bolivia potatoes were boiled, then dehydrated and frozen so hard they splintered like glass. In the center of the milky white semitransparent product was left a hollow space into which sharp crystals projected.

A "bitter white" *chuñu* was made by leaving potatoes in flowing icy river water for some weeks, then drying them out on a sunny bank and freezing them. They were pressed under heavy rocks and stored in llama-wool bags.

Ordinary "black *chuñu*" was made by freezing potatoes on high open ground out of the sunlight. They were sprayed with water periodically and after the proper interval, were spread out on grass beds and trampled. Potato-freezing time in the Andes was always a colorful spectacle, like wine-pressing time in Italy. Girls, their long many-colored dresses pulled high on their calves, pressed the water out of the potatoes. After repeated freezings with alternate thawing and trampling, the potatoes were reduced by the final freezing into small black marbles, hard as pebbles, which were kept under reed mats.

Chuñu keeps for years without deterioration. Often while still frozen hard, it was (and is) ground into flour for soups and purées, sauces and puddings. The flavor of *chuñu* in such preparations is superior to that of fresh potatoes.

The potato always played a great role in native medicine. Some cures were as superstitious as our cures for warts. Jaundice could be cured by mixing powdered *chuñu* with black cow urine and three lice and drinking the concoction on Tuesdays and Fridays. To cure rheumatism, you carried three potatoes in your pocket with a ball of tree resin. Potato applications supposedly helped heal bone fractures, and potato flour was added to hot baths to cure disorders due to "fright," to which the Indians, like psychoanalysts, ascribed a large assortment of sicknesses. In Europe (after 1500 or so) people believed the potato to be an aphrodisiac. Shakespeare mentioned this.

Slices of raw potatoes, treated with salt or vinegar, were (and are) pasted on the temples to cure headaches. Rubbing healing wounds with *chuñu* flour, powdered brick, and vinegar, would prevent scars. If potato was ground up with willow ash and olive oil, it was supposed to prevent rabies. Because potatoes are good retainers of heat, they were used in hot poultices to alleviate gout, cure rash, pimples, erysipelas and other skin disorders. A cold poultice applied to burns prevented blisters.

The great early Spanish ecclesiastic and chronicler, Father Bernarbé Cobo, one of the first to go to the New World, who made special studies of the potato, believed firmly, as do all modern Peruvians, that if you ate slices of raw potato with your meals, you would not suffer from indigestion or heartburn. (Several raw-food cults in California harbor this same idea.)

2

The house a man lives in, his furniture, tools, methods of preparing food, the plants and animals he utilizes tell a great deal about his society, about marital, clan, village, and political relations. Primitive though most houses were in South America, they reflected individual skills and more mental alertness than buying a prefabricated house or getting food in cans at the corner store.

However primitive the early homes, they were built by persons who lived in them and who showed great ingenuity in utilizing available materials for protection against the elements. Most of rural Cuba still lives in *bohíos* such as Columbus saw on his arrival. In South America, thirty million people or more still live in homes little different from those of their ancestors a thousand years ago. Only in major Andean cultural centers did early homes evolve into more impressive structures.

A few dominant types of houses prevailed: rain-resisting houses in the humid tropics; wind-resistant houses in Patagonia; heat-resisting houses in equatorial regions; cold- and snow-resisting houses in the Andes. The character of construction varied according to local materials: trees, leaves, and grass in the Amazon; stone and adobe in the treeless portions of the Andes; animal skins in the treeless, stoneless Pampa and parts of Patagonia.

The family on the Pampa which used the shell of a giant prehistoric glyptodont had a finer—and prefabricated—dwelling than did their neighbors. Some cave dwellers were more comfortable than those who built homes.

Simple was the placing of a horizontal pole between stakes or tree crotches and leaning palm leaves against it—common among the Brazilian Botocudo, and tribes of the Mojos-Chiquitos. The Siriono of eastern Bolivia made lean-tos large enough for as many as fifty people. The Purí of the upper Xingú leaned branches on both sides, as did various Montaña tribes and the Caingang of Brazil.

In rainless places houses were often little more than shade ramadas, branches over four upright poles. The Goajiro of Venezuela used cactus thatch. The Charrúa used mats affixed to uprights as windscreens. Many Chaco tribes used bulrushes similarly and the Mataco merely heaped grass against uprights. The Nambicuara stuck palm branches in a protective half circle.

Rectangular mat-tents were constructed by the Paraguayan Guayaquí and the Aimara of the highlands.

Light dwellings utilized small poles or saplings in different ways, covered with branches, grass, leaves, skin, mats or bark, sometimes clay and straw.

Hundreds of tribes constructed square, rectangular, or oval gable-roofed dwellings, often having two doors, one for men, one for women. Sometimes the roof was extended to make a veranda.

Conical tepees, often covered with sod, were rare, though the Ona sometimes built them, especially for ceremonial centers; also the Timbirá of eastern Brazil. The Caingang and the Chaco Guaranoco used a center pole, four tilted poles, and palm covering, with interior apartments screened off for each family.

Tairona and Colombian peoples also used a center pole. Sometimes a double circle of uprights was used for strength, especially in the Guianas, perhaps because of tropical storms.

Other peoples used rafters meeting at a point, without a center pole. Circular or conical roof houses usually had perpendicular walls.

In general, nomadic hunting and gathering groups—as the people of Patagonia, where either rain or drought, wind or cold made agriculture almost impossible—as today—built temporary shelters though—as did the Alakaluf of the south Chilean archipelagoes— they left the beehive style bent-pole frames for later comers to recover with bark or skins. Doorways were sealed with flexible reeds or branches to keep out wind and rain, through which people could walk and which then sprang back into place.

This beehive or dome hut—which Rivet identified as typical of Australoid peoples—had wide distribution there in the far South. The Yahgan beehive was a circle of bent saplings tied in the center, and covered with grass, ferns, branches, bark, or skins.

The Ona, Tehuelche and Pampan Querendí used two upright poles covered with sewn guanuco skins painted red, the dwelling open on the off-wind side. Skin-covered dwellings were also common among the Chilean Auraucanian.

Groups such as the Timbirá, Chavante, Pemecamecra and numbers of Chaco tribes, also used beehive construction, though chiefly for ceremonial purposes. Nambicuara beehives were often twenty feet in diameter.

The archipelago Chono, the Uruguayan Charrúa, the Paraná delta Timbú, the Brazilian Ahueicona and Botocudo all made circular beehives, while those of various Chaco tribes were elliptical.

More solid frame structures were often built even by peoples commonly occupying more flimsy dwellings—with posts, beams, rafters, ridgepoles, crossbars. Even the Alakaluf—constantly flitting from one deep fiord to some stormy island sea channel—for initiation ceremonies and whale feasts, built relatively enormous buildings, though in the prevalent beehive style.

More settled peoples in the Amazons and Andes sometimes built large apartments housing whole clans, two hundred people or more, and men's clubs and ceremonial fraternities called for large structures. Some houses in the northwest Amazon utilized six posts, ten secondary posts, 72 roof poles, 76 transverse poles and nearly 200 bundles of thatch. The Yamamadidí and Mangerono of the Juruá-Purús rivers built conical houses 130 feet in diameter, 70 feet high, to accommodate 250 persons.

A single central pole with circular thatched roof reaching to the ground was used by the Guaporé River tribes; dwellings were often one hundred feet in perimeter. Elongated houses on the style of double lean-tos, with roof to the ground, were found among numerous Chaco and Mojo-Chiquito tribes, the Brazilian Carajá and Guiana Carib. The Tupinamba elevated this type to its most sophisticated form—dwellings 500 feet long, 50 feet wide, 12 feet high, able to accommodate 200 persons. They were vaulted and had flat ends.

Hans Staden, the German cannoneer taken prisoner soon after the first European settlements in Brazil, described their dwellings near present-day Rio. "Their huts, are about fourteen feet wide and all of 150 feet long . . . [and] about twelve feet high . . . round at the top and vaulted like a cellar. They roof them tightly with palm branches . . . each couple, man and wife, has a space in the hut on the side . . . of about twelve square feet . . . each couple has its own fire, [prepared its own meals and manioc beer]. The chief . . . has his dwelling in the center. The huts usually have three doors, one at either end, one in the middle . . . so low people have to stoop."

Most frame houses were thatched, a type found all through the Amazon tropical forest, the rain forests of South Chile, and in many Andean coast and upland areas. In Ecuador and Colombia roofs were of grass thatch, woven mats, or palm leaves; the walls were branches, cane, palm or thatch, or wattle and daub. Tairona houses (Colombia) had stone foundations; among the Chibcha, supports were of stone.

3

Solid construction was found chiefly in the Andes, though often clay huts were built elsewhere also. Wall materials were mud, clay, adobe, stone, or wood. Adobes might be conical, bread-loaf, hemispherical, ball-shaped, rectangular, square, usually held with binder of some sort. Puddle adobe was often tamped between temporary molds; this, if plastered over, provided a durable construction even for rain and snow country. Stone walls were of rough boulders, or split and selected stone, dressed blocks and slabs. *Puca*—rough stones set in clay—was much used; such house walls were usually from ten to eighteen inches thick and from six to seven feet high. Wooden beams and logs were used in many buildings, though stone beams have been encountered, even stone-slab roofs, often corbeled. But the massive Machu Picchu ruins—though intermediary floors were often of solid stone—having been roofed with thatch, today are roofless. Where rainfall was not great, mud roofs, reinforced with straw, have been resistant for centuries. Many Tiahuanaco stone-roofed houses were subterranean, sometimes two stories underground. Others were two or three stories high, with huge stone slabs serving for both ceilings and floors, usually from one to four apartments per floor, with large storage spaces, attics or lofts, and roof-suspended storage platforms. In many villages special "flute houses" were built to store musical instruments and ceremonial costumes.

4

Village planning existed even among primitive tribes, with regard to wind protection, possible flooding, defense, water and food sources, recreation grounds, etc., but also with an eye for community togetherness. The Shabióa and Carajá village houses were in regular street rows, or on one long street, the usual pattern for villages facing rivers. Tropical forest villages, ranging from twenty to 2,000 persons, were often surrounded by stockades, as were many Jívaro and Araucanian villages and numerous other groups, from Venezuela to Paraguay.

Where war was a peril, homes were often fortresses, and whole villages were sometimes palisaded. Moats or ditches were often used, as among the Witoto. Among sedentary agriculturists, villages often built hill forts with bastions and concentric walls, having loopholes.

Staden described the Tupinamba coast settlements: "Few villages have more than seven huts. . . . The savages fortify them as follows: They make a stockade of split palm trees about nine feet high . . . so thick no arrow can pierce it, but leave loopholes to shoot through. Outside this stockade, they build another of high stakes set close together, so no man can creep through. It is the custom to set the heads of the men they have eaten on the stockade at the entrance."

Houses, especially in the highlands, were often painted, especially when stuccoed, but not many were decorated, though paintings and petrographs have been found in caves throughout the continent. The Tupí-Cawahib painted outer walls with figures of jaguars, dogs, eagles, snakes, frogs, children, and moons. Some Guiana peoples painted designs on posts and walls. Beautiful are the Peruvian Chanchán stucco arabesques of the post-Christian period.

In the highlands, of course, nearly all temples, public buildings, schools, etc., carried pictorial decorations or carvings, and houses often had painted or in relief, animals on door jambs and lintels; in some places, clay, carved wood or metal llamas or birds were put on the rooftops, as often today, in Huancayo and elsewhere in Peru, where Christian saints have since been added. The Coricancha temple in Cuzco, 12,000 feet about, walled with perfectly dressed stone, was decorated inside with hammered gold and silver and ornaments.

In Sacsahuamán (also at Quenco near Cuzco) stone bleachers overlooked the wide parade and fiesta quadrangle.

At Machu Picchu were a series of bathrooms on descending levels, served by aqueducts bored through solid stone, each with a tub cut out of solid rock, with angled stone seats and recesses for soap and ointments—designs that would be considered ultramodern today. Such baths were a common feature of houses in Cuzco and other Quechua cities. Many buildings in Cuzco were served with running water, and part of the old conduits are still in use there. The famous Inca baths in Cajamarca were equivalent to a good-sized swimming pool and are still operating today. Those at San Agustín, Colombia, were cut out of native rock and carved with figure designs.

5

House furnishings ranged from almost nothing to the elaborate and elegant. Many peoples slept on straw mats (often painted or decorated), bark, branches, skins, or woven blankets; in hotter insect-snake country, in hammocks. Platform beds were widespread, sometimes with a separated footrest between forked uprights. Such beds were usually about twenty inches high, twenty inches to ten feet wide. Among some groups, virgins had beds (screened off with mats) six and a half feet off the ground. Typical was the Jívaro bed, with separated footrest made of four upright forked posts, two crossbars, the rear one slightly higher, with split bamboo between, covered with deerskins. The Chibcha, Choco, and Cueva screened their

96

beds with cotton cloth. Among the Aimara and Quechua, a solid clay or clay-stone bench was built at one end of the room and covered with mats, skins, or blankets, where the entire family slept.

Hammocks were made of long bark strips tied at both ends (Ipurina), interlaced buriti leaves (Timbirá and Sherenté), cross-strings between heavy side cords (Witoto), netted (Tucuna), long warp threads joined at intervals (Chiriquano), loom-woven (Carib, Arawak). Palm fiber, also Chambira, Tucuma, and Caraguata fibers, and cotton and wool were also used. The Carajá used hammocks also as capes. Among other groups, hammocks were used only as baby cradles, also as burial shrouds. Numerous Amazonians used tent-shaped mosquito netting; some had completely sealed sleeping rooms. Members of one tribe customarily buried themselves in the sand to sleep and protected only their heads. The Choco used wooden bolsters.

Wood-block stools were used in the western Amazon, though sometimes reserved for only honored guests, chieftains, and shamans. These stools sometimes rested on two wide side feet or had four legs, and were often oval or slightly hollowed. Four-legged seats carved in animal shapes were used in the Guianas, the upper Xingú, and by the Incas. Two-sided stools were made by the Jívaro, also many mountain peoples. Carved turtle-shell stools were used in the Guianas. The Chibcha had stools with backs. Where there were forests, log and back benches were common. The only tables of ancient vintage, except among the Incas, were used in southwest Brazil. Eating was customarily done sitting cross-legged around mats.

In the Manabí ruins in western Ecuador were found stone U-shaped stools supported by carved animal figures. Throughout Inca-land stone seats, often carved, were common. In Machu Picchu such carved seats were located at convenient intervals beside long flights of stairs, always with a fine eye for a panorama of city or landscape. Similar stone seats were often found along Inca roads and the mountain-carved stairs, for rest, and nearly always provided a breath-taking view of the majestic canyons and mountains and rivers.

Jars, wooden boxes, stone bins, baskets, sewed hides, etc., were used for storage. Enormous stone bins were used to store maize, potatoes, meat, and vegetables at all the mountain *tambos** or inns

* These inns were mostly for couriers on official business. No one traveled in the later period of the Inca Empire without a permit, regularly checked.

along the Inca highways, a food supply so great the Spaniards lived off little else for years.

Many tribes had no fireplaces, at best scooped out hollows in the ground for fireplaces. But stone fireplaces were built in the Guianas, and underground earth ovens or barbecue pits were widely used. ("Barbecue" is an Arawak-Taino word.) In east Brazil, clay stoves were common, and in the Andes pottery braziers with three top burners and lower side openings for fuel were customary household equipment.

Charcoal was universally used for cooking, often for heating. Llama dung was burned in the Andes. Fire-fans were made of feathers (west and southern Amazonia) and plaited mat-type fibers, some very fine and flexible with thick woven handles, all over the continent. Various types of oil lamps and resinous or bark torches were used.

Many kitchen implements were provided. Manioc preparation had special presses, graters, and other tools. Wooden and stone mortars and pestles, some ten feet long, were universal. Guiana mortars were hourglass shaped and painted with geometric designs. *Metates*, grinding stones, and rolling-pin-type mashing stones were common. Among the Jívaro and Witoto, signal drums were a part of every household. Like the old tin dish pan in the United States, they saved lungs in calling children and men in the fields, or out fishing.

6

Pre-Spanish building reached its greatest magnificence in temples and public buildings. Some of the most stupendous of these belong to the long-buried Chavín culture. At Puerto Sipe, one of the oldest temples located on the coast, boulders were covered with fired clay. The ruins of Cerro Blanco and Puncurí in the Nepeña Valley (Peruvian coast), probably almost as ancient, on or around platforms and sunken courts with conical adobes and split stones, had plaster reliefs, paintings, and ornamental columns. Various pyramid temples have been unearthed both on the coast and in the highlands.

Chavín de Huantar in the northern inner Andes was a crowning glory of the era: with platform buildings, terraces, sunken plazas, and terrepleins, obelisks, monoliths, and statuary.

Pucará in southern Andean Peru had a sunken enclosure surrounded by a series of walled-in rooms in a horseshoe circle, each with two slab altars, with numerous statues and carved slabs.

At Pachacamac on the central Peruvian coast—visited and violated by Hernando Pizarro—the Pyramid of the Sun covered 12 acres and was 75 feet high. Upper terraces were painted with murals.

We would know more about the early peoples and their architecture and art and society had it not been for the fanatic zeal of the Conquistadores and early Catholic monks to wipe out all such centers of "idolatry."

Early large stone carving has been uncovered in Colombia at San Güetán and the Tierradentro areas, also in the Nariño and Pitamayo departments, and carved stone tablets have been found at Guayas and elsewhere on the Ecuadorian coast. In Manabí, huge U-shaped stone seats have been found in Peru at Huamancha, Cajamarca, Callejón de Huaylas, and Aijá, with here and there complete statues. The southernmost recorded stone carving, other than petrographs, is found on ornamental pillars on northwest Argentina. The greatest pre-Inca center subsequent to Chavín was at Tiahuanaco in Bolivia, made of dressed stone slabs, with stone staircases, had painted walls and stone sculpturing.

7

Incan building skills created memorable Cuzco in the Andes—massive palaces, temples, arsenals, granaries, and schools built around two main squares. In some buildings enormous blocks, 16x24x36, weighing tons, of various shapes, were fitted glove-tight.

Corners of buildings were carefully locked with ledges or projecting tenons fitted into section joints. In few instances was cement employed, though the Spaniards feverishly tore one building apart, believing gold had been used in the mortar. The Tiahuanaco people used copper cramps set in T-shaped cramps, for joining, or else drilled holes in adjacent stones and poured in melted copper. Corbeled arches were employed. Floor stones in Inca buildings were cut with depressions for uprights.

Sacsahuamán, a tremendous structure above Cuzco, was built of gray Yucay sandstone, and the carefully fitted walls were of diorite porphyry, a hard stone not easy to process. Black andesite was used for more showy buildings.

8

Roads and bridges were evidence of important intercommunication, and many peoples in the Guianas, Brazil, Venezuela cleared highways frequently 23 feet wide, even built causeways across swamps, often surfaced with pounded earth. Short stone paved roads were built by the Tiarona villages in Colombia. The Atacama and Duiaguita of northern Chile, but perhaps after the Inca conquest, built roads ten feet wide, with stone.

The magnificent Inca highways (to be described in a later section) were usually wider and well paved and stretched for thousands of miles north and south through the Andes and along the coast, and from jungles to the coast.

Simple bridges, if no more than a tree trunk across a stream, existed everywhere. Less advanced peoples made them of logs, sometimes with supports in the water, as the Timbirá tribe in Brazil. Handrailings were common in Guiana and eastern Brazil. Cables with a hand-cable support were used among the Chaco Botocudos. The Paez of Colombia utilized arched bamboo poles with crosstie flooring, also handrails. Ferries also existed—balsa or reed canoes.

But here as in the other arts, the Quechua surpassed all others. Fiber-cable suspension bridges were supported by tall double stone towers on either bank, often anchored behind, and crossed above gorges thousands of feet deep. Other Inca bridges were made of long stone slabs or big beams with crossbars and poles. Pontoon bridges made of balsa canoes topped with a regular roadbed were built. Breeches buoys were also used, a basket with a loop handle, pulled back and forth on a cable with guide ropes.

9

Terracing, irrigation, reservoirs, and canals were other tangible records of advanced ancient life. Few works of man are more stupendous than the Quechua stone-faced farm terraces that climbed up the sheer Andes for ten thousand feet and more in almost every valley in Chile, Argentina, Peru, and Bolivia, many still in use.

In the Mojos area of eastern Bolivia irrigation canals—one 20 feet wide and 6,600 feet long, another 10 miles long—paralleled the raised highway. The ancient Casiquare canal connected the Negro and Orinoco Rivers. The Chicama Valley canal on the coast of Peru was carried across the valley by a high causeway, and required the moving of millions of tons of earth, making possible more cultivated area than today. Water was also carried in grooved stone troughs and often through bored holes in stone mountains. The flow into intricate side canals was regulated by movable stone-slab gates.

In Cuzco all streams were controlled by stone beds and walls, and the water supply was guaranteed by a reservoir, the construction of which is one of the engineering marvels of all time. The Inca engineers bored through a stone mountain to divert a river into an enormous cavern, where hundreds of thousands of gallons of water were always available and which were distributed to fields and through an intricate system of underground conduits to the temples and houses of the city. This, plus the underground drainage system, made Cuzco probably a more sanitary place than it is today. Tiahuanaco also had underground drainage canals, likewise early Chavín peoples had other canals for running water in buildings, and also drainage canals.

Some relief maps have survived. The Xingú tribes made maps on the sands, indicating rivers, trails, and villages. Rock carvings near Rio Casiquare, Venezuela, were probably maps. The Inca had enormous clay relief maps of the entire empire, and parts of such maps as well as models of buildings have been preserved in modern museums.

All architectural and building skills were based on much mathematical and astronomical knowledge; the New World discovered "zero" and the "decimal system" long before the Old World.

The Inca perfected to a high degree statistics and accounting, census-taking and mnemotechnical methods. Many a carving of astronomical events, many an astronomically oriented building, the curved walls (quite rare) in Cuzco and Machu Picchu, and sundials, all suggest the high mathematical precision behind early skills. Architectural remains of buildings, known to have been built with reference to the position of certain constellations, have revealed time shifts of star positions with reference to the earth, which in due time may throw light on the heavenly processes and on the antiquity of the Inca structures.

Certain number motifs—the number of steps, platforms, the laying out of planted fields, etc., throw light on early mystical numerology. This, too, may rest on intricate astronomical observations.

Most stone carvings left merely pictorial records, though often not merely decorative but informational. The carvings at Yenán, Chavín, and elsewhere may ultimately be deciphered as were those of the Near East.

Picture writing—as Garcilaso de la Vega indicates—certainly existed among the Inca, though examples have perished, for by such means Atahualpa was accurately informed of the armor, arquebuses, slings, and horses of Pizarro.

Unfortunately the great Peruvian archives of *quipús* have disappeared along with their keepers and interpreters. These were knotted cords of varied colors, used to record dates, vital statistics, economic data, tax assessments.

Bennett observed that simplified *quipús* are still used by upland herdsmen to keep track of the number of animals, newborn young, and deaths. The Pehuenche sent *quipús* to their enemies, indicating the blood money demanded for offenses; if the strands were red, it was a threat of prompt vengeance. Use of the *quipú* spread as far north as the Guianas—for use in keeping track of future dates; a knot being untied each day till the last one, representing the day of the celebration.

Besides wiping out the *quipú* records, the Spaniards also destroyed Quechua music and musical instruments (though Garcilaso de la Vega noted that some 600 native melodies actually were incorporated, tagged with Christian verses, into church hymns). But the large drums (*huáncares*), the melodious harps (*antaras*), the shrill whistles (*pincullos*), the strident guitars (*vihuelas*) were outlawed, fortunately never successfully. This suppression and others were told about in detail in that great "J'Accuse" of colonial cruelties, *La Nueva crónica de buen gobierno,* by Felipe Poma de Ayala and somewhat later by Juan Santa Cruz Pachacuti in his *Relación de antepasados del Perú*—this in contrast to official apologists, such as the bigoted Father Francisco Vitoria, who lectured and wrote with such furibund piety in defense of slaughtering the Indians and wiping out their "idolatrous" culture in his *Reelecciones de Indios* (1526–1546).

10

All actual written records are post-Conquest, but these throw much light on the activities of the peoples prior to European invasion, and provide considerable historical data of varying degrees of inaccuracy. Some are in native languages.

Most outstanding is Garcilaso de la Vega's great work, *Comentarios Reales.* Son of a Spanish captain and an Inca Ñusta mother, he was born early during the Conquest, met many participants in the early struggles, saw many ruins since destroyed, and knew intimately the history, oral literature, and legends of his people; also he ties in with United States history, for he participated in the conquest of Florida: his first book was *La Florida.*

The brother of Inca "Emperor" Tupac Amarú (murdered by Viceroy Toledo) wrote *Relación de la Conquista del Perú.*

An early drama, *Ollantay,* to this day a Peruvian classic, bears evidence of having been largely a translation from the Quechua tongue.

Cieza de León's *Crónica del Perú* is a tremendous and fascinating account. He reached the New World as a youth and for fourteen years traveled, having many incredible adventures, on horseback through the whole Pacific coast and mountain area from Peru to Central America.

Impressive too, inspired and imaginative, was Juan de Betanzos' writing. He came to know Quechua intimately, served as official interpreter, and published several volumes of Christian doctrine in Quechua and a dictionary, before writing his *Suma y Narración de los Incas,* of which, unfortunately, only eighteen chapters have survived. After Pizarro's death, he married one of the Conquistador's mistresses, Anas (baptized Angelina), a sister of Atahualpa and a Ñusta or Sun Virgin. She was the mother of Francisco Pizarro, Jr., the only son of the Conqueror not legitimatized.

And so, soldiers, explorers, friars and priests, lawyers, poets, bureaucrats and officials wrote about pre-Spanish life in the New World, and many with a broader sympathy and understanding than is revealed today in our ruling nationalistic countries. Some have already been mentioned, as the chronicle of Pedro Pizarro, to which should be added the *Relación* by Francisco Pizarro's own secretary.

Bartolomé de las Casas, who reached the Americas in 1506, was close to native life and fought for Indian rights and against enslavement. Gonzales Fernández Oviedo (1478–1557), one of the greatest scholars and commentators, though also a Crown official, was an indefatigable observer, though not oversympathetic.

Polo de Ondegardo, who died in 1675, was a prolific writer, though with an official slant. He covered the whole area of Inca life, religion, history, customs. There are numerous chronicles of Spanish prisoners, as that of Francisco Núñez de Pineda y Basuñán, whose *Happy Captivity* tells of his seven-month stay in the hands of the Auraucanians.

Alonso de Ercilla y Zúñiga (1533–1594) wrote the greatest epic of the times, still the chief Chilean classic, his famed *La Auraucana.* He fought against the Auraucanians, was outraged by Spanish brutalities, and wrote his great poem right in the field, scribbling much of it on drumhead leather, so that it quivers and pounds with action and sincerity. His heroes are the great Indian leaders, Lautaro and Tucarel, his heroine the beautiful native Guacolda. His feeling of tragedy was similar to a much later and worse-written book in English, Helen Hunt Jackson's *Ramona*.

The Colombian peoples were told about by Conquistador Jiménez de Quesada, founder of Bogotá, in a vivid, if Church-tinged attitude. His *Epitome of the Conquest of New Granada* was surpassed, at least in volume, by Juan de Castellanos (1522–1606) who wrote *Elegies of Illustrious Indian Men,* history and ethnography, in 150,-000 verses, the longest poem in the Spanish language. Other chronicles of New Granada soon followed: Juan Rodriguéz Fesle, Pedro de Aguado (1591), who told about the Venezuelan El Dorado, and Bishop Luís Fernández Piedrahita of Bogotá, who rewrote the early history in such a "new," copious and lively style, he has been called "the Inca Garcilaso of Colombia."

The prehistory of Ecuador is told extensively if belatedly in the three-volume *La Historia del Reino de Quito* by Father Juan de Valverde, who has been savagely criticized, though with considerable injustice. He claims to have based his work on his own personal investigations on the spot, plus three previous chronicles, one by Cacique Jacinto Collahuaso, whose manuscripts and books were burned by official persecution soon after the Father saw them.

The conquest of La Plata, a much later event, was narrated in verse by Martín de Basco Centinera in 1602 in his poem *La Argentina,* and thereby he named a future country. P. Lozano was probably the first chronicler of the Guaraní of Paraguay.

The story of Brazilian Indians was told by Amerigo Vespucci, Staden, the companions of Magellan and other explorers and conquerors. Carvajal told the Orellana story. In the late sixteenth century Fernão Cardin told about the Brazilian Indians—*Terra e Gente* and the 1530 *Armada* of Lopes de Souza and Frei Vicente de Salvador. For several centuries the long-delayed conquest of Brazil's interior made almost every account a story of life there as it was lived long before the conquest.

These are merely a few highlights of the vast literature available. But besides such records, millions of descendants still live in the ways of time immemorial, their life and culture crystallized, little changed in the onflow of history, relatively untouched by the Conquest, surviving through the era of the republics and the arrival of this dreadful modern age of ours, which so circumscribes the freedom and happiness of man. These many South American peoples live in much the same way they did four thousand years before the

104

coming of the Europeans; their language little changed, their dress, their food, in many instances their tools, no different. Walking with these peoples through the mountains, along the rivers, deep in the Amazon rain forest, in the Guiana wilds, we may travel back through the long past, through days and years not without their peculiar wonder and beauty—and even glory.

6

▐▐▐▐▐▐▐▐▐▐▐▐▐▐▐▐▐▐▐▐▐▐▐▐▐▐▐▐▐▐▐

Far South Peoples

Among the peoples of South America who changed the least over the millennia were the inhabitants of the southern end of the continent—usually designated the "marginal tribes"—though marginal tribes existed throughout the continent, the Amazon, Guianas, and Caribbean, and north in Mexico, as for instance the Lacandon and Tarahumare.

The inhabitants of Patagonia and Tierra del Fuego were first seen by the Magellan expedition, in an area roughly triangular, 1,200 miles long, 600 miles wide at the upper base, the Rio Negro. The choicest livable portion was the southern part of Tierra del Fuego, above the Beagle Canal, and there are found most of the ancient kitchen middens and shell mounds of early dwellers—apparently permanent camping sites were established in that locale. But all over the region have been found well-preserved remains in lava caves, in the grasslands, as well as by the shore which has steadily risen since before man's occupation.

Those remains record no agriculture, for heavy rainfall in the west and drought on the eastern plateau, made farming marginal and difficult, as it is today. From the beginning these were a hunting and fishing folk and remained so.

The first archaeological discovery, a huge grinding stone, was made in 1578 by Francis Drake's crew while digging a grave. In 1895 a mylodon (giant sloth) skin, associated with human artifacts, was found in a cave above Ultima Esperanza ("Last Hope") inlet. This and later discoveries on the north shore of the Straits of Magellan proved that the earliest men hunted the mylodon and an early type of horse. They used stone scrapers for working wood and bone but had no pottery. These men, at least 8,700 years ago, also used barbless blades with tapering stones, and had bone-flaking tools, bone awls, crude chipping tools, and fashioned flat lava disks, perhaps as small workbenches. They cremated their dead.

How many centuries later they began using stemless triangular stone points, rounded at the base, we do not know. By then they had also discovered the *bola,* thrown to wrap around the legs of guanacos, rheas, and other birds and animals.

Gradually over more centuries, tools became more perfected. In what is called the Fourth Period, beads and other ornaments were made and worn. These later descendants, if such, laid the bodies of the dead out in stone cairns, and sometimes painted the skeletons with red clay.

The so-called Fifth Period, just before the historic post-Columbian era, showed greater refinement of tools and weapons. Combs and scratchers, bark-strippers, shell-knives, harpoons, fishline sinkers, chopping stones, and whetstones were made.

Well north of the Straits, Milíciades Alejo Vignati, among others, found decorated or incised pottery, drills, stone club heads, "ceremonial" axes, engraved stones. Francisco de Aparicio found cave paintings and petrographs in the Santa Cruz region.

The "canoe people" of Patagonia were the Chono, Yahgan, and Alakaluf, of whom there are still a few survivors.

The Chono lived mostly on the shores of deep fiords and twisted channels below Chiloé as far south as the Taitao Peninsula. A few shared the big Corcovado Gulf with more northern peoples. They used bark canoes; later, leaky three-plank boats caulked with bark or moss.

They often raided the Chiloé island Auraucanians to seize metals, and the island people raided the Chono to get girls and slaves—a reasonable exchange that could have been arranged on easier, if less pleasurable, terms. The Chono also raided the "Huilli" ("South People") for slaves and sold them, sometimes for flint axes and adzes, to the Chiloé islanders in the north.

The Chono did a little gardening (particularly potatoes) and some herding. But mostly they lived on shellfish, seals, birds' eggs and stranded whales, and drank seal oil, but apparently no alcoholic beverages.

Cormorants were captured at night by means of bark torches and clubs. Seals were hunted with nooses and long heavy clubs. A goose called *canquén* was driven ashore with pebbles when molting and unable to fly, where it was killed with clubs. They also had bone-tipped spears and lances, polished stone axes, and sometimes used bows and arrows. They bred small shaggy dogs, which they used for hunting fish, and whose hair they wove into jackets. Robert Gray, the first American to sail around the world, noted a similar use of dog's hair by Indians near Puget Sound.

Their beehive houses were of poles stuck in the ground, bent to a central point and tied together with strips of woodbine, and covered with boughs, bark, or skins.

The women gathered all fuel, dove for sea urchins and caught shellfish. The men put up the huts, killed seals and cormorants.

Their clothing was simple. They wore woven dog's hair, bark, woven down or feather capes reaching slightly below the waist, a kelp penis covering, but no shoes or headdress except ceremonial feather crowns. They painted their bodies and faces red, white, and black, scarred their faces and bodies for permanent decoration, and wore shell-teeth and bone necklaces.

The tops of their heads were always tonsured for they believed that if an enemy got possession of their top hair, he could destroy them with black magic by putting it between two stones and dancing about it and periodically pounding all night. To cause death the enemy would tie it with whalebone to kelp in the sea or toss it into mountain trees. No one looked at flying birds, for that would bring bad weather, of which they had far too much, and nobody threw kelp or shellfish into the fire or into the water for that would "anger the sea." Pains were cured by massaging, spurting water from the mouth, mouth-sucking, and grease ointments. Wails, moans, and daily sea-diving also helped.

Sometimes they took a mother and her daughter as wives. When a child was born, the father cut off all his hair.

The dead were buried in caves, headmen being provided with a platform. Usually the bodies were laid out extended, but some skeletons have been found in embryonic posture, the knees drawn up to the chin.

Sometimes in religious fiestas, presided over by a "devil," deep groans rose to a wild chorus. In frenzy, first the men, then the women, ran about with firebrands in their mouths, trying to burn anybody they could. Sometimes they slashed each other with mussel shells. Often they danced and sang all night.

2

Much more is known about the Alakaluf ("Westernmen with clamshell knives") who lived in the wild stormy region south of the Chilean Gulf of Penas and on the western islands of Tierra del Fuego Archipelago. Essentially a forest and canoe people, they avoided open meadows.

They, too, lived on shellfish, sea lions, porpoises, marine birds, fish, and a few land animals, such as the muskrat, *huemuls* (small deer) and guanacos, which they killed with a harpoon on a handle or a saw-toothed spear. They ate some plant foods, algae, vegetables, fuchsia seed pods, wild *aleng, panguë,* roots, and fungi. Birds, especially cormorants (the *Guanay,* which provides the famous guano of Peru), were particularly important in their diet.

The hunters blackened their faces and hid until night when the birds roosted, then caught them quickly, preventing noise by holding the bird's head tightly under its wing and crushing the skull with their teeth. On other occasions two canoes were used. One party frightened the birds shoreward with shouts toward shore torches, where the creatures were clubbed to death. Big, flightless steamer ducks, so curious they would always investigate a low whistle, were easily snared with nooses.

Blue petrels were caught by thrusting a small bird with a string on its leg into a hole where eggs were laid. Old birds fastened on him and were drawn out. Plaited rush nooses were hung near swan hiding places.

Poles were used to dislodge shellfish. They also had fishnets, animal-trap nets of sea lion thongs, hoop nets, spears for sea urchins and mussels, harpoons and lines, axes and knives. Open mesh baskets and bark buckets were in common use.

Their large oval two-door houses, about 13x8, nearly six feet high, were a complicated interweaving of ground poles and light hoops of Magellan fuchsia, *canela* or cinnamon tree, or cypress. A framework was covered with sea lion skins, about a dozen being required. Any holes were plugged up with fern fronds, grasses, or twigs. Branches or fern fronds, sufficient to keep out wind and rain, covered the doorways. The fire pit was in the center. The family slept on beech or cypress branches. Large initiation club houses, 40 to 60 feet long, more than 13 feet wide and over 10 feet high, were sometimes built with numerous inner enclosures.

Like the Chono, the Alakaluf wore short skin capes and sealskin pubic coverings; for adornment, tubular bird-bone beards, perforated snail shells and marine worm tubes and flat bone necklaces. Their split-ribbed canoes were made of strips of bark and were 12 feet long, two feet wide, with thwarts and crossbraces. Open mesh and tight coil baskets (*diayos*) were made from *chep-pach* rushes for carrying fish and berries. Shells were lashed to stones for adzing and chopping. Used in hunting and fishing were shellfish poles (*ayorquis*), hardwood clubs, cinnamon-wood fish prong spears; spears with whalebone points, saw-tooth spears, bows and arrows, stone slings, double noose bird snares. Their harpoons had a whalebone head and a sea-lion-skin line.

Spears (*tan-tarrh*), arrows, and red-painted clubs were stuck in the ground about a carved wooden figure as a declaration of war or a warning of impending attack.

At childbirth the husband stood guard at the spherical hut, red paint on his face, white feathers on his right shoulder, a whole kelp goose skin on his breast. The umbilical cord was cut with a choroshell knife, and this, with the placenta—except for a snip the father wore in a leather bag about his neck for several months to insure the child's welfare—hair from both parents, parrot feathers and a live ember were wrapped in hide and buried underneath the hut. The newborn baby was washed with sea water and the parents fasted for two days.

A seal hunt or a whale feast was a great occasion. Often families from far and wide were invited and a special house was built for them.

As Martin Gusinde described it, shellfish poles, painted white, with red spots and bands and red handles, were planted in a circle about the central hearth. The night before, the men stayed there apart from the women, and sang. In the morning they painted their faces, chest and arms white, with a red stripe across the chest. A boy, but no woman, went along.

After finding a sea lion cave and harpooning and clubbing the animals they took sexual satisfaction with the boy, then returned home with the canoes loaded down with meat and hides. Before reaching shore, they shouted "Ahha ha ha hoo," and all women went into the huts and covered the doorways with skins. Near the landing the boy was thrown out and swam ashore. The men then went to the men's house, avoiding the women. The boy, however, entered the women's huts. The following night men and women slept together as usual.

The women, who always gathered the shellfish, worked busily the next day to supplement the feast, and the men spent the day building the big feast house (*yinchihaua*) with four entrances and two fireplaces. They and all the boys slept there that night, the women and girls in the regular huts.

The men prepared the feather headbands, and a chief solemnly buried a piece of seal meat. They sang and danced and horsed around. Faces and bodies were then painted in various fashions according to age and experience. The most experienced men painted red vertical stripes on their faces and white stripes on their cheeks, with an inverted *T* on their foreheads. The women used no paint.

In the morning they hit the first woman who poked her head in. The women then fetched water, and the men emptied the buckets on the first comer. The water was drunk through bone tubes.

During the day the men and boys occupied the center of the feast house, the women and girls the ends, sitting cross-legged. If they dozed or leaned over weary, the men struck them. If they didn't then sit up properly, they were bound hand and foot. Food was cooked in the women's houses and brought over for serving. That evening all had to bathe in the sea. Cheeks were painted red and the older men danced with heron-feather headbands (*chepanas*). Boys stood guard at the doors with sticks to keep the women out. Afterwards all sang the seal song or the whale song.

> We sing upon the mountain,
> Over our heads and bodies we put the *chepana,*
> We enter the big house to paint the fish poles,
> The condor is flying at the top of the sky.
> Today we will not go out, tomorrow we will not go out. . . .

At the last refrain, a rounded piece of wood hanging from the ceiling almost to the floor was struck, and initiates had to dodge it without moving from their seats.

Two men with tied hands pulled at the ends of a 25-foot harpoon line, and three women were called by name from the huts to jump over it and back three times to the tune of a special jumping song. By threes all the women jumped. Any failing to get over was beaten by one of the men wearing the heron *chepana*. Afterwards a boy and an old man staged a wrestling match.

During the ceremony a chosen man slipped off into the woods and disguised himself as the *Aac-ai*, spirit of evil. He painted his body black with black stripes down his face and remained naked except for a white band with a single black spot and a white goose skin over his chest. Shouting *hu-hu-harh-hu haruh* as he approached, he struck every woman and girl he could catch with his club. Those inside the lodge beat on the walls to scare him away.

The next day the women occupied the feasting lodge, while the men and boys used the regular houses, but all returned at night. The women kept their heads lowered till they were chosen.

3

The Yahgan—five regional groups with distinct dialects and numerous subkinship groups—lived on Tierra del Fuego along the Beagle Canal and on islands south to Cape Horn, though they often roved as far north as the Straits of Magellan.

A sturdy folk, mostly they went naked, though the women always wore a small pubic bird-skin covering held in place by waist strings. Sometimes in inclement weather, skin capes were worn. They greased, oiled, and painted their heads and bodies; red (peace) from burnt earth, white (war) from clay, or black (mourning) from charcoal. Their hair hung loose, cut in forehead bangs with sharp-edged mussel shells and combed with an otter or porpoise jawbone or whalebone, brushed with bundles of stiff roots.

Their beehive houses were simpler than those of the Alakaluf. They traveled in gondola-shaped beech bark canoes, caulked with celery strings or moss and mud, ribbed, and with hardwood thwarts. A fire was carried amidships in an earthen, shell or stone hearth, for warmth, light, cooking, and signaling. The latter was accomplished by throwing on *Notofagus betuloides* (evergreen beech) branches to create dense smoke. One signal signified sickness or an accident; two, a grave emergency; three, a death; four, discovery of a stranded whale. The hot coals were handled with two-prong tongs.

Food, mostly from the sea, rarely animals, was precious, a gift of the Supreme Being, Huataunehuá, and to wolf it down or waste it was considered sinful.

The sexes were kept separate from the age of seven, but some premarriage cohabitation occurred, and if a child resulted, mechanical abortion might be practiced. Puberty and initiation rites, lasting from weeks to months, were solemn and festive, the most pivotal ceremonies of Yahgan life. Each candidate was painted in the required ritualistic manner, and given a special painted staff and feather headband. Sponsors, of both sexes, were appointed for each novitiate to give him or her advice concerning moral conduct, kindness to the aged, and responsibilities of adulthood and marriage. Violations would affront Huataunehuá and bring harm from Yetaeta, the chief evil spirit. Initiates had to undergo severe endurance tests, but in the end were given many presents, including a scratching stick. The rites ended, after much feasting and dancing, with a mock battle between the sexes.

Monogamy prevailed, though occasionally polygyny, especially when a wife became old or infirm, but no polyandry. Divorce was rare, but not prohibited. Marriage festivities lasted a week, then the couples departed in their own canoe to spend several months with the bride's family before going to live permanently with the groom's kinfolk.

Sons- and daughters-in-law were not supposed to speak to their parents-in-law or vice versa, any communication being done through a third person, usually an aunt or uncle. When in the same hut, the married children must keep their backs to their parental in-laws; it was improper to sit beside them or even look at them. At least this avoided many mother-in-law problems.

Dietary rules were followed by both parents before and after birth, and sexual relations were not renewed for six weeks or so. Children were named after the place where they were born, but thereafter never called by name; indeed, no one was ever addressed directly by name—a magical dread perhaps.

A hospitable people, they were generous with food and presents. A visitor crouched by the fire without greetings for a considerable while. No man visited the hut if the woman was alone.

Boys practiced with spears, bows and arrows, slings and at stone-throwing, and, as did their elders, engaged in much wrestling singly or in groups. Before more formal wrestling matches, each combatant was massaged by a medicine man, who corresponded to our modern "trainer," but he had far more magical powers.

There were various games: swinging, rolling down hillsides, one-legged endurance hopping, and a boy-girl game in which they crouched in separate rows and did a rocking type dance imitating a canoe going through waves and chanting *"Tchenalora, tchenalora."* Adults also joined in blindman's buff, tossing burning sticks, ring-around a captive trying to break out, a ball game in which a feather or grass-stuffed sealskin ball had to be kept in the air with hand-palm strokes.

Each Yahgan had a guardian spirit—*yefachel*—assigned to him by the shaman at birth. An owl's hoot portended murder or death. Waste, bones, shells could not be thrown into the water but had to be burned. They had some sixty special prayers, besides im-promptu prayers, to Huataunehuá for curing illness, providing food, good weather, etc. Prayer was in an archaic "thee" and "thou" language. Medicine men (called to that vocation by visions) were aided by dwarf spirits and by Huachellaquipa, a female spirit. Young shaman candidates were schooled for some weeks and obliged to fast, sing, hold a motionless position, and sleep little. Besides curing, the shaman prognosticated and influenced weather, helped bring luck to hunters and fishermen. He was the leader of all rites and fiestas.

The great Yahgan epic revolved around the Yoalox brothers, one stupid, the younger one clever, who always won out by goodness and better sense. The Yahgan had many tales, about birds, foxes, otters and seals, and about dread cannibal beings, *Lacuma* water spirits and *Hanush* giants.

4

The Ona (meaning "north people" in the Yahgan tongue) occu-pied all Fireland (Tierra del Fuego) north of the Beagle Canal; a few even dwelt north of the Straits. Two probably related groups, the Selknam and Haush, were barely able to understand each other. Doubtless Magellan saw them, but the first description was given by Pedro Sarmiento de Gamboa in 1580. Intensive studies were made of them and the Yahgan by missionary Thomas Bridges from 1857 on, and by the Salesian fathers, who built up a large museum in Punta Arenas. The great authority about both peoples, of course, was Martin Gusinde, who worked in the '30's of this century. John M. Cooper, the leading United States fieldworker and writer, started in 1917 to visit the region. Numerous excavations have taken the story back for thousands of years, and a recent report on the Alakaluf by Carleton Coon, vividly describes this dying people.

The Ona were a land or "foot people," not seafaring, and lived chiefly off guanaco, hunted with bow and arrow, but also killed *tucos,* foxes (not often), eels, and geese. They hunted five kinds of ducks, gathered berries, fungi, and grass seeds, which were ground up and mixed with water or grease. They did eat seals, whales, limpets, and crabs, but fished only in shallow water with whalebone hooks, bone-headed spears, nets, and weirs.

Their conical huts were primitive. They wore skin-capes, guanaco, fox, or woven dog hair—a guanaco fur forehead band, guanaco skin moccasins, and, in heavy snow, guanaco leggings. They made "shoes" by tying on to their moccasins bulky bundles of twigs—called *xoshe que xamni.* In very severe weather, they sometimes wore, beside the capes, guanaco skins, the fur inside, from armpits to knees, held in place by a thong belt.

Most of their tools, weapons, and arts resembled those of the Yahgan, also puberty rites (*cloquitin*), sex and marriage habits were similar. After death, the soul (*cashpi*) went to live beyond the stars and never returned except in dreams, though a shaman's soul was always available to his successor.

The Supreme Being, quite bodiless, Temauquel, commissioned Quenos, the first Ona ancestor, to shape the universe. Sometimes the first morsel of food was thrown out for Temauquel, and to get him to stop a storm a glowing ember was thrown out into the snow. Quenos gave the Onas their land. C'aux, the mighty hunter, then divided it into thirty hunting preserves for as many clans. Quanyp, the hero, overcame the evil devils Quenuque and Chasquels, "the grand cannibal." "North" always battled "South," and the Moon was the wife of the Sun. The mountains as well as rivers were transformations of early Ona ancestors.

5

North of the Straits and on into the Pampa lived numerous people; chiefly the Auraucanians (latecomers from central Chile), the

Puelche and Tehuelche, the "giants" seen by Magellan, and the Querandí, centering in the La Plata delta, but ranging well into Patagonia and cross-country to Córdoba.

There were dozens of Tehuelche tribes: The southernmost were the "Anoricacua," the northern ones the "Payni-quén." Near them lived various small non-Tehuelche tribes, such as the Caucahué, Huilliche (perhaps Auraucanians), and Poya, the latter two near Lake Nahuel-huapi, as described by Gerónimo Pietás. The Poya were also "gigantic." Very ancient petrographs have just been discovered there, apparently showing men mounted on what appears to be an extinct horse, or horselike animal!

The Puelche (in Auraucanian, "eastern people") or "Genaquín," i.e., "Nation Folk," were widely distributed from the high mountains to the Patagonian coast and in much of the Pampa. We know considerable about the pre-Columbian life of the Auraucanians and of the Querandí, near modern Buenos Aires, but it is nearly impossible to sieve out facts about the pre-Columbian life of the present Tehuelche and Puelche, for they were early intermixed with the Spanish and Auraucanians, quickly mastering the use of the horse, which altered their entire economy and habits. But many tools, adornments, ideas, myths, and theological concepts are undoubtedly derived from earlier ages, although from what era or how greatly modified it is difficult to be sure.

Archaeology has told us much about the Querandí ("People who have grease"), a very tall robust folk, early exterminated, for they bore the brunt of Spanish invasion. A fierce battle was fought in 1536 against Pedro de Mendoza, which has been vividly described by the earlier wanderer from 1534–54, Ulrich Schmidel. A generation later, they were badly broken by Juan de Garay, though he was killed by them in 1583.

They were probably a branch of the Guaicurú, and had no agriculture but fished and hunted the guanaco, deer, rhea, mostly with bolas, though they often ran down their game, or used spears and bows and arrows. They wore fur sex-aprons and ear plugs, and made skin and matting windbreaks. As a sign of mourning, they amputated fingers, a practice found also among our own Plains tribes.

Among other delta and littoral peoples were the Guaraní (a branch of the Paraguayans); Güenóa (who stuck themselves with many fish spears as a sign of mourning); Yaró (medium sized with

116

FIG. 1. SOUTHERN PAMPAS INDIANS (TEHUELCHE) AND THEIR HOMES. (University Museum, University of Pennsylvania)

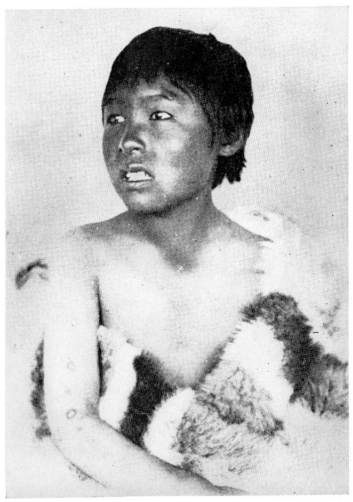

FIG. 2. ONA BOY OF TIERRA DEL FUEGO, IN GUANACO ROBE. (University Museum, University of Pennsylvania)

FIG. 3 (*left*). AMAZON BORORO GIRL, WITH PENDANT OF GIANT ARMADILLO CLAWS. (University Museum, University of Pennsylvania)

FIG. 4 (*right*). AMAZON BORORO YOUNG MAN, WITH FLOWERED HOLIDAY HEAD DRESS. (University Museum, University of Pennsylvania)

Figs. 5 & 6. Witoto Girls (Amazon Rain Forest) in Body Paint for a Holiday.
(University Museum, University of Pennsylvania [Paul Fejos])

FIG. 7. AMAZON BORORO WOMEN AND CHILD. (University Museum, University of Pennsylvania [David M. Newell])

FIG. 8. AMAZON BORORO MEN IN A FORMAL WRESTLING MATCH. (University Museum, University of Pennsylvania)

RAIN FOREST TYPES

FIG. 9. TABA MAN.   FIG. 10. PILAGA MAN.

FIG. 11. PILAGA MAN.   FIG. 12. PILAGA WOMAN.

FIG. 13. PURI OF S.E. BRAZIL. (Artist's Concept of a Ceremonial Funeral Scene, c. 1700). (Collections of Yale University [after Rujendas])

FIG. 14. ONE OF THE FAMOUS SHRUNKEN HEADS MADE BY THE JIVARO OF THE BOLIVIAN JUNGLES. (Collection of the Leyden Museum, Holland)

FIG. 15. URU (NOW MOSTLY EXTINCT) FISHERMEN, ON LAKE DESGUADERO NEAR LAKE TITICACA. BOATS ARE MADE OF TOTORA REED. (University Museum, University of Pennsylvania [Max Uhle])

FIG. 16. SUSPENSION BRIDGE OVER THE URUBAMBA RIVER, OF WHICH THE BASES AND CABLE SUPPORTS ARE INCA (PRE-CONQUEST) OR EARLIER. THE BRIDGE IS STILL IN USE. (Author)

FIG. 17. THE CALASASAYA COURT OF ANCIENT TIAHUANACO, PRE-INCAN MYSTERY CITY OF BOLIVIA, WITH A MODERN CHURCH IN THE BACKGROUND. THE BUILDERS ARE AN UNKNOWN PEOPLE. (University Museum, University of Pennsylvania)

Fig. 18. The Great Gate of the Sun, Tiahuanaco, Bolivia. (University Museum, University of Pennsylvania [Elena Hosmann])

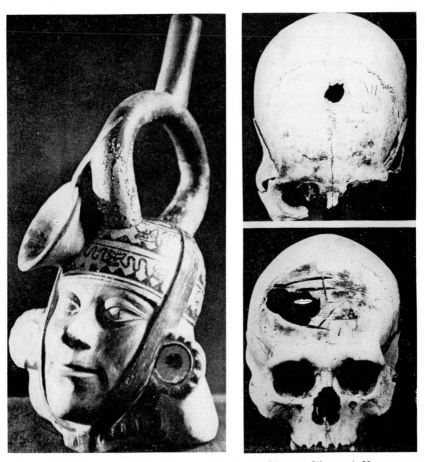

FIG. 19 (*left*). MOHICAN (MOCHE) POTTERY BOTTLE, THE DESIGN A WARRIOR'S HEAD—CIRCA A.D. 20–70. (University Museum, University of Pennsylvania [A. Guillen])

FIGS. 20 & 21 (*right*). SKULLS FROM CUZCO, PERU, PROBABLY PRE-INCA, SHOWING HEALED AND SUCCESSFUL BRAIN SURGERY, DONE TO RELIEVE PRESSURE. (University Museum, University of Pennsylvania)

FIG. 22 (*left*). MODERN AIMARA INDIAN WOMEN OF PERU, DOING A RITUAL DANCE, BALANCING 20-FOOT
POLES. (University Museum, University of Pennsylvania [Frances Toor])

FIG. 23 (*right*). MODERN AIMARA BOATMAN OF LAKE TITICACA, PERU, SHOWING UNCHANGED DRESS AND
APPEARANCE. (University Museum, University of Pennsylvania [Elena Hosmann])

Fig. 24. A Modern Quechua, Descendant of the Incas, in Front of a Cuzco, Peru, Church, Built on Inca Foundation Stones. (Grace Lines)

FIG. 25 (*above*). A MODERN QUECHUA HERDSMAN AND HIS LLAMAS IN FRONT OF THE WALLS OF SACSAHUAMAN, THE INCA FORTRESS. (Grace Lines)

FIG. 26 (*below*). THE TOWERING WALLS AND TERRACES OF SACSAHUAMAN, FROWNING ABOVE MODERN CUZCO, PERU. (Elizabeth R. Hibbs)

FIG. 27. THE TERRACED WALLS OF MACCHU-PICHU, THE INCAS' GUARDIAN FORTRESS OF THE INNER ANDES, HIGH ABOVE THE URUBAMBA RIVER GORGE. (Grace Lines)

FIG. 28. THE SAPA (SUPREME) INCA, IN HIS CEREMONIAL DRESS, WITH LLAUTU FOREHEAD
FRINGE AND CARECUENQUE FEATHERS, HOLDING A SYMBOLIC AXE (A MODEL BUST). (University Museum, University of Pennsylvania)

thick large-jointed legs; the women used fishbone and feather labrets); Bohané (who lived in palisaded villages); Chaná (who spoke a guttural language, painted the bones of the dead with ochre and grease, and buried children in urns: they made excellent pottery); the Mbeguá (farmers, when not fishing, who wore nose, ear, and lip plugs), Carcarañá, Corondá, Queloazá, Colastiné, and the Timbú (probably kin of the Carcarañá, an island people; a favorite food was earth fried in fish grease, and they were cannibals). In the early 1500's they were reported to have had 400 16-man canoes.

On the other side of the Pampa, the Huarpe of Cuyo, a tall, thin type, were considerably influenced by Quechua culture. They built semisubterranean houses on lakes, stone *pirca* houses in the mountains, stick and reed-mud houses on the plains. Good hunters, but mostly agriculturists (chiefly maize) often using artificial irrigation, for Cuyo is a dry area. They constructed balsa rafts from bundles of totora reeds, an art probably borrowed from the Urú near Lake Titicaca. They wove textiles and were good pottery makers, following Andean styles. A distinctive type was a kettledrum-shaped pot, though similar jars are found in early Tiahuanaco remains. They were also marvelous basket makers, which they decorated with tinted wool tufts. Baskets, vases, and goblets were woven so tightly they held water.

They painted parts of their faces green and both sexes used feather adornments, especially in fiestas, and staged three-day drunken orgies with chicha beer. Their chief deity was Humuc Huar.

6

The Charrúa—there were many subtribes—occupied all Uruguay and large parts of Argentina and Brazil, a tall people with "sad, taciturn faces." Their tools, spears, and so on were largely derived from the over-all Patagonian culture, except that their bolas were star-shaped. They made globular handled pottery, polished or incised, and sculptured stones. Their numerical system was based on four, so that five was "four and one" (*betum yu*); eight was two times four (*betum arta sam*); but separate words began again with nine, ten, etc.

They wore deerhide aprons in summer and fur robes, painted with geometric designs, in winter. They tattooed their faces with blue lines and added paint. For war, they painted their jaws white. Copper was used in their perforated nose holes, lip plugs, ear plugs; and pendants were of shell, bone, or bright feathers.

Their nomadic homes were four poles stuck in the ground, roofed and walled with mats, but in the dry season they merely stuck up a single mat as a windbreak.

They built enormous 40-man cedar canoes, beautifully carved, which they rowed in unison and singing, standing up, with long paddles decorated with bird feathers.

Their cooking pottery was of black sun-dried clay, polished and incised with zigzag lines; they also had stone urns and utensils. Hunting was done with bow and arrow, darts, bolas, pebble sling-shots, and spears; enemies' skulls were preserved as drinking cups.

Their death rites were elaborate. In their grief they cut off fingers. The dead were buried in a circle of stakes, along with nets, skins, clubs, and spears; the bones were later disinterred and preserved. "They carry the bones of their deceased relatives wherever they wander," remarked the early Jesuit, Pedro Lozano, "for love makes this stinking cargo very light." The Apache of our Southwest did this as well.

The death of a father was particularly painful; his sons remained naked in their huts for two days, eating only tinamou, fish, and eggs. Friends jabbed many sharp rods into their arms from wrist to shoulder, and the eldest [son or friend] went thus impaled into the woods and dug a deep hole, covering himself with earth up to the chest and remaining there the entire night. He returned to the hut, removed the rods and lay motionless for two days without water or food. For several weeks he spoke to no one and ate only food brought to him by children.

7

The Pehuenche (Pine People), the Araucanians of the high Andes, probably occupied eastern Andean foothills and high portions of Patagonia in very ancient times, though most Araucanian intrusion into Argentina took place after the Conquest. The main body of their culture was on the Chilean Coast, stretching for nearly a thousand miles, from Coquimbo on the edge of the dry northern desert, through the Vales of Paradise, and on into rain and lake country to the Ancud or Corcovado Gulf, and out to Chiloé Island.

What the dance was to the Quechua and other highlanders, music was to the Auraucanians. They were practically the only people of the Americas to develop more than a pentatonic scale and use intervals smaller than a semitone. The Auraucanian had music for every conceivable occasion, or it was quite as often spontaneous: when a traveler left and when he returned, for the harvest cycles and the changes of season, for religious fiestas, and for all the life periods and life's events: birth, puberty, marriage, sickness, death, the hereafter. There were many work songs, folk songs, and cradlesongs.

Their music has inspired many modern Chilean composers including perhaps the most notable, Carlos Isamett, and outstandingly in his symphony *Wirafún Kavellú*, "Galloping Horses," and also his piano composition *Pichi Purún*.

They developed many original instruments. A brief account of them is given in *Music in Latin America* by Nicolas Slonimsky, the outstanding authority in the field, and more extensively by Isamett himself, with illustrations, in three volumes of the *Boletín Latino-Americano de Música*. Two types of flutes, among others, were used, besides Panpipes: the *pifulca*, a small reed pipe, and the *trutruca*, several yards long, but capable of emitting only one lugubrious note. Unique was the *quinquilcahuë*, a double bow made of two strips of wood or animal bone, bent with a bowstring and interlocked like a two-ring chain. The *huada* was a fruit or gourd shell filled with seeds; the *quilquil*, an animal horn; the *pinquilhuë*, a vertical flute; *cultrún*, a flat drum. Hollow-tree drums with languettes were also played.

There were four main groups of Auraucanians, besides the various emigrants to Argentina. The Picunche lived north of the Bío Bío River as far as Coquimbo, and in the drier parts used artificial irrigation. South were the Mapuche and below them the Huilliche ("South People") but not necessarily the same as the Huilli, often attacked by the Chono. The Pehuenche ("Pine People") lived in the dense pine forests of the Andes on both slopes. The designation "Auraucanian" ("Muddy Water") was first used as the name of a local setting, by Ercilla in his great early epic. The Quechua called them Auca ("Rebel Enemy"). About 50,000 Auraucanians lived on Chiloé Island. A very early description is provided in the second volume of Miguel de Goicueta's early narrative of Juan Ladrillos' expedition to the Straits of Magellan in 1558.

Their language provided flexibility and much subtlety with numerous words for essentially the same object or idea, by shifts in the plural form or by shifting certain letters—for example, *t* to *tr* to *ch*; or *r* to *s* or *d*. Also, there was an elegant leader or upper-class tongue.

Araucanians lived in small settlements of three to eight houses (*rucas*), dispersed on high ground but within sight of each other; they were a kinship clan (*cuga*) under a headman. The *Cugas*, according to Ricardo Latcham, Chile's most notable anthropologist and archaeologist, bore such names as Sky, Sun, Stone, Grove, Jaguar, Snake, Condor, etc. The houses were built at community "bees" with proper celebrations. Some were 33'x66', though the chiefs' houses were often larger. Each house had a separate fireplace for each wife. People slept on skins and used bundles of reeds, skins, or else stones for pillows. Cut tree trunks were used as chairs, though customarily they ate, with much etiquette, seated on the ground.

Mapuche men wore a wool *chiripa* (still worn by Chilean gauchos), a sort of loose diaper; a *chamal*, a rectangular cloth from the chest or waist down; and a *macuña* or poncho with a head slit.

The woman's *quepán* was woven cloth pinned over one shoulder, leaving one breast exposed; this cape reached to the calves or lower and was held by a belt. Over her shoulders she wore an *ecul*, fastened in front by an enormous silver *tupu* or brooch.

All went barefoot. Ercilla described the Gulf of Ancud Huilliche as using pointed woolen caps. Hair was bound by brightly colored woven wool fillets or *tarui*, though caciques used a silver band and large silver earrings. Women wore *llanca* necklaces of polished malachite and azurite, shells, or silver. Some of these were extraordinarily beautiful. A string was added at the birth of each child, and women with large families became very weighted down. They would never part with their *llancas* for love or money, for each string guaranteed the health and soul of the child. *Llancas* also served as currency.

The Araucanians, though the fiercest fighters of South America, were almost wholly vegetarians, so that contentions by certain United States pacifists that a vegetarian diet would diminish bellicosity does not seem borne out, in this instance. However, among themselves the Araucanians were very pacific, good-natured and full of fun, and had a fine sense of humor, though not perhaps as imaginative as some early peoples. They were settled agriculturists and had much knowledge of scientific cultivation, though they used no fertilizers, so far as is known, but allowed fields to lie fallow for a year to three years, depending on the crop.

According to John M. Cooper, they had thirteen main food crops:

1. Maize (*zea mays*). Nine varieties.
2. Potatoes (*puñe*). 30 varieties. On Chiloé, 100.
3. Kidney beans (*degul*). 14 varieties.
4. Squash (*pencha*).
5. *Madi* oil seeds. The oil was used extensively in cooking.
6. *Chili* peppers (*trapi*). Many kinds.
7. *Quinóa* (*dahué*). A grain.
8. *Oca*. A root crop.
9. *Mango* (Malay). *Magú* (Auraucanian).
10. *Teca*. A barleylike grain.
11. Peanut *Mani* (Arawak). This, according to Latcham, was introduced by the Quechua. Some, however, believe it was a post-Conquest crop. But *mani* were cultivated almost everywhere in the New World, from Mexico south. (*Cacaguate*, Aztec.)
12. Strawberry (*quellén, llahuén*).
13. *Heuquén*. A barleylike grain.

Beans and corn (the stalks served as poles for climbers) were often planted in the same field.

Tools were primitive: a shovel-shaped instrument; three-pronged pitchfork, with a stone-weighted handle; pointed stick, wide and rounded at the top for stomach pushing; dibbles and digging sticks. Men broke the ground, women followed behind sowing seed. Chicha beer and food were served for the communal planting. The same at harvest time.

Land was held communally, but each family had its own house and plot in perpetuity, and products were family owned. Polygamy was practiced, and each wife was entitled to the products of her own garden plot.

The Auraucanians were highly skilled, either one sex or both, in basketry, rope-making, weaving, dyeing, ceramics, the mining and smelting of gold, silver, and copper, stone-perforating and polishing.

Girls were promiscuous until after marriage. Cross-cousin marriages were preferred because they "avoided discord" and, for the same reason—family harmony—sororal polygyny, the marrying of sisters, was practiced. More prosperous citizens had from four to ten wives, even up to thirty according to historian Antonio Sors, who wrote about 1780. A widow automatically became the wife of her oldest stepson, or her husband's brother or nearest male kin.

The marriage rite was featured by the kidnaping by the groom of the bride after a rough melee between the two family groups. After three days in a hide-out, he brought her to her mother's house where the bride price was then paid and a wedding fiesta celebrated, that lasted from four to six days with much feasting and the singing of special ballads.

There were payments and repayments, often complicated, in the case of divorce, adultery, or remarriage, compared to which the U.S. alimony systems seem simple. Customarily the wife on separation kept younger children, the father all grown-up children.

For child delivery women retired with a friend or midwife (the latter were quite skilled) to a hut near the sea, a lake or stream, and gave birth in a kneeling position, then immediately bathed the child and herself. After an eight-day seclusion, she attended a naming fiesta, with the sacrifice of an animal, whose blood was poured over the umbilical cord, laid in a hole before it was covered over. In some places, a tree was planted over the cord and given the same name as the child.

Cradles were made of poles with nets or were hammocks. No sexual intercourse was practiced until the child had cut some of its teeth. Walking poles helped the child learn to use its legs.

Boys were exposed very young to hardship, cold baths, long runs, fasting, swimming, the use of weapons, and *chicha* drinking. Disobedient children were given datura and lectured.

Coffins were elaborately carved hollow trees in dugout shape, which were buried or hung in trees. Intricate grave posts were carved. Bodies of killed warriors were cremated and their ashes brought home for burial.

The human soul (*palli*), designated by half a dozen words according to attributes and circumstances: e.g., In-the-Body, Out-of-the-Body, Before Death, After Death, Body Shadow, Ghost, etc., lived in the depths of the Andes in a contented state, though one legend said they had to live on Black Potatoes, not a prized food variety. Chiefs' souls lived in volcanoes or the Milky Way, "The Road of Fairies," but revisited their people as large bluebottle flies.

Though the Mapuche recognized the *vitanmapu*, or folk country or nation, with three major political-race subdivisions, only lesser and local chiefs existed. The smaller divisions, about fifty below the Itata River, exclusive of Chiloé, were called *aillarequa,* which was made up of nine or fewer clan groups, each headed by a *toqui,* his name being derived from his symbol of authority, the hidden battle-ax, which was brought out only on the occasion of war. The *levo* (clan) was divided into *cavi* of four hundred persons each, in turn subdivided into *pichicavi,* (small *cavi*) usually headed by a *huilmén* ("noble rich man," though he was not always "noble" or even "rich"). Each small *cavi* was made up of any number of *cuga* or settlements.

There were blood-brother fraternities, ranging from two persons up to allied *cuga,* with initiation ceremonies involving prayer and animal sacrifice.

War victory was celebrated by the dancing of both sexes about a *canelo* or laurel tree, with enemy heads adorning spears. Captives were flayed alive, sometimes enslaved. The heart of an executed captive was sucked and bitten by the headman; his skull became a drinking cup, rattles were made from his dried skin, and flutes from his longer bones. Reports of ritualistic postwar cannibalism have never been adequately confirmed.

The Supreme Being was *Gúnechen* (variously spelled) though some groups exalted *Pillán,* who had power over both good and evil. All catastrophes, eruptions, earthquakes, sickness, and death were ascribed to his power, though death more often was considered to be the result of sorcery. He was sometimes prayed to before the great hockey games which attracted thousands of spectators and were featured by lively music, betting, and much drinking.

Most evil, however, was ascribed to the malevolence of the *Huëcurú,* or evil spirits. These had individual names, such as Twelve Suns, Whirlwind, Two Feet, Green Toad, Master of Worms, etc. Twelve Suns always advised a girl whom she should marry and who would make her pregnant. If she did not heed, the marriage was likely to prove barren and unhappy.

Living Mapuche were said to be descended from the handful of survivors from the great flood, resulting from the quarrel of two enormous serpents, Caicai, who raised the sea, and Tren, who tried to raise the mountains higher. Some humans were changed into fish, sea animals, and rocks, but a few managed to take refuge safely on the mountaintops.

Gos: God of the Chaco

THE Chaco "Hunting Ground" is a vast central plain between the Mato Grosso plateau and the Argentine Pampa, from the sub-Andean mountains to the Paraguay and Paraná Rivers; south to the Córdoba and Guayagán mountains of Argentina, all dry hot country, but traversed by mighty rivers; besides those named: the Pilcomayo coming down full tide from jungle rain-forests and Andean snows of inner Bolivia, the Bermejo, Juramento, Salado, and Dulce, also Andean fed. Many other fairly large streams eventually lose themselves in great marshes and lagoons or perish in the sands. Only the north-flowing Paripití, which disappears in the great Izozog marshes, then re-emerges beyond as the San Miguel river, belongs to the Amazon fluvial system. Water is also found in great lagoons, water holes, stone pits, natural reservoirs, and springs. However, in the east, a rainy system from October to May deposits fifty inches annually, even in the central portion twenty-five inches.

At times when a cold south wind blows, temperatures may fall below freezing, but the highest temperatures of South America have been encountered along the Salado and Pilcomayo rivers, where 120 degrees are not uncommon.

The pre-Conquest Indians were wild and warlike. The most dominant advanced "race" was the Guaraní, though mostly they lived east of the Chaco proper in what is modern Paraguay. The Spaniards and Portuguese were led into this inhospitable and dangerous Chaco region chiefly because this was the one feasible route to the "land of the metal and the white king"—legendary ruler of a realm of gold and silver, rumors of whom started an early gold rush with expeditions under such explorers as Sebastian Caboto (1526) and Walter Raleigh later. The Portuguese sailor Alejo García, aided by Guaraní, got through about that time but was murdered on the way back, a fate that also befell Juan de Ayalos (1537–39). By then, of course, Peru was in the hands of the Pizarros. But major expeditions from La Plata continued to move through, including that of Álvar Núñez Cabeza de Vaca, particularly against the powerful Mbayá, so that gradually the area was subdued, though parts have never been seen by white men, except from the air, to this day.

Save for accounts by early daring travelers, little authoritative is known about the pre-Spanish peoples. But early life can be inferred from post-Conquest survivors, and a few modern anthropologists and linguists, such as Theodore Koch-Grunberg, Erland Nordenskiöld, Max Schmidt, Herbert Baldus, Robert Lehmann-Nitsche, Alfred Métraux and Enrique Palavecino. Archaeologists have scarcely touched the area, though there have been some important finds.

Apparently there is no connection between pre-Spanish ceramics and that of today. The early ceramic art seems to be derivative from Andean cultures, quite likely some from very early Chavín culture; or else from the Guaraní to the east. Early gold, silver, and copper objects, even among the Guaraní, seem to have been brought in from the Andes in exchange for deer and wildcat skins, rhea, and egret feathers. Nordenskiöld listed Chaco traits derived from Andean peoples: spades, knuckle-dusters, war clubs, slings, wooden knives, toothed wooden scrapers, feather fire-fans, wooden bowls and spoons, woven ponchos, shirts, girdles and headbands, sandals, netted hoods, shell-bead spangles, wooden combs, clay vessels carried by a string or with handles, games of chance, the tsuca game, rawhide drums, long wooden whistles, eyed needles, lidded calabashes, fire-engraving, tie-dyeing, knitting techniques, etc. But these arts are widespread in South America, so more definite proof of the place, time, and method of borrowing must be established. No wooden whistles of the Chaco types have ever been found in the Andes. Some of these accomplishments seem more like to have been borrowed from the Arawak to the northwest or the Guaraní to the east: such as the looms, hammock, nets, certain feather ornaments, *urucurú* dye, basketry, etc., yet even such arts among the Chaco Botocudo, Puré-Coroado, and Camacán were very distinctive.

On the other hand, initiation rites of the Chamacoco seem linked more with those of the Ona and Yahgan, probably also the pleasant terrorizing of women at fiestas by "devils" and mummers, but these habits could have come also from the Arawak and other tropical tribes. Among cultural traits common with the Fuegian peoples, Nordenskiöld listed: skin mats, leather bowstrings, notchless bows, sewn skin cloaks, and shields, leather girdles, hairbrushes, ostrich neck bags, twisted skin thongs, hockey. To these Métraux adds: moccasins, decorative designs on skin cloaks, barb-headed harpoons, and bolas.

To summarize: the Chaco gatherers, hunters, and fishermen dressed in painted skin capes, lived in flimsy communal houses, largely lacked basketry and weaving, but excelled in the making of netted bags. They lived in small kinship bands and used magic, as did their shamans, to expel or control evil spirits and sickness, had extensive puberty initiative ceremonies.

The Guaicurú were the most numerous Chacoans, their language the most widespread. Three subgroups: the Codollate (Codalodi), Guaicurutí (Napipinyiquí), the Guaicurú (Guazú or Mbayá) sometimes called Eyiguayequí ("dwellers in palm groves"). Each major group had numerous subtribes and sub-subtribes, such as—not to put down an endless number of unpronounceable long names—"people of the Rhea Country" (between the Jejuy and Apa Rivers but originally farther south), "Mountain people," "Red Earth Folk" (lower Apa and south of Sugar Loaf), "The Hidden Ones" (near the Branco River), "Bush Dwellers" (northernmost Chaco tribe), "Those of the Arrow Region" (headwaters of the Branco), the "Water People" (Lower Bermejo), the Guachí (eleven sub-tribes), and Abipón. The Payaguá (four subgroups) were bold river pirates and fishermen, often island dwellers, though many were famous growers of maize, sweet potatoes, gourds, and tobacco. They wove beaded baskets and traded far and wide.

Another Chaco linguistic family was the Machicuya (Mascoi) or Enimajá (with some six sub-dialects) northwest of Puerto Casado; the Casquihá, inland from the Paraguay River and along the Salado and Galván rivers; the Sapaquí and Sanapana, south of the Salado;

the Angoité, from the Paraguay to Montelindo rivers and west to Palo Blanco; the Lengua, with ten sub-bands. There were other groups in this general area, possibly Arawak, whose linguistic affiliations have never been identified.

The Lulé-Vilelá tongue was spread from the Bermejo to the Salado. Later, according to an anonymous document of 1690 and by the account of Father Antonio Machoni (1732), the tongue was spoken by five main tribes believed to have come in from the Tucumán and Santiago de Estero upland plains, but later authorities, such as Canals Frau and Métraux believe the reverse, that they invaded the Andean foothills, there taking over La Candelaria culture.

The Vilelá-speaking peoples comprised a dozen subgroups; "Those of the Excrements" (Vacaa); "Hole Dwellers" (Ypa); "Foxes" (Ocolé); "Bowmen" (Yecoanita). Also in this area were tribes with other tongues, such as the Malbalá and Matará.

The Mataco-Macán language family (first visited by the 1628 Ledesma expedition) were a solid block across the whole Chaco from the Andes to the Pilcomayo, almost to the Paraguay River, also down much of the Bermejo. There were four main subdivisions. The Lengua, related to this group, got their name (post-Conquest) from their flat labrets, that made them appear to have two tongues.

The Zamuco (four major language groups) in the Chiquitos region, beyond the Bermejo and toward the Santiago range, had outpost groups, such as the Moro, that ranged through the unknown northern Chaco plains, forest, and marshes.

There were many curious, still unidentified tribes on the upper Paraguay, apparently immigrants from the Inca empire, mostly agriculturists, such as the Chané (possibly a post-Conquest migration), who grew maize, sweet potatoes, peanuts, *mbocayá* palm fruits, and raised ducks and hens in pens. They went naked but had cotton cloaks which they stored in clay-sealed ollas. The men wore large wooden ear-lobe discs (*Orejones*) and the women crystal stones, finger thick and finger long, through their lower lips.

The Artán, upstream from Puerto de los Reyes, farmed only sporadically, for their land was periodically flooded or else covered with sand. They also went naked. The men inserted hard fruit husks in their lips, and the women tattooed their faces by means of a sting-ray tail.

Métraux has described the interesting food cycle of the Pilcomayo Indians. In spite of its forbidding aspect, the Chaco actually had more available food plants and trees than the jungle forest areas, also prolific animals, birds, and fish life. From November to January (summer), a period of great joy and much visiting, the Pilcomayo feasted on algaroba seed pods, which they converted into beer, and rich chañar and mistol fruits. At the end of summer, *poroto del monte* beans, tasi and tunas headed the bill of fare. Farm crops of maize, pumpkins, and watermelons were enjoyed, plus many wild fruits. Toward the end of the season, when the rains stopped, the women busily spread out fruits and pods on skins to dry for the winter. April, May, and early June (fall) was a period of plenty, for dense schools of fish came up the river. The surplus was smoked and stored or traded. Even as late as dry July (winter) some fish could still be caught. But midwinter—August and September—were hard months, though in August the Indians still had some *anco* (pumpkin and squash) and algaroba pods. Then they ate *tusca* pods and dipped into their stores of fish and fruits. There were also *sachalimonas* (mountain oranges) and *sachasandia* (Capparis). They gathered various wild squash and gourds and bromelias. A favorite wild food in this season was the "fox-tripe" which, when cured, had a chestnut flavor. Many wild roots and tubers were dug up.

In other places wild palm trees provided various types of food nearly the entire year. In marshy regions, wild rice was gathered by shaking the ripe kernels into canoes.

Farming everywhere was primitive, chiefly by means of a hardwood digging stick, with flat or beveled end; some with hooks to pull down out-of-reach fruit branches, and among many peoples a shovel blade lashed to a five-foot handle. The Chamacoco women used club or paddle-shaped sharp-edged sticks to harvest terminal palm shoots, and forked sticks for snipping off edible leaves.

The Guachí on the Miranda River planted their crops in flood lands as soon as the river receded. Agriculture at best was not easy; it was the prey of capricious rainfall and bad storms, blights, birds, parakeets, wild pigs, sometimes vast locust plagues. The hardest task for the Mataco farmer was the building of thorn hedges twice a year to keep out marauders. Clearing away brush and trees was also laborious. When harvest reached the ripe stage, the Mataco maintained regular guard duty to scare off birds and animals.

The Lulé and Vilelá south of the Bermejo, a dry area, dug deep pits for ollas in which reserve water was kept. They also dug deep cisterns and wells with ladder footholds. As a last resort they used the water in the hollow axils of caraguatá leaves, and bulky *cepoy* tubers were mostly liquid. Some good farming peoples, after they got hold of horses following the Conquest, turned into nomads.

During the fishing months, even inland tribes came down to the rivers, which sometimes meant war, though usually peaceable arrangements were made, even to the lending of fish weirs and nets. Sometimes maize or other products were paid to enjoy such privileges. In general, the arrangements were more civilized than among many so-called modern countries.

In places fish were so thick they could be scooped out by hand. Small streams were dammed, and the fish caught at leisure. The Ashluslay and Lengua used conical wicker baskets. The only hooks, of bone or wood, were used by the Lengua and Casquihá. The Mataco used large wooden hooks for catching caimans. Net-fishing was prevalent, both nets on scissor poles and on bent flexible rods. When the fish came swarming in, the Indians often constructed parallel or diagonal fences; the fish were driven in by striking the water with long poles, which made loud reverberations. Men and women below the outlets caught the frightened fish with nets or stunned them with short round clubs. The fish were threaded through the gills and hung on a cord about the waist. After each cold dip the fishermen warmed themselves beside platform fires.

The Lengua caught eels and lungfish with slender spears, even by hand, using a band of small bones to provide a good grip. The Mataco, Tobá, and Pilagá speared fish with wire-tipped bamboo poles. The Bermejo-River Mataco used a fifteen-foot harpoon with a detachable bone tip with lateral flanges, which could be drawn up by a cord in the hands of the fishermen. Fish were also secured with blows or a harpoon-type arrow. Pilagá fishermen shot from tree platforms overhanging the water.

None of the Chaco peoples used poison. The Mataco and Chorotí lured fish within arrow range by tossing in leaves or branches. In shallow lagoons, where there was danger of being gouged by the ferocious spiny palometa fish, caraguatá fiber stockings were worn.

Hunting was especially important to non-river people, such as the Mataco bushmen. Sometimes they set dry grass on fire, flushing out animals and small rodents which they clubbed. Animals barbecued in the fire were eaten on the spot. Later, the Indians hunted the deer who came to savor the salty ashes or the new grass. The Bermejo hunting parties—100 strong—set parallel bush fires and killed the animals as they tried to escape at the ends, or sometimes built corrals with gates closed by ropes as soon as the frightened animals had stampeded in. Indians often decoyed animals by imitating their calls. Blinds were used for both fish and game, also spring and pole noose-traps, sometimes pitfalls, especially for jaguars, though they were also hunted with spears.

The Mbayá shot white-lipped peccaries with arrows or clubbed the dangerous creatures. Or sometimes the animals were driven into the river or a brush-covered ditch where they could be more easily slaughtered.

Among other animals hunted were anteaters, foxes, armadillos, capybaras, iguanas, and the huge tapir. Otters were stalked with dogs and clubbed to death.

The Mataco warriors who killed an animal had the right to the carcass and dictated how it was to be divided up and to whom. The Mbayá hunting leader always received the heart of any slain animal.

Water birds were often captured on their roosts. Sticks were rained upon them and they were confused with torchlight. The Mocoví captured rheas, sometimes covering their own heads with grass or palm leaves to sneak within arrow or bola range. The Pilcomayo River Indians put on rhea feathers and imitated the bird's motions so successfully the creatures never took fright. Rheas were also driven to a fence concealed in the brush and killed. Hunting charms were worn in leather pouches. The rhea charm consisted of a bird's neck and grass, leaves, and food eaten by it. The Pilagá painted themselves black, believing the birds would not see them. Rubbing the body with special herbs also brought good luck; some herbs may have attracted birds. To fool the rheas the Lengua planted a wooden egg in the ground and sat on it.

Wax images were also used as charms, and special rattle dances often preceded hunting expeditions. The Mataco and Lengua scattered the head fathers of killed birds to confuse live birds.

Most Chaco Indians believed properties of the animal were transmitted to the eaters, hence some creatures, having unpleasant characteristics, were taboo, though old people could eat any animal. It did not matter, for instance, if oldsters became sluggish by eating armadillo flesh. Skunk and fox flesh were eaten only by the Mataco aged.

Deer marrow could be eaten by them, but not by young warriors. Some Indians never ate peccary lest they get toothache, or their teeth would chatter like those of the enraged animal. Livers of any game animal also caused tooth decay. The Tobá feared that the collared-peccary flesh would give them nose ulcers.

Meat was roasted on a spit or boiled or covered with straw and soil in an earthen oven over a wood fire. Intestines were squeezed, and the half-digested contents eaten. The Casquihá made a sausage out of chopped rhea liver, blood, and grease stuffed in the bird's esophagus or bladder, and boiled under ashes. Fish were cooked on a split stick held over the fire. The Tobá coated fish with clay to bake it under ashes. Wild tubers were boiled or roasted, then cooked in water, particularly the xiwielax creeper. Many pods, fruits, and roots were cooked in ashes and eaten with fish grease.

Algarroba and tusca pods and mistol fruits were crushed into a mush with water, and the mush sucked, except for the inedible seeds and spines. Cakes were made of algarroba flour. Chañar fruits were boiled, crushed in a mortar, and kneaded into balls. Palm fruits were eaten raw or crushed and boiled to make a mush, or were roasted in ashes, then boiled with syrup. Maize was roasted in ashes, or boiled and roasted, also made into cornmeal mush.

The mountain orange seeds were so bitter, they were pounded and peeled by hand, put in a bag and immersed in water overnight, then rewashed numbers of times, finally mashed in a mortar. Boiled and sun-dried, these seeds became stone hard and could be preserved all year. Sachasandía fruits had to be boiled five times in different waters to eliminate the poison; similarly "string beans," *protos del monte,* to get rid of bitterness. Pumpkins were halved, sun-dried or smoked, the seeds roasted. Manioc was grated on wooden rasps. Fish were scaled with a square, sharp, hardwood tool.

Food was seasoned with various peppers, ash from the *vidrera, saldillo,* and the *oe* bush, or with salt traded from Quechua regions.

Plates and spoons were made from horn or calabash and fruit shells. Oval clay dippers were used by the Pilagá. The Moscoví molded rawhide spoons.

Storage places were built above low platforms and enclosed branches, but much food and many objects were hung from the hut rafters in net bags, clay pots, or on suspended, near-ceiling platforms.

3

Houses were crude stooping affairs, built by the women, with tree trunks, thick ends down, branches intact, interlaced and covered with palm leaves or grass. This gave no protection against hard rains, but better-constructed, larger communal houses, had many apartments, each with its own door. Many tribes built separate huts for cooking and taking siestas.

The Pilagá and Ashluslay built ellipsoidal houses, facing each other across a wide street or plaza. The Mbayá houses were end to end in a horseshoe about a plaza, kept scrupulously clean.

Bulrush mats were used for roofs, that extended to the ground, supported by uprights of decreasing height. The mats could be raised or lowered according to the weather, and rain expanded them so they were soon waterproof.

The Caipoterade and Zamuco also placed mat cabins around a central plaza. The Paraguay River Tobá built flat-roofed houses with rush-mat walls, and, for camping out, bulrush mats were laid on flimsy stick frameworks or were stretched from a low branch, and a ditch dug to drain off rain water. Sometimes, as with the Mataco, branches or grass were merely planted against sticks.

The northern tribes built the best houses, with gable roofs supported by parallel rows of uprights. The back roof wing reached almost to the ground, the front made a porch.

The Guaranoca built seven-foot-high conical houses nine to twelve feet across. The frame was held up by a central post, covered with leaves, twigs, and mud. Big communal houses were constructed by the Guaná and Paresí, with arched roofs reaching to the ground.

Villages were located with an eye for security, proximity to water and food, preferably at the edge of bush land for possible escape in case of an attack. Only the Casquihá built on hilltops. Villages ranged in size from fifty persons to 1,000, as among the Ashluslay. The only club houses or ceremonial centers were built by the Pilagá and Ashluslay. Each house in their villages had a high front fence, lined with sheds facing the dwelling. The Chamacoco made palm-trunk floors.

Furniture consisted only of skins or mats, which also served as beds. The Chamacoco, Morotoco, and Guatá had mosquito swatters of stiff cloth attached to short handles. Some Chaco pottery, especially near the Andes, was made with skill and beauty. Receptacles were built up by adding successive clay coils, at intervals scraped inside and out with a wooden scraper or corncob and smoothed with the backs of the fingers. After shade-drying, the objects were fired over a bark or dry-wood fire, once the designs and colors had been applied, though black pottery was often made by smearing *palo santo* resin on hot surfaces. The Mbayá and Guaná made Greek frets and other geometric patterns, curves, volutes, and conventionalized foliage. Mostly the tribes made cooking pots, long-necked water jugs with vertical side handles, bowls, or basins. Large water jars were carried on the back with a tump line. Gourds, sometimes with a star-shaped lid, were also used for water bottles, bowls, dippers, spoons, and containers, and were often incised or burned with designs: animals, mountains, trees, musical instruments.

4

Aside from skin or cloth cloaks for cold weather, nearly everybody went naked. Only a few northern tribes used blankets. Bands, aprons, breech clouts, fringed girdles were worn. Robes for cold weather were made of skins, sometimes as many as fifteen were sewed together, the fur inside, the outer surface painted black with geometrical red patterns—squares, lozenges, zigzags.

The Mbayá men wore skirts, with designs and snail-shell spangles; wool belts and bands embroidered with blue beads and studded with large brass plates, sometimes with bells. Jaguar skin jackets, with or without sleeves, were prized possessions among the Tobá, Mocoví, Abipón, and Mbayá. Bermejo and Pilcomayo River women wore wool or deerskin skirts, held in place by a caraguatá fiber cord or, among the Mataco, by a wide leather belt. The Comaguá women wore cotton skirts, and the Mbayá and Guaná women a sort of loose diaper, though out of doors swathed themselves from head to foot in a large cotton blanket or, when working, a small one to cover their breasts. These blankets were beautifully striped, sometimes studded with shell discs. Chorotí and Tobá women used a cylindrical tunic clasped or pinned at the shoulders. Tobá children wore woven palm leaf capes; some were made of painted fish spines.

Headgear consisted chiefly of various feathered bonnets or tiaras, sometimes held on with red woolen bands ornamented with shells or beads or geometric patterns. The Tobá, Abipón, and Mbayá used bird skins, often with spread wings, sometimes with the beak over the forehead. Many kinds of feather or basket sun protectors for head or eyes were used.

Sandals were mostly Andean in form, a sole held by leather straps, but the Tsiracuá and Morotoco wore rectangular wooden sandals—the only examples in all South America. In bush country deerhide leggings were worn.

Ornaments were varied, ear plugs, wooden or shell, twirled palm leaf, deer hoofs, tassels, reed tubes, brass discs, were used by many. Lengua shamans attached mirrors to the plugs so as to see the reflections of spirits. The Mbayá wore silver crescent or animal-shaped pendants, and the men hung heavy palm-nut strings from ear to ear across the back of the neck. Only the Mocoví used nose plugs. But many tribes had labrets in the upper or lower lips, usually of wood, rimmed with silver or copper. The Payaguá labrets were sometimes six inches long. The Mocoví punctured their cheeks with a series of holes from nose to ears into which they stuck feathers "as if wings were growing on their faces." Snail and shell necklaces were valued, some as long as 65 feet, worn in many loops; also necklaces of beads and feathers, fore and back, were used. Mbayá males wore bracelets and armlets of palm leaves, feathers, and metal plates, also feather leg bands, and other peoples wore circlets as charms, such as deerskin with the hoofs. Rhea feathers were often used on the legs as a protection against being struck by serpents. The Mbayá and Chamacoco used feather chokes.

Styles and hair-do's often varied according to sex, age, and sexual status. When boys were initiated by the Guaicurú, their hair was shaved except for two concentric crowns and a center tuft. Warriors wore a crescent crest from ear to ear, or a crown around shaved heads. After puberty Mbayá women shaved their heads except for a semicircle of cropped hair on the crown, dyed with red urucú. The Guaná, men and women, shaved parts of their heads in various styles. Males of many tribes wore queues, with tassels or wrapped rigidly in a fillet. Facial hair was invariably pulled out by the roots.

Tattooing was almost universal, the higher the social status the more elaborate and intricate the patterns on face, breasts, arms, bellies, and buttocks. The Mbayá, who had developed the art of body-painting beyond that of other peoples, used a fish bone with black genipa juice or cabuigo palm ash for coloring. Leather stencils were sometimes used to paint on patterns.

All river people had boats. The notorious pirates, the Payaguá, made dugouts ten to twenty feet long, with sharp bow and stern. War vessels accommodated forty men. Six or eight men standing at the stern wielding nine-foot paddles could drive them at seven knots an hour. The Guachí canoes, built for two or three persons, could outdistance any sailing vessel.

Boatless peoples, whenever they had to cross a river, often made reed rafts or bull boats of deerhide, with upturned edges, which were towed by a good swimmer holding a leather thong in his mouth.

5

Mataco men wishing to make their wives pregnant drank much bird broth. But during pregnancy both sexes abstained from many foods. The Tobá and Pilagá parents wouldn't eat the legs or brains of game lest the baby be bowlegged, or its skull would not bone over. During this period the man never handled any cutting tools lest the child have a cleft lip, and wore no necklaces lest the infant be strangled by the umbilical cord. Just before confinement, the man loosened his belt and clothes, and the women rubbed sting-ray fat on their bellies, to make delivery easier.

A Mataco woman sat on the thighs of a squatting woman and gave birth while clinging to a post. The Ashluslay women gave birth in a squatting position in a special birth hut, a custom perhaps originating because the newborn child had a better chance of survival in fresh clean quarters.

Among the Casquihá the navel cord, cut with a bone knife, was sent to the father who put it on the rooftop if the child were a boy, but burned it if a girl. He refrained from eating meat for eight days and was careful not to get his feet wet. Chamacoco women gave birth unassisted out in the brush, cut the cord with their nails, and spat in the baby's eyes lest it be blind, as the shaman also did later on. For a month thereafter she lived only on young palm shoots and pigeon flesh and drank only boiled water. Sexual intercourse was not resumed for two years.

Following birth, the Abipón father lay in bed and fasted for many days, refrained from snuffing tobacco, ate no capybara flesh or honey, and would not swim rivers. A similar *couvade*, as it is termed, was observed for five days by Tereno fathers. If the child's father was a chief, the whole village celebrated for a week. Old Mocoví women wearing horsehair wigs staged a mock parade imitating warriors and presented the baby with miniature bows and arrows and spears. On the eighth day the child's ears and lips were perforated. The Abipón had even more hilarious performances in which the girls whipped the men.

Abortion, especially among unmarried girls, or at the first pregnancy, was common, either by mechanical means, such as pressing on the abdomen until the foetus died, or by potent drugs. Twins were killed as a bad omen. But the Lulé killed only one, on the theory that the other was due to adultery. How they ascertained which one was legitimate is not known.

Infanticide was common whenever a child was malformed or was inconvenient, as on the eve of a hard voyage, or when food was scarce. Yet parents doted over their children and would sacrifice greatly for them.

Training began as soon as the child could toddle, usually in the form of play imitating the work of the elders, for instance, a tiny tot fetching water in tiny jars.

At thirteen, the Mbayá boy was initiated as a warrior. He painted himself red and white, put on feathers and ornaments and beat a drum, and chanted all night and day. The following sundown, a shaman pricked his penis and jabbed his body with a jaguar bone. The blood was smeared over his whole body. Many cruel tests were devised, and the novitiate had to show his courage by not flinching. Sometimes the ceremonies were conducted around a sacred tree.

Juan Francisco Aguirre, in Volume VII of his *Diary,* told of a ceremony of the Payaguá, who initiated boys as warriors at the age of three or four:

"I saw them celebrating a child of about three . . . son of a chief. . . . They put out 400 *varas* of tent cloth and set out forty small palm trees, and made an avenue of palm branches to them. At the base of them, on four long sticks, with boards in the center, they made a hollow of stakes and mats like a small cart, so it was called, which was beplumed and adorned. After several days and nights of drinking, singing with taborets, and making wounds with ray-fish spines, the celebration ended with a procession . . . in which the padrino, or godfather, carrying the child—both extremely painted—got into the cart, which was carried on shoulders along the street, three steps to the right and to the left, then was returned to the place of palms. . . .

"During this procession tumult reigns; some throw *abalorios,* straw wreaths, fruits, balls of thread toward the cart, for whoever can catch them; and there are others who water it with their blood, the most sacred being that from the member, mixed with water. This is the gift for the distinguished child who, they hope, will become their leader; then children of the same age, denied, not enjoying, the illustrious rite, were selected as soldiers [for the future chief]."

Among the Chamacoco, boys were taken into the bush for a month where old men taught them tribal law and the ethical code, and imparted secrets of ritual which they were pledged never to disclose to the women under pain of being clubbed to death.

In Lengua puberty rites, at the girl's first menstruation women headed by a choir leader, in time to chants, struck the ground with staves, on which were tied bundles of deer hoofs. The leader (like the majorettes of modern bands) went through strange contortions or pretended to tear out her hair. The men formed circles, chanting to the rhythm of gourd rattles. Files of boys in rhea plumes, wearing masks to represent evil spirits, wove in and out, jingling deer hoofs and uttering shrill cries, trying to get at the girl, only to be beaten off by the women.

Among the Chorotí, the puberty celebration, as Rafael Karsten noted, lasted a whole month, during which the girl kept her whole body covered and remained in her hut. Every night the mother and other women circled outside, banging their staves, while shamans shook rattles and beat drums. It was the equivalent of the modern coming-out parties.

6

Among the Pilcomayo and Bermejo river tribes, girls enjoyed complete premarital sex freedom. Provocative, fickle, brazen, they always took the initiative, choosing their sex partner for the night by putting their hands on the boy's shoulder and dancing behind him or else seizing him by the belt. Some had private huts in the bush for sexual purposes.

In contrast, according to Martin Dobrizhoffer, an early authority, Abipón girls remained virgins until married.

Among the Mbayá were males who dressed and spoke like women, did only female labor, pretended to menstruate, and served as prostitutes.

Among the Chamacoco, a young man first married an old woman and abandoned her when he tired. Adolescent girls married old men, but had to wait for the husband's death before remarrying.

In most tribes the male had to "buy" the bride with necklaces, clothing, weapons, animals and game, skins, wild honey, etc. Child marriages prevailed among the Mocoví, Guaná and Mataco. Sexual play proceeded to intercourse at the age of puberty.

Except among the Abipón, there was scant marriage celebration, but some drinking and dancing among the Lengua. The groom "kidnaped" the bride from the feast, and a mock pursuit ensued. Among the Abipón the bride was conducted to the groom's hut under a canopy of blankets held by eight girls, was greeted by the groom, then was returned to her parents. She then collected all her belongings and took them to her new home (though they soon took up permanent residence in the mother's house). A boy on the roof beat a drum; guests crowded in to drink. Among the Tereno, painted adorned girls carried the boy's weapons to the bride's house, and he was brought there later by a band of singing, dancing youths. The pair then sat in a hammock, woven by the bride for the occasion, and drank together while women chanted songs.

In a few tribes there was considerable divorce. A Chamacoco man might marry as many as thirty times. But nearly everywhere woman's status was high; they were independent, not subservient, were rarely abused or beaten, often had much authority at home and in village affairs.

A Mocoví wife, keeping watch over a dying husband, struck him with her fists, crying out, "You unfaithful cruel man! Why are you leaving me? You were a skillful hunter and a brave warrior. You have killed so many enemies! Where shall I find another your equal? Don't you feel sorry for your children? Who is going to bring them food? Now they'll have to shift for themselves." Other women wailed and chanted.

If witchcraft was suspected, straw was piled over the defunct, and two arrows were shot into his throat and heart, with incantations that the unknown sorcerer be stricken.

In the Abipón deathbed dance, rattles were shaken and lamentations shouted. A female shaman pounded a drum near the dying man's head and sprinkled water on him. If witchcraft were suspected, the man's tongue and heart were extracted, boiled, and tossed to a dog, which was then killed. Final laments to the sound of rattles, drums, and shrill hisses by all married women, who with disheveled hair "leapt like frogs and tossed their arms about. This was kept up for nine days, after which the wailing and groaning gave way to a festive chant."

7

Hockey was a favorite Chaco game, played with end-curved sticks and a wooden or rope ball on a 100-yard field with two brush-heap goals. The players often wore shin guards. Big gambling stakes added to the enthusiasm.

Dobrizhoffer described a game (Abipón, Mocoví) in which a dumbbell-shaped stick about thirty inches long was hurled at a given mark "in such a manner that it strikes the ground every now and then and rebounds."

Mbayá and Mocoví youths, naked with jingles or peccary hoofs about their wrists, staged boxing matches. Coaches and umpires were employed, and the bout was ringed about by older men with spears. Women also boxed, and sometimes, as among the Payaguá, men versus women.

Among the Mbayá, races were heralded a day ahead by a boy beating a drum, shaking a gourd rattle, and chanting the news. The competitors, painted and wearing feathers, staged a plaza parade.

Another contest was shuttlecock, played with a ball of corn leaves and feathers. José Sánchez Labrador described a "ring and pin" game: 56 or 60 rings tied on a string were thrown into the air and caught by a stick.

Mbayá girls played at deer-hunting, fending off boy "hunters" with deer horns. Other hunting games were played: "deer," "jaguar," "vultures," "peccaries." A popular game (Tobá *et al.*) was for a "leader" with a firebrand to burn the last child in a linked line, which moved snake fashion to fend him off. Girls, clasping hands, wound up to symbolize a tree, which a boy simulated cutting down by switching their legs, until the whole group tumbled down in a screaming giggling heap.

Miniature weapons, dolls, cat's cradles, trigger tubes for pellets, buzzers, bullroarers, hoops, stilts, and string figurines were common toys.

Tsuca or *Tsucoc* (Quechua derived) was a favorite gambling game among the Pilcomayo. Two, four, or eight could play. Twenty-one holes ("houses") were dug, each holding a stick—a "fox" or "bird." The middle hole, the eleventh, was a "lake" or "river" and falling into it cost a penalty setback. Two "dice" with burned symbols on a convex face, were thrown twice, after striking the left shoulder each time and uttering vociferous advice. If four, two, or no convex side came up, the score was 4, 2, or 1. But an odd number of convex sides gave no score, and the next player then took over. Each player indicated his score by a colored arrow pointing at the proper "house." Once past the "river," he captured the "fox" in every hole he reached. Capture of all the opposing forces and arrows scored game.

Singing was often formalized, certain sounds to a three-beat rhythm, or the repetition all night long of a pair of words such as *"peitolo yavali"* (Lulé, Isistiné), or a monotonous melodic recitation of "epics" (Mbayá). Pilagá women songs were incredibly obscene. Each Pilagá had his individual song, which was handed down from father to son.

The only known instruments were rattles (gourd, deer, or peccary hoofs), turtle shells castanet style, shells, fruit shells, jingles, bows (Andean in origin), drums, flutes. Drums were clay cooking pots, or hollowed wood pots, partly filled with water and covered with rawhide. Players sometimes used a drumstick in one hand and a rattle in the other (Mbayá) and emitted "vulture beats" or "jaguar beats."

8

Visiting was a matter of great etiquette, sometimes accompanied by lengthy speeches and flowery formalities and rigid ritualistic conduct, until ordinary friendly contact was established. Other groups had very terse greetings and farewells, though omission of these almost sharp words would give much offense. An Ashluslay (and others) on arriving at a strange village spent the first night shaking rattles and singing chants about his friendly intentions. Travelers setting off on trips were given a singing farewell, perhaps with dance steps, the same on his return.

In his four volumes of travels, Felix de Azara wrote telling how, when a Lengua traveler returned and death had intervened in the family or village, he was greeted by two wailing Indian women: "They employed among themselves a singular form of politeness when one of them returned after an absence . . . the two Indians weeping before saying a word; any other action would be an insult, or at least proof that the returner was not welcome."

9

Political organization was simple: a chosen chief who might or might not be also a shaman, but respected for his wisdom, skill, and courage, though the post was often hereditary. He presided over councils, headed hunting, fishing, and war parties, acted as judge

140

in cases of theft, a very rare crime. He received no special reward and was expected to share whatever he had with others. Often, though, he received token gifts of the chase and fishing and war plunder, and was frequently tendered special dishes.

A few tribes had military societies, such as the *hecheri* of the Abipón to which membership was gained by tests of fortitude. On being admitted, the new member was given a new name, which was pronounced over and over by a band of women striking their lips with their hands. The initiate was obliged to speak thereafter to his fellows in a sort of "pig Latin," using redundant syllables, and there were many secret words.

The starting of war was preceded by many conferences in which the chief consulted the opinion of the more influential, or allied groups, in which the leader of the expedition was chosen, usually a younger man if the chief had grown old, but usually a relative of his. A fiesta was then held with drinking and dancing to celebrate the anticipated victory. Various taboos, such as no sexual indulgence, were observed, and Pilagá warriors could not eat the head, legs, or grease of any game. The war leader had to see that the necessary weapons were prepared, and sent out scouts to spy on the enemy. The Lengua notified other bands of the place and time of reunion by sending red arrows. The party was led by the chief or appointed commander, accompanied by shamans, for the alliance of God and war is universal. Flute players went along with all Mbayá forces.

War trophies were heads or scalps. Enemy bones were often made into pipes and whistles; skulls served as drinking cups. A Mocoví warrior attached a new feather to his spear every time he killed an enemy.

The victors were received by women dancing with red feathers (Tobá, Pilagá) who received the scalps and danced with them, making ludicrous dialogue of derision.

The warriors put on feather masks, painted themselves red with black stripes across their bodies, wore ankle charms, and danced around a pole or planted spears on which the scalps or heads were hung.

Male prisoners were rarely spared, though some people kept slaves or sold them as slaves, or else held them for ransom. Captured women and children were incorporated into the tribe, though treated as slaves; and their children, even by members of the conqueror tribe, were considered slaves. The treatment of slaves, however, was rarely harsh; sometimes they were favored over their owners. Thus Abipón masters would go hungry rather than deprive a slave of food. In general they had almost complete freedom except for their assigned tasks. It was understood they would never run away and few did.

10

The Chaco Indians had a vague belief in a land of spirits, and it was dangerous if ghosts lingered around. The hereafter was commonly a projection of the village, but more grandiose. This realm was "in the west" (Lengua), or "beneath the earth" (Mataco), "a gay place of eternal sun" (Tobá). The Mataco believed that souls became successively ghosts, birds, spiders, and bats before vanishing forever. But the souls of those stabbed in a drinking bout became mosquitoes or flies, then ants which turned into grass.

The Indians had a Supreme Being (denied by missionaries), deities and demigods. The Lengua believed a BEETLE made the universe and populated it. The Chamacoco sang every night to the female *Eshetunhuara,* mother of spirits, who dominated all, kept the sun from burning up the earth, and provided water. The Sun, moon, planets, stars, rain, lightning, rainbow, comets, wind, etc., were often deified. The lightning provided husbands. Comets were "evil" spirits. Eclipses were caused by a huge bird wing; thunder, by birds.

The Tobá believed the thunderbolt was an old hairy woman, who could return home only by flying on a fire (lightning) kindled by an earthly friend. The Mataco talked of "the Big Fire that Burns at the End of the World."

All natural phenomena, celestial and terrestrial, were accounted for by poetic and imaginative aetiological tales. The Abipón called the Pleiades "Our Grandfather." During the period of the year they were not in sight, the Indians said he was "ill," and his return was greeted with rejoicing, a feast, and magic rites, for this return marked also the season of the ripening of the Mbocayá palm nuts.

The Mocoví asked the Moon for physical strength, and if at the same time ugly noses were pulled, their shape would be improved. Menstruation was the result of girls having intercourse with the Moon (Mataco).

Epidemics were caused by mountain, swamp, forest, and river demons. The *Hacumuyi* spirit (Lengua) aided farm labor.

A whirlwind spirit danced in dust clouds. A female spirit in the hill brush and spirits dancing in glades at night were particularly dangerous.

The Mascoí said a huge horned armadillo lived underground. This, according to the Chamacoco, caused the Great Flood. Pilcomayo Indians, Juan Belaieff relates, told of a caiman, big as a kapok trunk, and of a glittering star snake that passed through the river rapids at night. An endless huge serpent, if seen by a Tobá or Mataco, caused sickness and death, and a big swamp anaconda carried off human victims on its horned tail.

Rites, ceremonies, dances, special body adornments were celebrated to propitiate deities and gods, drive off evil spirits, and cure sickness. Some tribes held joyous rain dances, especially when there was no thunder.

Dream interpretation was very important, some believing that a dream represented the soul's adventures while apart from the sleeping body.

The universe was divided into strata: three, according to the Chanaco, each with a different color.

Métraux gives the following description of a religious feast of the Vilelá.

"The assembled shamans designated a young man to impersonate a god called Gos ["spirit"] . . . a girl to be the god's wife and . . . boys to be his servants." Ten or twelve painted poles were planted near two huts specially built for the holy couple. "On the appointed day, the youth of the village, covered with feathers and smeared with paint, came to the sacred spot carrying jars of beer. They danced and addressed prayers to the spirit, begging for rain, after which Gos, with his wife and servants, emerged from a grove where they had hidden the day before. The boy . . . wore a huge tapering headdress of straw, provided with 'horns,' his whole body concealed under skins and bundles of straw. His wife was naked except for a net apron, and her followers wore only feather belts. . . . All concealed their faces behind small painted sticks. The divine couple and their escorts danced around the poles, shouting, grimacing and striking the poles with painted sticks."

8

Men on the Spit

W<small>HEN</small> the Hispanic explorers reached the east coast of South America, the great Tupí-Guaraní family of peoples were in process of a northern migration that had taken them as far as the mouth of the Amazon and had displaced other tribes, particularly the far-flung Gê of Western Brazil, who continued thereafter to thrive chiefly on the Brazilian steppes as far north as 3° south, along with the Tapuya, possibly related, though linguistic proof is lacking. Among other groups of the area were the Bororo, Guató, Botocudo, and a dozen others, from the primitive, shy yet warlike Patashó hunters to advanced farming folk like the Camacán.

Archaeological evidence indicates the region was originally inhabited in remote prehistoric periods by other peoples, neither Tupí nor Gê. Ancient pottery shards, particularly in Apinayé territory, some of superior decorative style, have been found, but the more modern Gê made no ceramics.

Long before the Gê, other earlier folk along the coast and river banks left kitchen middens in *Sambaquí* mounds, a Tupí word meaning "hills of shells," some of which were built up of sand, fern fronds, and mussel shells 300 feet high. Some remains excavated from the Sambaquís, particularly those inland, have great antiquity and seem contemporaneous with the nearby Lagoa Santa finds, perhaps dating back to the Pleistocene, though the chief investigators of the Sambaquís, Antonio Serrano, Everado Back-

144

heuser, Theod. Bischoff, Benedicto Calixto, Leon F. Clérot, Hermann von Ihering, J. B. de Lacerda, Albert Löfgren, Jósef von Siemirandzki, Antonio Carlos Simeons da Silva, and Carlos Wiener, have quarreled about the dating of deposits. Most agree, however, that those containing *Azara prisca* (fox-dog) remains belong to the lost Lagoa Santa culture. In these are found very ancient stone artifacts, particularly hexagonal or oval axes, roughly fashioned by heavy blows, though some were polished. Chipped stone knives and scrapers and hammers complete the list, but no pottery at all.

However, the stonework of the middle period around Rio de Janeiro and Espiritu Santo yielded highly polished objects and some pottery. More recent deposits relate to the various cultures encountered by Europeans, probably those driven out by the Guaraní stocks just before the Conquest, but the Guaraní also left some records in the Sambaquís. José Imbelloni considers that some artifacts in more southerly sites were of Fuegian origin.

2

Lagoa Santa man was discovered by Pedro Wilhelm Lund, a Dane who went to Minas Gerais to die of consumption, but lived out a full lifetime and made some of the most notable anthropological discoveries on this continent. His first find was in the Sumidouro cave, and feverishly he investigated hundreds of caves, finding a great number of human skulls and bones in conjunction with Pleistocene fossils, such as the *Arctotherium brasiliensis, Palaeolama weddelii* (llama), *Hydrochoerus giganteus, Hippidum neogaeum, Machaerodus neogaeus,* and others. The question of dating involved concerns how long did such extinct mammals survive in the New World, and whether the human bones were deposited while the mammals lived.

In more recent years in the Lapa de Confins cave, Dr. W. Tansley discovered a Lagoa Santa cranium, dolichocephalic, hypsicephalic, pyramidal, prognathous, and with a shallow elliptical palatine vault —probably older even than Lund's types. In a Campo Alegre rock shelter, Anibal Mattos discovered fossilized bones of eight individuals and, deep down, arrow points and a flexed Lagoa Santa type of skeleton, knees against the chin, in conjunction with various rock implements, grinders, irregular axes, pitted stones for crushing palm nuts—all similar to finds in the oldest coastal Sambaquís. In the Lapa Vermehla cave, considerably afield, were found petrographs on calcareous rocks.

3

The later Gê and others had primitive agriculture that stressed sweet potatoes and yams, sometimes peanuts, rather than manioc and maize. Several tribes cultivated Cissus, a grape-type vine, unknown to the Tupí or later whites. The Timbirá, as described by Francisco Paul Ribeiro, were accustomed to hunt and gather during the dry season, then return to their villages to plant crops, including peanuts and a midget corn, which were harvested by June. A plentiful food time was the season when *sapucaia* fruits were ripe. Gathered honey was kept in skin bags. For some peoples, toads, lizards, and bamboo worms, which caused visions, were considered great delicacies—as Auguste de Saint-Hilaire, the notable explorer, observed much later.

The Gê peoples had some crude weaving, of cotton, human hair, burití palm, and other plant fibers; various types of basketry, some excellent; and feathers were used in innumerable ways. The Botocudo wore a diadem of flaring yellow feathers set in wax.

Tools were primitive: a crude planting dibble; shell, bamboo, and piranha-teeth scrapers. Stonework was limited, though the Carajá, at least, had stone axes since time immemorial, one type being anchor-shaped, as indicated in petrographs. Bows and two-feathered eight- or nine-foot arrows were blunt for birds or had sharp wooden barbs for jaguars. The Carajá and Acroá used poisoned arrows. Grooved darts were relied upon by some. The most important weapon, however, was the bone- or wood-tipped lance.

The preferred tactic of war attack was to launch a shower of arrows, then charge in with lances and clubs. Cayapó women went along to hand their husbands the arrows. The Botocudo, according to Walter Knoche, used caltrops, four-pointed ground spikes, to block attack, but this may well have been after the arrival of the horse.

They played many games. The Timbirá, Sherente, and Camacán staged races dragging heavy decorated logs or tree trunks, a sport probably derived from utilitarian contests during house-raising bees. Wrestling, hockey, tug-of-war, hoop-and-pole, rubber ball games, shuttlecock were known.

The Machacali communicated with the dead in dreams, and a men's society impersonated them, dancing about an adorned sacred pillar and simulating spirit voices by whirling bull-roarers and blowing whistles.

Yurema was drunk by the Carirí to induce ecstatic visions, the same effect as eating bamboo worms. The Carirí had three gods: a Father and two quarrelsome sons. One was Badze (Tobacco). The Cayapó and Bororo shot arrows at the sky during eclipses, perhaps in a desperate attempt to ward off expected catastrophe.

Scarification, massaging, flogging, artificial sweating by means of hot rocks, smoking, sucking sore places, bloodletting were used as cures, though disease was believed to be chiefly due to sorcery.

The only musical instruments were drums, trumpets, rattles, whistles, flutes, decorated bamboo poles for striking the ground to provide rhythm for dancers. Timbirá village sites were actually selected so as to provide proper dance space. The most picturesque fiestas were perhaps the Parrot Dance of the Machacalí and the great Anteater masquerades of the Apinayé, Sherente, and northern Cayapó.

4

The Guato of the upper Paraguay have survived into modern times. Excavations have turned up three-stop bamboo nose flutes and notched rasp sticks. According to Max Schmidt, who uncovered platform mounds on the Caracara River, each family owned an acurí palm grove which provided wine from the sap, fermented overnight and sipped through a reed in modern ice-cream soda style. More primitive were the Guayaquí who roamed east Paraguayan forests.

The Bororo (including the Otuque) centered in Mato Grosso, but extended into Bolivia and western Goyaz. While the man hunted, the wife collected seeds, palm nuts, and edible roots and carried the game home: peccaries, tapirs, jaguars, rabbits, and birds. They lived in conical huts with a central pole supporting slanted poles; more permanent structures had a crossbeam resting on two forked uprights. In larger apartment houses, each family had its individual fireplace and oven. All quarters contained a platform bed, reed mats, pots, roasting spits, rock crushers, spindles, and bivalve shells for spoons and scissors.

Babies were put in hammocklike mats which could be rocked while the mother worked. Children went naked. The youth initiate was provided a penis sheath, a girdle with shell discs, a cotton-thread necklace, a lower lip bone plug, and ear ornaments. On festive occasions flags with red and black geometrical or animal designs were affixed to the penis sheath. Women wore a gray sex band, a black one when menstruating, attached to a girdle or form-fit corset. Bodies were painted with red urucú for aesthetics and to ward off insects, or with resin (a curative for sores and bites) to which feathers were affixed.

Women plaited hair with cords; cotton was plaited for arm, wrist, and ankle adornment. Both hair and cotton were spun on a shaft with a shell or clay disc serving as a whorl.

The Bororo fought with bamboo-tipped *seriba* palm arrow, using a human hair wrist guard, arocira wood, and fish spine knuckle-dusters.

They drew hunting scenes on the sand, filling in outlines with gray-white ash, and using black sand to depict animal eyes and spots.

Music was made with deer-hoof and gourd rattles, elaborate trumpets with bamboo resonators, polyglobular trumpets of three or four gourds joined with wax, flutes without stops, and bull-roarers. Gourd rattle war dances were frequent, also a jaguar dance, in which the animal's skin was worn, together with jaguar claw and teeth necklaces.

Robert H. Lowrie, a leading Bororo authority, described the Bari Soul of the Dead fiesta, when the souls came back to earth as *"bope, macrebop* or *huaicurú,"* causing falling stars, sickness, but foretelling the future and setting up food taboos.

Folk tales were imaginative. A jaguar spared the life of a man in return for his daughter. But the jaguar's grandmother, a caterpillar, made the wife laugh herself to death from her tickling. The husband performed a Caesarian operation and saved the baby twins, Bacororo and Ituborí. They burned the grandmother in revenge and ruled thereafter over the East and the West, the heavens of after-life.

The brothers Meri (the Sun) and Ari (the Moon) were pranksters. They put out fire, but it was saved by a toad. The Indians chased the pair up a tree and killed Ari, whose body was eaten by a canid, but the Sun Meri killed the animal and re-created the Moon from Ari's bones. Myths about the Sun and Moon were innumerable.

5

The tribes of Caingang—a name not used until 1882—stretched from São Paulo to Rio Grande do Sul, some half a dozen or so peoples, also related to the Gê. Originally known as the Guayaná, and so called by Hans Staden, they dwelt mostly on the open shore and open plains, such as Piratiningá, avoiding forests which were preferred by the incoming Tupinamba, though one tribe, the related Caagua ("Forest Dwellers") roved the jungles between the Paraná and Uruguay Rivers. The Caingang were found in numbers along the Piquiry, Iguassú (clear to the Falls), and Negro Rivers.

All these peoples were agricultural, raising red, white, and violet maize, pumpkins, white beans. They cleared out brush and trees, which they broke down with clubs and burned. Women did all the planting and harvesting. They also hunted and fished and gathered pine-nuts, wild fruit, and larvae. The pine-nuts were eaten toasted, made into dough for bread, or were soaked in sealed baskets for six weeks, then made into soup flavored with tart malaguet leaves. They had a clever double-noose system of climbing tall palm trees. *Ortiga brava* and other fibers were spun and processed, were woven into fabrics by hand or on simple looms. They made black clay pottery, large pots and roasting pans, and conical base jars that would stand up in the sand. Their seven-to-nine-foot bows were made of *Pão d'arco* or black *ipé* wood, were dressed down with flint flakes, smoothed with umbauba leaves, smeared with grease and wrapped with *cipo embé* strips. The arrows were of light white *palo alecrim*, with burned or pointed heads tipped with monkey or deer bones (perhaps also with stone points). Decorated war and work clubs often had cutting edges.

They went naked except for shiny brown bark belts, but in winter often used a square cloak or *curú*. They tied up the penis and tucked it under the belt. The women used fiber skirts, a black-dyed bark belt and a feather sex-apron, or else a looped bark strap fastened to the belt front and back. Both sexes wore strips of peccary hair or bark around the ankles.

The dead were cremated with elaborate rites, and periodic keening parties were held for a whole year. A cult of the dead—described by Herbert Baldus—thereafter conducted rites whenever requested by a relative. There was much horn-blowing, earth tube-beating, singing, stamping, and dancing. Participants stood face to face crying *"xogn, xogn."* Offerings of honey and maize were made, which, when fermented, was poured into a long trough and a feast spread beside it. The chief mourners, however, remained in their huts, painted with black stripes, and drank beer until senseless. Other intoxicants were made from maize, sweet potatoes, pine-nuts and palm fruits.

Their legends relate that the Great Flood left only the summit of Crinjijubé mountain unsubmerged. Two early folk heroes swam to it with firebrands in their mouths but were drowned, and thereafter their souls lived in the heart of the mountain. Some members of the tribe did survive on the summit, until *saracurá* birds, aided by ducks, filled in the sea with dirt carried in baskets in their beaks. All Caingang who had taken refuge in trees turned into monkeys.

Before disposal of a dead body, the shaman rattled his gourd over it, warning the soul of other-world perils. It would reach a road fork, one road leading to a gigantic spider web, the other to a boiling pot trap or a slippery bank above a swamp harboring a huge crab. If able to avoid such disasters, the soul reached a forested underworld heaven, where night and day were reversed, with an abundance of tapirs, deer, and other game. There the soul was rejuvenated. After another happy lifetime, it became a mosquito or ant, the death of which was the end of all.

6

Among the five major Gê branches were many subtribes, some now extinct, as well as other loosely related peoples. The Southern Cayapó, a most primitive group, occupied the Paraná tributaries in the Mato Grosso. The Guitaca, three or four subgroups, were scattered among the coast from the Circara River to Cape São Thomé and near Rio de Janeiro, and possessed the fertile Campos de Goaitacazes as far as the mouth of the Parahyba. They tracked down game until it fell exhausted, and speared sharks, the teeth of which were used to tip their arrows. They built houses on piles or in trees. Subtribes of the Timbirá were particularly good road builders. From each village four roads rayed out (used also for races) in the four directions for ten miles or so. These were twenty-three feet wide, and far-flung trails were also kept in excellent condition, all-important for log racing.

The Sherente, another important sub-subgroup, were sternly monogamous (though with some explicable sororal polygyny) and had strict sex and marriage laws.

The division of labor between the sexes among all the Gê and Caingang was precise and equitable, though with varying degrees of sex status. All groups had "wantons" who were promiscuous. Two were always taken on Sherente hunting trips, but were also required to cook.

The Canella (Neo-Brazilian) had lifelong paired male friendship, a dichotomy that may go back to prehistoric times. A youth chose a boon companion, or they chose each other for comparable diving and swimming or other ability, and thereafter they became inseparable. They hunted and fought side by side, and sometimes even temporarily exchanged wives, if the latter were willing.

The Sherente had four male societies (to which boys were inducted at the age of eight) which carried on sports, fiestas, and war activities. Each society had its own sacred clearing and stands of *buruti* and *babassú* palms where trespassing was forbidden.

There was only one female society, which arranged name-bestowing festivals. Among the Apinayé, godparents were appointed for every child at the age of five and had serious obligations.

The modern Canella have many handicrafts that seem derived from older times. They made accurate wax images of rheas, tortoises, deer, and armadillos, used attractive decorated forehead bands and sashes, feather adornments, and patterned baskets, mats, gourds, clubs, and other objects with pleasing geometric designs. Racing logs (Sherente, Timbirá) were intricately carved and colored. Body-painting with five-tine forks and stencils, was a highly developed art that used such motifs as stars, hourglass shapes, triangles, and dots. Different designs indicated sex, virginal and marital status, age, and social standing. They made music with buzzer discs, horn trumpets, rattles, and whistles (also used by warriors).

Sorcerers (Apinayé, Sherente) denounced as such by the chief or shamans, were put to death. Sickness was due to "soul loss, soul intrusion, or sorcery." The soul of a human, animal, or plant caused definite troubles; a deer soul quickened the pulse, that of a tortoise slowed it down. For every intrusive beast and plant soul there was an animal or plant antidote. Anti-deer medicine was made from an antler-shaped plant. Shamans were advised by stars; those most adept at healing belonged to the "Mars" cult.

Among the Sherente, earth, sky, sun, moon, and the underworld were eternal. Vultures peeped through sky slits at the earth. The Sun and Moon lived in separate heavens.

The Purí, Coroado, and Coropó—related culturally—had tribal offshoots between the Serra de São Jozé and Onza, both spurs of the coastal Serra do Mar, and along the Xipotó Novo, Pomba and Parahyba rivers. The Purí (three subdivisions) lived from the Parahyba to the Serra de Mantoueira and upstream along the Rio Dolci.

The Coropó lived on the Rio da Pomba and on the south side of the upper Parahyba.

The Purí were nomads whose favorite food in the dry season was the larvae of the *bixo da taquara,* kept in bamboo tubes, and used as fat for preparing corn cakes. They baked food in earth ovens or boiled it in green bamboo tubes. The Coroado, who tonsured their hair, were slouchy farmers and mostly killed game or gathered bush products.

They slept in hammocks woven from cotton or *embauba* fibers. All went naked, but used feather, animal teeth, and seed adornments. Until married, girls wore black strips around wrists, legs, and knees and ankles. Both sexes, according to Wilhelm Ludwig von Eschwege, were tattooed by pinching the skin and pushing through a needle and thread with pigment to make circular designs or outlines of animals and birds.

Mostly their handicrafts were similar to those of all the Gê groups. They broke the bones of their dead so as to cram them into large jars, which were buried in the deceased's hut, which was then burned down. If the deceased was a chief, the whole village was abandoned. Male relatives cut off their hair in mourning; women painted their bodies black. The soul went to a happy grove of sapucaia trees full of game.

Johann Baptist von Spix and Karl Friedrich von Martius described Coroado and Purí dances in their *Reise in Brasilien;* the men in a front line with bows and arrows, the women in a row behind: "In the first three steps they put the left foot forward and bent to the left side; at the first and third step, they stamped with the left foot, at the second with the right. In the following three steps, they advanced the right foot, at the first and last bending to the right side. . . . As soon as the song was concluded, they ran back in disorder as if in fright; first the women with their daughters, then the men with their sons. After this, they resumed their former order and the scene was repeated."

The Botocudo, according to Pedro de Magalhaes, occupied the coast from Ilheos to Porto Seguro, probably having come originally from the interior Sertão.

To build huts they pounded in a circle of stakes and covered them with grass or bark, or for more temporary purposes stuck palm fronds in the ground so as to make a domed roof.

They collected *inga* pods, *feijão do monte, maracujá* fruits, *araticú, imbú,* guayaba, *jabuticaba,* cocos and *sapucaia, issurá* palm shoots, the nettle and *genipa* fruit, and bush pineapples. They broke coconuts with a stone and chiseled out the white meat with a bone tool. Larvae were obtained from bottle trees. They had a great yen for honey. Clever hunters, they used blinds and imitated cries. Fish were baited by crushed roots and shot by special bows of coco palm and featherless arrows.

Both sexes went stark naked, the penis in a leaf sheath or bound in cotton thread and held against the abdomen by a belt. They wore large cylindrical wooden plugs in the ears and lower lips, and feather ornaments affixed with wax or by cords. They painted their faces red with *urucú* and their bodies black with *genipa*, except the legs, though sometimes they blackened only half the body with "jaguar spot" circles, "fish-scale crescents" and "bird-step" streaks.

The inner bark of the bottle tree was used for making strong thread. The bark was thoroughly chewed by the women, dried in the sun, then immersed in *tinta capichaba* juice for 24 hours to dye it violet, or in *genipa* juice to dye it black, *urucú* to dye it yellow or red.

Women gave birth in the bush unaided, took a bath, and came back alone. They knew much about medicinal plants, purges, diaphoretics, skin-healing herbs, and pain-alleviating concoctions. Wounds were smeared with the stringent tannin juice of the cotton tree. For smallpox, the body was rubbed with *habarandi do matto*. Bloodletting by means of a bamboo splinter was common, usually from a temple vein.

They played on perforated "nose flutes," with two stops, grass funnels with a transverse grass blade across a small aperture, armadillo tail whistles, and bamboo stomping tubes. They often broke into song when cavorting. Usually they danced in a circle, hands on the shoulders, stomping and singing, sometimes hopping. Their dances dramatized the day's events, the sky road of souls.

Animism was prevalent, and possible celestial catastrophes, such as the Moon falling into the earth, were greatly feared. Eclipses were due to the quarreling Sun and Moon getting into a black rage.

The Botocudo, for instance, worshiped a manlike sky race, the Maret, visible only to medicine men and those they favored. The Maret granted extraordinary powers to favored protegés and helped shamans cure sickness. Also they could turn people into animals. Too, they became very angry if anybody abused the Botocudo. Their chief was a white-haired giant with a red beard, who sometimes killed women with his huge penis.

A sacred *maret* ghost post was erected in each village, the upper part carved with a fierce visage looking east, the body of red heartwood, head and limbs of white sapwood. By this pillar the spirits descended in response to chants.

7

In the Gê region were other non-related groups, some studied at various periods from 1614 [Claude de Abberville], some not investigated until early in the last century, such as the Mashcali, Patashó (linguistically related), the Camacán, Tapuya, Carirí, Pancararú, Taraniu, Jaicó and Guck [perhaps Caribs originally from Guiana], the Carnijó, now called the Fulnio. Many others became extinct.

One major stock was the Guaraní, linguistically allied to the Brazilian coastal Tupí, but though in Paraguay the Guaraní tongue prevails today, more than Spanish, also in adjacent Bolivian and Brazilian areas, little is known about their pre-Columbian habits. Scant archaeological work has been done.

Two prehistoric patterns have been found in the Paraná delta, where huge conical Guaraní funeral urns have been unearthed, and at a third center upstream. But the earliest remains, if apparently Guaraní, reveal little or no continuity. The Paraná littoral has yielded molded clay figures and some incised or painted pottery (red on white, white on red, often with black incised accent lines) of poor quality, though designs and decorations of humans or animals serving as handles on relief show talent, realism, and sensitivity for the flora, fauna, as well as admirable geometric and other stylizations. One handle, at the Malalvigo site, for instance, was a delightful fierce-eyed tufted parrot—a favorite Guaraní topic. Another handle was a competently made owl—eyes, horns, and beak. Few examples of bone or stonework have been found, though in 1912 on the upper Paraná, F. C. Mayntzhusen came upon crude stone drills, knives, hammers, polishers, and quartz lip plugs, and also needles, weaver-daggers, spatulae, fishhooks, flutes, perforated shell discs, and teeth necklaces. All metal objects, chiefly gold and silver, originally came from the Incan empire, and imported chest pendants of silver or copper were used by the more privileged.

Mostly the ancient Guaraní went naked, though women wore a loin cloth, and some (this may have been post-Conquest) a sacklike cotton dress from breast to knees. In colder sectors, skin cloaks were used. Priests and chiefs had feather capes and diadems.

The Guaraní lip ornament was usually a long T-shaped stick of *jatahy* resin occasionally of stone or bone, and the men wore huge shell necklaces, the women triangular shell earrings.

The first Spaniards waxed delirious over the Guaraní women, and the early ranchers accumulated large harems.

The Guaraní slept in hammocks and had four-legged benches carved out of a single log.

Food and utensils were kept on roof-suspended shelves or hung on wooden or bent deer-hoof pegs or hooks. Goods were transported in twilled baskets often reinforced by a light wooden frame made of pindo leaves or in bark nets or skin bags.

When a guest visited the house, the women wailed about his dead relatives and recalled their heroic deeds. The guest covered his face with his hands and wept with them. The more important the guest, the longer he had to wail, groan, and weep.

Their villages consisted of from four to eight rectangular houses, each perhaps 165 feet long, with a roof thatched with grass, palm leaves, or bark and held up by a ridgepole resting on a line of posts that marked off each family's quarters (about twelve feet square). Villages were fortified by a series of moats with bristling spears planted, and by two or three stout stockades.

The women particularly were able farmers. Land was worked on a community basis, but with small family plots. Virgin fields were opened up about every five years, by the slash and burn method, as in the early days of the United States frontier. The chief tool was the dibble, and planting time was regulated by the Pleiades.

Nearly all tropical domesticated plants, except cayenne pepper, were grown, but chiefly sweet manioc, sweet potatoes, beans and corn, plus tubers, peanuts, pumpkins, bananas, papayas, and watermelons. The *misolia* herb was grown as an antidote for snake bite.

They also gathered pine-nuts and palm fruits, honey, butterfly and beetle larvae. They trapped game in deadfalls that crushed the animal, or in spring snares, some strong enough to capture tapir or deer. Parrots were noosed with a long pole. Muscovy ducks were domesticated. They hunted—also fought—with large bows and arrows tipped with hard *taquara* wood or human bones, and sword-edged clubs with basketry sheathed handles.

They fished with wooden hooks and fiber nets and probably also used poisons and drugs.

Maize cakes—*chipas*—were made; corn dough wrapped in the leaves of the *guaimi atucupi* was cooked under hot ashes, or else boiled inside green bamboo. Manioc tubers were dried to pound into flour for wafers, or were boiled and roasted. Manioc starch was obtained by grating and washing the mass in water. Palm pith was crushed, strained, and dried. Most meat was broiled on a spit. Broiled fish and game were sometimes ground in wooden mortars into a powder known as *piracui*. A type of tree ash was used for seasoning.

Maté tea was reserved chiefly for shamans, and tobacco was smoked in cigars or in clay pipes, examples of which have been found in old remains. Drinking bouts—for hunting and fishing expeditions, harvest time, and eating a prisoner—were frequent. A fermented *chicha* beer called *caguai* was made from maize or sweet potatoes by means of the yeasting of chewed corn or caaory leaves.

War prisoners were sometimes allowed to live for years, even be married and have children, before being eaten—a great occasion when it occurred. Music was made with gourd rattles and pounding tubes, the last wielded only by the women. After the killing, children crushed the victim's skull with small stone or copper axes and scooped out the brains and dipped their hands in the blood. Flutes were made from the victim's bones. Every one touching or eating of the corpse assumed a new name.

A girl at first menstruation had her hair cut short and was sewn into a hammock for three days, then had to do hard work under the supervision of an older woman, until her hair grew back. Child brides were not uncommon, and it was a frequent practice to give little girls to older men.

At a husband's death, his wife and female relatives threw themselves wailing on the ground, sometimes from such a high point they were injured. The remains were crammed into large chicha ollas and buried under the hut, which was then abandoned or burned down. Where danger of contagion was suspected the whole village was burned down. An *Añan* demon devoured the souls of the dead when they passed by his hammock.

A shaman's spittle could cause death. His chants could even control the stars. By expert sleight of hand, among other tricks, he cured sickness. After death, a shaman's bones were kept in superelegant hammocks in a special hut and were consulted as oracles.

According to the old-time Guaraní, at the beginning there was only darkness where Eternal Bats fought. Our Great Father "found himself" and, in company with Our Father-Who-Knows-Everything, created the earth which he propped against an eternal cross-stick, then created himself a wife, our Mother, whom he generously shared with his assistant. She bore twins, Our Elder Brother and Our Younger Brother; the latter, offspring of the assistant, turned out to be weak and stupid.

The mother was killed by a jaguar—a folk story known all over the Amazon—and the stars took revenge. Elder Brother stole fire from the Vultures for mankind and taught them ceremonial dances. Another version states that fire was stolen from the Heavenly Rhea. The Sun and Moon were also offspring of Our Great Father. The Moon (masculine) was smeared with black *genipa* dye after he had homosexual relations with his brother. Eclipses were caused by the Eternal Bat or by a Celestial Jaguar gnawing at the Sun or Moon.

8

The far-flung Tupí-Guaraní peoples were spread into the farthest reaches of the Amazon; some nine major groups lived widely in the Bolivian jungles; some eight in the Guianas. In Para were, among others, the Amanayé; on the Tocantins River, the Anambé, the Cupé-rob, the Aracajú, the "red-eyed" Jacandá; on the Pacaya River, the Paracona (wearing black-seed and bird-bone necklaces); on the Nhamundá River, the Apoto ("Fire People"); on the Tapajoz (but originally from Mato Grosso), the Cahuahib, later known as the Parintintín, "The Stinkers," who wrapped their penises in tubes of stitched-together *Arumá* leaves.

The Tapurapí were isolated from the main body of Tupí-Guaraní in Central Brazil, west of the Araguaya and north of the Paperapé River—an extremely dense tropical region—living in villages of about two hundred persons. The village communal houses (four to eight families) formed an oval around a large ceremonial men's house (taacana) 20 by 65 feet, and all houses had a quadrangular floor, with bent poles tied to a roof beam forming an arched ceiling; walls and roof were covered with *buruti* palm and banana leaves.

They cleared and maintained unusually large farming fields—individually or co-operatively—a work festival was known as *apacurú* —but all land was divided into family plots. Their crops were sweet potatoes, sweet and bitter (poisonous) manioc, four varieties of maize, squash, beans, papayas and cotton, but manioc flour was the great staple. Planting, except for peanuts and cotton, was just after the first October rains. All produce belonged to the wife, who did much of the work. After two years, fields were abandoned; after four or five years, the village was moved to a new location.

Wild fruit, *piqué* and *andaroba* were gathered. Meat was a luxury unless they were able to kill monkeys, jaguars, armadillos, deer, peccary, and coati (a kind of raccoon), or wild fowl such as ducks. Turtles and turtle eggs were appreciated.

Basketry, gourd-carving, and feather work were fine arts. Wrist, leg, and arm bands, of string or crocheted, often dyed red, were worn. Men used wooden lip plugs. Bodies were dyed, also tattooed, with extraordinary designs. The prepuce was tied over the penis with a palm fiber, and all pubic hair and eyebrows in both sexes was pulled out.

Children, though conceived by sexual intercourse, were spirits of thunder, or night, of monkeys, pigs, fish, or insects. Both parents during pregnancy painted their bodies black and their hair red. After some months sexual relations were broken off, and if the wife had relations with others after that all were "fathers." Childbirth was assisted by the wife's mother and two male relatives, while the husband took to his hammock, eschewing all liquids. Families were limited to three children; any births above that were done away with.

At twelve the boy tied up his foreskin, cropped his hair, and painted his body black. He replaced his mother-of-pearl lip plug with a bone plug. His legs were scratched till they bled profusely, so he would grow strong. He was richly adorned and given a red macaw feather diadam and had to dance steadily for twenty-four hours. At fourteen his hair was allowed to grow again and was tied in a tail at the nape of the neck.

At the first menstruation, the girl's body was painted with black designs, and until after three menstruations she could have no sexual relations; after that she was wholly free until married. After virgins began sexual intercourse, they cut their faces with a paca tooth, tattooing them in a blue quarter-moon.

Boys married right after the pubic rites, girls often when only seven or eight, usually to much older men. Cousins could not marry. Monogamy was strict, but only after the first child. A widow enjoyed free sexual relations for some months, then was supposed to marry again.

The only musical instruments were rattles and bamboo ground thumpers, but singing fiestas were frequent.

Men and women belonged to one of eight fiesta groups (*taataup huaá*) which celebrated many events, especially abundance of honey, maize, or meat.

There were special songs for harvest fiestas, as the Cao, or sweet manioc fest; that for the masked rain dance was a special falsetto voice song; the truly "Big Sing" was at the four-day-and-night Thunder Fiesta, which marked the end of the rain season. Special singers sang the verse, and all the men and women the chorus; the women in a high key a phrase behind the men. The shamans had their own special "Battle with Thunder" song. Everybody danced as they sang, bending slightly forward, stamping time with one foot. Dances, according to the ceremony, had different groupings and patterns.

No alcohol was imbided, but they made much use of tobacco for religion, conclaves, and pleasure, as a stimulant and medicine. It induced dreams and trancelike visions and also greatly enhanced the powers of the shaman. Shaman souls were pure thunder, and the shamans had great authority, but if they failed to effect cures or to get rid of sorcery or were malevolent, they were killed.

The people feared to go out at night because of the malignant spirits who killed by setting the hair on fire or who drank human blood, particularly the white-haired Topuí, whose half-gourd canoes made the sound of thunder and whose arrows were lightning. Ghosts and animals were often transmigrated human souls, for instance, a frog was a chief, a pigeon a male, a paca a woman.

The Guajá or Huazaizara, wholly nomads who built only occasional flimsy shelters, were distinguished by feathers stuck on shells in their ears with wax (*huazai*); the tribe's name meant "Owners [*zara*] of Ear Tufts." They used huge bamboo arrows and stone axes.

The Tenetehara, who lived in the northwest in hardwood, rubber, *copaibá* and palm jungle, were first visited on the upper Pindaré River in 1615 and 1616 by La Ravardière and by Benito Maciel. They were good farmers.

Masturbating boys were whipped; incest was taboo; the ghosts of rapists wandered homeless forever. Pubic ceremonies were elaborate. The Tenetehara were monogamists, with considerable prepuberty marriage.

They believed in powerful forest spirits, especially in mighty Marancauhua, who ruled the forests and punished any wanton kill-

ing of peccaries. In their folklore, Gamba, another spirit, is related
to animal tales. His daughter spurned the man he had arranged for
her to marry, and eloped with a wood-tick. The jealous father tried
to rival his son-in-law by floating to the ground on a leaf, but fell
to the earth with a jar that put him out of commission for good.
The tortoise was always a trickster, and there were eerie tales about
the "Rolling Head" at animal fiestas.

9

The most extensive Tupí-Guaraní division was the Tupinamba,
from São Paulo to the mouth of the Amazon. They had twenty-seven
villages on Maranhão Island, and in many areas stretched far inland.

The inland Tupinamba (some seven tribes of Tobayara) were
bitter enemies of those along the coast. Also located between them
at intervals along the coast were allied or even distinct groups. South
below the Parnaíba River, the subgroup was the Potiguará. From
the Paraiba to the São Francisco, the Cactá. The Tupiniquín reached
from Canamá to Espiritu Santo and along the lower Paraiba. Over
all this vast region the culture was fairly uniform.

The Tupinamba proper built houses even larger than those of
the Guaraní, always on hilltops. Some structures were 500 feet
long, accommodating 200 persons, with thatched roofs reaching to
the ground, so they looked "like overturned boats."

Their farm products were similar to those of the Guaraní, though
poisonous manioc was their staple, and they raised four varieties of
varicolored corn. Other crops were *cara, maigará* and *taia,* and they
had access to many more delicious wild fruits and nuts—most with
names meaningless to an American reader. They located the watery
edible roots of the ombó tree by the sound made when striking the
ground with a stick.

They were also fond of roasted fat-bellied *tanajura* or *ishá* ants,
which they lured forth with magic spells. Another delicacy, roasted
and stored as a food reserve, were guará eggs and oysters collected
from mangrove roots. Likewise their game was more varied; monkeys, agouti, and many birds; and river and sea fish were abundant.
In August, *parati* fish came up the river to spawn in such dense
schools they could easily be driven into the canoes by striking the
water with a stick. Funnel-shaped baskets were also used, and fishermen even dived and caught fish in their hands.

Small rodents, wild pigs, agouti, armadillos, and caimans were domesticated, also ducks, turkeys, pigeons, and parrots. Tapirage (color-changing of feathers) was practiced on parrots by using frogs' blood to make new feathers grow in red or yellow. Small animals were sometimes so beloved, that women nursed them at their breast along with their babies.

The Tupinamba dugouts, bark canoes, and rafts showed high skills. The softwood trunk of the *ubiragara* could be fashioned into a canoe in a few days. Large dugouts could hold sixty men, canoes as many as thirty. They paddled standing up, with lanceolate paddle blades. Rafts, reed bundles on transverse sticks tied with vines, accommodating a dozen persons, were used on big rivers and along the coast. Small fishing rafts (*piperi*) were made of round lightwood sticks tied together with creepers.

Though naked, they made up for it by showy adornment. Men wore high diadems of parrot or other bright feathers that sometimes streamed far down their backs like capes. Also they often wore enormous red guará feather capes, and feather necklets, bracelets, and anklets; sometimes whorls of feathers on their hips. Both men and women coated their bodies with sap or honey then often sprinkled chopped feathers (or red or yellow wood chips) all over themselves. Necklaces, belts, and garters of coiled shell beads were worn. Shell necklaces might be thirty feet long and heavy. Warriors made necklaces of the teeth of enemies—as many as 2,000 teeth. Spiked fruit shells served for combs.

The Tupinamba employed cosmetics, palm oil ointments, and sapendus root or fruits for soap. T-shaped labrets of semiprecious stones and often similar stones in cheek perforations were worn, as described by Vespucci and others. Both sexes were tattooed with pottery-like designs by rubbing pigments into wounds made by a rat's tooth or a sharp shell. The tattooing was extended each time an enemy was killed or a prisoner sacrificed. Body painting often by professional artists was extravagant, chiefly black and red, but often blue and yellow on the face.

At puberty a girl's head was shaved, she stood on a whetstone while her back was tattooed. A string was tied around her waist, and she fasted in a concealed hammock for three days. At the second menstruation, her breasts, stomach, and buttocks were tattooed. After the third period, she could resume normal work.

Sex relations were free until marriage. After her first intercourse, the virginal string was broken. A youth could have no sexual relations until he had killed a prisoner.

A girl usually married her uncle, or some other relative of her mother, though the uncle's claim first had to be relinquished. But a husband, if not her uncle, became her father's servant, helping him to build houses, clear and cultivate land, hunt and fish. Thus a father preferred to have many daughters, rather than sons. The bride-purchase price was high, too. Often marriage was delayed for years, and thereafter the husband remained in bondage until his father-in-law died.

Once freed, he could take other wives—chiefs had as many as thirty—without having to do service. Each new wife, Staden noted, had her own "fire" and cooked the husband's food so long as he cohabited with her—"and thus he went the round of them." Sometimes, however, wives lived in separate houses, even in different villages. To avoid servitude some young men temporarily married an old woman so as to obtain a second desirable wife without paying for her so heavily.

Women gave birth squatting on a flat piece of wood or leaning against a wall and surrounded by women, who gave little or no assistance. It was the husband who acted. If delivery was difficult, he pressed her stomach; if it was a boy, he cut the umbilical cord with his teeth. When it was dry, he sliced it into bits and tied a piece to each main house post so that the boy would propagate a large family. Thereafter the father took to his hammock for some days, eating no meat, fish, or salt, and received the visits of friends who expressed sympathy for his plight. He was not supposed to do any hard work for some time, but performed magical rites for the child's welfare.

The child was usually named after an ancestor he or she was supposed to resemble. Animal figurines, a miniature bow and arrow and a grass bundle, symbolizing future enemies, were tied to the male child's hammock. Female babies were given *capibara* teeth to harden their own teeth.

Men retired at forty, thereafter doing no hard work. The old were treated with great respect.

The dead were wrapped in a hammock or bound in a foetal position and crammed into a big chicha olla, which was buried under the house in a stick-lined grave along with food. A fire was built to keep off evil spirits. Women mourners cut their hair, men let their hair grow on their shaved foreheads, and both sexes painted their bodies black.

A widow could not remarry until her front bangs reached her eyes.

The souls of brave warriors killed in battle or eaten by enemies went to live forever with a Grandfather in a beautiful western land, where all except the wives of notable warriors were banned, and also all cowards.

Time was regulated by the Pleiades. The Tupinamba had named nearly all the constellations—chiefly after animals—and had many legends about them. Dates of future events were calculated with knots or beads on a cord—in short, the Inca quipú.

The chief purpose of war was to obtain slaves, a high status honor, or to obtain human food. Flesh-eating was the leading theme of oratory, poetry, and religion, and joyous fiestas were held at the time of the killing and banqueting. Warriors, usually traveling by canoe, were always accompanied by musicians. They fought with tapir hide shields, bows and arrows, and unique two-piece clubs with round handles and sharp duo-edged blades. Attacks were accompanied by ferocious yells. Stockaded villages, if not taken by surprise, were besieged, and fire arrows used to burn thatched roofs. They tried to disarm opponents, and take them prisoner rather than kill them. All enemy corpses were roasted and eaten on the spot, but the sexual organs were brought back as trophies.

On the return, prisoners were exhibited in friendly villages, where they were subjected to derision and vituperation. The prisoners proudly expressed their desire to be eaten, the proper fate for the valiant. Before being brought into the home village, the prisoner had his head shaved by women who bedecked him with feathers and tied about his neck a thin cotton rope, with beads on it, to indicate the months before death.

As prisoners were marched in, women snatched them from the men and celebrated their capture with dances and derisive songs referring to their execution and devouring. First they were led to the graves of the recent dead and required to clean them. Temporarily they were given the hammocks and ornaments of the dead, for otherwise the heirs could not use them lest they too die.

Each prisoner was required also to dance before "the hut of sacred rattles." About once a month prisoners were subjected to humiliating public exhibitions, required to dance, and were subjected to jeers. In his presence, various portions of his body were allotted beforehand to the carousers. In cases of great animosity, however, as Georg Friederici noted in his *Die Behandlung*, fingers or limbs were sometimes cut off, roasted, and devoured in the victim's presence.

Yet otherwise prisoners were treated like honored guests, fed the best food, allotted fields to cultivate, often given the daughters or sisters of their owner to wed, and might live for years before being eaten. No guard was kept over them, for it was rare that one attempted to escape, since he would be a "man without a country," who, if he returned to his village, would be contemptuously killed. Children of such were eventually eaten also, sometimes at a tender age. Mothers who objected were considered subversive and disloyal to the tribe—the "Communists" of their day. Female captives, if not taken as wives, were free to cohabit promiscuously, but in the end, unless beloved by an influential leader, were also eaten.

Hans Staden, taken prisoner soon after the Conquest, saved himself by using "White God" magic to cure a chief, described many cannibal feasts, which often lasted for days.

"When they first bring home a captive, the women and children beat him, then decorate him with gray feathers and shave off his eyebrows and dance around him. They give him to a woman who . . . has intercourse with him. If she conceives, the child is kept until fully grown, then, when the mood seizes them they kill and eat it.

"They fed the prisoners well . . . while they prepared the pots for their drink. They also bake special dye-pots in order to paint him and make tassels to tie to the club with which he is to be killed, as well as a long cord called *musurana,* to bind him when the time comes. . . . The drinking vessels are filled a few days in advance. . . ."

Friendly villages were invited, and "when the guests were assembled, the chief . . . welcomes them and asks that they help eat their enemy. The day before they commenced to drink, the *musurana* was tied about the victim's neck, and . . . they painted the death club, called *ihuera penne.* . . . It is about six feet long, and they cover it with a sticky mess (and) . . . powdered *macuehahua* bird eggs. A woman . . . scratches designs in the powder. . . . When the *ihuera penne* is ready, they hang it on a pole in an empty hut and sing in front of it all night.

"Similarly they paint the victim's face, the women singing while one woman paints, and when they begin the drinking . . . he drinks with them. . . . They rest the following day and build the execution hut in which the prisoner sleeps under close guard. Then, well before daybreak, they dance and sing in front of the (death) club. . . . Afterwards they take the prisoner from the hut, which they tear down and clear away. Then they remove the *musurana* from the prisoner's neck and tie it about his body . . . numbers of them hold on to the ends. They leave him for a time, with stones beside him which he can throw at the women running around him . . . boasting they will eat him. These women are painted, ready to snatch his cut-up quarters and run with them around the huts, a proceeding which provides great hilarity. Many celebrants paint their bodies gray with ashes.

"A fire is built about two paces from the prisoner which he must tend. . . . A woman brings the *ihuera penne,* waving the tassels, shrieking with joy, and running to and fro before the prisoner. . . .

"The chief thrusts the club between the slayer's legs, a sign of great honor (to be thus chosen). The slayer seizes it and addresses the prisoner thus:

"'I am the one who will kill you, since you and yours have killed many of my friends.'

"To this, the prisoner replies, 'When I am dead, I shall have many to avenge my death.'

"Then the slayer strikes him from behind and beats out his brains."

Another early voyager, Samuel Purchas, noted that in the "butchering rites," sometimes the prisoner was nimble enough to dodge the death blow for a long time. He told of one prisoner with a skull so hard they could not smash it. Later, the Indians called the whites "soft heads."

"Women seize the body . . ." Staden related, "and scrape off the skin, making the flesh quite white and plugging up the anus so nothing will be lost."

Métraux adds that "old women rushed to drink the warm blood, and children were asked to dip their hands into it." Mothers smeared their nipples with it, "so even babies could have a taste of it."

"A man cuts up the body," Staden reported, "removing the legs above the knee, and the arms at the trunk, whereupon four women run with the four limbs around the huts with joyous cries. After this they divide the trunk among themselves, devouring everything that can be eaten. . . . A brew was made of the paste in the bowels, and the brains and tongue were a great delicacy. The fingers and fat around the liver and heart were allotted to distinguished guests." As the flesh roasted, old women licked the grease running down the wooden spits.

The prisoner's skull was stuck on a stockade post. "The slayer takes a new name," Staden continued, "and the chief scratches him with the tooth of a wild beast. . . . He must lie in his hammock all day, but is given a small bow and arrow, so he can . . . shoot into wax, lest his arm become feeble from the shock of the death blow." For three days he was not allowed to walk but was carried. He could eat none of the meat and had to stand on wooden pestles, while an eye of the victim was shown to him and was rubbed against his wrist. The dead man's lips were given to him to wear as a bracelet. After he was given a new name, his house was looted. On returning to a normal life, he tattooed himself with an agouti tooth to record the great event.

However repugnant the procedure seems today, nevertheless the human body provided the optimum healthful nourishment, for it had the precise minerals, organic compounds, and vitamins required. Thus cannibalism at least gave warfare a practical, grim *raison d'être,* although one unknown to the practicers of it.

Headshrinkers

To give an adequate picture of the thousands of groups and as many languages of the teeming pre-Columbian peoples of the Amazon, the larger number of whom have been projected into modern times, would require a hundred volumes even for a superficial account.

The archaeology of the Amazon, scarcely investigated and even then mostly by persons not scientifically prepared, throws little light on the early peoples of the vast series of groups who were spread out along the eleven thousand tributaries of the enormous continental river-sea, from high mountains down to Marajó Island, a grassy plain as large as Denmark.

The stone walls along the coast of that island—apparently to protect crops against flooding, for the entire island is only three feet above the river and is often inundated; also the remains in some hundred burial mounds with three-level deposits, some of which have been examined—suggest a one-time advanced economic and social organization. Some students believe it was largely an Arawak culture, established by invaders from the Guianas, which gradually spread upstream. There are still pockets of Arawaks as far as the Andes in Bolivia, Peru, and Ecuador.

Looking at a Lake Araří mound in 1877, Domingo Soares said that pottery—white slipped and incised—"covered the ground like a great mosaic," and a later investigator collected 3,000 specimens in a week. In 1934 Teso de Severino found, on an *iguapé* or inlet of the same lake, gray clay pottery fired orange-red and glazed with native resin and bearing highly stylized and anthropomorphic motifs, chiefly female. Everywhere he and others found innumerable triangular convex clay sex coverings, perforated for a string, all delicate and thin and beautifully decorated.

Interest in Santarém pottery and early artifacts was aroused in 1922 when a cloudburst washed out the streets and exposed many early remains. Similar pottery was then found on the Xingú and all the Tapajoz tributaries, to the west as far as Serra de Paritines, and a few specimens even well north of the Amazon, perhaps traded with early tribes there, but all told, suggesting a widespread related culture of considerable antiquity.

This is an amazing fantastic rococo type of pottery suggesting that of parts of Central America: it has extravagant designs, elaborate free-wheeling surface decorations of animals, birds, and humans that seem to be struggling forth from the original clay of creation and poised for flight or combat.

Many seated figures on this pottery had haggard features and painfully twisted mouths, small arms looped on sides, legs, or chest, and wide sloping legs. Some had a diadem-like headdress, oblong nose and big, outspreading ears.

The middle Amazon sites have been little investigated. In Manaos in 1870 Joseph Beal Steers saw barefoot parading soldiers wearing down the exposed rims of buried burial urns. Most middle pottery is inferior, and the cultural tie-ups have not been successfully established.

2

Though pre-Conquest all life in the Amazons had a certain uniformity imposed by the jungles and savannas, but localisms were marked, and languages, arts, legends, and customs quite as varied as in modern Europe but far more numerous. Each group of peoples was unique, and their primitive arts often breath-takingly beautiful, or, just as likely, very crude. Many objects reveal a fascinating blend of the utilitarian and aesthetic—i.e., "classic"—and they mirror the spiritual and moral aspirations common to all mankind, the agelong story of tragedy and eternal hope.

Though there were wide differences in the kinds and styles of musical instruments, there was a lack of range, a lugubrious monotony, to all their music and their songs, which mostly depended on loudness, shrill penetration, or bizarre effects rather than subtle skills, or else sank to an endless moaning refrain within a pentatonic scale—or even fewer notes—that seemed to emphasize mournful despair rather than joy, though these endless repetitious chants, if almost stupefying, were often integrated with the most joyous festivals.

Mostly their literature, their legends and myths, reflected marvelous imagination, often spiritual seeking. They had the most varied sex customs and sex taboos, involving puberty, cohabitation, marriage, property holding. If some sex habits appear to us distorted, from the point of view of personal satisfaction and psychological balance (often also of rational social well-being), many were more sensible, more beautiful, less tortured than those in our own modern society, still distorted by early Puritanism and other aberrations.

If other practices and customs seem odd to us, these sprang both from the local environment and ancient tradition. The mainsprings would be more intelligible if we could slough off both contemporary and historical provincialism and prejudice, also our poisonous self-superiority and rigid nationalism. As Chesterton said long ago, the African savage wearing a red feather for fiestas, is impelled by the same childish motives of self-adornment, personal distinction, and show-off as the silk-hat promenader in a Fifth Avenue Easter parade —except that the feather is more beautiful and probably called for individualized artistry.

Even today flocks of gaily chattering naked Witoto trot through Amazon river towns—healthier, more beautiful than the greedy petty traders and the sniveling third-rate officials—people uprooted and dislocated, who have behind them the power of colonial and national conquest but are without vital cultural roots and enjoy little self-expression beyond petty power and the grossest enjoyment. Though the Witoto go naked, they walk proudly and confidently, considering themselves more elegantly attired in their fine body painting than mestizos and caboclos wearing ugly cotton prints or ramshackle denim or khaki trousers. The Witoto women, with their intricate geometric body painting—black, red, yellow, and white, the lacelike tracings of birds and plants that cover their breasts, bellies, sex, and buttocks do indeed make them more attractively clad—and more appropriately considering the climate—than the human misfits of imperial transition, who belong neither to the past nor the future, but who have lost their physical and moral integrity in the twilight of history's tragic crosscurrents, even though personally they are sustained by a feeling of superiority to the "savages." For morals have always been, and still are, confused with mere clothes, especially by the pharisees of Western Christianity.

3

These Witoto of the Para-Paraná and upper Caqueta Rivers are an independent language group, possibly remotely related to the Tupí. Julian H. Steward flatly calls them "Tupí-speaking," and J. Alden Mason lists them as a definite subdivision of the Guaraní-Tupí language family. The matter is not that clearly established, though likely they belong to some major phylum if scientists ever get around to looking into the matter.

The main Witotoan group—there were seven subgroups and related dialects were spoken by twenty more—split asunder another still-surviving language family named after the *Toucan*, the *Tucano* —who resided in separate geographic kingdoms, but culturally were akin. Both the Witoto and the Tucano cultivated bitter manioc, resorted extensively to hunting traps and nets—in this they were very adept—and for fishing they used weirs, baskets, and hollow-log traps instead of harpoons and javelins.

William Curtis Farrabee says they made nets six feet high and 1,000 feet long to catch larger animals. They also stupefied fish with barbasco and other drugs. Both peoples used two stones instead of a boring stick to make fire. Both cooked on pottery stoves instead of flat plates. Both slept in hammocks rather than on mats or platform beds. The women of both peoples went naked, but men wore a bark breechclout, instead of the usual penis sheaths. Both blackened their teeth for beauty and to prevent "worms." Face and eyebrow hair was removed by a caustic sap. Both the Witoto and the Tucano wove wild basts with their fingers, instead of processing cotton thread on looms.

The Witoto fields, where a special work house was always built, were half a mile from the village. Besides manioc, they cultivated plantains, bananas, yams, sweet potatoes, an exclusive variety of peanuts, papaws, pineapples, mangoes, and palm fruits, tubers, beans, coca, tobacco, some maize, and cotton. Cacao was collected wild.

Coca was toasted, pulverized, and taken with leaf ashes, often in lieu of food. Tobacco was smoked in long cigars or mixed with water and drunk, or taken as a powder by mouth or as snuff. Two friends would blow snuff into each other's noses by a double V-shaped pair of tubes.

Their most important game-meat was monkey flesh, though turtles and turtle eggs were important, and they hunted capybaras, pacas, wild pigs, tapirs, agoutis, small anteaters, armadillos, deer, parrots, and frogs. Birds, including parrots, were killed with blow-guns and poisoned darts.

A Witoto village consisted of from one to ten enormous thatched multiple family houses, sometimes with an inside dance space. They kept their dwellings clean with palm-leaf brooms.

The village was an expanded local exogamous patrilocal family, bearing the name of a bird, animal, star, or some other totemic appellation.

Art was crude, some carving or decoration on house posts, dance staves, utensils, tooth beads, gourds, and nuts. Baskets and pottery had pleasing designs and ornamentations.

Agreements at family conclaves were solemnly sworn to by the ritual of licking a stick covered with tobacco juice and pepper.

Young prisoners were adopted into the community, but older ones were eaten, for they were "like animals," and at times food was scarce and salt was lacking. After a masked dance-song-and-speech fiesta, the victim was stretched between two posts and stabbed or lanced. They ate human flesh with a tobacco cud in the cheek and vomited afterward. The skull was hung up as a trophy, leg and arm bones were made into flutes, the teeth into necklaces.

There was considerable infant betrothal. A Witoto youth gave his future father-in-law a load of firewood and a big bag of coca, and had to demonstrate his hunting and fishing skill by working for him for six months. The dead were wrapped in hammocks and buried under the house floor.

They made big hollow-wood signal-drums, "male and female," with two holes at the end of a long slit, which were beaten with rubber-headed sticks and produced only two notes, but could send complicated code messages for eight miles. Other tribes on the upper Amazon and in the Montaña area had similar drums, and the Span-iards were often astonished to discover that Indians hundreds of miles inland knew all about them days ahead, even knew their dress and appearance, the weapons and animals they had. The Witoto also played three- and multiple-tube Panpipes, bamboo and animal bone and human flutes, with a center and back trumpet hole, used leg and stick rattles, and castanets.

According to Gunter Tessman, they celebrated seven major fiestas a year. Besides the cannibal feast, there was a masked Whirling Log feast at which they danced on a pivoted log—perhaps a planting fiesta. In a strictly male "Renewal Fiesta," masked figures blew trumpets of spiraled bark, to celebrate the start and finish of a building. In one fiesta a ballgame was played with a rubber ball. Tessman told of a house dance, featuring decorated rattle staves, possibly a "Feast of the Dead."

They believed in a "Father Above" and a malevolent "Satan Below." Ancestors were also worshiped. Deification was extended to the Sun and his wife, the Moon; animism and demonism were potent, and the jaguar and boa were listed as evil spirits. Demons, driven from the earth by a great flood, went underground.

People, also animals, originally emerged from a hole in the ground and were children of the Earth God. Sky-God gave them manioc. How to plant the stalks and grow it was discovered by the daughter of a virgin sired by a manioc plant. Stories of sacred virgin births, just as in the story of Christ, were universal in the New World from the Aztecs to South America. There was also the typical flood story, tales of female warriors (Amazons), and many animal yarns. The capybara and agouti, according to Steward, were tricksters.

Shamans, with spirit helpers, both bird and animal, caused and cured disease, chiefly by sucking out the foreign object or spirit, though herbs were also used, as well as rattle-shaking, trumpeting, sleight of hand tricks, shouting and imitating bird and animal cries. According to Farrabee the shaman was paid for his services. He controlled the spirits of condors by their claws, snakes by their skins. He could change himself into a jaguar and do away with enemies. Often he used actual poisons—a magical "ball," injected into an alien body. He relied on coca and tobacco for visions. All death, even if accidental, was due to supernatural evils.

4

The Curaca, or chieftain, of the Jívaro clan on the banks of the big Santiago River in the Ecuadorian jungles, was so pleased with his new wife Ninguita, from the Sepa clan, that he let her carry the hamper of food and the gear on nearly all his hunts. But she had given him no children as his other wives had. To remedy this, he ordered a tobacco fiesta in her honor.

Buxom, with broad, good-natured face, Ninguita, unlike the girls of his clan, did not cut her luxuriant black hair in bangs or braid it, but parted it in the middle and let it flow freely over her bare shoulders. Nor was her lower lip perforated for the usual wooden plug. Her only clothing was a one-piece skirt held in place by a belt of shells, but she wore a necklace of animal teeth, bamboo cylinders in her ears, and tight forearm bracelets of dyed fibers and copper.

She was skilled at necessary tasks. Men did the weaving and basket-making; women made pottery, and no one could spin a ball of clay into coiled ropes to form any desired utensil or a big jar for *nijimanche,* or manioc beer, more deftly. She incised the clay with zigzag decorations and geometric designs of animals, warriors, and gods and colored them with red copal or urucú. She was adept, too, at making a fire with a bamboo drill and chicken feather fan, something taught the clan long ago by the giant Humming-Bird.

For the tobacco fiesta, Ninguita set about planting manioc for the *nijimanche* that would be needed. For five days she and her friends danced or squatted near the cuttings and chanted prayers to Nunguí, the earth goddess, and made pleas to the rats not to eat the tender shoots. While the crop was maturing, Ninguita removed her bracelets and did not paint her face or body with the usual black genipa sap, merely traced a salmon-colored line across her nose and cheeks with bixa dye and wore a red bixa flower in her hair. The first ripe manioc cut, she painted red and wore against her groin.

At the fiesta everybody danced and sang to the music of a small rawhide drum, bamboo flutes, and clay rattles. The Curaca wore a brand-new *utiapa,* or wraparound skirt, his chest bare. He painted his face with red and black horizontal stripes and braided his hair into three strands with toucan feathers.

Ninguita had to drink tobacco juice, which made her vomit but produced beautiful visions and was supposed to guarantee fertility. The Wishinú, or medicine man, squatted to one side, seeing visions from cayapi, the powerful drug he had taken, chanting spells against evil spirits, performing fertility rites. The clan banqueted on chickens, young pigs, and monkey stew, fresh corn and quantities of manioc beer.

After the fiesta, the Curaca led Ninguita to the platform bed in the big clan house, which was an elliptical 40x80-foot structure, with gabled palm-thatched roof supported by inside posts and ten-foot walls of strong staves impervious to enemy spears or blowguns. The bed was made of smoothly fitted split staves resting on rods in notched stakes, a foot above the ground. A separate bar near the fire served as a footrest.

Nine months later, Utijuanga, a male child, was born, destined to become the greatest head-hunter of all the Jívaro clans. Due birth ceremonies were observed, and an old man was stationed on the river bank to blow tobacco smoke across the water to discourage the Anaconda, the great white river snake, from slipping ashore and swallowing the infant. The parents abstained from all magical foods known to contain the divine but fickle soul-essence.

When the Curaca came upon a sloth hanging from its brown cecropia or mulberry tree, he killed it with a poisoned dart, shrank its head, and did a *tsantsa* victory dance with it suspended about his neck, shouting insults to drive away its evil spirit lest it harm Utijuanga. Along with the child, Ninguita suckled a newborn puppy, which was to be his boon companion as soon as he could toddle.

One of the first things the boy learned was how to weave the thirty-inch hexagonal baskets, interlined with palm leaf to make them waterproof. Other baskets were made of bamboo-like reeds, in which tapirs lived. This huge horselike animal aroused little Utijuanga's admiration, and he vowed to kill one someday, till he learned that it was taboo to harm them, for it was believed that the tapir's spirit would always return to plague the clan. He soon knew all the animals, snakes, and birds, all the trees and plants, too—which ones were good for curing sickness.

He learned to spin and weave, then to knit. For cloth goods, raw cotton from the cotton tree was fluffed and fed from an overhead hamper on to an eighteen-inch chonta-wood spindle, and the yarn was woven on a vertical frame loom. The women dyed the cloth with vegetable saps.

While at these tasks, Utijuanga was taught history and religion. The Jívaros, the largest group in the entire Amazon basin, jealously guarded twenty-five thousand square miles, mostly north of the Marañon in the shadow of the Andes. Long ago, the Jívaros had mined gold—this is one of the richest gold-bearing regions of South

America—and traded it to the Incas for goods. For more than a thousand years, longer than any empire had even endured, the Jívaros had maintained their independence.

Utijuanga loved the legends about the jaguars. Once, a jaguar, married to a Jívaro girl, killed her. His mother raised the two children secretly, and they went to heaven as twin stars. Later, they came back to earth and killed their father to avenge their mother's death, then returned to the sky on a chain of arrows they shot ahead of each other.

Utijuanga learned that the gods Cupara and his wife were parents of the Sun. For the Sun's wife, they created out of mud (not a rib) the Moon, and she was very fair. The Sun and Moon had numerous progeny, both animals and plants. Manioc, the Jívaro staff of life, was their child. So was the sloth, who was the first Jívaro. The Supreme God was Cumbanamá, but immediate human affairs were governed by Tsaratuma, the Universal Essence in All Things, who commanded lesser gods and spirits. This Essence was in the Rain God atop the mountains and in the Anaconda god in the rivers. It animated the Earth Mother. When Utijuanga went with the men to set out a new banana grove, they prayed to Shacaima, husband of the Earth Goddess.

At fishing time, Utijuanga helped make astrocaryum palm fiber nets. The clanmen repaired a dam of loose rocks on a small side stream, then gathered wild cinnamon or barbasco to stupefy the fish. Beating the branches on flat rocks till the sap oozed, they tossed them into the water well above the dam. In less than a quarter of an hour, fish began leaping out of the water and swimming frantically downstream to the dam where they turned over helplessly on their sides. Utijuanga leaped into the water with the others, women and girls too, shouting, laughing, getting well doused, and came tearing out with a fish in each hand and a third in his mouth.

Utijuanga was never happier than when he made his first blowgun. He polished and split a piece of chonta-palm trunk, put the halves flat side up on forked stakes and grooved them with a jaguar tooth. The two pieces were then bound with tough fiber about a round chonta rod, which he worked back and forth with fine sand and water to smooth the bore, a three-day task. When the two halves fitted snugly, he glued them together with quick-drying latex and wrapped them end-to-end with ivory-nut fiber, coated them with resin by means of a warm machete blade, stained the gun black with *sua,* and gave it a high polish. He now had a weapon which could send a *tsenac,* a twelve-inch palm rib dart, through hardwood half an inch thick at ten feet and was accurate up to a hundred yards.

He was ready for his first hunt. To prepare the poison darts, the sharp ends were smeared with goo kept in a small gourd. This sticky mixture was curare, containing strychnine, vine saps, ground pepper berries, roots, leaves, and mashed spiders. With the other hunters, he took datura to induce a dreamlike trance to find out from the spirits how to make the hunt a success, and he painted his face red with bixa. In monkey-skin pouches they carried bone-and-shell good-luck charms and red toucan feathers and ornaments to put on in case they dropped in at another clan house. Ninguita and the other women carried the huge baskets and cooking jars, with *nijimanche,* manioc, and plantains.

They were off at daybreak, treading so noiselessly through the jungle that even by the keenest ears they could not be heard a few feet away. First they inspected their spring-pole snares and guillotine traps and a camouflaged pit with sharp chonta stakes and lasso for catching jaguars. There was no game in them, but a magnificent golden yellow jaguar, with black rosettes, bounded off in long grace-ful leaps. They killed three monkeys out of a large troop and that night feasted on monkey meat, seasoned with capsicum pepper.

The next day, they bagged two more monkeys and visited a friendly clan house. Moving on, they killed a capybara, the world's largest rodent, a spindly legged creature four feet long and weighing a hundred and fifty pounds.

They came upon a tailless, three-toed sloth hanging head down. Utijuanga drove home the spear that killed it, his first prize. Sloth meat is delicious, but his father said this one had the soul of an old man, an enemy of the clan, and bade him shrink the head. This was Utijuanga's first practice in this art.

One day the Curaca took his son behind a palm-leaf blind and taught him new birdcalls. A large macaw answered and came close. With the jaw of a piraña, which has tiny sharp teeth like a file, the Curaca notched the dart deeply, so the poisoned arrow would break off in the wound, and wrapped cotton around the blunt end to make it tight in the blowgun and balance it in flight. He sighted briefly, blew out his cheeks, and the blue-green bird plummeted to the ground, paralyzed in the heart. Inside of an hour they killed a dozen poorwills and toucans.

Each day, the Curaca explained to Utijuanga the traditions of his people and dangled a *tsantsa* or shrunken head before his eyes to instill in him a determination to avenge past killings of his clan brethren. Until their enemies were killed and their heads shrunk, the sacred ancestors would show malevolence toward the entire clan. Evil spirits would ruin their crops, their hunting and fishing, so that to kill an enemy was a noble deed that brought security and prosperity to the entire clan. The better to impress this on Utijuanga, his father had him fast for two days, then drink datura to induce a hypnotic state in which everything told him would remain indelibly impressed on his brain all his life.

The boy went on his first head-hunting expedition when he was thirteen. The warriors, fearsomely painted, first danced and drank much *nijimanche,* then went forth armed with spears and triple-disc ceiba-wood shields. It turned out badly. His father, the chief, was killed, but they saved his body.

The burden of vengeance now fell on little Utijuanga, and he practiced with blow-darts and spear incessantly. A year later, preparing to go out by himself, he drank guayusa, a purgative and emetic, to gain vision and strength. Successful in surprising his father's killer, he drove his spear deep into his back and cut off his head.

On the way home, he paused in the forest to shrink the head. First he put on his toucan feathers and braided a magic belt out of the dead man's hair. Slitting the skin up the back with a sharp bone knife, he peeled it off the skull, hair and all. He sewed the lips together with palm fiber and dunked the skin in a boiling solution of astringent saps. Then, putting hot stones and sand inside it, he shrank it to the size of a fist and pressed the features with a wooden spatula back into their original shape. He then smoked it and polished the skin.

On his return to the clan house, the folk danced and painted his legs with pigeon blood and black *sua* sap. For six months he prayed and fasted, mostly in solitude, then his uncle staged an elaborate fiesta, inviting friendly neighbor clans by way of the booming *tundui,* the hollow-trunk signal drum.

The warriors danced around the *tsantsa,* affixed to a spear planted in the ground, and lunged at it fiercely with their weapons. Finally Utijuanga hung it about his neck on a cord and danced alone, shouting insults at it. He felt a great upsurge of victory and prowess. He was a man now, with full clan rights. The Wishinú or medicine man imbibed his usual narcotics and pronounced that the gods had directed the clan to take Utijuanga as its Curaca.

None of the girls in the clan appealed to him. "Like your father," said Ninguita, "you won't be content until you get a wife from outside." But before making a raid on a hostile clan to carry off a girl by force, he visited the friendly Cambanaca clan. His eyes fell on a lovely strong girl named Pantoche, and he knew she was the one he wanted.

Three days later, painting his face with care, cutting his bangs neatly, and putting toucan feathers in his braids and ear plugs, he dropped in at the Cambanaca clan house again. His hosts seated him ceremoniously on a two-sided stool. When Pantoche served him *nijimanche,* he poured it out disdainfully and angrily threw the delicacy of stuffed bird intestines she brought him onto the ground. These deliberate insults informed her he was greatly interested in her.

For his third visit, he collected muspa leaves and sweet-smelling herbs, dried them before the fire, and ground them into powder. He took along gifts, vanilla beans, a wooden comb, a shell necklace, and his mother added her prize possession, an obsidian mirror gotten from a Quechua trader long ago.

This time, when Pantoche brought him *nijimanche,* he smacked his lips with great relish and rubbed the magic sweet-smelling powder on her shoulder and down her arm. She did not repulse him, so he massaged her breasts with it. They did not kiss, that was not the Jívaro custom, but they caressed each other with pleasure. She made delighted birdlike cries over the mirror and other gifts.

Pantoche made Utijuanga a devoted wife, and as time went by she selected other wives for him, as befitted a leader of his clan. Over the years he became known throughout the Jívaro land as its greatest hunter and fighter. He alone brought in more than fifty *tsantsas,* so there were many feasts to insure health and good crops. The stomachs of his clansmen were always well filled.

His greatest tragedy was the death in a clan raid of his eldest son, but he had others by Pantoche and his various wives. His third son by her, Tinahuache, was handsome and stalwart, and Utijuanga took him on all his hunts and spent many hours dangling a *tsantsa* before him to teach him his patriotic duties. But when fifteen, Tinahuache fell ill with dysentery and, in spite of the Wishinú's trances, prayers, and brews, soon lay at death's door.

Desperate, Utijuanga raced off to his closest friend, the Curaca of his wife's clan, the Cambanacas, to get help from the Wishinú there, famous for a potent remedy known only to himself. But on the way home with the Cambanaca medicine man, Utijuanga was bitten by a fer-de-lance and died quickly in agony. His body was brought to the clan house where everybody wailed. None was more grief-stricken than faithful Pantoche and Ninguita.

The Cambanaca wise man cured Tinahuache, soon he was as strong as ever, and he became head of the clan.

After special funeral rites, the Curaca's body was placed upright in a hollow log slung from the rafters, and preparations were made to depart from the clan house of death to a new site. On a stream a league distant, they built new dwellings and cleared the jungle to put in crops. But each week they brought food to the dead man in the old building, until, at the end of two years, he became a jaguar. After that Utijuanga roamed, tawny and deadly, through the forests of Jívaro land, the finest, most fearsome creature ever seen in those parts. Someday, perhaps, he would be killed by some daring warrior, who would make a necklace out of his teeth and inherit his tremendous strength and courage.

The local Wishinú was jealous of the rival tribe's medicine man and, soon after Utijuanga's burial, he resorted to potent drinks and announced that his visions had informed him that it had been the Cambanaca chieftain who had sent the evil spirit which had caused the snake to bite Utijuanga.

Tinahuache was horrified, finding it difficult to believe that his father's best friend and a relative of Pantoche, his mother, could have been so malevolent. But no one, not even a chief, let alone a new one and young, could gainsay the Wishinú in such matters, and so the two friendly clans were caught in a death feud. Henceforth Tinahuache had to dedicate his life to killing the Cambanaca chief and shrinking his head.

And so the cycle carried on as it had for a thousand years and more.

10

World of the Anaconda

ONE great Amazon family, the Caribs—dreaded cannibals—had spread over the north of the continent and were in process of taking over the Caribbean when Columbus appeared. Anthropologist John Gillen of Duke University has listed eighty Carib dialects and some thirty now extinct, or 110, in the Guiana-Venezuelan region alone. There, with sixteen language groups, they dominated the Mount Roraima area, that center of prehistoric horrors made famous by Conan Doyle. Another eleven major Carib tongues, with dozens of dialects, were spoken in the Maracaibo-Magdalena sector; still others in the Cauca and various Colombian river valleys.

The Carib may have originated in the Chaco, though J. Alden Mason believes in the upper Xingú and Tapajoz River areas. Caribs also lived in Mato Grosso and eastern Peru, but the bulk of them came to share the general Arawak regions in lowland Ecuador and Colombia, northern Brazil, and the Guianas.

The Arawak, the "Jaguar people" with similar customs, were far more widespread, especially in the eastern Andes and Montaña, from Bolivia all the way to Venezuela. Indeed, they were the most important linguistic family of all South America, with hundreds of sublanguages and dialects.

Their original point of diffusion may have been in the Guianas, though some authorities believe the diaspora might have begun far south in the Paraná area, where numerous Arawak tribes, speaking six languages, also lived. They spread to many parts of the highlands. The upland Urú-Puiquiná languages were allied to the Arawak. One group, the Chango, reached the Pacific coast via Chile, and in ancient times the Arawak may have held a considerable part of the western coast. Another band, the Chana, reached Uruguay.

There were numerous groups along the Jurúa-Purús and in the Bolivian Chiquitos area. Here the Araná—some seventeen language groups—were first definitely identified as Arawak by Paul Ehenreich in 1897.

In fact, the Arawak lived along all the great inland mountain rivers and tributaries from the mighty Ucayali to the Urubamba, Madre Díos, and Colorado, and were called *Anti* or *Chunco*, "Wild People," by the Quechua-speaking Incas—as they still are today. In the Uaupés-Caquetá region, where Irving Goldman identified ten major divisions, Arawaks were also found from the mouth to the upper reaches of Amazon, on the Xingú, and in the north in the dense jungles of the Rio Negro, as far as the lower Igut and Rio Branco regions; they spread all through the northwest Amazon area.

Thus the main Arawak habitat was from middle Amazonia to the Orinoco, and they occupied most of the British Guiana coast, besides the Carib. There were eight other major language groups, in the general Guiana area, also some 55 other tribal units never identified. Of the Guiana Arawak, John Gillen listed thirty tribal divisions.

From the Guianas they spread through the entire Caribbean, reaching Florida long before Ponce de León sought the Fountain of Youth there.

Some authorities believe the Jívaro headshrinkers are related to the Arawak. Max Schmidt and Mason definitely classify them thus; Rivet was doubtful. The great linguist Rodolfo R. Schüller, who published scores of monographs and books between 1906 and 1936, suggested that the Arawak, Carib, Chibcha (northern Andes) and the Maya should be included in one vast language phylum, but evidence is scant.

North of the Amazon, one of the more interesting and widespread Arawak jungle peoples were the Manão, after whom Brazil's largest interior city was named. They occupied a large region of the southern tributaries of the Rio Negro down to that river's mouth, and also extended well into the Uaupés-Caquetá area. They were first observed by the great explorer Cristóbal de Acuña early in the seventeenth century. Like most Arawak, they were possessors of *urucú*, makers of excellent manioc graters (traded far and wide), fine *cachibanco* hammocks and "curiously worked" clubs and shields—this according to Father Samuel Fritz in 1606. They were also traders of Iquiari river gold. They encrusted their noses with shining shell discs and tattooed their faces as high up as their eyes. Because of the color of the tattooing, one group became known as the "Black Mouth," *Jurí pixuna*.

All the Arawak north of the Amazon lived in conical roofed houses. The Jurí took refuge against mosquitoes in small earthen oven cabins. Canoes were made from the huge trunks of the *iacareva* or *angelim*. The men wore fringed *miriti* shirts, but the Pasé tribe preferred a *sapucaia* bark apron. Uainumá women and others were clad in a fringed bark apron, wore ear plugs, long labrets, and woven bands around the arms and below the knees.

All celebrated great fiestas—as when the *pupunha* fruit brought migrating waterfowl to the lakes. One Manão fiesta—at the first March full moon—included a cruel religious penitential flogging that made the blood run copiously, and which both men and women endured, however severe, without the slightest whimper. According to Métraux, the Jurí and Pasé used fiesta masks.

2

Not enough archaeological investigation has ever been made to establish a cultural continuum from early times, though here and there are some possible pottery links. In general earlier artifacts were considerably superior.

The leading authorities in this field are Walter Edmund Roth, W. Ahlbrink, whose 27-volume Caribbean Encyclopedia was published in Dutch in 1931, and Theodor Koch-Grünberg, who published from 1900 to 1934.

Nordenskiöld identified some Marajó island pottery as definitely early Arawak. At the beginning of the nineteenth century, Alexander von Humboldt found in an Orinoco River cave in quadrangular palm-leaf baskets, six hundred Atures skeletons, the bones dyed red or varnished with aromatic resins and wrapped in plantain leaves. Unfortunately his collection was lost.

The principal records of prehistoric dwellers have been found in caves, buried wells, graves, *sambaqui* shell mounds, open surface sites, painted or incised rocks near rivers, stone alignments.

Many belts have been found, also stone mortars, pestles, flint utensils, clay idols, and funeral urns, as in the Canucu and Pacarima mountains, and on the Demerara, Rupunumi, Courantyne, and Potaro rivers.

The Guianas and Northern Brazil were one of the richest South American areas for cave pictographs and petroglyphs. A few examples, gleaned mostly from John Gillen's excellent summary, must suffice: On Cerro Pintado, near the Orinoco Artures rapids in 1887 Jean Chaffanjon found, picked in granite porphyry, designs of lizards, centipedes, squarish men, a bird, "bizarre figures," and a 400-foot serpent. Elsewhere have been found petrographs of suns and moons; a figure being taken to the moon; paintings of monkeys, red human figures in sandstone, frogs, caimans, birds, and circles. At Ihla da Pedra on the Rio Negro, below the Branco, engravings of men, birds, and animals are frequent, as for instance "thirteen men dancing in a row." On the Quitaro River, a sun with a human face. On the Berbice and Courantyne Rivers, engraved figures ten feet high; on the Rio Branco near Marau incised designs 400 feet high; on the Suqudari branch of the Ireng River, carvings on sandstone of the sun, snakes, spirals and circles and, further up in the Huaeteipú mountains, fifty yards of dressed white quartz rocks were lined up to lead to a nearby cave with long red-and-white wall-painted figures. According to Charles Barrington Brown (1876) these represented a Carib jaguar killing.

A large share of all designs, chiefly Carib not Arawak, represent dangerous animals, heavenly bodies, flying of "grotesque" human figures—all with a mythological ritualistic flavor.

3

Though numbers of minor tribes have been studied intensively, the separate patterns of Arawak and Carib cultures have never been satisfactorily disentangled, and habits and artifacts are usually lumped together, with references only now and then to local tribes of one group or the other.

In the upper Uaupés-Caquetá region, from the Andes to the Rio Negro; from the upper Caquetá to the northern Guavaré River, though Spanish travelers and missionaries went through there from the early sixteenth century on, the people have never been satisfactorily identified.

The Uaupés River was first mentioned by Hernán Pérez de Quesada, who led expeditions through there in 1538, and by Phillip von Hatten in 1541, but neither described the people they called the "Uaupé." Portuguese leader Manuel da Gama Lobo de Almada sent in various missions, all of which soon gave up the ghost. The following century, the Jesuits and Carmelites set up missions as far as the Rio Negro and Branco, but were driven out in the early eighteenth century. In 1881, a few Franciscan missions were established on a permanent basis. Irving Goldman has noted that, except near the missions and early rubber-gathering posts (which on the Putumayo wiped out 80 per cent of the population prior to 1920) "no profound changes appear to have occurred as a result of white contact," except for some trading of fishing equipment and increased manioc production, a female occupation. Also, some European pigs and fowl came in.

Manuel María Albis did look into the Andaquí of Colombia as early as 1861, and Alfred Russel Wallace, who visited the Rio Negro and Uaupés in 1853, described the languages and cultures, but nothing competent was turned out until Theodor Koch-Grünberg began contributing to scientific journals in 1908. Goldman, by personal investigation and close examination of previous authorities there, identified some ten major Arawak language divisions and half a dozen main Carib languages. But no archaeological material has ever been pulled out. However, certain cultural traits suggest prior Tupí presence, so the Witoto and Tucano may have been derived from them in ages previous.

Among the Uaupé the multifamily house, rectangular or circular, often 70 feet long and thirty feet high, prevailed, in small 20-to-100-person settlements. These houses lasted not over five years, the period required to exhaust the soil and to move on. Location of settlements with reference to friendly neighbors was determined by water, food possibilities, flood safety, high banks being preferred. For defense they were usually surrounded by moats. Stairs with handrails led up steep banks and swamp paths were made with felled logs.

Each house had a wide corridor, and dance floor, flanked by sleeping apartments. The front part was both parlor (or dance space) for guests and the burial ground. The rear, the women's quarters, were for manioc processing. Most houses had attics for storing fishing and hunting gear and weapons. Doors could be swung up on a pole for ventilation. Cubéo houses particularly were kept scrupulously clean.

Every family had a hammock, cooking pots, water gourds, trays, manioc pressers and graters, hourglass pot-holders, baskets, low

184

stools. The chief's quarters contained heavier equipment; large clay and wooden jars, a flat manioc oven, a juice crusher, and long guest benches.

Uaupé pottery, usually black, was rarely decorated or glazed, but was polished with pebbles. Big chicha ollas were enveloped with basketry. Liquid containers were mostly calabashes lacquered black with urine-soaked manioc leaves, then incised. The Arawak had elaborate patterned resin-embellished, quartz-toothed manioc graters. Basketry was checkered or twilled. Hexagonal baskets woven of different colored strands served for flour-sifters, trays and manioc processing; for drying chile, for storage and toting. Pounded bark cloth was used for masks, usually white and a bit macabre, also for pouches, aprons, breechclouts. The Tucano did no weaving, but the Carib and Arawak made light tucumá-fiber hammocks on looms, and the Yahina made knitted wallets. Fish-lines of palm fibers were braided into cords and ropes.

Bitter manioc, an unfailing crop, was the staple food, planted in slash-and-burn fields just before the rainy season and maturing in eight months, though replanting was done almost any time. Cultivating, gathering, and processing took up at least 75 per cent of the woman's time, and when chicha was prepared, all of her time.

The gathered tubers were washed in the river and carried to the house where they were peeled with knife or teeth, then grated on a board inset with stones. The woman sat down, placed the board on her stretched out legs, bracing it against her abdomen and a house post. Holding two roots, one in each hand, she scraped them with alternate up and down motions of each arm. The grated mash piled up at the end of the board and was then pounded through a tight-woven basket on a tripod, which drove out the liquid starch containing the deadly prussic acid and left the thickened mash, which was pressed in the long *tipiti*, then was put through a coarser sieve, whereupon it was dry enough for the oven. To make flour, the manioc was dried on a stove, being stirred with a wooden paddle to prevent scorching. Well wrapped and kept dry, the flour could last almost indefinitely. Dried under ashes, the starch lost its poison and was used for gruels, mush, and in other ways.

The women also gathered ants, grubs, berries, and roots whenever the men, usually only in the dry season, went out for game: peccaries, tapirs, pacas, deer, caimans, monkeys, armadillos, agoutis, and birds—using the lance, blowgun, bow and arrow, snares and traps. The paca was hunted at night with flares, and the tapir before sunset at salt licks. Whenever a long expedition was planned, women went along and set up camps.

Fishing, a daily task, was far more important. The best seasons were during low water drought or during the spawning at the start of the rainy period. Fishermen used three- or four-tined spears, a five-foot red shaft arrow with bone head, weirs, nets, basket traps, and poisons. Fish lines were often suspended, with worm or berry bait, from overhanging tree boughs or from poles extending out from canoes. Night-flare fishing was common. The guaracá was the most popular catch, but 100 edible species were available.

Fish were stewed or boiled with chile, or roasted in leaves in hot ashes, barbecued, or smoked. Dried fish was powdered with chile to make "butter" for manioc bread. No group could eat any bird, animal, or fish after which it or any individuals were named. Cooking was done in each family but meals were communal. The prepared food was brought to the dining commons, with trays of manioc bread, and the encircling men and boys always ate a little from each serving, sometimes with appropriate praise. Gorging was in bad taste, and care was always taken to leave plenty for the women. Often while eating, the men passed back tidbits on manioc bread to the women.

Guests were received with formal etiquette. The visitor stood at the door not speaking until invited in, then took a step forward, where he greeted each person present by his kinship name, then sat down on a stool near the door. The women set out manioc and chile sauce, of which the visitor ate sparingly, then went back to his stool where he was served a calabash of chicha.

Where people came en masse to a fiesta, the male visitors formed a line outside the door, the male hosts a receiving line inside, and each visitor as he entered, had to exchange long harangues with each greeter. Women always entered by the back door. If a man did so by mistake, he was coldly ignored till he recognized his faux pas and re-entered correctly.

Women went naked, but men wore at least a pubic covering. The Carib made a wide bark-cloth girdle or breechclout. Elaborate feather headdress of toucan, heron, and parakeet feathers, with a monkey tail behind, were worn at fiestas. Everyday attire included jaguar teeth or white quartz necklaces, spine-joint belts, feather anklets and bracelets, knee and ankle woven bands. Both sexes

painted on elaborate body designs. For fiestas, the women accentuated their jaws with red *genipa,* but on workdays, to keep off insects,
they painted the whole face red. The back was merely spattered
with *genipa,* but careful designs were painted on face, breast, thighs,
and legs.

4

The Cubéo, a distinct language, but apparently having some relationship in vocabulary with the Arawak and also the Panoa, south
in Bolivia, were a fierce cannibalistic outfit. They believed that
three groups (corresponding to their three tribal dialects, at three
different rapids on the lower Uaupés) had emerged as paired anacondas, who shed their skins and became human brother and sister,
then sought others in marriage. The first male named all the succeeding sibs or kinship families, such as "Fat People," "Manioc
Graters," "Jaguar Children," "Scabby People," "Wasp People" (eaters of wasp honey), etc. Incest restrictions were strong, and exogamy
practiced, with "cross-country" marriage often preferred, via brother-
sister exchanges.

Childbirth was always in the manioc patch, never in the house,
with assistance from the mother-in-law and older women at the first
delivery; thereafter she had each child unattended and cut or bit
off the umbilical cord herself. When she was ready and announced
her visit to the garden, the husband remained in the house for five
days eating only stale manioc and water, avoiding any contretemps
that might harm the child, such as stumbling or dropping anything,
lest the infant would also fall and be hurt.

The infant was bathed in tepid water, painted with protective
genipa on the second day, spotted with red to resemble the jaguar,
so the animal would not devour him and so as to give male boys
daring and character.

The mother observed the same food taboos and also avoided acci-
dents. Jealous earth monsters and river monsters, such as the anaconda, were anxious to kill the child, and if parents ventured near
the river they would be killed, so great precautions were taken and
various safety rites performed. The chief, with an old man, charmed
all fish and game to prevent their hurting the infant. Many apos-
trophes were addressed to such malignant creatures: "You spiny
fish, don't let your spines lodge in the little one's throat."

The child was not named for six months. An old man, holding

the infant on his knees, chanted the history of the sib. He dipped his index finger into milk from the breast of the father's sister and touched the child's breast to make it grow; then touched the nose, so the child's soul would be able to escape from the body at the time of later death. The Cubéo chanted:

> Milk of our soul,
> That the little one may grow,
> That we may see him grow,
> Milk from the calabash drank
> The child, born of "the great fat one."
> A little child . . .

Puberty rites were simple or nonexistent and included food taboos. At a tender age boys were taken berrying or fishing and were shown the sacred Ancestor Horns, trumpets or flageolets, made of tree or tubes of bark and bearing the names of ancestors. Women were never allowed to see them. The Horns were played, everybody bathed, and when the troop came home all the women hid in their manioc patches. The men then whipped the boys three times across the back, abdomen, and behind the knees, hard enough to draw blood. Then the men lashed each other until exhausted. Finally the women were called in and whipped to the songs of the ancients and the sounds of the trumpets, blown outside, unseen.

At death—always due to sorcery—the body was wrapped in the dead man's hammock, legs drawn up to his chin, put in his own canoe, which was cut in halves, one half for a cover, along with a calabash, cane, fish-line, bows and arrows, food and tobacco, and was lowered by ropes into a dance-floor grave as a male relative blew tobacco smoke into the far corners.

Only the widow went into mourning, but six months later a group keening with black masks and other paraphernalia was held. Among the Tucano, the ceremonies assuaged grief by the presence of "ancestors" and "Beings of this world," including fish, insects, animals, and birds, and drove the dead man's ghost out of the house. Thereafter, the dead person's name was never again mentioned by a living soul. Dead enemies were eaten in a victory dance. But the penis and scrotum were cut off, smoked, and worn by a dancing warrior over his own genitals. After the dance, his wife ate the penis as a guarantee of fertility.

Yet these people were very tender toward their children. Koch-

Grünberg described them, and drew them: one a plump baby, learning to walk by means of an underarm ring suspended by three cords, by which the child was held in by a cloth passing under his crotch. The children had many games, often based on mythological tales. They spun tops, walked on stilts, and played catch with rubber balls.

Dances, enlived with manioc beer, coca chewing, and cayapi, were frequent. Tobacco was also chewed, drunk in liquid concoctions, or smoked, often as cigarettes in a long two-pronged cigarette holder. In the Circle Dance, men, women, and children lined up in the order of size, the tallest in the center, each with his left arm around his neighbor's shoulder, then entered the house and formed a big circle. Singing and pounding with hollow staves, they danced seven side steps, a halt to sway forward and back, more side steps.

In small-group dances, instead of pounding with staves, the men played Panpipes or long flageolets. In the Panpipe festival five men, embracing each other's shoulders, danced side by side with sharply accented steps. Women joined in by thrusting their heads under the men's arms. A flageolet dance was often done by two men only.

Among the Tuyuca, the "Clay People," a Tucano tribe—after a food-gathering expedition, half a dozen men blowing trumpets led the heavily laden women into the village. Music was much loved and often played without dancing, but only by males for no woman was allowed to touch a musical instrument. Elaborate Panpipes were made and played individually or as part of an orchestra of five instruments in different keys. Flageolets ranged from small reeds to five-foot paxiuba palm tubes, and there were also ten-foot trumpets flaring at the end. Reed or bone flutes emitted many tones. The usual tree-trunk and rawhide drums existed.

They were an artistic folk, realistically decorating masks, religious objects, pottery and baskets and house posts with human forms, fish, birds, and animals or geometric patterns. Sometimes they cleverly reproduced creatures from palm leaves. Gourds and stamping tubes were often exquisitely carved.

Among the Tucano besides a vague Supreme Being, the folk hero-god was Guhuai, a trickster who liked to transform people and objects into animals. He created rivers, taught farming, fishing, all the arts, dances and ritual, but sought to kill every mortal who obstructed his schemes. Mortified by ingratitude, he lived morosely in solitude on a distant mountain. He was always having trouble with his wives, Indian girls who were always unfaithful or deserted him, until, in despair he created a wife out of a tree. But she eloped with a fish.

There were also a large assortment of river and forest creatures, mostly malevolent. Parents frightened children with the dread two-faced abuhuhua, hairy cannibals. Some such demons were Siamese twins, become so by raping a female, or by a female demon seizing a man. Others cut a hole in the roof of a victim's head and sucked him dry leaving only his skin hanging on a tree.

White anacondas menaced menstruating women, also women after childbirth, and short, fat, river demons seized men who failed to fulfill properly the taboos of the birth-rites.

The ghost of the dead had to be driven out of the house by burning chile peppers but lingered around the vicinity trying to carry off blood relatives. Wicked people were transformed at death into birds, insects, or beasts. A shaman or chieftain's soul always entered into a jaguar, could do so even when living. Every jaguar who attacked a human had such a soul, and the angered tribesmen sometimes either killed the jaguar or the suspected shaman—even so, his soul would merely enter another jaguar and be more menacing than ever.

Shamans could be of either sex. These had tremendous powers in tribal affairs, in sorcery, in supernatural matters, for they could manipulate the souls of men and all creatures. The shaman's body contained invisible black palm needles he could shoot into victims. Before a novice shaman was accepted, he had to produce a thunderstorm.

Animal tales mostly revolved around contests between the tapir and a tortoise. Folk hero tales and stories of struggles with forest monsters were common, also tales of ancestor exploits.

The moon was personified, always trying to copulate with young girls—the proof of success was the first menses. The moon also pawed over fresh graves and prevented the theft of his lamp (the ending of an eclipse).

5

Guiana culture had many similarities. There lived nine Tupí tribes, thirty main Arawak tribes, and 108 Carib tribes, as well as the independent Ahuaque Caliana, Macú, Mirá, Macuá (Saliva) and Guaharibo (Shirianá), plus some fifty-five tribes never identified.

Many of these peoples were first described, somewhat fancifully, by Sir Walter Raleigh who in 1595 journeyed five hundred miles up the Orinoco in search of El Dorado. The following year, a companion, Lawrence Keymys, explored the coast and carefully identified and located the various tribes, rivers, and products, paying particular attention to the Oyapoc, Maroní and Courantyne. But the first thoroughgoing account was provided by Robert Harcourt in 1613. There were various Dutch and French accounts also, still largely unknown to English-speaking scholars.

But very few intimate or systematic studies of individual tribes have ever been made. Walter Edmund Roth's notable studies from 1908–1929 chiefly emphasized the material aspects, though in 1915 he did publish a lengthy paper on animism and folklore.

Even less has ever been known about the plateau, and northern Brazilian tribes or those in Venezuela. In all this area, food was scarcer than in northwest Brazil, but largely the same except for different kinds of seeds; and wild rice was gathered in the Orinoco marshes. There, more use was made of lizards, grubs, frogs, and frog and insect eggs.

House furnishings included elaborate stools and benches, from the wood block "loaf" to those intricately designed and carved. One Arecumí and Macushi (Carib) stool was a solid half-circle trunk, with protruding carved animal head at one end, its tail at the other. One such stool had an anvil shape, with hourglass openings cut through on each side.

Another Macushi and Pantamona (also Carib) type is like a miniature table with deeply incised two-sided supports and a base with four square "feet" upturned. Many were made with stylized animal head and leg supports. A most amazing double crocodile head stool with a concave seat was made by the Huarrau of the Orinoco delta.

Head deformation was practiced by Dutch and French Guiana people. Sometimes teeth were filed. The Carib, rarely the Arawak, used lip plugs, and the Murá men on the lower Urubá river used them in both lips. Cheek perforations were made by the Carib Acochuá. Ear lobes were generally perforated for pendants but the Tarumá Arawak of the Berbice River, and some other groups, also perforated and decorated the ear helix. Carni River Caribs shaved the whole head except for a topknot, much as do modern North African Berbers. Other hair styles were a double part, with the center hair caught in a net or wrapping at the back. Sometimes forehead bangs made a complete circle around the bald head. Two-bar combs were used, and crab oil was used for hair dye. The Carib glued white down on their foreheads. Pubic hair was generally removed. Facial tattooing was frequent among the Arawak, body tattooing among others. The Arawak painted the whole body; the Carib and Huarrau only the face, with such dyes as annatto, *urucú*, and *genipa*.

Headgear was frequent and varied; peaked palm-leaf hats, basket-like crowns with feather patterns, cotton fillets and forehead bands, with tassels, knots, feathers, bird, and insect wings.

Women were clever spinners of cotton, using a bone or calabash spindle which was rolled fast against the lifted thigh then allowed to revolve freely in the air, the yarn being held aloft in the right hand. Thicker three-ply yarn was first looped around the toes and leg, then spun. Multi-ply yarn, sometimes not cotton but palm and tree fibers, bromelia, silk or other grasses, was spun on the thigh but sans spindle, though one tribe used a bow-driven spindle.

Hammocks were woven on a continuous warp, often separated by shed rods or wooden laminae, with semilooped weft. Sometimes shuttle-spools and leveling bars were used.

Blowguns had inner tubes, and poison—chiefly curare—was smeared on darts and arrows. Many gums, glues, and resins were available. Considerable intertribal barter for such weapons, instruments, also foods was carried on.

Tobacco was prepared with pulverized fresh water algae and baked in cakes on a casava pan, or mixed with black nitre earth. The Macushi poured pepper water into their nostrils; the Arawak used it as an enema, introduced by an animal bladder syringe.

The warlike Carib stimulated valor by dances, invoking the jaguar spirit, drinking manioc beer, with worms from the putrid brains, heart, and liver of a dead jaguar. The weapons were smeared with the pus. The war summons was carried by small trumpets and arrow-trail markings.

Other dances, to the tune of flute and drum, celebrated the hummingbird and other birds. The Carib had special dance and assembly halls.

They enjoyed clay trumpets, wooden flageolets, bamboo side o: nose-blown flutes; big bamboo blowing flutes; gourd, wooden or clay ocarina type instruments; nut-shell and wood whistles; three- to ten-reed Panpipes, and clarinet trumpets, with reed vibrators;

clay, wood, or bamboo gourd rattles; dance stamping sticks sometimes with attached rattles; various kinds of drums, including a
friction drum sounded by a rasp stick drawn through a hole.

They had the folk heroes similar to those further inland. Originally heroes made animals out of magical trees, and they killed
supernatural shapes, as in Teutonic dragon tales.

Legend said the *bunia* bird taught the Carib the use of plants.
The shamans conducted ceremonies to aid manioc and tobacco
growth and to prevent diseases, and gave tribal advice. Fetishes of
beeswax, clay, or wood were used by the shamans.

There were many bush spirits (*canaimá*); grotesque *hebú,* clown
spirits served as the butts of human jokes. Celestial and star lore was
greater among open savanna tribes, who reckoned the seasons by
them—particularly the Pleiades. Months and years and future dates
were recorded on knotted quipús or cords. Each day or each period
of time before the given date a knot was untied. Future dates were
also recorded by a bundle of sticks, and as each time period elapsed
a stick was taken away. Pegs in boards were similarly used.

11

Zipe, Zaque, and Oncoy

COLOMBIA narrows northward to the Isthmus of Panama, the crossroads of South America, of north-south, south-north migrations. There, eventually, may be discovered many secrets of early man in the Americas.

Southbound migrants spread along the Colombian Andes. The seaborn Tupí, Carib and Arawak, mostly, but not entirely, by-passed this route in their surge north.

Four main Andean ranges carve northern and western Colombia. The most westerly—the Serranía de Bandó—was covered with dense rain-forest, not so different from the low hinterland. The next two ranges have numerous lofty peaks and deep-cleft but fertile valleys, such as that of the Cauca River. The innermost range curves east, embracing the Maracaibo Basin, and strikes well into Venezuela. As Wendell C. Bennett pointed out, Colombia was also an Andes-Amazon link; there the highlands, not rising to such vast heights as further south, presented less of a barrier. There jungles, foot-hills, and mountains flow into each other easily. Also, since Colombia is nearer the equator and climate less affected by altitude, there were less violent differences in temperature, hence less break in the flora and fauna. In spite of the rich potential of archaeological wealth, next to nothing has been excavated, though that little is significant even if done mostly by nonprofessionals and largely confined to the lofty western third of the country—but not enough to establish any reliable chronology, merely some mapping of cultural limits. Difficulties of timing are accentuated by the non-comparable culture of the various areas.

As yet only tenuous possible relations have been established either in Amazonian, Venezuelan, or Incan cultures, though here and there are definite intrusions of later Inca artifacts. Indications of Amazon origins are round houses, four-legged stools, urn burial, effigy urns, leg bands, art motifs, portrayals of jungle animals, birds, plants, etc.

The southern Nariño zone is indubitably linked with Ecuador and the adjacent Putumayo jungles. The three-color negative ceramic painting is related to the Tuncahuán style; it certainly was not Incan in origin. There are a few similarities with the earliest periods in north Andean Peru, perhaps with the great Chavín culture. For here in south Colombia (as at Santa Marta to the north) begins the stone-carving tradition: slabs, pillars, statues, underground rooms, box graves, also a monochrome type pottery with many urn variations. The stone carving of San Agostín and Tierradentro show remarkable similarities with Chavín workmanship. Later Quimbaya ceramics suggest Mochican work (Peruvian coast); the double spout is characteristic of Nazca ware (south Peruvian coast); and the three-color negative pottery, according to some, suggests the "middle period" of Andean development, i.e., pre-Inca.

Thus far, outside the allied central Andean area, eight geographic centers, with occasionally overlapping styles (save for the strictly *sui generis* artifacts of Nariño), have been mapped. Even the pottery in these sites is localized; tall tripod vessels (San Agustín), short tripods (Quimbaya); tetrapods (Quimbaya-San Agustín-Nariño); two-color negative painting in three areas but nowhere else; three-color negative painting in two sites; incising with white paste in four sites.

2

The main Quimbaya archaeological area in the rolling hills of central Cauca valley and adjacent Quindío has yielded superb ceramics and gold work. Shaft and chamber graves are three to eighty feet deep, some with cut steps, arched gable roofs, and supports with painted designs. At one period cremation was practiced. Superb gold work has survived, sometimes alloyed with copper (*tumbaga*) processed by soldering, melting, forging, mold casting; solid or hollow ware, made with wax forms—*cire perdue* and *repoussé* designs; also wire filigree work, with different quality gold in a single object to provide contrast: nose rings, half-moon, round or elongated; jars, bottles, vases, idols, breastplates, diadems, pendants, bell bracelets, beads, brooches; tweezers; masks for fiestas and mummies; scepters with bird, animal, or human heads.

Later period pottery suggests some Peruvian influence. Among objects recovered have been "whistling jars"; incised, highly polished brown ware with globular shapes; or double-open bowls and tall cylindrical urns; jars with intricate figurines either standing or seated on benches, legs out or knees drawn up. Clay stamps were found, for cloth or body painting.

In Bolívar Department—the Simú River region—have been discovered elaborate large human figures, amazingly competent, curved to the sides of ollas. The females use ear plugs, necklaces, short skirts bellied at the waist, the naked torso incised to show intricate tattooing.

The largest circle of stone columns was found near Tunja in the Chibcha area. These same early people used stone-slab covers on graves or cremated bodies to ash under bowls.

The gold work here was definitely Chibchan, hence very late—excellent but inferior to the Quimbaya gold breastplates and figurines, with more and finer wire work and filigree than elsewhere. Scenes with cutout figures were arranged on flat platforms. The sophisticated textile designs were probably applied by rollers. Pottery was mostly one color, or red on white, some decorated with incision, or else by pinching, appliqué, occasionally modeling.

Early Nariño pottery in the south was beautiful, in two colors, red or black on light yellow or white, and various combinations, with elaborate, casual, yet reiterated motifs: lovely formalized black-faced monkeys and other animals. Clay ocarinas have fine stop and scroll designs—red on cream.

Henry Lehmann, who has done the only reliable scientific work in this area, is not convinced that the late pre-Spanish dwellers there—the Guambía-Coconuco group—were related to the people of the earlier archaeology.

The Tairona, Inca (not those of Peru), and Cágaba, lived in the remote, vast, and very lofty Sierra Madre de Santa Marta in the northeast corner of Colombia, among heavy forests sloping to tropical jungle. Some forty sites have been excavated. At Santa Marta on the coast, extensive stonework survives, ring houses, vaults and tombs of fitted dressed blocks. The ring house platform was 16 to 65 feet in diameter, made of an inner circle of carved slabs on edge; an outer row of wedge-shaped slabs placed horizontally. Dressed slabs in steps led to an inside threshold stone. Terraced building platforms were also cut out of slopes, faced with stone walls, and with large rectangular dirt-walled courts. Slab stairways and paved streets 16 feet wide connected buildings, sometimes crossing streams by means of stone-slab bridges. Stone-lined pits served as reservoirs.

The two types of pottery were: (1) thick red ware, with appliquéd figures; (2) thin black ware, better made, with fine-line incision and varied double-orifice jars and effigies; also wire-framed clay whistles, flutes, rattles, pestles, and figurines.

Stone objects for religious services were of polished jade; there were also stone *metates, manos* or rolling pins, mortars, pestles, pierced stone weights, polishing stones, polished axes, carved ceremonial batons, pendants, animal-shaped amulets, four-legged tables, beads, and triangular faces.

San Agustín, ancient place of stone carvings in southwest Colombia, was Andean in culture, related to Chavín in Peru. There in 1797 Francisco José de Caldas, a local scholar, examined "great numbers of statues, columns, temples, tables and an image of the Sun, all of stone and in varied shapes." This culture, it was later found, extended over a considerable area, mostly in present-day Cauca Department.

The records of those peoples were made by rock-scratchings in caves and on the flat stone slabs over tombs, by bas-reliefs of human beings with turned-out feet, as well as frogs, monkeys, and large quadrupeds—as at Alto de Tablón above the Magdalena River; where were found cylindrical stones, with human faces, sometimes with arms, one outstretched, the other folded over the body; many well-carved statues with large canine-like teeth, surmounted by a symbolic clay "soul" figure. Very realistic warriors and musicians were carved, with strong free movement in execution. Also, a more "modernistic" type, in which the earlier forms are tamed to less dynamic expression. Statues are in relief, or incised and painted black, white, red, and yellow.

Though Andean, the representations were reminiscent of many in Amazon pottery, and ended in a circled trunk or bird beak. Three sculptures showed short loincloths, penis cords, necklaces, ear discs, bracelets, and leg bands; on the head, birds, wreaths, capes, or hats; in the hand, a club or spear, shield, hammer or staff. Posts were carved with snakes, lizards, and tadpoles, human figures or faces, quadrupeds, and monkeys. Replicas have been found in gold leaf. Sometimes, instead of a secondary figure or a face over the head—the soul—a trophy head hangs over the breast, or a wavy ribbon from the mouth ends in a small head.

These statues served as grave markers or as caryatids on temples, perhaps were representations of the deities, as were those found at baths or springs and overlooking fields.

Temples were ten by fourteen and a half feet or so, usually roofed with a single slab sustained by wall columns and caryatids, with hard earth floors sloping to a center idol. The walls were often painted with geometric designs. Sometimes there were cellars, lined and roofed with large stone slabs.

The builders of the old stone centers at Tierradentro also disappeared. The Andaquí and Paez, living in the region when the Spaniards came, were a more primitive people. The ruins there have extensive galleries and underground chambers, excavated out of soft granodiorite, which were entered by shafts with well-made straight or circular stone stairs. The walls are covered with white cement, intricately painted black, red, or orange. In one tomb at Loma Alta, a decorative frieze circled under the stone slab roof, and had fine sun figures, with radiating lines. Many chambers had niches for statuettes separated by carved pilasters, with grimacing faces, painted black on white. At Segovia the underside of entrance slabs were carved with eyes and animal mouths. Stones were carved or dressed with polished andesite, and other hard-rock tools, points, chisels, gravers, knives, scrapers, and axes, some with sculptured feet. Also, long stone pestles were common.

Plain and incised pottery was made, usually brown on red, or orange on red; numerous kinds of fold and flare urns with very extraordinary but simple geometric designs. Crude tripod pots were also made, a few figurines and spindles.

The builders of the stone-reared San Agustín and Tierradentro, reaching back to the Chavín era, thousands of years before the Spaniards, were not the "moderns" there—the Chibcha and Tairona, who for all their remarkable talents, were less "progressive" than the great ancients.

3

The lofty fertile basins of Cundinamarca and Boyacá were the paradises of the region; here was the center of the noteworthy if little known Chibcha civilization, that was in flower when the Span-iards came, chiefly along the upper Magdalena tributaries, the Blanco, Bogotá and Chicamocha rivers. The most recent Chibcha artifacts, though inferior to many of earlier epochs, nevertheless show some of the most advanced skills of the continent, but these people left no permanent construction, except for a few stone foundations, so that Chibcha culture though highly concentrated, because of the rival splendors of Cuzco, Chichen Itza, Monte Albán and Tenoch-titlán, has been downgraded, mostly ignored by chroniclers and students to this day. Bennett remarks, ". . . the Chibcha culture of Cundinamarca Boyacá achieved an intensity comparable to that of the central Andean pattern." However the Inca Empire repre-sents the ultimate expression of a pattern whose roots lie deep in the archaeological past. The Chibcha culture has no such demon-strable antiquity—"though of course this may be due to the paucity of archaeological research."

Most of what is known about them—and it is scanty—comes from Gonzalo Jiménez de Quesada's account, as completed by Oviedo: *Historia General y natural de las Indias,* and Juan de Castellanos' blank verse, *Historia del Nuevo Reino de Granada,* "full of clear, exact prosy ethnography."

The latter was a soldier (who became a priest) at Tunja from 1561 to 1607. Fray Pedro Simón, though not writing until 1604, provided the fullest account of the Chibcha. Later writers during that century were less reliable.

The Chibcha achieved a considerable political organization with outstanding leadership and were reported to be able to mobilize armies of 50,000 men, though the Spaniards never reported having to fight such hosts. There were two sovereign states. The southern, the larger, was ruled by the Zipe, the northern by the Zaque.

Allied with the north, loosely federated, were several other Chib-cha groups with various subdivisions. Also, a small priest-ridden realm of the Tundamá peoples—Iraca—maintained complete inde-pendence.

The Zipe kingdom proper had six districts under local chiefs, usually relatives of the ruling Zipe, and some twenty minor political units. The Zaque realm—some eight districts—centered in Tunja, the capital city, and ruled extensive subordinate areas on the Upía-Meta-Orinoco river section to the southeast and included Boyacá (later to be the site of Bolívar's famous 1819 victory).

Though both Zipe and Zaque realms stretched well down into jungle country, the main inhabited portions were more than 8,000 feet high, reaching up to more than 10,000 feet, or as high as maize or potatoes could be grown profitably.

The over-all Chibcha population was estimated by A. L. Kroeber to have totaled about a million, the same as in the area today, exclusive of modern Bogotá.

The two main groups lived rather peaceably, though they had frequent trouble (as did Spaniards later) with the wild naked Mazo and Panche of the tropical hill slopes, who deformed their own heads. These were bow and arrow people, who seized skulls as trophies, and were said to eat their enemies, their first-born, and even their own dead. Nevertheless, much trading was carried on. Other neighbors, some speaking Chibcha dialects, if also backward, were less bothersome. As with Cuatemoc in Mexico, the successor of the slain Zipe was tortured to death by Quesada to try to force him to reveal his treasure-trove of gold. The second Zaque was similarly executed. The Chibcha were not archers, and for war purposes used darts and spear throwers, four- to six-and-a-half-foot spears set in cane shafts, and two-handled clubs, often with four cutting edges—*macanas*—in close-up fighting. Small shields lashed to the forearm were used. However, they largely employed mercenaries from the Panche and Mazo tribes to do their fighting.

Pre-Spanish legends tell of fierce dynastic wars in each kingdom and steady territorial expansion. A typical historical yarn, told by A. L. Kroeber and derived from earlier sources, was about a Guatavita ruler, in the district of a high tributary of the Fruza River in the Zaque realm. He impaled the lover of his favorite wife, made her eat his flesh, and had his minstrels compose and sing songs about it. He forgave her, but she threw herself and girl child into a lake. The ruler ordered a priest to dive for her and bring her back. He returned, saying she was living with a dragon snake. "Bring back the child," the ruler ordered. The priest went down again, but the little girl he brought back was dead and blind. The dragon had plucked out her eyes.

Hunsa-Huá, a Zaque ruler, fell in love with his sister. When she became pregnant, the mother beat her and threatened to kill her. She and the brother fled following a dart from his sling, and reached Zipe territory safely. The child was born but turned into stone. The pair traveled south as far as the great Tequendero Falls, where they grew weary and also turned into stone. Since then all Zaque rulers have married their sisters.

The Zipe heir apparent was trained for six years—"six" and "twelve" were basic holy numbers—and during the last six months was kept in the dark in a temple, not allowed to see daylight and let out only at night. He had to abstain from meat, salt and pepper, and could have no sexual intercourse. Frequently he was whipped. Finally anointed with gold dust, he was set adrift in a raft.

One legend tells that the Zipe, having no close kin to succeed him, lined up possible young candidates naked before a girl. The one who showed no erection was selected as heir.

Their mud-daubed, cane-walled house, with gabled or conical roofs resting on posts, on rare occasions had stone footings. Towns were enclosed by palisades, with observation crow's-nests. The people slept on elevated crisscross canes, covered with cotton blankets, and used low chairs or stools, cut from single wood blocks.

They wore two cotton cloth pieces, the lower wrapped around the waist, fastened by a *tupu* pin. More distinguished people wore clothing painted with red or black designs.

Land was privately owned and inheritable, and men and women worked in the fields side by side, using wooden tools. White, yellow, and purple potatoes were grown, also white, yellow, pink, red, black, and tan corn—six magical colors. It was ground on concave *metates* and the dough was boiled or toasted in balls wrapped in leaves. Corn *chicha* was drunk copiously. *Quinóa*, manioc, *aracacha*, sweet potatoes, beans, squashes, tomatoes, and *aji* or chile were planted as well as coca and tobacco. Cotton and most fruits were secured by trading, often from the Panche. Meat played a minor role in diet: rabbits and the cavy, for deer could not be killed without the ruler's permission.

They beat gold, or gold and copper (*tumbaga*), sometimes gold and platinum or gold and silver, into sheets over forms, or cast it into flat figures, filigree effect. *Repoussé* was much used. Vegetable acids were employed to eat away all surface copper.

The chieftain's litters were huge, with sheets of gold, and attendants cleared the path, putting down rugs or strewing flowers. Good roads ran from town to town and to temples, most of which had baths. The Curaca's doorway was hung with gold sheets that clanked in the breeze.

Little of this gold came from Chibcha territory, but being greatly coveted by the nobility and priests as wealth, church adornments, and for ritual and burial, was traded in considerable quantities for salt, cotton cloth, and emeralds washed out at Somondoco.

The gold marts were part of the great international fairs on the Magdalena and Suárez Rivers. Cast gold was made into coinlike discs, measured for value in the curve of the index finger against the first thumb joint. Larger discs were measured with a string. The thickness must have been standard for it is not recorded, so it is now impossible to gauge the actual content. Pubic rites lasted a "sacred" six days during which the girl sat in a corner with her face covered. Chastity was unimportant, rather despised in fact, though wives were required to be faithful. Polygamy was practiced and a noble might have a hundred wives, who lived all in one room, with him in another.

4

Priests trained for a "sacred" twelve years, fasting in a special building, eating maize once a day, observing complete continence, frequently drawing their own blood. Finally, candidates' ears and noses were pierced curaca-fashion, and they were personally ordained by the Zipe or Zaque, who presented them with a painted mantle and a carved calabash for his coca.

On taking his place in the temple, the priest had to remain celibate and eat little, though coca, tobacco, and datura were taken to induce visions. He fasted frequently. He must sleep but little and be taciturn. His life was a perpetual penance. However the Iraca priest-chief had wives.

The priests threw ashes from a mountain peak to draw rain clouds. They foretold events, a service for which they might receive several capes or a bit of gold.

There was also a class of wandering "wizards," mostly old men or women, who sold cures, poisons, abortion potions, aphrodisiacs, diagnosed illness, located lost objects, and interpreted dreams, after first becoming intoxicated with tobacco, datura, *tyhyqui, yopa* or *osca*. These herbalists and soothsayers—a similar profession existed among the Inca—still operate throughout the Andes as far south as Bolivia.

There were many wayside shrines, also in mountain caves, beside rivers and lakes. Some places were holy centers—the town of Chía, for instance, was named after the moon. Offerings of gold, cloth, chicha, fruits and vegetables were made. The only animals sacrificed were guacamayos and talking papagayos. Their heads were kept as mementos.

Gods requiring gold as their chief offering, such as Bochica and Chibchachum—"Chibcha Staff"—came to be worshiped chiefly by the goldsmiths. The god Bachuë, who protected crops, usually received incense gum; Cuchabiba, "The Rainbow," emeralds and beads from the sick or a woman about to give birth. *Chicha* was given to the "Nencatacon," patron of weavers and cloth painters.

Human sacrifices were largely reserved for the sun, who had many temples. Sun sacrifice victims were captives, slaves, and children of the best families. Also small children were brought for sacrifice from the distant Marachore. They were kept in the temples, were always carried, never allowed to touch the earth, were put through ceremonies and singing, in which they wept. They were cut open, the heart and viscera removed, the head cut off. Another ceremony occurred with the building of a royal dwelling. The posts were pounded up and down on a child, while earth was poured in.* Rulers were always buried with live female wives and slaves, previously stupefied with datura.

A September maize harvest fiesta with weeping masks was staged. At New Year's (March and June moons) garbage was burned and all hearth ashes thrown out. Special pilgrimages were made to the sacred "Snake God" at Guatavita Lake—a twenty-day trip—and to four other lake snake shrines.

A creator, Chimi-ni-guagua, began to shine in the eternal dark-nothing and made large black birds, then the Sun and Moon. The Iraca version was about a Sugamuxi cacique and his nephew who, when all was still dark, created men out of yellow earth and women out of a tall herb, then his nephew became the Sun and he the Moon.

The Zaque citizens told of the "beneficent female," Fura Chogue, who emerged from Iguaque Lake near Tunja with her three-year-old Son, whom she married when he grew up. They had four to six children at each birth, and thus rapidly populated the land, whereupon the two of them returned to the lake as snakes.

The goddess "Mother" Huitaca, who taught pleasure, dancing, drunkenness, and every sexual freedom, was turned into an owl; but some stories say the Moon.

Chibchachum, angered by his worshipers, flooded the savanna with

* This habit was one practiced by both certain African and Polynesian royalty and chiefs when house raising, and appears to be widespread and ancient.

two rivers and from a rainbow hurled his golden staff at Tequendama, creating the waterfall there, then vanished underground where he still supports the world. When he shifted his shoulders, there were earthquakes. The resemblance of many of these myths to those current among the Incan Quechua is marked.

The culture hero Boshicha, or Xue or Lord (a resemblance is indicated to Nahuatl or Aztec), a messenger of Chimi-ni-guagua, came from the far east, traversed the Zipe and Zaque domains north, east, south, and west, and died among the Iraca, leaving in his wake many valleys from his mighty tread and deep caves where he slept. He was old and bearded, with long hair, went barefoot, wore a knotted mantle and taught virtue, charity, and observance of religious and secular law; also, spinning, weaving and cloth painting. His powers were inherited by an Iraca ruler, who was able to cause rain, droughts, and epidemics.

5

The remarkable Andean culture, centering at Chavín de Huantar in Huari Province, Peru, which flourished probably 4,000 or more years ago, was the first flowering of a truly superior civilization to appear in all South America. Only two or three later civilizations, for which it laid the basis, surpassed it.

But until forty years ago, it was all but unknown, just part of man's universal ignorance. No mention of it, save of various temples, not culturally identified, was ever made by earlier chroniclers.

The indefatigable Cieza de León remarked in his *Crónica del Peru* about the Andean "fortress" which "in many places has carved faces and human figures all beautifully adorned." In 1624 Antonio Espinoza wrote that it was comparable to Rome or Jerusalem. Other passing travelers mentioned a "fortress castle" on the upper Marañon, but made no investigations.

The great Italian naturalist Antonio Raimundo saw at the site in 1873, an enormous stele carved with a "Supreme Deity," and in 1880 Charles Wiener, the French artist, published a crude engraving of the upper portion of the temple there.

The long ignorance about the Chavín culture is not surprising, for mostly the evidences of it were deeply buried. Both Jesuits and Augustinians were especially zealous in stamping out all "idols" and tearing down old temples stone by stone, another possible reason for the dimness of the old records. But the disasters that overtook great Chavín were more likely natural—for most remains of that civilization in the Andes have long been buried under layers of flood silt, landslides, lava, and volcanic ash—convulsions occurring thousands of years ago and on down through the centuries. In other instances, later peoples constructed new temples on top of Chavín temples.

Also, Chavín's inaccessibility, deep in a wild gorge of the inner Andes, long discouraged visits by scientists.

Not until 1919, when Julio C. Tello, dean of Peruvian archaeologists for many decades, led an expedition there, was the importance of the place appreciated. He recognized very quickly that this was no extension of Central American or Maya culture, but locally generated after long evolution, perhaps by peoples up from the jungles. It was probably thousands of years older than the oldest Tiahuanaco culture in Bolivia beyond Lake Titicaca. It was also different from the later Ica, Nazca, and Mochica developments on the coast of Peru.

For twenty years after Tello's investigations, most North American archaeologists and anthropologists remained unaware of or unimpressed by his findings; or else, like Philip Ainsworth Means, woefully misinterpreted them. Many are still unready to accept the tentative early dating of the culture. Nor did they like Tello's implications of possible Amazon origins, for they cling sternly to a reverse thesis. Nearly all the art motifs at Chavín except the condor, are derived from jungle plant and animal life.

This mighty bird, the largest on earth, soaring high through the clear upland air, matching its flight with the highest mountains, this free open-heaven world, must have filled the newcomers from darker forests with a greater wonder at this new lofty realm they had occupied. The condor was symbolic of the Supreme Being himself, free from earthly chains, soaring above the highest mountains and out of sight into the blue empyrean.

Doubtless sometime—since back-dating is now feasible and reliable—the true periods of Chavín culture will be established, though at present the energies of the world's peoples are too taken up by trying to create new ruins rather than examining those available, now silent and daily deteriorating, with cumulative loss for man's knowledge of his past and his evolution.

Chavín de Huantar, in a narrow gorge beyond the first snow-clad cordillera, fifteen miles southeast of Huari, lies on the side of the mountain at the junction of two torrential streams that form the

Puccha River, tributary of the great Marañon. Across from it are other ruins; above it, ruins considered even more ancient; and it is twenty miles from Recuay and the remains of still another civilization, a reflowering centuries later, but distinct enough to provide a separate nomenclature, one which may have contributed much, probably via the coast, to early Tiahuanaco in far-off Bolivia.

Tello found Chavín mostly buried under modern cultivated fields, which were strewn with archaeological items, shards and stone figurines, carved jaguars and condors. He found fine pottery incised in low and full relief, a deer bone with beautiful designs, figurines encrusted with turquoise and shells. Other dressed and carved Chavín stones had been used in contemporary dwellings for foundations, lintels, walls, and sashes.

Everything indicated that in remote early periods Chavín had been repeatedly struck by major catastrophes, earthquakes, landslides and floods. Hence it was some time before he realized the magnitude of his discovery. The construction covered about 850 square feet on a terraced mound overlooking the river across which extends a monolithic bridge of the same era, constructed with huge stone cubes. The site included numerous underground galleries and a maze on different levels of drainage conduits, terraces, platforms, a great main square, the "castle temple," the chapel of the condors. An archaeological setback occurred in 1949 when the place was reburied under a landslide.

Local people told Tello that the rock-hewn channels were not merely for drainage but to provide a pure water supply and that they had been bored under the river through solid rock to provide water to the lesser ruins on the opposite bank.

Magnificent stone steps, adorned with a bird of prey, rattlesnakes, and fish-lizards and guarded by a lone cat-demon, lead from the lowest terrace (through one end of which one of the stream cuts), up to the main "sacred" square, paved with polished stone and centered by the tall "Lanzón" or stele of green diorite, now known as the "Tello obelisk." Other stairs led to a narrower third terrace fronting the massive dual-tower temple, with its projecting animal heads and exquisite relief frieze of jaguars, condors, and snakes.

Inside the temple another mammoth monolith, the "Raimundi Column," was supported by stone roof slabs. The interior was a labyrinth of dark galleries and chapels carved with animals, birds, and having alabaster urns and stone chests.

Three chapels to one side of the temple adjacent to still higher irregular terraces were evidently later additions not conforming to the original plan of the site—they had cylindrical columns, and were richly adorned with bas-relief steles.

Such magnificent construction as that at Chavín could hardly have been an isolated expression. Tello confidently predicted that other sites would be uncovered. He himself soon proved that the culture was ramified through all the Marañon headwater area and down to the famous Pongo de Manseriche, where the great stream bursts through the inner wall of the Andes.

He and others found Chavín tombs, artifacts, and constructions at Yayno, Llamellín, Cotush, Chalhua, Yaco, San Marcos, Huamán Hüayna, Hacal Gayoc, and Pacopampa. In the Callejon de Huaylas alone, some 400 stone statues were discovered. At the headwaters of the Cotush he found a remarkable collection of plates and bowls with flat bases, oblique rims, geometric, and animal designs. The artifacts and structures of the entire basin were homogeneous—they were ancient "Chavín."

Much later, Tello discovered and uncovered the beautiful temple and steles of Kuntur Huasi near Cajamarca. On the upper platform, four magnificent statues were found. This religious center was supplied with water by the massive and elegant Cumbé-Mayo aqueduct, a prodigious stone-carved enterprise. Its walls were profusely carved with symbolic designs and Chavín-style inscriptions; it was lined with niches and stone altars and figures.

The enormous temple, largely hidden under cultivated fields, was dedicated to the Condor Cult—hence its name—and was located at the crest of a mountain slope on typical massive superimposed platforms. The whole mountainside was terraced; stone walls filled in with loam, similar to later Inca work, a gigantesque undertaking for farming and burial. The famous Las Ventanillas burial ground had tombs carved out of solid rock. One royal burial there was of a seated personage, legs folded back, surrounded by six snake-motif gold plaques, thirty-two small rectangular gold plaques, a gold necklace, and turquoise, plus a clay cup perhaps for food for his long journey.

Presently evidences of Chavín culture were found all along the Peruvian coast, mostly buried, frequently with edifices of later civilizations on top of them.

The brilliant amateur archaeologist and wealthy *hacendado,*

Rafael Larco Hoyle, who came upon the first site in 1939 in the Cupisnique Valley, dubbed this the "Cupisnique" culture and identified it as the offspring of Chavín. According to Carrión Cachot, it dated 3,500 years back, although 848 B.C. is also given. Ten or so other sites were uncovered in the Cupisnique area and six more nearby. Burial and other remains yielded ceramics and plant reproductions, such as beans, potatoes, *caiguá* gourds, domesticated dogs and llamas and several unidentified jungle animals. The Cupisnique discoveries spurred feverish surveys, soon sites were located in every northern valley—such as Pacasmayo and Chiclayo. Sometimes the black Chavín-style ware was mingled with that of other periods and peoples. One of the most exquisite, sophisticated examples of black Chavín ware was found in the almost unknown (archaeologically) Piura of northern Peru: a tall vase with a round, slightly flaring base bearing severe incised geometric designs. The body of the vase, narrowing upward slightly, had on four sides three connected oval niches, twelve in all, with women's breasts formalized as eye-and-beak-bird designs. An open ring and a tube-like neck surmounted these. Fussy-duddy Means called this superb artifact "the ultimate stage of aesthetic dissolution."

Even before this, Tello proved that the vast burial site further south at Ancón (the ancient Lancón) a bathing resort south of Lima, which had excited scores of earlier investigators for generations, was actually Coastal Tiahuanacoid in nature. The tombs contained pottery, carvings on stone, wood and bone, basketry, ceramics, textiles, silver, gold, copper, and bronze objects. Other southern sites were soon located.

Farther south, a Chavín settlement was discovered on the seashore at Supe, with its mat-rolled mummies and red-painted skeletons and fishing gear, with evidences of maize, yucca, and bean cultivation, at Maracas, even on Puná Island. The lowest levels at Ancón also are seen to be Chavín in style.

Bennett has listed twelve major Chavín coast sites, by no means a complete list, and some represent a score of separate excavations.

The coastal Chavín culture, mostly lacking stone, has informed us through burials, mummies, skeletons, bones, and artifacts, that the people wore loincloths, caps with rich adornments, bone ornaments, bone, stone, and shell beads and necklaces. Stone necklaces had a magnificently carved center stone. Some early skeletons wore bone rings, artfully designed, on every finger.

Thus the Chavín people, coast and highlands, sculptured and carved porphyry, granite, slate, turquoise, lapis lazuli, quartz, shells, bone and wood ornaments, animals, birds, receptacles, benches, and mortars. Anthracite coal was polished to make mirrors. Reliefs on gold were made by, among other methods, bone-pressing and often imitated highland stone carving.

Textiles, mostly cotton, were woven with an interlacing technique, sewn with bone needles, and painted or printed with roller and flat stamps which were also used for body patterns. In some places monkeys were favorite subjects.

6

The most impressive coast centers found thus far have been in the Casma and Nepeña Valleys—which Larco Hoyle considered the initial diffusion point of all Cupisnique culture. Other authorities disagree, however.

The Nepeña temples are superb edifices on superimposed platforms with low-relief of murals. At Cerro Blanco, where the temple was covered over completely and topped by a Moche temple (about A.D. 1), three distinct Chavín epochs were disclosed, including the topmost major temple, built on a clay platform of split stone and conical adobe in the form of a gigantic bird, likely a condor, alighting with outspread wings. Everywhere walls were decorated with reliefs or stucco painting on red, yellow, and black. Entire walls are taken up by a single enormous stylization of animals or birds or combinations.

The pyramidal temple of Puncurí, built of conical adobes and clay columns (the third Chavín edifice on the site), rises majestically above split-level platforms with wide stone staircases guarded at the bottom by a fierce cross-fanged jaguar who also keeps watch over various carved granite objects and the tomb of a sacrificed woman.

Three temples were found in Casma Valley; at Moxeké, Sechín and Pallca. Moxeké is stupendous, erected on three vast platforms, the top one with statue niches, above which was a vast walled courtyard. Behind this, above four lesser steplike platforms, rises a massive dual windowless temple, each half surmounted by a domed tower.

The gods in the façade of the upper platform were thirteen feet high, seated figures mostly, with hands across their stomachs, fingertips not quite touching the surface polished and painted. They wore belted tunics with serpent hems. Alternating with the niches were panels of intricate stylizations of interlaced serpents.

Underneath Moche and Chimú temples at Sechín were found 87 monoliths, 22 of them 15 feet tall. Some had been wrenched out of place for some 60 feet by a prehistoric landslide. One carved monolith depicts a warrior with headdress, plumes, and snakes—striking for its stark economy of execution. This site, some authorities state, is attributable to no culture but its own.

The pyramidal Pallca temple, of Casma Valley, rises above terraces covering over 40,000 square feet, the whole surrounded by a thick wall and a balustrade of polygonal stones and adobe. The terraces are approached by three staircases. Nearby are the remains of habitations. To the east, about two miles, are several smaller pyramidal temples. Many tombs were excavated, yielding charcoal, many utensils and Chavín pottery with animal adornments.

Still another significant discovery was at hand—the extensive Paracas burial site on the Pisco Bay peninsula—which Tello characterized as "the highest manifestation of all aboriginal art. . . . A new horizon has been opened for the study of ancient Peruvian cultures."

At the necropolis there, covering about 30,000 square feet on Cerro Colorado, the contents of more than 500 graves have been examined. Also numerous buried living apartments. These open on a series of patios, leading to the graves, and contained a kitchen, small oven, and storage bin. The graves have yielded well-embalmed bodies seated in baskets, wrapped in many windings of mummy cloth, ceremonial and decorative objects of bone, shell, and gold of superior workmanship, great quantities of clothing and textiles, admirably dyed and with harmonious designs of high quality. Once again, however, Chavín influence is not certain.

In due time evidences of Chavín culture appear to have been discovered in Ecuador at Chordeley, Zig-Zag, Azuay, Elena-Pata, and near Quito. At Chordeley a breastplate bore a humanized puma head. Dr. Marshall Saville found fine carved stone slabs and remarkable gold objects at Sisig. It was also confirmed that a stone city of San Agustín in Colombia had kinship with Chavín civilization.

Other Chavín remains were found as far south as Cuzco, Ayaucho, and Arequipa provinces in Peru and at Moxos in Bolivia.

Despite these numerous discoveries, the knowledge of the Chavín era is still meager, the surface barely scratched. As Means complained fretfully in his *Ancient Civilizations of the Andes* (1931), there are probably vast numbers of unknown sites, and even those known—a whole series (he throws out many names)—have never been scientifically investigated; nor has the northern part of the Titicaca basin from La Paz into Peru been explored. Hence the reliable facts about relations between coast and Andean cultures as yet are insufficient to lay the basis for more than conjectures; and he might have added also, insufficient for a proper understanding of the evolution of the famous Tiahuanaco cultural horizons in Bolivia.

He does point out similarities—square-edged reliefs, for instance—between the Chavín sculpturing and the "Weeping God" of Tiahuanaco, the latter a depiction of Viracocha, the Sun God. Yet unpardonably he ascribes the Chavín culture as having been derived from Tiahuanaco II, the latest period, the work of the same people, with the same cult, the same art, the same traditions, but with an interval of a century or two between them. Actually Tiahuanaco II probably flourished thousands of years later than that of Chavín. He even believed Chavín was derived from Chimú and Nazca art! Incredible! Means was a prodigious scholar with considerable field work behind him, but nearly all his conclusions are muddle-headed, and his rigid arbitrary chronology, still accepted by some North American archaeologists, is absurd.

In nearly all things he accepts the early beliefs of Sir Clements Markham, a most fallacious writer, that Chavín art was a "senile art," and he hoped that the transition will be found "from the earlier and simple style of Tiahuanaco to the more elaborate and corrupt work" of Chavín. He even has the bald temerity to cite "the laws of aesthetic evolution."

His mentor, Markham, had even less data to go on, and what was worse, he was a hopeless prude. In his voluminous translations of the early chronicles (which most English-speaking scholars are prone to use rather than go to the originals), he suppresses or puts in an entirely new version whenever sex or copulation are mentioned. Even when not relying on Markham, Means' whole theory of the evolution of later Inca civilization is ludicrous.

Actually, the early Chavín world was almost coextensive, through trade routes, with the vast area of the Inca empire thousands of years later.

These enormous early Chavín temples all reveal a mature, vigorous if uniform art, with profound sense of rhythm, harmony, and proportion and, as Means pointed out in his unconvincing effort to prove the lateness of Chavín art, it had an almost fanatic urge for bilateral symmetry. There is no doubt that it does indicate well-schooled architects, artists, and artisans. Architecture, sculpturing, ceramic, and metal techniques—all were superb. Forms and decorations were often imitative of wooden and gourd utensils from jungle areas. But more elaborate classic forms, higher up, have designs of a far more advanced character.

Mortars were beautifully carved and designed—condors, four-footed jaguars—often were urn shaped, but mostly straight-sided. The Chavínites carved many stone chests, replicas of wood chests. These and other objects were often of onyx, alabaster, turquoise, quartz, etc. Pottery designs were simple, but showed moons, half-moons, crescent moons, suns, stars, jaguars, owls, condors, jaguars or jaguar-like spots, maltese crosses.

Much fine gold work—earrings, finger rings, nose rings, bracelets, plaques—was found at Chavín, Paracas and Kuntur Huasi: at the last place, a collar of gold plates with serpent heads.

They worked the hardest stone competently. Granite of many kinds, often towed from great distances, was quarried, polished, and carved almost as if it were chalk, with complex images and symbols. Secondary stone often used was black slate. Anthropomorphic styled heads of birds, jaguars, and serpents, agents of Oncoy, the Supreme Being, provided the thematic and mythological bases of the Chavín religion—most human figures, animals, and birds, with their flaring toothed mouths, seem ferocious, yet they also brought life, for at their feet were carved the prized plants of the hot selva, from where they must have come; manioc, peanuts, cotton, chilies, etc. Humanized bird heads had a hair-knot; sometimes shown as a serpent or as jaguar claws. Feathers circle the eyesockets; they have thick beak-like noses and the face wrinkles are stylized snakes.

Humanized jaguar heads had a long protruding mouth, a long thick nose almost to the elliptical eyes, with tail-like curls for eyebrows and cheek hollows. Long sharp teeth project downward over the jowls.

Humanized serpent heads, square shaped, were even more fantastic. Eyes were on opposite sides; mouths, with triangular hanging-out tongues and down-jaw fangs, were designed of looping, twisting serpents. As Bertrand Flornoy pointed out in his book on the Incas, these three animal and bird shapes synthesized the early Chavín concept of everlasting supernatural forces and their own identity with them; an attempt to fuse their own beings, their own faces and bodies, with these creatures and thereby with the eternal mystery. Their art symbolized the on-going of existence, for thereby they also revered sacred ancestors, the creatures from which they were personally descended—a realization of biological evolution long predating Darwin's scientific proofs.

The Supreme Deity, Oncoy, the Pleiades, according to both Tello and Carrión, was the god of alimentation.* In June this constellation was directly overhead and marked the winter solstice, which began the Chavín calendar year. He was often shown surrounded by three stars and bearing the useful fruits of the Andes and the jungles.

He is depicted in glory on the Tello Obelisk—a hermaphrodite lizard-dragon and jaguar, with massive, baleful-eyed head and eight down-jabbing tusks. From the massive penis, in the form of a puma head, issues a many-branched flowering plant. The genitals on the opposite side are female. The rest of the body is a fantastic but beautiful mélange of human "tigers," mythical demons, decapitated head and sun-faces. Along the back is a prone human with one arm touching the first of ten figures that stretch on to the dragon's tail. In Oncoy's paws are the jungle fruits: chili, manioc, cotton. Jagged interlocking teeth along his gastric tube—the very framework of the whole body—indicate his colossal appetite. In the Chavín religion, hunger was emphasized in all the arts and the depicting of the gods —an insatiable hunger never alleviated—hunger for food and hunger for the deeper meanings of life. Ahead of him fly three eager messengers: a jaguar, a parrotlike bird (or condor?), and a small river fish. The whole crouching figure mysteriously provides an impression of tremendous power and velocity.

Even Means is forced to admit grudgingly that the allover design has unusual beauty. "The immense intricacy of details, the feather-like and snake-headed side ornaments, the fang-motif, the feather motif, and the puma-face motif, being all arranged with masterly precision and balance . . . an imposing richness of embellishment."

Quite evidently the Oncoy carving is an effort to fuse man with

* The jaguar was identified with the Pleiades by a number of early peoples.

the world about him, with the animals and plants, with the stars in their courses and the heaven beyond. It is also likely that here is an attempted synthesis of the entire Chavín religion and philosophy, the yearly and epochal time cycle when once a year at the summer solstice the Pleiades briefly appeared in the eastern night sky to measure the passage of the days and the year and the wheel of the sun. It represents everything from the realities of earthly life, the basic essentials of that life, on up to the soul of man and his relation to the universe. Here are echoed the reliable periodic manifestations of the sidereal system; here is the index of the unalterable cosmic law, over and beyond ephemeral man and his activities. The pattern, the order of Chavín life was that of eternal life, with which they wished to be joined and interblended, as well as with their Supreme Being, who embodied the whole concept. All their art was an effort to make this eternal order familiar and to hand it on to future generations. And into it entered the timeless abstraction, over and beyond earthly and spiritual utility of art for art's sake. They wished "to create a worthy setting for their gods; mountains were ripped open, earth leveled, stones quarried and engraved, gold melted and impressed with carving. . . ."

"The old Chavín civilization," remarks Carrión Cachot, "was homogeneous in the arts, in ritual, in religion, in race and probably in language. The mother tonque probably had its origin in the forest language, possibly the Acaro, and this in turn gave rise to the Aimara, Cauqui, etc. Chavín is thus the trunk, the root of the great Peruvian family which in later eras produced such great cultural centers as Paracas, Moche, Nazca, Chanca, and Inca; to which civilization it bestowed a unity of race, language, religion, and philosophy—for they are found united by the same foods and the same apparatus, the same common woes and joys, by the utilization of this generous land so magnanimous with the people who once worked it. Thus the Inca empire was merely the crowning civilization that had evolved over a span of 4,000 years, made great with the inventions and progress of hundreds of generations. Its wise social and political organization crystallized the efforts and hopes of thousands of years of experience and common endeavors."

12

Fire on the Andes

TIAHUANACO (Bolivia) was a temple, a city, a period, a style, a culture. Better said, it is a word for at least two cultures. How closely related they are is disputed; how old and how they arose, are also disputed. The time period has been placed from 20,000 B.C. (by a Chilean archaeologist) to some time A.D. (Means). Later dates, but probably B.C., seem indicated, at least for the Tiahuanaco II period, which may have been derived from new peoples, not a refinement of the work of the original builders. Very little has been excavated—mostly by Max Uhle and Arthur Posnansky—and that chiefly restricted to the more obvious edifices. Anywhere, a few feet down, more carved stones are encountered. In fact, the stones for the statues of St. Peter and St. Paul, which after three centuries are still gracing the local adobe church, were found in this way near the portico. Early in the sixteenth century, Juan de Vargas dug up a big store of silver stools and flagons, gold beads, bangles and a huge, gold, human head.

All that is definitely known is that Tiahuanaco, prior to the Inca period, represented a mighty thrust toward art, architecture, religion, social organization, and greatness.*

Mostly the whole matter of origins remains conjectural. Both Cieza and Cobo stated that the resident Indians had no idea who

---

* For several years, extensive new excavations and reconstructions have been carried on, and the Bolivian revolutionary government has erected a magnificent museum at the site.

had built the center, and the cultures succeeding Tiahuanaco have seldom been studied (i.e., the era intervening prior to the Inca Empire, generally called the "Chullpa Period," after the two-story towers of adobe or rough or dressed stone, occasionally carved with snakes or animals, which stand on so many hilltops. These places were used later by the Aimara and Colla for burial of VIPs. There are innumerable Chullpa sites in the Titicaca basin, but Harry Tschopik, Jr. notes that the outstanding sites of Sillustani and Quitumpú show no evidence whatever of Inca or Tiahuanaco derivations. Where Inca pottery does appear, it indicates later conquest).

Were the first builders the Urú (probably Arawak; at least Rivet strongly believed so), who came into the area, also into Chile, very early and who, to this day, claim to be the oldest race on earth, predating even the sun?

The chief authorities believe that the architects were ancestors of the present-day Aimara and Colla. Likely both peoples were widespread there for ages, though there is doubt about the Aimara, for some were settled at Julí, on Lake Titicaca's shore, by the Incas, where they prospered and expanded. To this day on nearby Copacabana Peninsula, there is celebrated the greatest annual fair and religious fiesta of the continent—which goes back to prehistoric times—to which people come with goods and soul-searching even now (thousands of miles through the Andes). But the Aimara language is so widespread in all Bolivia and the entire Titicaca region, that the people can scarcely be accounted for by mere Inca resettlement. They must have been rooted thereabouts as anciently as Tiahuanaco, if not actually at that site.

Edgar Lee Hewett has a low opinion of "the sullen" Aimara. "I cannot conceive of the Aimara as sufficiently virile to have built the great Tiahuanaco establishment." They had only "vestiges of a rudimentary sun cult . . . an elementary deification of the great lake and its islands." He gave all the glory of Tiahuanaco to the Collas. True, the Aimara, until their confidence is won, are like Yankees, silent and standoffish, but this can scarcely be a measure of their innate abilities or virility. A proud people, they have shown tremendous tenacity for centuries in preserving their language, customs, and identity against great odds.

Tschopik, a real authority, tries to explain their dourness which impressed so many outsiders, as being due to the fact that travelers have had contact with most of the Aimara in towns, and on *fincas* and haciendas—the ones grossly exploited by whites rather than those of the free *ayllu* or commune, where a more genial, even gay, spirit is observable in spite of harsh conditions. Luis Valcarcel, in his *Mirador Indio* has noted the same difference in attitude of modern hacienda *yanacones* or serfs among the Quechua, in contrast to those still living in independent *ayllus*.

For all of the Aimara, Tschopik notes, "the struggle for survival is an ever-present reality. . . . Basically an agricultural people, they must contend with poor soil and a limited choice of crops in a region where a harsh climate makes farming precarious. The land, the crops and the flocks comprise all-absorbing interests, but this makes for monotonous daily routine. . . . Recreational activities are few and infrequent." *

The ancient peoples, whether Aimara or not, had the same handicaps, which makes the rise of great Tiahuanaco culture all the more remarkable.

2

Tiahuanaco was set on a flat treeless plain fourteen thousand feet high, lacking in resources, except for a coarse grass that permitted animal husbandry, an area where food crops did not prosper. The endless red earth is monotonous, and this undoubtedly was reflected in the people. Even villages—utilizing the earth in adobe walls—blend with the soil so closely that they are scarcely visible a short distance away. The plain, mostly sodden under leaden skies, is surrounded by grim barren mountains, though in the distance rise the lordly snow giants, Sorata, Huayna Potosí and Illampú. Even the hard, volcanic, andesite stone, used in the Tiahuanaco II period, had to be hauled in from great distances, some blocks weighing a hundred tons. The temples and dwellings covered one-sixth of a square mile.

Statuettes of brown sandstone or adobe were scattered far and wide across the plain, some only a few inches high. These are still sold to visitors by Indians who may be local descendants of the ancient builders, and quite a few objects are genuine. There are innumerable slabs, steles, and statues. The latter were mostly provided with teñons for wall installation. More "realistic" statues had flat faces, prominent cheek bones, jutting jaws, and flaring lips, and

* Visiting the Colquiri mines in April 1961, I found the Aimara workers, though heartlessly exploited, highly intelligent, good-humored, and warmly friendly.

wore headbands. "Conventionalized" statues were large monoliths. Reliefs were carved in gates and on pillars—rather cubistic—with incised textile-type patterns. Later "decadent" manifestations were pillar statues and crude heads, showing human faces, lizards, salamanders, and toads; also geometric designs with stylized heads and faces. Both the classic and late period suggest that textile weaving must have been an important industry, though no examples have survived.

The stones on the various buildings are well dressed, well fitted, usually with angular notches and copper cramps, as Father Cobo noted so long ago, speaking of the "perfection of workmanship": the stones had a "smooth flat finish than which nothing could be better." Carved stone slabs were used for decorations in nearly all periods, ranging from the cruder efforts of Tiahuanaco I, through the precise, tailored, stereotyped work of the classic period, to the "modernistic," or as some writers prefer, "decadent" work, of the last period. However the last shows greater individual freedom and imagination.

The construction is centered by the Acapana, a stone-faced natural hill, surmounted by a stepped pyramid fifty feet high, with reservoir and living apartments on top. Northwest was the later Calassaya, 425 by 424 feet square, constructed of dressed stone uprights walled in with similar well-cut stones, and containing a large inner sunken court. West of this, the "Palace"—195 by 180 feet—was surrounded by double walls. To the east semisubterranean edifices were built with uprights and smaller building blocks. Means, who saw the place only in a tourist fashion, thought these were erected by the first builders; Bennett believes it was a post-Tiahuanaco II construction, utilizing rubble from older buildings.

Well outside the center was Pumma Puncú, a platform of sandstone and basalt blocks, with low seats, which Means believed was the beginning of a never-finished edifice, but more likely was an arena or parade ground that once upon a time was entered by means of large monolithic gates now tumbled down and out of place.

The most dramatic feature of Tiahuanaco was the great "Gate of the Sun," with the "Weeping God," serving as the entrance to the massive Calassaya staircase. It was made from one gigantic stone, and the door entrance was rectangular, not in the rhomboidal (Incan) form. Some claim the figure is Viracocha, the Sun God, but it may well have been a portrait of a mighty ruler. His arms are outspread in a gesture of authority, and his four-fingered hands clutch a spear-thrower and a quiver with two spears, perhaps a megalomaniac ruler's desire for self-perpetuation. He is dressed in an elaborate tunic fringed with puma heads, and is in the center of a frieze of personified birdlike figures in rectangles, all racing toward him, each with flowing headdress and what seem to be a staff or perhaps the royal symbol of authority used by messengers or runners. Perhaps the momentous message of war?

3

Cultural links of Tiahuanaco with Inca, coastal, and Chavín cultures have been hotly disputed. Bennett discards any direct link with Chavín, apparently much older, and he withholds opinion on whether the basic cultural impulse in the rise of Tiahuanaco came from the coast, or whether Tiahuanaco development provided the spur to much coastwide expansion. There is evidence of give or take —perhaps both—with the earliest Nazca civilization of south coastal Peru. Also there seems to be a relationship—perhaps roundabout— between Tiahuanaco and the post-Chavín-Recuay culture. The source would seem to be Recuay, not, as Means believed, Tiahuanaco. The whole matter merits further fieldwork and study. However there was indubitably a coastwide spread of classic Tiahuanaco culture—that has been dubbed "Coastal Tiahuanaco," Middle Ancón, or Epigonal, as far north as Chicama. Whatever such diffusion there was, the Epigonal was absorbed, blended into a new cultural product, a revised style that spread even further north, perhaps into Ecuador. But the whole hen-or-egg question cannot be answered at present, though it would seem that a center so stupendous as Tiahuanaco must have been a great culmination or else a major diffusion point, probably both, considering the many ages it spanned.

Part of this whole jigsaw is the esoteric Chiripa culture along the south shore of Titicaca (reliable dating has never been established) which has no discernible relation to any other society. As described by Alfred Kidder II, the outstanding authority, it was a village society—fourteen double-wall houses, claystone foundations, and sliding panel doors, facing a central plaza—a type of construction encountered nowhere else in the highlands.

The belief that Tiahuanaco was the fountainhead of later Inca culture was first suggested by Father Cobo who visited the Bolivian site in 1610. His theory is unverified, though Means, without presenting evidence, believes certain very ancient parts of Sacsahuamán, the fortress above Cuzco, are of Tiahuanaco inspiration. If so, this is the only evidence to date of any spread into the Peruvian area. Also Means lays great stress on a single apparent Tiahuanaco artifact found at Cuzco—somewhat pointless considering the developed trade of the Andean region as far back as prehistoric records are available.

John Howland Rowe, a more reliable authority, says bluntly that "Inca civilization" was the product of a long development in the Valley of Cuzco itself; probably true to a point, though only one pre-Inca period has been unearthed, the Champata, featured by crude walls of undressed stone, laid on end, sunken courts, and no carving, just black pottery with appliqué or incised designs. Champata may be of Chiripa origin. Tello, however, traces Chavín influence, sans any stylized Tiahuanaco connection. Bennett, always reliable—and conservative—declares that Champata is very early and "certainly does not explain the later Incan development." Nor does their belief, as Rowe implies, that the earliest Inca period rose as an isolated phenomenon—quite the contrary.

Without trying to link up Tiahuanaco with other areas, it is observable that the Tiahuanaco I builders used only red-brown sandstone found only three miles from the site. That culture had limited geographic range, nowhere else apparently except on Titicaca and Coati islands in the lake—indicated by the simple incised and colored pottery of attractive shapes and designs and a few animal imitations. Flat bowls had handles. But here again, the chicken or the egg problem exists.

Mountainous Titicaca Island, with its score of bays and coves, is one of the most picturesque on earth—as Adolph E. Bandelier so vividly described it and as any present-day traveler can easily verify —and was and is a sacred Aimara center. The island is covered with *comida de oso*—"bear food"—a spiny yucca, useful for food, medicines, and other products, and some twenty additional medicinal plants are also gathered there. Besides, it had a teeming bird life. Compared to Tiahuanaco proper, the Titicaca region, though so high and often bleak, was paradise. For Valcarcel it was the great mother area of highland cultures and peoples—and also of the Inca forebears.

Classic Tiahuanaco had little more diffusion than that of the earlier era. It scarcely reached beyond the north shore of Titicaca, though Pucará in Puno seems to have been a center.

<h1 style="text-align:center">4</h1>

"Coastal Tiahuanaco," not widespread but prevalent until Inca times, left beautifully shaped and decorated pottery that has a certain gayety, with smiling serpent-jaguar heads and genial faces, sharply contrasted designs and colors, mostly geometric. The llama is a common topic, suggesting Andean origin. In similar style were gold, silver, copper, and bronze objects—cramps, tools, axes, knives, brooches, clasps, fiesta or religious masks; all were angular, rigid, conventionalized. This Tiahuanaco influence was of sufficiently long standing for a new defined character to evolve—as in the Ica, Nazca, and Moche-Chimú cultures.

The Chimú culture and rule extended as far north as Ecuador. It left one of the clearest records—chiefly on clay which has survived because of the dry climate—of any ancient people, a story of the occupations, habits, amusements, beliefs, and resources of a remarkable society.

The colossal Chanchan—an amazing expanse of covered over adobe buildings and tombs—rose as an elaborate vast metropolis, which Hewett called "the Babylon of America."

César García believes that Chanchan flourished a thousand to fifteen hundred years before Christ and lasted down until the twelfth century. Means, of course, believes that it is a late after-Christ expression, partly coterminous with Inca civilization which took it over.

Chanchan and Pacasmayo replaced much older cities, such as Moche and Pacatnamú. Moche is still visible on the other side of the river, within sight of the ocean. The Pyramid of the Sun there was twice as high as any structure in Chanchan. It and the lesser Huaca of the Moon were both built of large rectangular adobe blocks.

The Chanchan burial ground, which people still rake over, scattering bones and skulls, hoping to come upon ancient treasure, is far-flung. It has been suggested that a subterranean passage led from the Palace to the burial ground of the sacred royal mummies, richly attired and feathered, with gold and silver jewelry, pottery, and numerous other articles, sometimes the skeletons of animals. Some sarcophagi are roofed with stone slabs or have tall pyramidal markers. But the pottery mostly was inferior to that of earlier Nazca and Moche work—peoples who developed two of the world's greatest art forms.

Chanchan proper was composed of numerous walled-in units, each more or less self-sufficient, with irrigated fields, stone reservoirs, fountains, pyramids, and gabled houses, adorned with alto-relievo or with thick stucco and wall paintings, niches for figures, and pleasing clay arabesques, mostly geometric—rhomboids, crosses, and stylized sea birds. The main platform-elevated palace of slanting walls, with its broad central entrance terrace, numerous apartments, galleries, and halls, had some doorways forty feet wide; quite a feat, since they were sustained only by strong bamboo and adobe.

Diked salt marshes were developed for growing totora reeds, so necessary for mats and boats. Local fishermen still use this type of vessel: a thick bundle of reeds tightly bound with vegetable fibers and with a space cut out for kneeling. In water, the reeds swell up and soon make a watertight contraption. When waterlogged, they are pulled upon the warm sand and allowed to dry out. Provided with a strong paddle, fishermen venture far out to sea, and even hundreds of miles up and down the coast.

The Spaniards discovered Chanchan soon after founding Trujillo nearby in 1535, and thereafter it fired the imagination of each and every investigator—Squier, O'Donovan, Markham, Bandelier, Uhle, Perfecto Velardi, Tschudi, Rubero, and Tello.

To complete one's picture of Chanchan one must visualize fifty thousand people crowded into the great plaza, with their wares, fruits, vegetables, pottery, vivid textiles, ornaments, and animals—from dawn to dark, when the night fires leapt up, illuminating the arabesques on the great buildings. One must visualize the august rulers and councilors in the palace, presided over by the richly robed Chimú Emperor himself; the priests swinging their golden censers in the temples, the hosts performing ceremonial chants and dances and touching their foreheads to the pavement in adoration.

5

Nearly ten centuries ago, Manco Capac, the first Inca Emperor, stood in the "Cave of Royal Windows" and looked out over a fair valley of the Andes near where two huge rivers run down to join others flowing into the Amazon. Such was the account of legendary history told in 1634 by Fernando Montesinos, about a hundred years after the Conquest, a version also repeated in modern survival legends.

Other versions are given by Garcilaso and various early chroniclers. The most common is that of four brothers, called *Ayar*, "Wild Quinóa," and four sister-wives called *Mama*, or "Mother." Individually they were: Manco Capac, Warrior, Salt, Chile Pepper; the women were Pure, Huaca or Temple or God, Aunt Weed, and Rahua. According to one account, all perished during the march, except Manco Capac and his wife Mama Occlo, or were turned to stone in divers manners.

Another record tells of the "Origin Tombs," composed of three small hill-caves, about eighteen miles from Cuzco. From the side caves emerged various prominent Inca ancestors: the founder of the Empire and his wife emerged from the central cave.

A much earlier account by Blas Valera took the story of the dynasty back to 1300 B.C. to a mythical Piruná Manco. But Manco Capac's story shines with brighter credibility.

Rowe accepts as established fact thirteen rulers from Manco Capac to Atahualpa. With the exception of Manco Capac—reputedly turned to stone, a common legend among many early peoples—the alleged bodies of the other twelve had been preserved:

1. Manco Capac (the Dawn Cave founder, *c*. A.D. 1200).
2. Sinchi Rocha.
3. Lloque Yupanqui.
4. Mayta Capac.
5. Capac Yupanqui.
6. Inca Roca.
7. Yahuar Huacac.
8. Viracocha Inca.
9. Pachacuti (one of the first great conquerors, 1438–71 A.D.).
10. Topa Inca Yupanqui (who carried the empire to the Pacific Coast to Chile as far as the Maule River; to Ecuador where was built the great coastal city of Tanebamba; possibly to the Galápagos Islands and the Amazon headwaters. He was a mighty road and bridge builder. 1471–93 A.D.).
11. Huayna Capac (1493–1525).
12. Huascar (1525–32).
13. Atahualpa (1532–3).

To this list must be added the brief rule of Inca Urcón, half brother of Inca Pachacuti. Pachacuti ordered Urcón's name stricken from the royal lineage—in the true style of a Stalin purging a Trotsky.

6

The people—that fine spring morning ten centuries ago—gathered outside the magic cave, as soon as the news of the arrival of the god-like stranger spread. The miraculous royal person and his sister-wife Mama Occlo (most Incas married sisters) had come, some said, from the island of Titicaca (Garcilaso's version); others said, from the Three Windows in the deep Apúrimac Gorge. Manco Capac (with three brothers and sister-wives) led forth ten marching tribes. Likely enough the survivor, Manco, and his wife, took over a town already existing in Cuzco Valley.

Various legends tell of their battles with the Hualla there, how one of the queen's sisters killed a Hualla with a stone bola, cut out his entrails and lungs, and blew them up to terrifying size as big as balloons (like a tale from Vasari), which so terrified the rest of the people, all fled from the valley. . . .

Manco Capac stepped forth commandingly into the early dawn—clad in plates of glittering gold and wearing a gold crown with bright feathers.

"I am the son of the Sun," he told them, and hurled his golden staff across the plain, farther than any other man could.

It stuck upright in the deep rich earth, humming like a song in the thin high air.

"There," he said, "we will build a temple to the Sun, to Viracocha, who makes the crops grow and brings all blessings. There we will build a city of stone palaces, a city more splendid than any the world has ever known."

They called it Cuzco—"Navel of the World."

They laid out two vast squares: the Joy Plaza for the fiesta of the people, jaguar dances, and condor dances; the Plaza of Tears, the "Holy Plaza," for Inca nobles and priests in great religious fiestas. There, in gorgeous processions, they and the warriors brought corn to the feet of goddess Mama Saca, or sacrificed llamas on the altars, or danced about the golden rope of the Sun God, carried each year to Lake Titicaca to be sunk in its waters.

They laid out four wide avenues, paved with stones in mosaic patterns that led out across the plains and mountains to the four quarters of their great empire, called Tahuantinsuyu.

Over the centuries they put up massive walls and buildings, with smooth-hewn blocks of dark gray stone that weathered brown and was cut in forms pentagonal, hexagonal, octagonal, twelve-sided even, often irregular or neatly rectangular, even square, but perfectly fitted together like gigantic jigsaw puzzles.

One twelve-sided stone in the later Huayna Capac Palace—"the chief or key to the whole edifice," is still in the great wall opposite the present "House of the Admiral." One stone in that wall bears carvings of what appears to be a mastodon and some other prehistoric creature. Cuzco became a city of forts, palaces, schools (richly carved), military academies, sports fields (*canchas,* a word still used throughout South America), "The House of Six Pumas," "The House of Seven Serpents," museums, zoological and biological gardens, prisons, storehouses, convents, and temples. Every street had its altar or shrine—Polo de Ondegardo counted 320 of them.

Above all other shrines was Coricancha (Garden of Gold), the Sun Temple, where the priests burned coca incense in twelve huge gold urns and sprinkled holy water brought in by gold pipes to the fountain of gold spouts. At dawn they chanted—just as the Sun struck through upon the golden disc encircled with emeralds, chalcedony, and turquoise, with its radiant Sun Face and flaming brow. Gold, early chroniclers state, was mixed with the mortar for the Sun Temple and for the later Emperor's Palace; the walls were lined with sheets of pure gold, and the Emperor's Throne was solid gold on a thick gold slab.

A stone schoolhouse covering five blocks was built back of the first royal palace, the Cora Cora. There were taught language, religion, history, and the reading of *quipús,* those knotted strings on which were recorded statistics and the census, but also poetry and other things.

The census was so exact, according to Garcilaso, that the emperor had a record of every pair of alpaca sandals beside every bed and hammock in the realm. The Inca had his best craftsmen make clay relief maps of every town and every province.

They built and they kept on building, till Cuzco was a great labyrinth of a city, a labor costing centuries of effort. Cieza de León described many of the dazzling buildings erected by Inca Yupanqui in the heyday of the city's splendor. As it expanded, other plazas, parks, botanical and zoological gardens, and schools were added. The gardens were adorned with life-size gold and silver images of every animal and bird in the realm.

Garcilaso named the twelve chief wards of the city, each an *ayllu* of the nobility, descendants of the Incas. And to house the people that surged in from all over the empire, numerous suburbs, mostly adobe, sprang up, such as Carminaqua, Cavaucac, Tocacache, and Colcampata.

After an attack by the Pocra, an adjacent tribe, which almost toppled Inca supremacy, a colossal fortress—the third great fortification of the city—was started by Inca Yupanqui on Sacsahuamán ("The Satisfied Falcon"), a crest high above the houses and palaces, a massive edifice which, according to Cieza, required 20,000 men to build, though another chronicler puts the figure at 30,000. Workers' houses were built nearby. Four thousand men worked the stone; 6,000 dragged the blocks to the site with huge leather and agave ropes; the rest worked excavating to bedrock and putting in foundations, placing the stones. The place was planned to be so well built "it would last as long as the world."

It was 1,000 feet long and 600 feet wide and some of the stones in its sheer lofty walls were as big as small houses.

"The walls," wrote Cieza, "were of enormous impressive stones. Some are 12x20 and others bigger than an ox, all fitted so delicately, that not even a *real* (a small coin) can be pushed between them. . . . I myself noticed one stone, 270 of my hand-spans around, and so high it seemed to have been born there, and all the Indians say the stone got tired when it got that far, and couldn't be moved from the spot. Had it not been dressed, one would have believed . . . that human strength was not great enough to have gotten it there."

Actually parts may be pre-Incan and may date back thousands of years. The building of the final great edifice, however, took most of the lifetime of Yupanqui, his son Tupac, and his grandson Huayna Capac.

Outjutting semicircular defense parapets with loopholes commanded every inch of possible enemy approach—a most impregnable construction, brilliantly engineered, both architecturally and militarily.

Beyond a wide parade ground, a polished stone throne—The Suchuma—and a small amphitheater were cut from the granite so the Inca could review his forces and preside over fiestas.

Alongside the many winding stone steps leading up to Sacsahuamán heights, on market and fiesta days, scores of other mountain peoples, arriving in multitudes, danced across a sea of blood-red *muccho* flowers, to the wail of *quena,* guitar, and harps. The women of one remote tribe wore short stiff flaring skirts, ballet style, their bare legs graceful as those of the deer. They danced with branches of white waxen leaves that fluttered loose and drifted in the thin air over the low roofs like a sea of white butterflies.

From the massive Sacsahuamán ramparts, pride of Inca might, one could gaze out over the stone city with its forest of towers, over the surrounding fields across the Tiger-Trail fields to the more arid plain and high barren crags.

At hot springs, also above the city, were carved from solid stone the splendid Inca baths. Not far away, hidden in a grove, were the Ñusta baths, and males who spied there were turned into stone by protecting Caullaca, Goddess of Chastity.

And from Sacsahuamán, two streams rushed down, the Huatanarú and Tullumaya, passing between stone channels, at places covered with stone slabs. Other water was brought in by stone aqueducts, partly still in use. It was a clean healthy city, a beautiful city, at its apogee more impressive than any other on earth.

Garcilaso waxed eloquent about all the "greatest and most superb of the edifices the Incas raised to demonstrate their majesty and power." Cuzco seemed to have been "reared by enchantment, by demons, not by men," for the "walls were more like cliffs than walls." All the more marvelous because the gigantic stones had to be transported over "steep mountains and abrupt declivities . . . from long distances" by "main force!" And how could they be fitted so accurately "that the joint often could hardly be discovered"?

Pedro de Ondegardo summarized it all: "That city of Cuzco was the house and habitation of the gods. Scarcely a fountain, a well or wells that did not speak of mystery."

It was a city of male mountains and uplifted crags, ancient fortresses and bold towers, of conquering warriors and imperial splendors, a city chained to the Sun forever with golden links. There the Sun ruled and still rules, and all Cuzceños through all history have been Children of the Sun. The gigantic altars of the Andes themselves are Temples of the Dawn, Temples of the Sun. Temples and Gardens of Silver. Temples and Gardens of Gold. Such is the chant of Peruvian poets.

7

It was from Cuzco and the later Sacsahuamán that over the centuries, the Inca armies—archers, slingers, knife-club wielders, and pikemen advanced south along both sides of lofty Lake Titicaca into Bolivia, on into Chile and Argentina. They marched north along the three lofty Andean ranges—the White, the Black, and the Blue Ranges, through lush upper Amazon valleys on to Ecuador and Colombia. Before campaigns and battle, they laid corn at the feet of Mama Sora, Mother Maize, and sang their Victory Chant:

> From his skull we shall drink;
> We shall adorn ourselves with his teeth;
> His bones will serve as our flutes;
> With his skin for a drum, we shall dance.

They sang the "March of the Inca Warriors," a grandiose beat of battle and victory, twined through with the tears of parting from loved ones and the grief of death.

They drove back the Pocras, then the Chancas, from the very walls of the city, and broke the latter's strength in open battle on Ichupampa Plain beyond Apúrimac. Over the decades, they moved down to the foothills, on down to the desert coast, where they overwhelmed the territories which once held the Ica and Nazca cultures and the far-flung realm of the Chimú. They made the terrific crossing of the Andes into Chile and camped under the snows of Aconcagua, mightiest mountain of the continent. In Bolivia, they built a war fleet of five hundred balsa rafts to carry ten thousand men down the Beni to invade the Amazon forests.

It was Inca Huayna Capac who battered down the great Ecuadorian empire of the Cara and probably took an Ecuadorian princess for his wife—Pacha, daughter of the ruler of Quito, mother-to-be of Atahualpa. And so the Incas made themselves masters of the Andes, the Pacific coast, and all the western headwaters of the Amazon. Only the Auraucanians in central and southern Chile and the Jívaro in interior Ecuador on the frontiers were able to hold them at bay. And on the edge of the great Argentine Pampa, they paused dismayed, not having the techniques or means of transportation to penetrate that vast and level expanse of awesome prairie.

8

The Inca ruled by divine right as a descendant of the Sun and had absolute powers, restricted only by custom and fear of revolt. Actually the primary tradition of the land and of the dynasty was the obligation to see that the people were well served, prosperous, and contented. The people, were not, as some commentators have maintained, wholly passive subjects, though imperial demands were inexorable and punishment severe and even drastic. But their collective system functioned with individual and village participation on a voluntary basis, a degree of freedom on the lower levels if not in higher affairs. In few societies has it ever been different, even today, though sometimes other illusions are cherished. The obligation of service to the commonwealth, with which the Inca was identified, was deeply imbued in the Incas, especially in later centuries, and a similar spirit of service also imbued the Supreme Inca, the nobility and governing circles. A certain doctrine and practice of civic rights prevailed, but more important in that early era, there was a guarantee of economic security for all.

This resulted in a few unique laws. Thus if robbery was committed, the local Curaca was punished on the theory that if he was administering his office properly, no one would have any reason to steal.

The Inca wore no distinctive clothing, except his special fringed *llautu,* but his attire was of the finest quality, and he enjoyed special deference at meals, fiestas, and all public appearances. Also he and his class absorbed a considerable share of the products of the empire, though perhaps a smaller proportion than in the modern state, democratic or otherwise, and he commanded large labor forces, for otherwise court luxury in sumptuous palaces could not have been maintained, Cuzco could not have been built, and the vast public works could not have been constructed or maintained.

As a symbol of authority, he carried a gold, star-headed mace, and two attendants carried the royal standard in pairs, small cotton or woolen pennants, with the royal arms painted on so thickly the cloth stood out stiffly. The emperor sat on a low redwood (in later eras a solid gold) throne, eight inches high. He was addressed as "Unique Inca," "Son of the Sun," "Lover of the Poor."

Court etiquette was rigid. Even nobles had to remove their sandals and carry a token burden on their backs and kiss the ground when coming into his presence. Estete, Pizarro, Cieza, Polo, and others observed and described this ritual. When he visited the provinces, his litter was decorated with drapes embroidered with the sun, moon, and serpents. The fittings were of solid gold, and it had two gold arches encrusted with precious stones. At the head of his column marched two thousand "slingers," able to throw darts or stones from leather slings. At the rear marched two thousand soldiers of high Inca caste. Closely guarding the royal litter were two thousand trusted Cañari royal guards in resplendent uniforms, from a conquered province south of Quito. When the Cañari finally gave in to Inca overlordship, the Emperor Topa Yupanqui told them, "No men in the empire are braver. No men are better fighters. Henceforth, only the men of Cañari shall guard the palace and the person of the Inca." They remained loyal for centuries.

At his death, the emperor's entrails were kept in a special receptacle, and the body embalmed with herbs. His favorite women and servants volunteered to die also, and were made drunk at a farewell dance and strangled.

The top nobility—the Incas—as distinguished from the emperor himself and his Coya or queen and his sister-wife—were all of royal blood, except for wives or concubines chosen from the Ñusta convents or a few commoners who married Incas, a practice frowned upon, and sometimes harshly forbidden by the Inca. The Incas were known as "Big Ears" to the Spaniards, because of the enormous ear plugs they wore, often of gold or silver, and were called Sinchi, a prestige title. In Cuzco there were ten or twelve Inca *ayllu*, usually kinfolk descended from a given emperor. The Manco Capac *ayllu*, of course, was very numerous. The number of Incas in the capital itself was given as anywhere from five hundred to more than a thousand.

The Incas were not idlers. They provided the top administrators of the empire and their sons received special training and periodically had to perform formal menial duties alongside the peasants, the sweepers of temples, the royal herdsmen. They became specialized in various branches of government, engineering, and economy. Doubtless some local administrators were also drawn from the Inca group, though governors and chiefs were usually hereditary. But there were plenty of tasks that obliged Inca officials to fan out over the empire and even to take up permanent residence far from the capital.

Not that all in the empire was always peaceable. Some local peoples who voluntarily gave obeisance to the emperor and the Sun God were allowed to retain their chieftains and curacas; sometimes given tribes ruled almost autonomously over considerable areas. This led to suballiances, to a jealous balance of power, on occasion to local wars—at least until the assimilative genius of the Inca had smoothed down the wild plumage. The empire in various periods was rent by dynastic struggles: this was true when the Spaniards came. The two half brothers Atahualpa and Huascar were at each other's throats to decide the issue of the throne, and this spelled bloodshed and much tragedy for the people. Over so many centuries, it was inevitable that numerous convulsions occurred, wars and even revolutions of a sort—though they were chiefly the palace-guard type of change-over. But the empire followed a course of expansion and consolidation, plus expanding growth and prosperity, so that such disturbances were absorbed in the general current of improved well-being.

Nor was it rule merely by royal whim, however absolute the Inca's authority. Ancient customs were strong and had to be respected, and there were recognized laws and governing methods which could not be set aside without trouble. Society and the institutions that had grown up had enduring validity and had to be respected.

Laws, if often severe, were reasonable and, according to Garcilaso, justly administered, trials being conducted with proper witnesses and defense procedures, though appeals from sentences were not allowed. Punishments consisted of public rebuke, loss of office, exile to the coca plantations, torture, and death. Death was imposed for stealing from the royal fields or herds, burning bridges, or breaking into Ñusta convents. But only the emperor or the governor could impose the death sentence; curacas who did so might be put to death themselves. Not many evildoers were imprisoned, though this was the fate for "traitors," doubtless a flexible category, who were cast into subterranean dungeons along with wild animals and poisonous snakes and rarely survived. Though the worst possible punishment for the proud Incas was believed to be censure or demotion, sometimes the penalty for their misconduct was more severe than that imposed on commoners. Adultery, for instance. The punishment might be relatively mild for commoners, but for the Incas it brought the death penalty to both parties. Adulteresses were usually hung by their hair from a lofty crag till dead: their chant was supposed to be "Father Condor, carry me hence; Brother Falcon, guide me hence."

9

The empire was divided, about 1460, by Inca Pachacuti into four administrative units: (1) central and northern Peru and Ecuador; (2) the southwest, including the coast; (3) the eastern forest; (4) Titicaca, Bolivia, northern Argentina, and Chile, by far the largest unit. These "Four Quarters" were administered by nonhereditary appointed military commanders (the *apo*) with headquarters in Cuzco, where the corners of the four quarters met. They acted as a State Council.

Each Quarter was divided into many provinces, not equal in area or population, but based on historical, tribal, or geographical expediency. Each had its local capital and religious center, and the citizens of each province wore a distinctive headdress, so that when they gathered in the capital they made a colorful spectacle. The province was ruled by a royal governor—*Toricoc*—who exercised both administrative and judicial powers. The governor's subordinates were curacas, classified according to the number of taxpayers, viz., *Hono Curaca,* Chief of 10,000, down to *Pacaca Curaca,* Chief of 100. Two types of foremen were responsible to the curaca, those supervising fifty and those over ten taxpayers. The statistical reports of these curacas were delivered by the governor on *quipús* every December at the great Raymi fiesta.

The emperor also had recourse to both open and secret Inspectors —*Tocoyricoc,* "He Who Sees Well," through whom he checked on any mistakes, dishonesty, or maladministration, and ascertained the need for public works or reforms.

Each province was divided into two or three *saya,* in turn divided into *ayllu* or communal landowning village units of varying size. Thus the empire—at least the central part—was well organized, administered according to annual census-taking, which divided the population into five age groups, the young and old (excluded from civic obligations), two middling groups, and teen-agers.

This precise organization did not mean interference, beyond a certain point, with local customs and habits. In the broken-up terrain, with so many small walled-off valleys and pockets of land, so

232

many varied peoples and "races," so many ancient traditions, there was no way to impose conformity of modes of living; the empire could hardly have survived any such attempt. To this extent there was the breath of freedom, of voluntary effort, in all local activities. As with most mountain folk, very likely, the air of freedom was in their nostrils from birth.

10

Through the long centuries, the Incas pulled together hundreds of dispersed tribes speaking many languages, organized them into practical administrative districts, and pushed the spread of the Quechua language. In the highlands were forty-three provinces, and on the coast at least thirty-eight from Túmbez to Anca. In Bolivia, in addition to the Aimara language districts, the Incas organized four non-Aimara-Colla districts, in some of which were settled colonies from other parts of the empire. Of these, the Chicha were important, because, as Cobo noted, they paid their labor tax by providing carved redwood logs for the sacrificial fiestas in Cuzco.

Among more important highland entities besides the Quechua (Warm Valley People of Abancay and Cuzco provinces) were:

1. Densely populated Huanacabamba, "Valley of the Field Guardian." Cieza wrote that they told him they had once been eaters of human flesh.

2. Cajamarca, "Town in a Ravine," once head of a powerful independent state, allied with the coastal Chimú, was possibly descended from the Chavín peoples long, long before. Their capital, the summer home of the Incas, was famous for its sumptuous buildings, hot baths, and strong forts. There can still be seen, and still used, the old Inca bath, really a small pool, cut from solid rock and supplied with water boiling from the mineral springs, and water cooled in an adjacent reservoir.

3. Chachapoya, a warlike people with unusually light skin, divided into various strong tribes.

4. Huayla, "Meadow," a group notorious for homosexuality, according to Cieza and Garcilaso.

5. Huánuco, "Eyebrow of the Mountain," a handsome city of eternal spring on the left bank of the Marañón. Today the modern city is located on the Huallaga River.

6. Chinchaycocha, "Lake of the Lynx," on the banks of Junín Lake. Llama-breeding country par excellence. According to Estete,

Huayna Capac brought balsas all the way from Túmbez to attack the island towns.

7. Yauyo, once a great Chavín center, a prosperous area with 10,000 taxpayers.

8. Huanca (including Jauja), 25,000 taxpayers. Builders of balsa rafts and round houses.

9. Angará. To bring these warlike people to more civilized peaceful habits, the Inca settled many colonists from Cajamarca and elsewhere among them.

10. Vilcas. The most important center north of Cuzco. Largely peopled by Antas, "Big-Ear" folk. Extremely important Huamanga (now Ayacucho) was the center. Emperor Viracocha married an Anta princess to strengthen his hand against the warlike Chanca.

11. Rucana, "Finger People." From these sturdy folk were chosen the emperor's litter bearers.

12. Chanca (Andahuayla), going back to Chavín days, was the most unruly of all the provinces, first and last. At one time they drove out every Quechua settler and, according to Cieza, during Viracocha's reign nearly wrecked the Incan state.

13. Vilacampa, "Valley of the Narcotic Berry." Here in the rugged mountains northwest of Cuzco, for forty years after the Spanish Conquest, the Inca dynasty there continued to maintain an independent state. Cobo and Antonio de la Calancha (1638) had much to say about this area.

14. Parihuancocha, "Flamingo Lake," was minutely described by Garcilaso and Juan Pachacuti.

15. The Chumpivilca, "Famous dancing peoples," paid their labor tax by dancing at court.

16. Arequipa, "Behind the Needle" (referring to famous slim Mount Misti), was easily taken over by the Quechuas after volcanic devastation.

11

Cuzco was located halfway between the great Apúrimac and Urubamba rivers, which flow together to become the Ucayali, one of the grandest Amazon tributaries, in places "more like a lake curving between distant banks and large islands." On its banks, just below the Inca realm, lived and still live the independent Chama Indians in a land of alligators and enormous turtles, white herons and scarlet flamingos, a gay folk always dancing, singing, and drinking *masato* wine, but good workers, too, who made and still make, the finest pottery in Peru, decorated with beautiful designs painted on by human-hair brushes.

Chama products were highly prized by the Quechua. Many tropical fruits came from there. Originally, the old Chama legend states, they had only black *genipa* fruit, which they made into mush, but one day two birds, Mashentari and Ruirú, visited a beautiful girl alone in her hut. The birds scornfully refused to share her *genipa* mush and told her to strike her knee with a stick. Ripe plantains tumbled forth. Next, Mashentari struck more plantains from her left knee, and from the other manioc, sweet potatoes, yams, and corn, and showed her how to plant them.

From the Chamas, the Incas obtained all these products and also turtle oil, palm oil, sarsaparilla, vanilla, cinnamon, balsam, salted fish, manatee lard, balsa flowers for mattresses and pillows, wax, cacao, and tobacco. Chama reeds and canes and bamboo were used to make mats, benches, and musical instruments. Their balsa wood was used for boats and causeways. The gray *chonta* palm wood, tough but springy, was required for spears and bows and arrows, tools, fish hooks, houses, and bridges.

To control this trade and keep out rude warlike tribes from the hot country, who, it is reported, at one time actually overran Cuzco, the Incas built a chain of fortresses all down the Urubamba River gorge. At first, the most impressive was Ollantaytambo. Others were built and, finally, Machu Picchu—"The Old Mountain"—a truly magnificent and incredible white stone fortress and temple city, with walls sheer with the two thousand foot cliff that rises on three sides from the Urubamba gorge, green with boiling spume far below the windows and ramparts. Circling all about the city, higher still in the sky, great snow giants of the Andes sparkle with never-melting ice.

Hiram Bingham of Yale, who discovered Machu Picchu, overgrown by dense semitropical forest for nearly four centuries, reversed the chronology, insisting that Machu Picchu is not a late settlement, but actually the fabulous Tampu Tocco, the original seat of Inca culture, which was expanded and embellished for half a dozen centuries: that from here the Quechua advanced upstream, planting new cities and building more farm terraces, and finally moved on to conquer Cuzco, which in turn may actually be much older, perhaps founded originally by other peoples.

The Incas managed to hide the existence of Machu Picchu from the conquering Spaniards during the entire three centuries of their rule. Legend has it that four Inca emperors, postdating the Conquest, hid out there and secretly directed revolts against the intruders.

Machu Picchu was reached from Cuzco down the Anta River, then the Urubamba gorge, beneath some of the most grandiose snow mountains of the entire Andean chain, such as Veronica and Cachicata, frosted with lavender glaciers. Right up to the snow line, all these mountain walls were terraced with stone and in many, crops and fruit trees still flourish. Palaces, ruined temples, fortresses, cities are everywhere—except for small modern towns—badly overgrown by jungle. Halfway to the old fortress is a still-used Inca suspension bridge, with modern steel cables substituted for the original thick fiber cables, but the stone river pier and the stone anchor towers of the ancient time are as intact as the day they were erected. The valley, in Inca days, was densely populated, with nearly every inch cultivated.

At Machu Picchu stone terraces stretch back from the cliff in dizzy ascent up the mountainside. Thousands of stone steps were cut out of solid rock, and polished stone houses were built with sturdy doors and windows and massive stone lintels. At every point where there is a fine view the Incas carved out lookout seats. They brought water through a marvelous mountain-bored aqueduct and cut sixteen bathrooms and shower stalls out of solid rock, with stone hand-holds and recesses for soaps and oils. Some of the bathtubs, with their corner seats, are as modern in design as in this present year of grace. The city was dedicated to Viracocha, the Sun God, supreme in the Inca pantheon, and they set up their stone sundial for the ceremony of Inti-Huatana, the "Tying of the Sun." It is near the Temple of the Three Windows on the Sacred Plaza. Back from the river cliff is the semicircular Palace—almost unique in the history of Inca architecture (save for the wall of the Sun temple in Cuzco) for they preferred straight lines. There lived the Ñustas— the Sacred Virgins. On the opposite side of the city are cemeteries and the Royal Mausoleum, where mummies of Incas were placed, clad in gold.

Below, along the river, they built a highway down to Quillabamba

236

in the jungles, thus making Machu Picchu the magnificent gateway to the rain-forest. It stood guard for centuries over the vast Amazon basin.

12

Dress and customs varied widely from village to village and province to province, although there were broad regional distinctions: coast, foothills, highlands, the eastern rain-forest. Clothing on the hotter coast was often made of cotton; that in the highlands of wool. Weaving both in the highlands and on the coast was competent and beautiful, mostly alpaca and vicuña wool with some cotton. Spinning was carried on at all hours—as it is today—the distaff being spun in the air or on the ground. The belt loom was first used by the coast Moche people—two parallel rods supplying the warp and fastened to a tree or post, the other belted around the weaver's middle, a type that soon spread to all highland Indians, though the Aimara used chiefly a horizontal loom. The heddle in both types was a light rod with loops which passed over alternate warp threads. Tapestries and heavy rugs were woven on a four-pole vertical frame, as was also the finest cloth, called *compi*.

On the coast particularly, fine hammered gold or silver was sometimes sewn to cloth in patterns or as sequins. The Quechua also did skillful feather-weaving.

In the highlands from puberty on, men wore a breechclout, a sleeveless knee-length slipover tunic and a large wool cloak, like a two-piece blanket, the ends knotted over the chest or one shoulder. Often a sort of headband or *llautu* was worn, but without the gold and fringe that featured the Inca "crown." The Aimara wore knitted stocking-caps. Other groups, especially the women, wore felt derbies and some a felt "stovepipe." Often they also used a woven headband and folded kerchief.

Women wore ankle-length wraparound dresses, with waist sash, fastened with straight gold, silver, or bronze pins at the shoulder, and a shorter cloak held at the breast by a pin with a large flat head that could also be used as a knife. Both men and women wore leather thong sandals or fur moccasins.

Jewelry consisted of large ear plugs, bracelets, necklaces with a large chest disc. Women wore no earrings or plugs, only their ornamental pins, and shell or seed necklaces.

Hair-do's varied considerably from province to province—as is recorded in decorative material and told about by Poma and Garcilaso. Poma's illustrations show Rucana and Colla males with long flowing hair. Mostly, male hair was cut with obsidian knives in forehead bangs and a long bob behind, so arranged as to cover the ears. Women usually parted their hair and let it flow long down their backs, though in some places they wore twin braids, or else numerous smaller braids, as among Aimara women. Combs were made of thorns set between strips of wood.

The face was painted for war and ceremonies, also in mourning—mostly cinnabar red and achiote purple. Some tattooing was done in coastal regions.

13

Family and conjugal relations were precise, the latter quite complicated, however. The words for brother and sister (applied also to cousins) varied according to the sex of the speaker. A mother had no separate words for son and daughter—both were "children."

Diego Gonzales Holguín (1607) listed most of the Quechua kinship terms. *"Cosa"* was husband, *"Quari,"* a man as opposed to a woman; *"Huami"* was wife.

Terms designated for parent group were:

> *Yuya.* Father, father's brother
> *Mama.* Mother, mother's sister
> *Cori.* Father's son (also nephew)
> *Ososi.* Father's daughter (also niece)
> *Huachua.* Mother's child or niece

Terms for the brother group were:

> *Huauqui.* Man's brother or male cousin
> *Para.* Man's sister or female cousin
> *Ñaña.* Woman's sister or female cousin
> *Tora.* Woman's brother or male cousin

Before giving birth, a woman often fasted (as did her husband), confessed to a priest, and prayed in the *huaca* or shrine. Midwives were used, though many deliveries were unassisted. Immediately after giving birth, the mother washed herself and baby in the nearest stream.

The baby was kept tied loosely in a shawl in a cradle till able to walk. It was weaned a year or two after birth, at which time an elaborate "hair-cutting" fiesta was held with relatives and friends.

238

The oldest uncle cut the child's hair and nails and gave it a name, which was used until maturity, when a new one was bestowed. All the guests brought gifts.

Education was chiefly a family matter, though some localities had male and female clubs where the sexes learned things appropriate to either boys or girls.

Only the offspring of nobility and curacas received formal instruction—a four-year course, which included language, religion, history and *quipú* reading. The Ñustas, or Sun Virgins, were also specially trained for four years. The girls were selected from all over the empire for their beauty and intelligence and put into the "convents" at the age of ten, where they were taught domestic economy, cooking, weaving, sewing, music, and art. On completing their studies, after due ceremonies, they became vestal virgins. The fairest tended the temples, although some of them were selected as first or second wives of the nobility or became concubines of the emperor.

At fourteen boys received a breechclout in a two-week puberty ceremony at the fiesta of the Raymi. The mother made the boy's new costume in October; in November he made pilgrimages to Huanacauri temple to sacrifice llamas and pray. The priests drew a line on the boy's face with the sacrificed llama blood and gave him a sling. The rest of the month the boy gathered straw for relatives to sit on during the ceremony and chewed up great quantities of maize to make the required quantity of *chicha*. Various additional sacrifices and religious observances were performed. At one point, a foot race was staged with other puberty candidates, down from the Anahuayas shrine, on a 2,000-foot hill. They were met by girls tendering them *chicha*. At another ceremony they were formally given their breechclouts; and, in another, weapons and many presents.

The girls' puberty ceremony was held, without much preparation or fanfare, at the first menstruation. After three days' fasting, she was bathed and her hair combed by her mother, who dressed her in new clothes and white wooden sandals. The oldest uncle then bestowed a permanent name on her.

Marriage for commoners was mostly monogamous, though this varied according to local custom, for many villagers took more than one wife. Wives were a help on the farm. The upper classes were wholly polygamous. The number of wives was an index of wealth and prestige.

Usually marriage was restricted to the village *ayllu,* hence endogamous. Exogamous marriages did sometimes occur, though often they created difficulties over patrilineal versus matrilineal rights and property. Numbers of such pairs, after the Conquest, brought complaints to the Spanish courts.

Only the Inca was allowed to marry his full sister, nobles their half sisters. But after this "first wife," they could take as many wives as they wished. There are indications that attempts to emulate the emperor resulted in considerable premarital incest between brothers and sisters and, when the boy married, sometimes the sister continued to live under his roof. The levirate was practiced with widows, who could marry only their husband's brother, though if he allowed it, probably she could seek elsewhere for a mate.

Sociability extended to the dead. The Incas had no fear of death or the dead. Embalming was a perfected art, and the individual was considered not so much dead as merely dumb and deaf, and the bulk of his personal possessions accompanied him to the artfully decorated sepulcher in which he was placed in a sitting position. The mummies of kings and the Sinchís were especially decked out in their most gala costumes, for from time to time they had to pay courtesy visits to the Sun: also, they were brought out to attend important fiestas. At the great Raymi fiesta they were seated in state on the great Aucaypata Terrace, with major-domos and aides, and delivered imaginary speeches and held imaginary conversations, carried on by their spokesmen and interpreters, speeches racy with irony and humor and wisdom. An Inca had to be more witty dead than when he was alive. At times also, the Great Dead were consulted through such interpreters and the priests as oracles.

In addition, one whole month, Aymarca, was the "Month of the Dead"—literally, "The Duty of the Dead"—and again they were brought forth from their tombs. It was a month of moaning, tearful dances, and funereal music, but it terminated in exuberant dancing and joyous music and sexual excesses. The dead were always an intimate part of social, economic, and political affairs, contributing their wisdom and reinforcing valuable ancient traditions. Their tombs, often caves, were usually in high places that provided a view of the mountains and overlooked the village, keeping guard over the affairs of the *ayllu.*

13

🔺🔺🔺🔺🔺🔺🔺🔺🔺🔺🔺🔺🔺🔺🔺🔺🔺🔺🔺🔺🔺🔺🔺🔺🔺🔺🔺🔺

Temples of the Sun

Lıke the Romans, the Incas built highways across the entire empire, a larger land empire than that of Rome, with roads superior for the most part to Roman roads. "Nothing in all Christendom," wrote an early Conquistador, "equals the magnificence of the Royal Roads across the Sierras." Nor were they to be matched in Europe until centuries later. Without such highways, the Incas could not have built the empire; they could not have governed it and it could not have survived.

The best roads, stretching for thousands of miles, were fifteen feet wide, paved with precisely fitted stones, in places carved from the face of 5,000-foot cliffs. They tunneled through stone mountains. They crossed over ten 10,000-foot chasms by fiber suspension bridges and traversed swamps by causeways resting on driven piles. Desert highways were flanked with adobe or stone walls to keep out drifting sands.

The main north-south highway stretched for 3,600 miles. North from Cuzco it followed the mountains past Cerro de Pasco and Cajamarca, site of the emperor's summer palace and hot-spring baths, to Quito, Ecuador, and Pasto, high in Colombia. A side branch to Pachacamac on the coast went through large prosperous towns. Hernando Pizarro used this on his first sortie out from Cajamarca. South from Cuzco, a highway passed Lakes Titicaca and Poopó in Bolivia (where a side road ran down to the Beni River, which was then more accessible by land than it is today), then ran on through

Chuiquisaco to Mendoza in northern Argentina and over the Andes to the Chilean coast, where are now located Copiapó, Santiago, and Valparaiso. It was this road which the last Spanish Viceroy Ambrosio O'Higgins reconstructed, together with ancient Inca *tambos* or inns for travelers. Another road from Cuzco ran to Arequipa, then south to Chalma, Copiapó, and on to the Maule River in Chile, well beyond present Santiago, to the frontier of the Auraucanians, whom the Incas, and later the Spaniards, could never subdue.

Another system—the Cuntisuya—linked Cuzco with the region of Peru's south coast. A fourth network extended east through the Urubamba gorge to the Amazon country.

Over swamps, roads were built up with sod and paved with stone. Tunnels were sometimes cut through stone mountains.

Chronicler Cieza de León described the Inca thoroughfares: "One of the things I admired most . . . was . . . how and in what ways it was possible to make roads so great and majestic such as we saw, and what man-power was sufficient to do it, and with what tools and instruments they could plane down mountains and break down the crags, to make them so wide and fine as they are; for it seemed to me, if the Emperor wanted to make another royal highway like that which goes from Quito to Cuzco, or goes from Cuzco to Chile, I really believe that with all his power he could not be that powerful; there were not enough men to do it. . . . If it were a highway of 150 or 300 or 600 miles it could be believed, however harsh the terrain . . . but some of these roads were more than thirty three hundred miles long and went through mountains so rough and terrible that in some places it is impossible to see bottom, and some of those mountains were of vertical stone, making it necessary to carve them from living stone . . . all of which they did with fire and with hand-picks. . . .

"In other places there were ascents so high and steep that stairs had to be cut to get up the highest ones, with wide platforms at intervals for people to rest. In other places were snow mountains even more to be feared, and this not in one place but in many . . . and through these snows and wherever there were trees and brush, the roads were made level and paved." He mentioned specifically the road from Lima to Xauxa through the rocky mountains of Harochiri, the snow passes of Pariacá, the steep descent to the Apúrimac, and the road across the Paltas, Cajas, and Ayaucas mountains. These roads were fifteen feet wide, and "in the time of the Incas they were spotless, without a single pebble or weed, for they were constantly cleaned. And alongside were large palaces and inns for warriors; be it in the snowy wastes or in the meadows, there were places where one could find refuge from cold and rain; and in many places, as in Collao, there were stone markers called *topos,* as those in Spain, but better made, about every four miles."

In many stretches travel was made more pleasant by specially planted fruit trees. Every fifteen or thirty miles, where some spot provided a beautiful outlook, they built a *tambo* inn for travelers, and storehouses to take care of the seven lean years. In ventilated bins, some carved out of solid rock, they preserved llama and alpaca wool, coca, dried meat, corn, beans, dried and frozen potatoes. There were also special inns for the emperor's messengers and mail carriers, the fleet *chasqui* runners, trained from boyhood to run up the steepest high mountains without tiring or getting out of breath. Each *chasqui* ran a few miles, then handed his messages to a fresh runner. In this way, they covered as many as three hundred miles a day, rain, shine, or snow, through desert heat or thin mountain air. The royal Inca service was often faster and more efficient than modern telegraph or postal service.

Over these highways passed travelers and foot soldiers and notables in litters; cavalcades of imperial llamas and alpacas, tended by skilled herdsmen—eight for each hundred animals. They still pass by, sometimes thousands of them at a time, stepping proudly with darting, tasseled heads and tinkling bells. Goods were also often carried by human porters, usually in a cloth hammock on the back. Large jars with liquids were carried on the back with a rope, and for heavier loads a tump line was used.

2

The accomplishments of the professional Inca architects, builders, and masons shine with glory in the imperishable historical record of man's long climb toward civilization. All were government employees, as were most craftsmen, and exempt from taxes (according to Cobo and Poma). They spent all their time on public works.

Lacking suitable paper for drawing plans, the architects made precise clay models (sometimes even in stone) of buildings, roads, terraces, bridges, aqueducts, waterworks. Whole towns were laid out in accord with such preconstruction models. Garcilaso told about this, and a few models have survived.

For measuring they used a double-stick slide rule and employed a plumb-bob, called the *hupayci,* with which likely they could also establish levels. Measurement units were:

Finger	*rocana*
Thumb-forefinger span	*yucu*
About eighteen inches	*capa*
Yard (re 32 inches)	*sicya*
About sixty-four inches	*ricara*
The land plot, of varying size	*topo*
Grain (measured by a gourd, wood, or silver container) re 26 quarts	*cculla*

The pan-balance was used, but there was no system of weights. Time was reckoned by the hour, by "one cooking," the period necessary to boil potatoes—*hochuaycoy.* Other time units were based on day, night, a ten-day week, months, seasons, solstice, equinox, planting time, harvest time, etc.

An abacus accounting board of stone, clay, or wood, was used, according to Charles Wiener, for calculations. Huamán Poma said that numbers from 1 to 100,000 could be manipulated by these boards with stone or seed counters. An illustration has survived showing a board with five five-pocket horizontal compartments, each with from one to five smaller holes. The decimal system used corresponded to that on the *quipús,* or varicolored knotted statistical cords.

The customary *quipú* had a base cord, usually about a meter long, to which were attached as many as 100 shorter cords, sometimes in separate clusters. "Long" knots, i.e., made by a number of loops, ranged from "1" to "9." Single-loop knots were for higher decimal units. Those beyond hundreds were carried over to the main cord. Units of tens of thousands were employed, giving results in millions.

Poma said they recorded, among other things, fiesta and patriotic dates over the years. Leland Locke believed that the *quipú* census records were arranged on the basis of one *quipú* for each five towns, with five recorded categories: taxpayers, married people, youths, old people, boys and girls. They were also used to record sales, statistics, tax assessments, economic data, and one chronicler claimed that even literature and poetry were preserved by *quipús*. They served to record tribute or taxes to be paid. Everyone, in this way, knew his precise assessment and was free from official abuses. On them were recorded vital statistics, births and deaths, so that there was an annual census, making possible the proper distribution of wool and other goods from state-owned industries and the proper resettlement of farmers.

Though all upper-class youths had to study to read the *quipús*, the knotted cords were a tool of nearly everybody. But, official data, being more complicated, the imperial *quipús* were prepared and filed by a special group of trained archivists—the *quipú-camayo*.

For moving and working stone, the Quechua employed rollers and ropes, bronze and wooden crowbars and levers, bronze chisels, stone and bronze axes and hammers, and they also cut stone with some type of saw. Polishing was done with sand and water. Temporary earth ramps were built to move stones into place on walls.

Mostly three kinds of stone were used: *Yucay*, a hard gray sandstone, as in Sacsahuamán, in Cuzco foundations and for interior walls; green diorite porphyry, as in Sacsahuamán; and black andesite, the most preferred for temples and palaces—though it was difficult to work and had to be brought from a great distance.

Most stone blocks had beveled edges, emphasizing the joints. Doors and niches sometimes had stone lintels, but more often ropewrapped poles. One story was the rule, but numerous edifices rose to two or three stories. Columns were occasionally used. Carved snakes, pumas, and designs were common about doorways.

Many towns grew up hit or miss—an irregularity often imposed by the rough terrain—but as the Inca policy of resettlement expanded, new places were preplanned. The most typical design was laid out in squares (an arrangement perhaps adopted from the Chimú) with one or more plazas or *canchas;* but because of the various levels, slopes, and irregular spaces, such ideal projects nearly always had to be modified. At Ollantay the town had to be crammed into a trapezoidal space, with the large *canchas* at the edge.

It can be stated—at least tentatively—that perhaps no other people in history utilized such a high percentage of their technical knowhow in practical application and for social welfare—so far as we can tell, well over 90 per cent, a straining for improvement and achievement that led to accelerated inventiveness. In contrast, so rapid in modern times has become the accumulation of scientific knowledge, that in the United States, the most advanced realm of applied science, probably not one per cent of our available knowledge is actually so utilized.

Indeed the Incas, though they would marvel at our technology, would likely look upon our competitive acquisitive society as barbarous and unjust, our social and economic concepts beneath contempt, our methods of land utilization (except for farm techniques), and our handling of farm problems, as ludicrous. That most Americans would hardly prefer to live under an arbitrary collective system, largely devoid of individual political expression, is equally obvious.

3

The superb Inca technology is well illustrated in their agriculture, both in its methods and its social organization. Cultivation went far beyond the domestication of plants, some forty species, a remarkable accomplishment in itself—and the adaptation of scores of food plants from other regions. For the Incas knew a great deal about scientific farming, types of soil, fertilizing, soil conservation, adaptation of crops to the soil, rotation, seed selection, drainage, and plant productivity in relation to population.

Gradually they built up the physical equipment, adding to the narrow lower bands of fertile watered valley soil, by building terraces, ever higher up the mountainsides. The steepest slopes did not dismay them, and the steplike fields often rose thousands of feet. Earlier terraces were crude, small, and irregular, seemingly family enterprises, but in later Inca periods, the whole official labor force was swung into widespread projects of building elaborate terraces faced with selected stones, often with cut stone, and scientifically filled in with layers of loose stone and gravel for proper drainage and topped with deep fertile loam. Steps or footholds of jutting stones were provided in these walls. They planted corn and coca, beans and potatoes, and cinchona for quinine to cure malaria. They also set out peaches, plums, apples, and other fruit trees.

Terraces were fed by artificial irrigation, because of the long dry season and the quick run-off. Early irrigation ditches were of earth though now and again supported by dry-stone walls. Later, aqueducts were sometimes cut through stone along the face of colossal cliffs, sometimes bored through solid stone mountains. Indeed, nothing was more marvelous than the Inca aqueducts, some of which are still used. By drilling holes and sealing water inside, the most refractory rock was split asunder. They also brought water to their homes and bathrooms.

Water was one of the chief keys of Inca civilization. It was the source of all being, along with the sun. From Garcilaso to Valcarcel, numerous authorities have believed that Lake Titicaca was the original source of Inca greatness, the generator of its people, its rulers, its customs, and its art; that all sprang from the water of that high, little, inland sea. The importance of water was inherent in the very language of the earliest peoples in the uplands. The Urú, the shadowy marsh folk, were "Water People." "Urú" meant water, and they bequeathed the word to their successors. In Aimara, it became "Uma." And how many "Water Peoples" there were: Usuna, Umayu, Umasuya, Umate (Omote). In Colla and Quechua the word for water—at least the prefix—was "Co," and so the Colla were also "Water People."

If water was so important to the earliest highland peoples, in the case of the Incas it held the inner secret of the survival of the empire, its growth and prosperity. It was basic to the whole economy for, if the Andes have some of the biggest rivers on earth, the mountains themselves are among the most barren on earth. The Quechua knew the music of flowing water nearly everywhere, but it escaped into the void like music into the air, leaving only a sweet echo, and the crops withered till the water was tamed and used. The irrigation system, far greater than anything existing in modern Peru, was the secret of Inca prosperity and success.

4

The Inca and many of the people, doubtless, had a sense of greatness and destiny. But the great Inca edifices, far-flung roads, public works—the memory of Egypt rises up—suggest a tyrannical world or abject serfs driven under the lash. However, there is not too much indication of this; few legends of cruel leaders or official injustice. There were difficult periods, disorderly periods, revolutionary periods, but in the more favored eras, life under the Inca, if the records are at all factual, was imbued with a joy, confidence, and love of labor, both in local units and on the national level. The impressive monuments of Incan industry seem rather an eager outpouring of body and spirit.

The people had to co-operate or die. Hence the great works of the empire connote an extraordinary social self-discipline which could scarcely have been imposed solely by autocracy. With the limited implements at hand, such achievements, even with compulsory labor, would otherwise have been impossible. They would have been impossible also had the people not been fully aware that such efforts truly answered local and national needs. Corruption, such as that in the United States, was not conceivable to the dedicated Quechua. The harsh mountain conditions imposed well-ordered work habits and foresight in storing food and preparing warm clothing and shelter to assure survival.

Apparently the Inca work tax was rarely onerous or too prolonged. Furthermore it respected and utilized individual and group talents and skills: villages renowned for music provided musicians; certain groups became litter bearers for the emperor and the nobility; others traditionally integrated the palace guard. The *mita*, or obligatory labor service, rather than being looked upon with aversion, apparently was accepted as an opportunity for displaying loyalty, a chance to see new places and people, to enjoy fresh experiences. Work was featured with numerous joy fiestas, dances, public feasts, often was done to the rhythm of chants, flutes, drums, harps. The musician was always as important as the engineer, the harvester, the foreman, or the chief. Though the empire lasted several centuries, and perhaps longer, it seemed for the most part in the springtime of life. Thus the massing of work forces, the *mita*, the building of irrigation ditches, was as much the compulsion of nature as compulsion by the state. It was the prerequisite of generalized well-being.

Modern Peru prefers land monopoly, oppression, and exploitation. The Incan motto was not to destroy or despoil but to build, to produce, to create. As always, the gulf between intention and deed often must have been great, the motives, methods and aims far from clear, and though the empire endured long, many portions were not so advanced. Many were ruled remotely and nominally. And those last to come under the imperial sway scarcely received attention comparable to those in the more central areas.

5

Farm methods and the tools are of special interest. Some gardening tools that have survived in museums are so simple, handy, and unusual, that a modern tool manufacturer could well profit by imitating some of them.

Foot plows, provided with handle and a footrest for pushing for certain purposes, seem superior to our ordinary iron spade. They were used for cultivating, seeding, and potato harvesting. Hoes (wide, chisel-like with a long blade and haft) were used for both cultivating and weeding. A clod-breaker (*humi*) was a doughnut-shaped stone on a long handle. Also, a boat-shaped board scraper was used to smooth fields or cover over seeds.

The only metals available for tools were copper and bronze—for the Incas had important tin mines. Iron (*quellay*) though known, was not used; perhaps methods of working it had not been discovered. Gold and silver were reserved for the Inca, the emperor, and the nobility. Platinum was mined and used only in Ecuador and Colombia, though a few platinum adornments were imported.

Techniques of mining and processing were well advanced. Mines were sacred, and special all-night dancing and chicha-drinking fiestas were celebrated at suitable times. Metals were treated by smelting, alloying, casting, hammering, repoussé, incrustation, inlay, cloisonné, soldering, and riveting. Metal plating was known on the north coast, perhaps elsewhere. The edges of tools were hammered and annealed with much skill. Silver was often incised with gold, shell or bronze, and vice versa.

Despite much artisan specialization, Inca society was overwhelmingly agrarian. From farming, from the soil and the cycle of the seasons sprang the whole superstructure of government, religion, art, and ethics.

The unit of village life and resettlement was the *ayllu,* originally perhaps based on kinship, which held title to the land and gave annual or lifetime occupation of houses and fields to individual families. The land was cultivated, planted, and harvested as a community enterprise, though the crops from each field remained in the hands of the family. The fields of absent members were similarly harvested, without cost to the planter except for food, and the product stored for him pending his return. Special fields in each village were set aside for the Inca, the priesthood, and for community hospitality to travelers.

Field boundaries were marked with official markers—*sayhua.* According to Cobo and Poma, tampering with them was punished by exile to the unhealthy royal coca plantations; a second offense brought death.

The exact origin of the *ayllu* is unknown, but it was a basic family, village, and landholding group on which most Inca social organization pivoted, and which has been handed on down to the modern communal landholding system. In later periods, for administrative purposes, the Inca found it convenient to combine the *ayllu* into two or more sections, called *saya*.

Farming was a communal enterprise preceded by religious rites and carried out with chants. The men did the digging, the women followed behind breaking up the clods. On state-owned lands, chicha was provided to the workers.

Both sexes also worked together harvesting, after which, another song and dance fiesta—the *amoray*—was held.

Coca (cocaine), almost a necessity for overexertion at high altitudes, was a state monopoly, restricted largely for use in unusual enterprises, in fiestas, and for ordeals by the army—not a widespread vice as today.

Most maize was planted in September and harvested in February. The sun priests fasted till the plants were a centimeter high; and, in places, a ceremony of sacrificing llamas, followed by dancing and drinking, was celebrated.

The soil was fertilized with llama and human dung, ashes, fish, bones and, on the coast especially, with bird-guano.

When droughts threatened, the people entreated the aid of Thunder God Ilyapa and held black-robed, wailing processions, with banners. Black llamas were tied to stakes and sprinkled with chicha and denied food and, unless the Thunder God sent rain in time, they died.

Crops had to be weeded, and animals such as deer, foxes, and skunks, birds (and humans) kept away. As the crop neared maturity, the man, wearing a fox skin over his head and carrying a tasseled rattle-staff and a sling, stood guard during the day; the wife kept night watch with a small drum for frightening off marauders and to summon help.

Many wild plants were collected, though the products—except for herbs, medicinal and dye plants—played no large part in the food economy.

Bunch grass *ichú* was important for roofs, brooms, rope, and ritual observances, and agave, or *acopa*, for strong cordage.

Among wild fruits often gathered were false-pepper berries for the most tasty chicha, *tunas* (two species), and the much prized *ahuimanto*. Leaves of the *hataco* and *pisoc-caquin* ("bird's foot") were eaten raw or cooked as savory additions. Berries and nuts were picked. Such delicacies as eggs, insects, larvae, particularly that under the *chachacomo* tree bark, were eagerly sought.

Fish, meat, and vegetables were dried, smoked, or frozen, and when eaten were broiled or roasted with chili and herbs. Soup (often thickened with *quinoa*), stews, and corn-meal dumplings were favorite foods, as was popcorn. Beer—a daily beverage—was made from corn, *quinoa, ocas,* and false-pepper berries. The fruit pulp was chewed and the mash spat into warm water and allowed to ferment. Men and women ate back to back, women facing the kitchen.

The Quechua had special stone rocker grinders, so that the heavy rolling pin crushed the maize or potatoes without pressure. Even little girls could easily keep the rocker moving.

Pottery of the later period was the finest in Latin America, though it is questionable whether designs ever surpassed the early Nazca and Moché work of thousands of years earlier. The Inca intaglio was possibly derived from the early Nazca. Quechua gourd designs were superb.

6

There were enormous royal herds of llamas and alpacas, tended by professional herders, though sometimes by women and children. These provided food, clothing, transportation, and sacrificial victims. There were periodic distributions to the villages of meat and of yarn. The Inca gave all newlyweds completely new alpaca wool clothing. At most villages these animals were provided with stone-wall refuge corrals.

Llamas were sometimes sacrificed on the altar; llama foetuses served as offerings and were buried under a new house, or used in other ways to bring good fortune and health. A special llama-mating fiesta was staged with a "white magician," a white llama, symbolically in charge of ceremonies.

Ducks, dogs, and guinea pigs were domesticated. The latter, living mostly on kitchen scraps, swarmed in all the dwellings, and everywhere were an important part of the diet. The flesh was tender and savory, with considerable fat along the vertebrae. Cobo observed they were—and any modern traveler can also discover—most tasty. Only in Huanca province did people eat dogs—though apparently only those sacrificed on the altar—which won them the contemptuous epithet, according to Poma, of being "dog-eaters," or *alco-micoc.*

Wild vicuñas and guanacos were driven between fences that channeled them into a narrow gorge where they could be easily sheared or killed. Numerous food animals were hunted, though foxes, pumas, and bears were chiefly killed because they were nuisances. But most wild game areas were royal preserves not to be hunted in except by special permission. One of the notable annual events was the great public hunt—the *caco*—the end products of which: meat, wool, hides, etc., were distributed equitably to the villages.

Some 10,000 Indians would ring a space up to sixty miles in circumference. Accompanied by beaters they closed in toward the center, forming concentric rings as the space narrowed. Designated hunters entered for the final kill. One such hunt in Jauja yielded more than 11,000 slain animals, even after large numbers had been set free, such as smaller creatures, females, and pregnant mothers.

7

The Quechua calendar—a corn calendar, an agricultural calendar, a religious and war calendar—began December, viz.:

1. *Capac Raymi.* The major religious celebration of the year, a splendid harvest ceremony, a puberty ceremony, with participation by the emperor, the nobility, and every citizen, honored Pachacamana—the Earth Mother.

2. *Huchuy Pocoy,* "Little Germination," or the "Quiver of the Child in the Womb," the nuptial month. A mock battle of newly matured boys was held in the Joy Square.

3. *Hatún Pucuy,* "the Great Ripening." Twenty guinea pigs were sacrificed and twenty loads of firewood were offered to the Sun in behalf of the crops.

4. *Paucar-huaray,* "Earth Ripening," "Underdrawers of Flowers," the flowering month.

5. *Aryihua,* "Golden Fruit," "Harvest Time," "The Month of the Corn Ear of a Thousand Colors."

The royal insignia were honored. A white llama, dressed in a red shirt with Big Ear ornaments, was provided with *yanacona* and *mamacona,* or royal attendants of both sexes, and was given coca and chicha. Fifteen ordinary llamas were sacrificed in its honor. It was never killed and received a royal funeral when it died.

6. *Hatún Cuzqui,* Aymuray ("Great Cultivation, Great Harvest"). The maize harvest was celebrated when the granaries were bursting with grain. Thirty llamas were sacrificed.

7. *Ahuacay-Cusqui* ("Warrior Harvest"). The month of health,

when the sun turned the dead fields copper-red. A great military parade and sun festival, with the presence of all of noble blood, was celebrated.

8. *Cauay Huarquiz* ("Water Fiesta"). Irrigation system celebration, sacrifices, music, dances, and chicha drinking. Cobo says this major fiesta was first celebrated after Inca Roca completed a particularly elaborate water system.

9. *Yapaquiz* ("Planting Time"). A thousand guinea pigs were sacrificed in honor of Frost, Air, Water, and Sun. Mummies of ancestors were taken through the fields to give their blessing to all the generations. This was repeated in November.

10. *Asituá* ("Purification"). Fiestas to ward off sickness. All deformed persons, sinners, and dogs were sent out of the city. Clothes were shaken out of the door to get rid of "evil" lurking in their folds, and warriors washed their weapons in the river. Everybody bathed. Four llamas were sacrificed, and their lungs examined to see whether the year would be prosperous and free of disease.

11. *Cantaray, Uma Raymi* ("Rain Month"). Ceremonies against drought.

12. *Aymarca* ("Maturity"). Preparations for the male puberty rites.

This calendar was based on both the solar and lunar year, though how they were reconciled is not known. Planting time (August, early crops; September, general crops) originally was determined by the flowering of a certain cactus but, later, more accurately by the sun. Four permanent Time-Markers, *paca-onaucoc*, two to the east, two to the west of the city were set up and observations were taken from the royal judgment seat (*osno*) on a raised platform in the center of the great Cuzco square. Similar time-markers fixed the December solstice and the day for the Raymí fiesta. Polo de Ondegardo claimed there were towers set to mark the beginning of each month, but his evidence is dubious. Equinoxes, according to Garcilaso, were determined by noting the shadows cast by a set pole. Among the coast peoples, astronomical and planting time apparently pivoted on the movement of the Pleiades.

8

Nothing was more remarkable than the organized system of resettlement practiced by the Incas, which in retrospect made later depression-day resettlement in the United States a childish, unscientific, and demagogic enterprise. This led to the setting up of new *ayllus*—usually tailored to a hundred souls—and new villages, the irrigating of new lands, and bringing wild areas under cultivation. If in the main the aims were laudable: to reduce population pressures, promote efficiency, increase production and hence welfare, its political implications must at times have been irksome and unwelcome, and the severing of long-established ties almost brutal.

One of the chief objectives was to bring less civilized people into contact with more advanced groups.

Quechua, being the best trained and most loyal, were sent out from the central provinces to peripheral parts of the empire, often were resettled in remote backward villages to teach more modern methods, husbandry, and living habits.

Such delegates were given the temporary title of "Inca" (were even allowed to wear large ear plugs and variants of the royal headband or *llautu*) and enjoyed certain privileges with respect to their persons and goods, violations of which meant severe punishment. But their superior status was ephemeral; they were supposed to become part and parcel of the new community, to spread not only technics but also the Quechua language. It did result in the rapid diffusion of the dominant language over nearly the whole empire, though perhaps less successfully in the long-rooted Aimara and Colla provinces, but as a designed and not haphazard effort, it had surprising acceptance.

Similarly, wilder peoples were moved into lands closer to the heart of the empire to absorb habits and arts. These more primitive outlying people—at least the upper class—were brought to the capital to be educated and trained. Some never returned, so Cuzco became a polyglot place like New York. The intrusion of more progressive culture into more colonial areas brings about displacement, and the population urge is always to the mecca of major population and opportunity, even in nonindustrialized societies. The parallel between the Quechua experience and that of New York and Puerto Ricans is not farfetched. The colonists, or *Mitima*, sometimes moved almost the same distance to an even stranger environment.

Much thought was given to the process. New settlers were introduced into areas similar in climate, altitude, and types of crops to those to which they were already accustomed. The vast heights necessitated much special consideration, for over the millennia, the highlanders had developed a 25 per cent greater lung capacity than most mortals, so that when they went to lower altitudes, part of the lung was not used, and thereby tended quickly to become infected with respiratory diseases. Similarly, lowland people moving into too high levels, felt lassitude, often became anemic, often suffered from heart trouble or other ailments. For this reason the Inca also built up three types of armies, designed for very high levels, medium levels, and for coast fighting, which were utilized outside of their habitat only in emergencies.

9

Fortunately at the more lofty altitudes, the people were mostly free from noxious or disease-carrying insects. The dreaded *verruga* disease was carried by a night-fly only and at around the 7,000-foot level. There were few poisonous snakes or lizards. It was not a realm of poisons in the animal or human kingdom, and the land was continually washed and freed of evil by the rains and rushing torrents.

The Quechua knowledge of biology and medicine was considerable. From native usage in Peru have been derived some of modern medicine's most notable remedies. Every animal—the fur, claws, feet, flesh, fat, penis, intestines, heart, liver; every plant, vine, tree, the roots, wood, bark, leaves, fruits had their designated medical uses, on the basis of either religion, superstition, or science, for effecting cures, a matter first extensively investigated by Cobo. More recently this vast medicinal panorama has been set forth in the monumental three-volume work, *La Medicina Popular Peruana,* by Doctors Hermilio Valdizán and Angel Maldonado (1922), a treatise indispensable for understanding Incan culture. There was a large class of doctors, *hampi camayoc* diviners, midwives, *curanderos* and mumbo-jumbo artists, who were paid for their services with food, clothing, gold, and silver.

Dentistry and gold filling were practiced in many places. Brain surgery, trepanning, was well advanced. By drilling the skull with a circle of overlapping holes and sawing out a rectangular window, the brain was entered, treated, tumors and pressures removed. Often the opening was later covered by a riveted metal plate.

Valdizán and Maldonado saw Peruvian medicine as being in a transitional state, half evolved out of a type of animal worship, the use of cures stimulated by desire for animal traits: courage and fierceness from the puma; ability to speak from the parrot. So they used the elements of the parrot's body to cure pathoglosis (speech defect, inability to speak, or dumbness), both congenital and acquired; similarly elements of the puma body to overcome timidity and weakness, whether congenital or acquired. They then anthropomorphized sickness itself and conceived of the transferral of the intrusive spirit or element causing illness to animals. They learned also by observing animal use of plants, and by such use, by trial and error, gradually evolved some empirical methods. Medicine was still mixed with much superstition and magic, a condition not entirely eradicated even among modern doctors. But the Quechua had achieved a remarkably accurate and vast knowledge of the scientific use of herbs and plants in curing sickness.

10

Considering the difficulties of terrain and the toil required to produce anything, though nature was often prodigal, the limited means and the tools at hand, the people lived lives singularly rich in recreation, music, and beauty. Their arts were not inconsiderable and, at least on the handicraft level and considerably beyond, the vast majority apparently had much talent. Little of Quechua literature has survived aside from legends, but the fragments written down after the Conquest indicate that it was extensive and original. Prayers, hymns, narrative poems, drama, and songs were recorded by Cristóbal de Molina of Cuzco, Pachachuti, Poma, and others. Molina recorded a hymn to Viracocha:

> Hail Conquering Viracocha!
> Ever-present Viracocha!
> Thou without equal on earth,
> Thou who did abide from the world's beginning to its end.
> Thou gavest valor to man, saying:
> "Let this be a man."
> And to the woman, saying:
> "Let this be a woman."
> Watch over them, that they live in health and peace.
> Thou who art in the highest heavens
> And among the tempest clouds,
> Give them long life
> And accept the sacrifice we give.
> O Creator!

The Quechua language was both onomatopoeic and compounding; nouns and verbs were formed by adding suffixes to the root, and more refined meanings by inserting affixes between stem and ending, making it more precise and a more subtle language than the Spanish.

Viracocha the Sun God, the Maker of Earth and Sky, the Creator of All, was initially without light. First he carved giant stone statues and gave them life. Not satisfied, he turned them back into stone at Tiahuanaco, Pucará, and elsewhere and, except for two assistants, drowned the rest in a flood. Next he caused a sun and moon to emerge from Titicaca Island. The moon was brighter until the jealous sun threw ashes in her face. At Tiahuanaco the God molded animals, then men his own size, out of clay, giving them their customs, language, songs, and food, and sent them forth to settle the different localities.

Presently he followed incognito, sending his two assistants along the coast and the eastern rain-forests, to see if people had obeyed his instructions. He went as an old man with a staff and at Cacha, where people disliked all strangers, he was stoned. Viracocha thereupon called down fire from heaven which melted the rocks. The people begged him to save them, and he put out the fires with a single blow of his staff. In appreciation they built a shrine in his honor on the burnt hill. He went on to Urcós near Cuzco, where he brought his people out of the mountain, and a still larger shrine was built. North, in Manta, Ecuador, he bade farewell to his people and walked out across the Pacific and disappeared.

An old widow had seven lazy sons, who lay in the shade in the fields all day, but ate ravenously. When harvest time came, there was nothing to eat. The widow cut off pieces of her sparse flesh and put them into the pot. When the sons had glutted themselves, she cried out: "You have eaten everything, even the body of your own mother." She flung ugly names at them and disowned them.

Thunder beat upon them, lightning embraced their house in flames. The mother was converted into a gigantic serpent that looped up black into the sky. She hurled thousands of lightning bolts in a furious battle to destroy them.

They were changed into Hail, Ice, Rain Storm, Snow, Wind, Thunder, and Lightning. To placate her, they stripped away all the fruits of the field to lay at her feet in the caves of Ice and Snow where she had taken up her abode, and ever after, *Ceatú,* the

Mother Serpent, loops up black into the sky, and the sons sweep down to ravage the fields to placate her and, after the fury subsides, all the Ychbi Occlos, the little folk of the lagoons, send out streams of colored light from their belly-buttons to form the arched rainbow of peace.

Many of the legends of the first Inca are intermingled with those of Viracocha and other gods. Later Incas also have special relationships with the deities. One of the latest legends in time was that about how the pestilence struck in Guayaquil, where Huayna Capac was carrying on a campaign around the shores of the Gulf. In a vision he saw his camp surrounded by a million ghosts preparing to attack. The emperor quickly hustled his army back to Quito to celebrate the great Raymí fiesta. There a messenger in a black cloak brought him a small, carved, lidded box—a *poto*—saying it was a gift from Viracocha, that only the emperor was to open it. A cloud of moths and butterflies flew out, and pestilence swept the camp. The emperor was one of the first to die.

Such legends told by early chroniclers were versions of memorized narrative poems, customarily repeated or chanted by trained bards and minstrels, but well known by the people. One "drama" of the Chanca War introduced a "neutral" Indian narrator to avoid jumping the scenes confusingly from camp to camp. The *Ollanta* drama, claimed to be pre-Spanish, is probably only a few centuries old, but likely was derived from an early Quechua drama, and the songs and other portions, Rowe believes, were little changed from the originals.

Many dramatic pieces were integral parts of dance fiestas, where trained actors chanted and a general chorus answered. Garcilaso gives a little gem:

> In This Place
> Thou shalt sleep.
> Midnight
> I will come.

Sarmiento gives a poem about the death of Pachacuti:

> I was born like a lily in the garden
> So also was I raised.
> As my age came, I have grown up,
> And, as I had to die,
> So likewise I dried up,
> And I died.

Much of the poetry is nostalgic, rich with allusions to nature, plants, birds, and animals. Some chants appear to be connected with medicine and curing, magic and sorcery.

11

Their great dances were part of their intimate life. Few nations—perhaps only some peoples in Africa, perhaps the Andalusians in Spain, but in a more individualistic way—have ever had such a great universal dance tradition as Peru. The dance was a basic form of expression, better than any newspaper or any doctrine—a medium by which individual emotions and ideas, family feelings, group and village feelings, religious and political ideas, could find fullest expression. They had personal dances and group dances, religious dances, agricultural and crop dances, patriotic dances, war dances, animal dances, bird dances, rain dances, and when injustices arose, as they do in all societies, they expressed their protests in the dance. They danced before the curaca, they danced before the Inca, telling him more vividly about their woes than they could have done in any illumined parchment scroll. Mostly the dances were light and agile, but placid in a deep sensual way. Neither Quechua music nor the dance hinted often at despair or fear; such notes have crept in since the Conquest. Thus, whatever their tribulations and at times misrule, they had at the root of their lives something later civilizations have impatiently sought and never found.

The sun, the gods, the hero-Incas were all there, intertwined in the legends, the dances, partaking of an integrated concept of creative power.

The clarity and luminosity of the upland light must have stimulated such clarity of soul and of ideas, and the sun, shining equitably on all, without any favoritism, seemed a "pillar and prop of the state." The great spaces, though stretching upwards toward the sky, because of the great height, provided amplitude of vision, celestial embracing, a continuous feeling of wonder.

There the sky and the sun ruled; and at night, the replicas of men, gods, plants, and animals in the stars and constellations—the Quechua nomenclature so identifies them and tell us how things all happened.

"For the Incas," remarked Valcarcel, the Peruvian who, along with Hildebrando Pozo, most deeply understood Quechua life, "the starry sky was the panorama of the Ecumene, the whole world, the universe, the cosmos. It was the world itself projected from below above. . . . The night was propitious for the flight of the Quechua soul to another universe where there was no death. . . . The celestial *quipú* was his Bible . . . his infallible oracle." And so, forced always to gaze up at the sky because of encircling mountains, he worshiped the sun by day and the great mystery by night. The mountains, the *Apú*, were also sacred, ever present in his consciousness, but his gaze, his very soul was channeled upward to the strip of sky above the crags. Distance, the horizon, the frontier, the realm of freedom for the imagination were not across great plains, but over his head, above him.

Here in Peru were encountered no ferocious or unpleasable gods. There were few hostile demons, such as existed in the dark Amazon twilight. There was no human sacrifice, few tortured prisoners, no cruel animal-baiting as sport. Brutality was mostly abhorrent to them, but etiquette and reasonableness were greatly cherished. They were simple children, perhaps, but wise, too.

Unlike the Aztec or some Oriental religions, theirs was not a religion of fear. The gods of agriculture, save a few who wielded the power of inclement weather, were mostly benign, mostly maternal, such as Mama Sara (Magic Goddess). Magical, picturesque, and beautiful legends cluster about all the Quechua gods. Nor did they look with fear upon the hereafter: there was no hell, no after-life punishment. They lived close to nature and interpreted it, the animals, the plants, the rivers, and mountains with warm affection; for they looked upon the earth, however hard they might toil, as a kindly mother; their deities far more helpful and friendly than fierce or malign.

What a glorious record those deities and creatures of the heavens left in the early pottery, from coast to highlands; likewise there appears sympathy for the doings and stances of animals and plants and birds, which are depicted with such loving care and delight! Even the marvelous fierceness of the jaguar, a universal theme dating back before Chavín, and the one notable "alien" creature in Quechua art, is depicted with loving understanding, an awareness of the animal's innate need for such fierceness, an affectionate acceptance of it. Even more deeply felt and understood on the pottery and in weaving is the spirit of the llamas who shared their love and labors, portrayed with such elegant and proud silhouettes. The wonder and awe of the mighty condor! The seductive glide of serpents! Here, unlike Chavín art, are no exotic plants or creatures, no fearful imaginary dragons and monsters.

All this came out of Titicaca—if we are to believe Garcilaso—the Sun, the Moon, the Inca, man himself emerged from that great lake atop the world. Or, if we accept other versions, all such manifestations came out of the bowels of the mountain, the caves of the mountain, the eyes of the mountain, the caves of dawn, the eyes brimming with the golden sunlight. They and the sunlight traversed the high earth and all the Paradise valleys, warmer than the heights. The valleys were carved by sunlight. The rivers were the moving light of the Sun. "Discover the meaning of the Sun in the Quechua legends," says one writer, "and you will have discovered the secret of Inca culture!"

Thus, the Quechua made a mystic union of Water and the Sun. They spoke of the "River of the Sun," "The Celestial Lord that Murmurs," "The River of the Great Serpent," the serpent being symbolic of both water and sunlight—"The Royal Sunlight." Their rivers brought life, they cleansed the sin of living, swept it away, swept away sickness and evil memories. The source of the "Sun Rivers" was always near the Sun; the source was the great Mountain God (or gods) Salcantay, Umanta, Panticalla, Sorata, Illimani—a thousand snow giants.

12

Among the old-time Quechua, remarks a Peruvian writer, with curious inversion, "It was the hand that made the man. The Quechua put his whole being into whatever he did." There may be something in this, for, according to Valcarcel, the Quechua and Aimara were ambidextrous, which if true is at least symbolical of efficiency and harmony. There was another paradox; their hands were especially skillful and patient at the most minute handicrafts, this in an empire of gigantic stones, but even those gigantic stones were smoothed to precision with patient loving care.

This balance between the right and left sides of their bodies was also symbolic of their technology on the one hand, their superb mastery of agriculture, weaving, metallurgy, animal husbandry, basketry, pottery, architecture, and engineering, and, on the other, their talents in dancing, singing, music, poetry, mathematics, and astronomy; the beauty of design that went into their basketry, their weaving, their pottery, their carved gourds, and stone receptacles.

Harmony and completeness, the full man, in a rich co-operative society.

Individualism was not expressed in *winning* the race, but in the *style* of the racing, the beauty of the technique, the perfection of the form and movement. The grace of doing was as important as the winning, or more so. Yet it was no art-for-art's-sake aloofness, for it required group appreciation and judgment.

13

The Inca government ruled not by guesswork but by exact information about the needs of the people, about production, the viable relation of man to the soil, and this in turn permitted taxation on a fixed equitable basis without favoritisms or exactions. In the same way the government knew the precise needs of their forces in the field—food, supplies, weapons—and they moved large armies across swamps, mountains, and deserts with clockwork efficiency.

The army, once it occupied enemy territory and won allegiance, converted itself into a corps of workers, engineers, and agronomists, who overnight turned barren fields into gardens, built aqueducts, roads, and buildings with astonishing celerity that won local gratitude and admiration. A gigantic "student-exchange" operation was instituted promptly. As already mentioned, Inca nobles were sent to the conquered provinces to study and work; the sons of local curacas were brought to the capital to be trained.

If the major tool of Inca rule and Quechua superiority was technology, it was technology—except in evil periods—for human ends rather than the more murderous ends or tyranny; rather did it aim not at personal enrichment but toward advancing the welfare of the state and the people. It sought to promote the good life.

On this basis the empire endured long, though its weaknesses were all too apparent, and it might have endured gloriously for many more centuries had it not been for a premature historical accident —the coming of the Conquistadores, the terrifying "Men from Mars" with their greed for gold, glory, and an alien God.

Clearly the Quechua and other groups were no mere enslaved people; they were not stolid oxen of toil. It was too great a culture to have been created in any such miserable fashion; it could not have survived for so many centuries on such a basis. It was rooted in the free *ayllu,* the obligations of which were economic, not obedience to cultural conformity. It lived in admirable equilibrium, and the whole great edifice (despite the privileges of the Incas) for the majority, rested upon justly imposed duties, just distribution, and just rewards. Wise foresight saw to the building up of ample reserves of food, clothing, utensils, arms—for periods of drought, war, and famine—a tangible system of social security that provided confidence in the future. With effort, the deepest, most rocky, most arid mountain slope could be converted into flowering gardens, a geometric exactitude of terraces surmounted by abundance and beauty, in a climate, which for all its coldness and sometimes blizzards, was sufficiently benign for flowers to grow most of the year, in some places all year, and for corn and potatoes—of specially selected species—to grow in some areas as high up as 17,000 feet.

As Luis A. Valcarcel has expressed it, "The men of the Andes possessed a happy confidence in their destiny; they had an expansive harmony with the cosmos."

The important thing for any people is not in any abstract labeling of society, but that their social forms, their customs, their way of life—individual and collective—evolve out of their physical setting, the resources nature provides them, out of their needs in the face of nature and man, out of the trial and error of centuries of experience. The Inca system did grow and evolve out of the necessities imposed by living in the Andes, and in its time and place it was one of the finer fruits of human endeavor on this planet, for on the whole it was a generous, equitable, and kindly society. Not often in any national complex have the cultivation of the soul and the human spirit achieved better harmoniousness, amity, or creative expression.

The Quechua colonist worker, the *mitimae,* as has been indicated, had special obligations. When he went permanently into a new community he took his family, all his worldly goods, his knowledge; he was a settler, and took unto himself a world of new unusual dimensions that called for dedicated efforts. It was a mutual enrichment for them and for the local communities, with new agricultural, irrigation, public works and buildings, to bring about more prosperous and civilized conditions, a more universal co-ordination with the empire, to make life less agonizing and more human.

The world could still learn much from the art and genius of Inca government.

In Cuzco, in turn, the outlanders from each new acquisition of the empire became the raw ore to be refined as quickly as possible into the true gold of citizenry.

All newcomers to Cuzco had to bring offerings for the court and the temples: fruits, animals, cloth, gold; but a *sine qua non* of such excursionists was a fistful of soil from the village plaza which he had to deposit with special ceremony in the great Aucipayta Plaza, which thereby became symbolic of the earth of all the empire; it was the empire in miniature, and the plaza in turn became a dedication to the empire, to the world, to the cosmos—a microcosm identifiable with the macrocosm. In turn, both the Inca and the Sun God had their bits of productive soil in every *ayllu* in the land.

But even in the capital, the outlander, whatever polish and understanding he acquired, lived according to his own customs, was encouraged to do so, which gave the city tremendous variety and richness. Assemblies there, where the distinctive provincial headgear brightened the multitude, were always picturesque and humanistic. Also, the newcomers placed their own favorite god in a special niche or altar in the Coracancha, the Great Temple of the Sun, as servitors to the Lord of the Universe. One God, Viracocha, the Sun, ruled the empire, but he was not a jealous god.

Appendix

MAP I

SCALE OF MILES

0   500   1000

THE MAJOR TRIBAL
AND LINGUISTIC GROUPS
OF SOUTH AMERICAN INDIANS
(1492)

267

MAP II

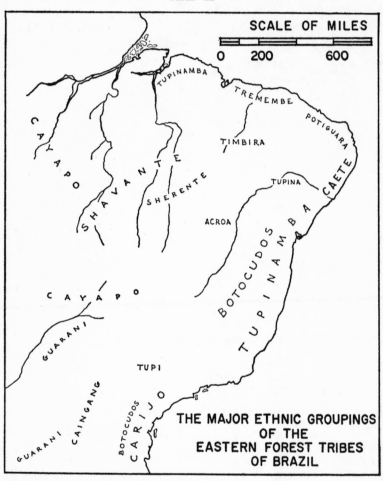

SCALE OF MILES

0   200   600

TUPINAMBA

TREMEMBE

POTIGUARA

C A Y A P O

S H A V A N T E

SHERENTE

TIMBIRA

TUPINA

ACROA

CAETE

C A Y A P O

BOTOCUDOS

TUPINAMBA

GUARANI

TUPI

GUARANI

CAINGANG

BOTOCUDOS

CARIJO

THE MAJOR ETHNIC GROUPINGS
OF THE
EASTERN FOREST TRIBES
OF BRAZIL

MAP III

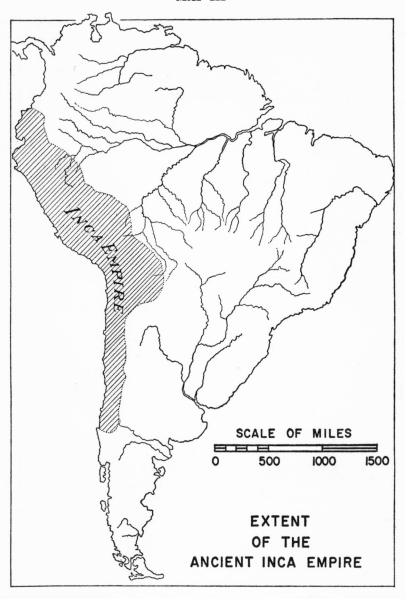

INCA EMPIRE

SCALE OF MILES

0   500   1000   1500

EXTENT
OF THE
ANCIENT INCA EMPIRE

MAP IV

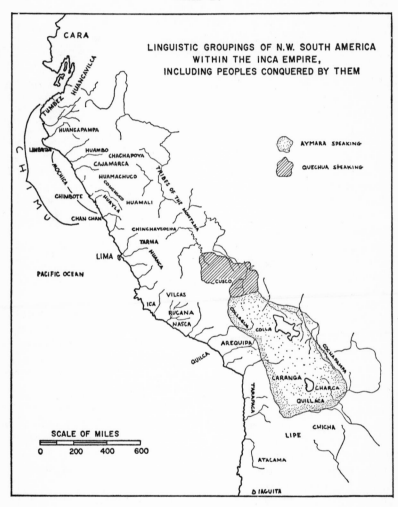

LINGUISTIC GROUPINGS OF N.W. SOUTH AMERICA
WITHIN THE INCA EMPIRE,
INCLUDING PEOPLES CONQUERED BY THEM

AYMARA SPEAKING

QUECHUA SPEAKING

CARA

HUANCAVILCA

TUMBEZ

HUANCAPAMPA

CHIMU

LAMBAYEQUE

HUAMBO
CHACHAPOYA
CAJAMARCA
HUAMACHUCO

MOCHICA

CONCHUCO

CHIMBOTE

HUAYLA   HUAMALI

TRIBES OF THE MONTAÑA

CHAN CHAN

CHINCHAYCOCHA

TARMA

HUANCA

LIMA

PACIFIC OCEAN

CUSCO

VILCAS

ICA

RUCANA
NASCA

COLLAGUA
COLLA

AREQUIPA

COCHA PAMPA

QUILCA

CARANGA
CHARCA
QUILLACA

TARAPACA

SCALE OF MILES

0   200   400   600

CHICHA
LIPE

ATACAMA

D IAGUITA

Glossary

Aac-ai. Alakaluf supreme deity.

Abalorio (Payagua). Straw wreath.

Abato. Plant. Leaves used for a stimulant.

Abipón. Chaco people.

Abracoma. Andean food and fur animal. A domesticated rodent.

Abuhuhua (Tisano). Two-faced hairy cannibal, mythical personage invoked to frighten children.

Acapeno. Tiahuanaco pyramid.

Acarajú. Tupí on Tocantins River.

Acaremba. Amazon timber tree.

Acaro. Amazon language.

Acatay mita (Quechua). Six-day avocado fruit festival.

Acaya. Amazon fruit.

Achera. Quechua plant cultivated for food.

Acochúa. Carib Guiana people.

Acope (Quechua). Agave.

Acroa. Brazilian backlanders.

Acshú (Quechua). Potato.

Adobe. Sun-dried brick.

Age of Mammals. The Tertiary. (*See* Geological eras)

Agouti (Acuti, Guaraní). Plump rodent used for food.

Aguari. Upper Amazon Tupí group.

Ahuaimanta (Quechua). A plumlike fruit. (*Physalis peruviana*)

Ahuaque. Guiana people.

Ahueicona. Amazon Indians.

Aimara. Bolivian highlanders.

Alakaluf. Chilean archipelago people. "Canoe people."

Alco-micos (Quechua). "Dog-eaters." Epithet applied to Huanca.

Alena. Tierra del Fuego flower.

Algarroba. The Carob. Honey mesquite. West Indian locust. Rain Tree. Sweet, pulpy pods.

Alpaca. Breed of llama. Finer wool.

Amanayé. Tupí group of Amazon delta.

Amara. Hardwood used for warclubs, etc.

Amaray. Quechua harvest festival.

Amarca (Quechua). "Month of the Dead." "Duty of the Dead."

Anahuac. Valley of Mexico.

Anambé. Tupí of Tocantins River.

Anán. A Guaraní demon.

Anco. Chaco pumpkin or squash.

Andaqui. Cambrian highlands.

Andesite. Hard feldspar, porphyry type of rock found only in the Andes and used in Sacsahuaman and Cuzco buildings.

Anericacua. Southernmost Tehuelche of Patagonia

Angara. Warlike people of Inca empire.

Anta. "Big Ear." Applied to Quechua nobles or Quechua privileged to distend their ears.

Anthropop. Pre-man ape types.

Anti. Arawak of Peruvian jungles.

Aparia. Indian chief, upper Amazon, 1542.

Apinayé. Brazilian backland tribe.

Apo (Quechua). Military commander.

Apoto ("Fire People"). Tupí on the Nhamundá River, Brazil.

Arana. Arawak people on Jurúa-Purús River and Bolivian Chiquitos.

Arawak. Widespread people from Uruguay to Guianas and West Indies.

Arecaché. Colombian food plant.

Areceira. Arcera. Brazil timber tree. Poisonous sap used medicinally.

Arecuní. Guiana people.

Argico. Plant providing stimulant.

Arí (Bororo). The Moon, a folk hero.

Ariranha. Large Amazon otter.

Aritica. Brazilian fruit.

Arrayán. Leaves used as dentifrice and aromatic.

Arreacha. Quechua food plant.

Arripurí. Indian chief, lower Amazon, 1542.

Arroba. Spanish weight, approximately 25 lbs. Portuguese arroba about 33 pounds.

Ashluslay. Chaco people.

Assai. Widely distributed important palm. Poisonous sap used to cure syphilis.

Association. Relation of artifacts, geological, plant, and animal remains found in juxtaposition with human remains or artifacts; relation to similar finds elsewhere.

Astrocarym. Fiber used by Jívaro.

Atacama. Northern Chilean people, desert and highlands. Also, the region.

Atahualpa. Thirteenth Inca, murdered by Spaniards.

Atlas. The first vertebra of the neck.

Aturé. Arawak people on Orinoco River.

Auca ("Rebel Enemy"). Quechua appellation for Auraucanians.

Aucapata. One of Cuzco's great central plazas.

Auraucano. Powerful nation of people, Central Chile and Patagonia.

Australoids. Aboriginal Australian and Tasmanian people.

Autochthonous. Formed in place now existing. Indigenous. Aboriginal.

Avara. Useful palm.

Aya-huasca. Narcotic made from spruce.

Ayar ("Wild Quinóa"). Four Inca brothers.

Ayecoc. Almond. A much prized Amazon nut tree.

Ayllu. Quechua clan and commune.

Aymara. *See* Aimara.

Ayorquín. Alakaluf shellfish pole.

Azara prisca. Foxlike canid.

Aztec. People of central Mexico at time of Conquest.

Babassú. Bussú. Palm. Important for fruits, oils, sap, green shoots, etc.

Bachué. Chibcha god.

Bacororo. Bororo folk hero.

Badze (Carire). Amazon tobacco god.

Bandurría (Ibis). Estrado Island sea bird.

Baracuna. Amazon timber tree.

Barba tobacco. Prized fine tobacco.

Barbasco. Wild cinnamon. A fish poison widely used.

Bari (Bororo). "Soul of the dead."

Batata (Taino, Tupí). Sweet potato. Later in Europe corrupted to "potato," an entirely different plant.

Belt loom. Loom attached to weaver's waist at one end.

Bixa orellana. Seeds providing red dye.

Blood types. O, universal; A, largely European; B, largely Asiatic; M, chiefly New World; N, chiefly Australian and New World; MN, chiefly New World; RH factor, chiefly western Europe, Africa; Diego factor, first discovered in Venezuela.

Bochica. Chibcha god.

Bohané. Argentine river and delta people.

Bohío (Spanish or Arawak). Thatched Cuban hut. Corruption of word also used in Tupinamba area, Brazil.

Bola. Stones, usually three, tied by cords or leather thongs at end of a riata and thrown to encircle legs of birds and animals and bring them down.

Bopé. Bororo soul.

Borhyaenid. Prehistoric carnivore.

Borón. Witoto group.

Bororo. Brazilian backland tribe.

Brachycephalic. Round-headed.

Bunía. A Guiana bird who taught Carib use of plants.

Buriat. Mongol people of Siberia.

Caatinga. Brazilian brush land; dry scrub country; Forest dwellers southeast Brazil.

Cacaguate (Aztec). Peanut.

Cachebanca. Arawak fiber used for fine hammocks.

Cacique (Tano, Arawak, Aztec). Chieftain or ruler.

Caco (Quechua). Public hunting party.

Cacta. Tupinambi group between Parayba and São Francisco Rivers.

Caeteti. Collared Brazilian peccary.

Cafushi. White-lipped, teeth-grinding Brazilian peccary.

Caguaba. Northwest Colombian highland and jungle people.

Caguaí (Guaraní). Chicha beer.

Cahuahil. Tupí tribe on Tapajoz River, Brazil.

Caicaí. Araucanian mythical serpent who raised the sea, causing the Great Flood.

Caingang. Brazilian southeast plateau people.

Caipoterade. Northern Chaco people.

C'Aix (Ona). Legendary mighty hunter.

Cajuy. Cashew nut.

Caltrop. Four-pointed ground spikes for stopping pursuers.

Camacán. Chaco group.

Cambrian. Earliest division of Paleozoic Era.

Cañagua ocú (Quechua). Toasted quinóa, a grain.

Canaimá. Guiana Carib spirit.

Cañarí. People south of Quito. Provided the royal Inca guards.

Canayurú. Prepared lacquer, Rio Negro region.

Cancha (Quechua). Sport field or plaza. Still used in much of South America.

Canela. Cinnamon; N. Brazilian Indians.

Canelo. Laurel or cinnamon tree.

Canibe (Caribe). Original name of Carib, corrupted by Spaniards. Means "brave," and provides our modern word "Cannibal."

Canoeiro. Brazilian Guaraní on Araguaya River.

Cao (Tupí, Tupinamba). Sweet manioc festival.

Caoana. Gold in aboriginal Hispaniola.

Capac (Quechua). About 18 inches.

Capichaba. Purple dye.

Capulí. Plum. Cherry.

Capybara. Enormous tropical rodent. Eaten for food.

Cara. Early Ecuadorian kingdom. Its people. Conquered by Incas.

Caraba. Crabwood.

Caracara. Patagonian bird of the falconiformes.

Carache. Lake Titicaca fish.

Carachú. Yucca.

Caraguatá. Fiber plant; Amazon Indians.

Caraque. Ecuadorean coast people.

Carbon-dating. Method of determining age of organic carbon materials by amount of radiation loss. "Carbon half life" is 5,568 years.

Carinjé. Perfumed wood. Amazon.

Carizo (Quechua). Reed.

Carnejo. Brazilian backlander.

Carudo. Reed-stemmed plant, with flowering clusters. Brazilian backlands.

Caruzo. See Carudo.

Cashpi (Ona). Soul.

Castelú. Brazilian board.

Caucasoid. Caucasian types. "White" race.

Caullaca. Quechua goddess of chastity.

Cavi. Small Araucanian political subdivision of 400 persons.

Cavy. The "guinea pig," edible rodent.

Cayuyu. Dwarf cashew.

Ccullá. Quechua grain measurement, 26 quarts.

Ceatú (Quechua). Mother Serpent. Bringer of storms.

Ceiba. Hardwood tree widely distributed, Mexico to far south in Latin America.

Ceja de la Montaña. "Eyebrow of the Mountain." Mid-Andean eastern temperate zone altitude.

Cenozoic. Era of recent terrestrial age. 75 million years. Includes Quaternary and Tertiary Ages.

Cere perdu. Use of wax molds in metal casting.

Chachalaca. A species of guan from Argentina to Texas.

Chachapoya. Warlike people of Inca empire.

Chacóa. Chaco group.

Chama. Ucayali River people.

Chamacoco. Chaco people.

Chamal. Over-all article of clothing worn by Auraucanian males.

Chamico (Datura). A narcotic.

Champata. Pre-Incan Cuzco culture.

Champlevé. Incised stone work.

Chana. Arawak, Uruguay.

Chañar. Pampa and Chaco fruit-bearing scrub bush.

Chanca. Unruly people near Cuzco.

Chanchan. Chimu capital near modern Trujillo, Peru.

Chané. Chaco immigrants.

Chanibera. Amazon Indians.

Chapina. Black potato dye.

Charrúa. Argentine Indians, lower river area.

Chasquel. Ona cannibal dead.

Chasqui (Quechua). Runners. Messengers.

Chaucha (Auraucanian). Yellow potato. Modern slang for a centavo.

Chavín. Early great Peruvian culture. Perhaps 4,500 years old.

Chayo. Early Chilean Indians, perhaps Arawak.

Cheluele. Chief Patagonian devil. Also called "Setibos."

Chepena. Alakaluf heron feather headdress.

Chep-pach. Rushes used for Alakaluf basketry.

Chía (Chibcha). The Moon.

Chibcha. People and culture of Central Colombia and possibly eastern Central America.

Chibchashím ("Chibcha Staff"). A God.

Chicha. Coast Peruvians.

Chicha. Peruvian beer. Made from molle, berries, corn, grain, chili, cactus, etc.

Chilco. Tierra del Fuego flower.

Chimi-ni-guagua. Chibcha creator God.

Chimú. Post-Moché, pre-Inca culture; Peruvian coast, Ecuador.

Chipas (Guaraní). Maize cakes.

Chique-chique. White flowered Brazilian palm. Paissaba.

Chiquicuano. Amazon Indians.

Chirimoya. Fruit, Brazil to Mexico. Scalelike shell, gray-white flesh with small black seeds dispersed. Tastes like granulated vanilla ice cream.

Chiripa. Culture north shore of Lake Titicaca. Pre-Inca.

Chiripa. Diaperlike breechclout used by Auraucanian males and modern gauchos.

Choco. Mountain or plateau Indians, upper Amazon.

Chomba. Palm wood used for blowguns, musical instruments, house building, etc.

Chono. Chilean archipelago Indians below Auraucanians.

Choque (Aimara). Potato.

Chorotí. Chaco people.

Chuchau (Quechua). Maguey.

Chullpa. Culture between Tiahuanaco II and Inca empire of Bolivia-Peru-Lake Titicaca region.

Chumpivilca. Bolivian people, famed for dancing. Provided Inca court dancers.

Chunca, Chanca ("Wild people"). Peruvian jungles.

Chuñú (Quechua). Frozen potatoes.

Cipo embé. Bark used by Caingang for binding.

Cloquitíin. Ona puberty ceremony.

Clovis points. Types of arrowheads or tools first found at Clovis, New Mexico.

Co (Quechua, Colla). Prefix meaning "water."

Cocana. Tupí tribes, upper Amazon.

Coconuco. Colombian highlanders.

Codalodi. Chaco people.

Codollate. Chaco people.

Colastine. Western pampa Indians.

Colla. Leading people and language, Inca empire, chiefly in Bolivia.

Comagía. Chaco people.

Comida de oso ("Bear Food"). A spiny yucca on Titicaca Island.

Compí (Quechua). Fine woven cloth.

Coniupuyara ("Grand Mistress"). Queen of the Amazons. Orellana's time.

Cora Cora. One of the royal palaces in Cuzco.

Coracenque. Probably the forktailed nighthawk. Feathers reserved for the Inca's sole use.

Corduru. Red timber tree.

Coricancha. Cuzco Sun Temple to worship Viracocha.

Coroado. Chaco Indians.

Coronado. Argentine Delta Indians.

Coropó. Brazilian Indians.

Cosa (Quechua). Husband.

Courontuné. Orinoco River people.

Coya (Quechua). Queen.

Cubéo. Uaupés River people.

Cuchabiba (Arawak?). Uaupés River group.

Cucurubitaca. Chaco food plant.

Cuga. Araucanian kinship clan, or settlement.

Cultrún. Araucanian flat drum.

Cumbanama. Jívaro Supreme deity.

Cupí-rob. Tupí Tocantins River people.

Cupisnique. Culture on Peruvian coast, roughly 850 B.C.

Curaca. Chieftain.

Curandero. Healer.

Curevá. Eastern Plateau Indians.

Curita-bimbi. Red almond tree (arcyocar armydatigerum).

Curú. Caingang cloak.

Dahué (Araucanian). Quinóa. A grain.

Damas del Sur. Peruvian and Chilean edible shellfish.

Datura. A narcotic. Chamico.

Degúl (Araucanian). Kidney bean.

Desert Culture. Nomenclature of prehistoric civilization in the Great Basin, U.S.A.

Diaguita. People of northern Chile and northwest Argentina.

Diargo. Alakaluf coil basket.

Diego factor. Blood type first encountered in Venezuela.

Dinosauria. Prehistoric reptiles.

Diptothomo argentinus. Supposed late Argentine hominid (Ameghino).

Dolichocephalic. Long-headed.

Ecúl (Araucanian). Female cape or shawl.

Elephas colombii. A New World Mammoth.

Elothera. Gigantic prehistoric extinct piglike mammal.

Embabúa. Brazilian fiber.

Embira (Bombax). Bark cloth. Cotton. White or red flowers.

Endogamy. Marriage within the family, clan, village, tribe, or nation.

Eninaje (Machicuya). Chaco linguistic family.

Epigonal. Late Tiahuanaco culture on Peruvian and Ecuadorian coast.

Epiphiti. Epiphyte. Aerial plant.

Escorzonera. Quechua medical root.

Esmeralda. Coast Ecuadorians. Also name of modern province.

Exogamy. Marriage outside the family, clan, tribe or nation.

Eyigayequí ("Dwellers in Palm Groves"). Chaco tribe.

Fasán Calla (Quechua). Popcorn.

Feijo do monte. Mountain bean.

Forno d'aqua. Mountain bean.

Fulnio (Carnejo). Brazilian backlander.

Fura Chogué ("Beneficent Female"). A Chibcha goddess (Zaque).

Gaianoca. Ch   )le.

Gama (Tupí)   irit.

Garúa. Peruvia.   `   ɛ.

Gatubí. Fruits.

Gaucho. Pampa cow   )y.

Gê. Brazilian peopl driven into hinterland by Tupinamba.

Genequín ("Nation folk"). Penhuelche.

Genipa. Black dye (*Bixa orellana*).

Geologic eras, ages, and periods.

(1) Cenozoic Era ("modern life"), 95,000,000,000 years.

  (a) Quaternary "Age of Man," 1,200,000 years, including Holocene period (recent, 250,000 years) and Pleistocene, 1,000,000 years.

  (b) Tertiary. "Age of Mammals," including
Pliocene, 16,000,000 years
Oligocene, 11,000,000 years
Eocene, 19,000,000 years
Paleocene, 17,000,000 years

(2) Mesozoic ("Middle" Age. "Age of Reptiles"), 130,000,000 years, including
Cretaceous, 60,000,000 years
Jurassic, 30,000,000 years
Triassic, 40,000,000 years

(3) Paleozoic. 300,000,000 years.

  (a) Age of Amphibians, 75,-000,000 years
Permian, 25,000,000 years
Carboniferous, 50,000,000 years

  (b) Age of Fishes, 80,000,000 years
Devonian, 45,000,000 years
Silurian, 35,000,000 years

  (c) Age of Marine Invertebrates, 145,000,000 years
Ordovician, 65,000,000 years
Cambrian, 80,000,000 years

(4) Proterozoic, 425,000,000 years. (Part of Age of Marine Invertebrates.)

(5) Archeozoic, 575,000,000 years.

Glacial ages. From beginning of Pleistocene, 1,000,000 years ago. (European name in parenthesis.)
Jersey (Günz)

Glacial ages (*Continued*)
Kansas (Mindel)
Illinois-Iowa (Riss)

(Upper Pleistocene)
Early Wisconsin (Würm I)
Late Wisconsin (Würm II)
Last period known as Mankato
in U.S.

Glyptodont. Armadillo-like prehistoric gigantic mammal.

Gos. Supreme spirit of the Vielela, Chaco.

Guachi. Important Chaco racestock.

Guaharibo. Surinam people.

Guaicurú. Pampa and Chaco people.

Guaimí atucupo (Guaraní). Leaves used in cooking.

Guaja. Tupí nomads. Brazil.

Guajiro. Venezuelan people.

Guanaco. Wild cousin and ancestor of the llama.

Guarabú, Guarabá. *Astronium,* red timber tree.

Guaraní. Chaco people. Still the prevailing language of Paraguay.

Guatabita. Colombian highlanders of the Zaque realm.

Guayana (Caingang). S.E. Brazil people.

Guayaquí. Paraguay people.

Guaycurutú. Chaco people.

Guazú. Chaco people. Subgroup of Guaicurú.

Guck. Brazil backlanders near Amazon mouth. Possibly Carib.

Gueloaza. Argentine people. Cf. Hueloaza.

Guenoá. Coast and delta Argentine people.

Guhaí (Tucano). Creator hero god, with power to transform people and objects into animals.

Gúnechen. Auraucanian Supreme Being.

Habarandi do matto. Botocudo cure for smallpox pustules.

Hacamuyí (Lengua). Spirit who aided farm work.

Hamaca (Arawak). Hammock.

Hanipi camayoc (Quechua). Doctor.

Hanush. Legendary Yahgan giant.

Hebú. Guiana clown spirit.

Hecheri. Abipón (Chaco) military society.

Het. Chilean and Argentine people.

Heuquén (Auraucanian). Barley-like grain.

Hogo (uncertain origin). Plum. Mentioned by Carbajal on lower Amazon.

Hoka. Race-group, Oregon to Tehuantepec, Nicaragua. Salvador.

Holocene Period. Most recent period of man. 250,000 years.

Hominid. Family of animals to which man belongs.

Homunculus. Supposed prehistoric small man-type (Ameghino).

Hono curaca (Quechua). Headman over 10,000 people.

Huaca. Any prehistoric archaeological object of a religious nature, or a temple.

Huaca. Sister-wife of one of first four Inca brothers.

Huada (Auraucanian). Shaking gourd, for music. Similar to Cuban *matraca.*

Huaicurú (Bororo). Soul of the dead.

Hualla. Early Cuzco people before Quechua.

Huancaré (Quechua). Large drum.

Huancavalica. Peruvian Ecuadorian coast people.

Huani (Quechua). Wife.

Huapa. Race-stock, California and Mexican border Indians.

Huarpe. Western Cuyo Pampa Indians.

Huarrau (Warrau). Inner Amazon Indians.

Huascar. Twelfth Inca. Heir of Huyna Capac. Half brother of Atahualpa.

Huayla. People of Inca empire; homosexuals.

Huayna Capac. Eleventh Inca. Father of Atahualpa and Huascar.

Huazai (Guaja, Tupí). Wax.

Huazaizara (Guaja, Tupí). "Owners of Tufted Ears." "Tufted Ears." Nomads of central Brazil.

Huëcurú. Araucanian evil spirit.

Huillí ("South People"). Chilean archipelago.

Huilliche (Araucanian). "South People."

Huilmén (Araucanian). "Noble rich man." Headman or cacique.

Huimba. Fine fluffy cotton.

Huitaca ("Mother"). Chibcha goddess of pleasure, dancing, drunkenness, and fornication.

Humuc Huar. Huarpe supreme being.

Huni (Quechua). Clod-breaker.

Hunsa-Huá. A Zaque (Chibcha) ruler.

Hupaycí (Quechua). Plumb-bob.

Hurón. A ferret.

Hutia (Tupí, Taino). Edible rodent of Cuba and adjacent islands.

Hypsicephalic. Very high-headed. Super dolichocephalic.

Ibiritanga. Hardwood used for war-clubs.

Ica. Coast Peruvian culture, below the Nazca.

Ichú. Bunch grass used by Quechua for roofs, brooms, etc.

Ihuera penne (Tupinamba). Painted war-club used to kill prisoner to be eaten.

Imbú. Brazilian fruit.

Inaga. Plant used for smoking rubber.

Inca. Quechua Supreme Ruler. Inca Roca. Sixth Inca.

Inca Urcón. Deposed Inca, not counted in royal lineage.

Incucha. Quechua medicinal roots.

Inga. Large pods. Good wood.

Ipe. Brazilian wood. Pao d'arco.

Ipí. Small fresh-water fish, Lake Titicaca.

Ipurima. Amazon inlanders.

Iraca. "Nation" of the Tundama, ruled by priests.

Isía. Fat ant eaten by Tupinamba.

Isistiné. Chaco group.

Issura. Amazon palm.

Itaborí. Bororo folk hero.

Itacolumite. A quartzite sandstone, Brazil only, often imbedded with diamonds.

Jabatica. Jabiticaba. Small fruit varieties of the Jabota tree, used for making canoes.

Jacandá ("The Red-Eyed"). Tupí people on the Tocantins River.

Jaibirú. Large stork.

Jaico. Southwestern Brazilian people.

Jataca. Quechua food and medicinal plant.

Jívaro (Jibaro). Ecuadorian head-shrinkers.

Joaz. Brazilian tree with golden blossoms and edible fruit.

Jobe. Plumlike fruit.

Jurema, juremú. Amazon timber tree.

Jurí (Arawak). North of Amazon.

Jurí pixuna (Arawak). "Black Mouth." Nickname of tattooed tribe of Arawak at and about Manao.

Kitchen midden. Prehistoric household trash heap and garbage pile.

Lacandón. Chiapas (Mexico) Indian.

Lacuma. Yahgan water spirit.

Lambayeque. North coastal Peruvian culture.

Lengua. Important Chaco group.

Lerma points. Type of pointed artifact and tool first found in Tamaulipas, Mexico, also in Venezuela and Argentina.

Levirate. System in which widow becomes wife of husband's brother.

Levo. Auraucanian political district.

Lipán. Southwest U.S. and northern Mexico tribe.

Lisa. Mullet. Brazilian ocean fish.

Llanca (Auraucanian). Necklace.

Llauhuén (Auraucanian). Strawberry.

Llautu (Quechua). Wool cap. The Inca's llautu was adorned with wool strands held by gold tubes.

Lloque Yupanque. Third Inca.

Lu. Useful palm.

Lucuma. Aboriginal Brazilian fruit.

Lulú-Velela. Widespread Chaco linguistic family.

Luqui. Luki. Highland potato, frost resistant.

Macacauba. Beautiful hardwood, used for cabinet work, also for charcoal.

Macacuya. Brazilian fruit.

Macambia. Water-storing plant of Brazilian droughtlands.

Macán. Chaco people.

Macana. War-club, set with sharp stone, glass, or metal.

Macha cali. Brazilian backlanders.

Machicuyo. Important Chaco people.

Machipero. Upper Amazon people.

Machúa. Type of bean.

Machu Picchu. The great fortress-temple city on the lower Urubamba River.

Macnú. Red dye.

Macrauchenia. Prehistoric animal resembling a combination of camel, horse, and elephant.

Macrebope (Bororo). Soul.

Macú. Guiana people.

Macuehahua (Tupinamba). Bird. Eggs eaten. Played a role in cannibalistic ceremonies.

Macuña (Auraucanian). Poncho.

Macurdu. Amazon tribe.

Macushi. Guiana Carib people.

Madí. Auraucanian oil seed.

Magú. Auraucanian mango.

Malbala. Chaco people.

Mama (Quechua). "Mother." Four sister-wives of first four Inca brothers.

Mama Saca. Quechua goddess.

Mama Sora ("Magic Mother"). Quechua goddess of maize.

Mamona. Castor oil bean.

Manaca. Amber plant used for curing syphilis.

Manão. Arawak group of central Amazon north of the river.

Manco Capac. First Inca.

Mancol. Useful palm.

Mangaberra. Latex for coating boats.

Mangerona. Western Amazon Indians.

Mango (Malay), Magú (Auraucanian). Tropical fruit, with long thin stone.

Maní (Arawak). Peanut.

Manioc. A tuber. Staff of life in Amazon area.

Mankato. Wisconsin glaciation about 11,000 years ago.

Mapuche. Auraucanian from Maule River to Bio Bio River, or so.

Mara. Harelike rodent. Pampas region.

Maraja. Useful palm.

Marata. Palm tree. Provided beer of same name. (Also called Masata.)

Marata. Beer from Manioc.

Maronta. Arrowroot.

Marouiní. Orinoco River people.

Masata. Manioc beer.

Mascoí. Chaco linguistic group.

Masculí. Indians of southwest Brazil.

Masculiné (Guaraní). The Moon personified.

Mata. Ecuadorian coastal people.

Mataco. Chaco people.

Mataco-Macún. Chaco people.

Maté. Herb used for tea.

Matrilineal. Tracing descent through female line. Usually newlyweds live with bride's family.

Mayabá. Much prized Amazon fruit.

Mayta Capac. Fourth Inca.

Mbayá. Important Chaco people.

Mbeguá. Argentine coast agricultural Indians.

Médanos. Stretches of Peruvian desert sand dunes.

Megatheria. Giant prehistoric ground-sloths. Pliocene period.

Merí. The Sun, Bororo folk hero.

Mesozoic Era. "The Age of Reptiles," including the Cretaceous, Jurassic, and Triassic periods. Lasted 130,000,000 years.

Metate (Nahuatl). Stone for grinding maize, etc.

Mirití. Fiber used by Arawak for clothing.

Mistol. Chaco fruit.

Mitimae (Quechua). Compulsory colonists of other areas under the Incas.

Moche. Capital and chief (arch.) site of Moche people.

Mochica. Language of Peruvian coast people, about time of Christ.

Moco. Rock cavy of guinea-pig type.

Mocoví. Chaco people.

Mogo-Mogo (Quechua). Food and medicinal plant.

Molle. False pepper tree. Piru tree. Red berries used for chicha.

Mongoloid. Race of people from northern China, Siberia, and the Orient, one of three major races.

Moratoco. Chaco people.

Mu. Mythical lost Pacific continent.

Muirapenema. Tortoise-shell wood.

Muleta oars. Crutch-shaped oars.

Murandaluguaburabura. Indian kingdom on lower Amazon, time of Orellana.

Murichú. Palm used for building houses, fences.

Mylodon. Prehistoric slothlike edentate.

Nahuatl. Mexican-Central American race stock. Included Aztec, etc.

Nambicuara. Amazon people.

Napipinizique. A Chaco people. Also called **Guaicurutí.**

Nazca. Pre-Inca, pre-Chimú Peruvian coast culture.

Nencatacóa. Patron gods of Chibcha weavers.

Neotrópica. South America as zoographic region.

Nijimanche (Jívaro). Manioc beer.

Nucay (Arawak). Gold in pre-Spanish Cuba.

Ñucchú. Red Flower of the Inca.

Ñusta. Inca vestal virgin.

Nustal. Chaco food plant.

Oca (Quechua). Highland wood sorrel. Roots eaten.

Oclla, or Mama Oclla. Sister-wife of Huayna Capac.

Ocole ("Foxes"). Chaco people.

Ocullo. Highland squashlike vegetable.

Olla. Large terra cotta jar.

Omagua. Amazon tribe.

Ombu, umbo, umbu. Widespread tree common from Patagonia into Amazon. Poisonous leaves, but roots eaten.

Ona ("North People" in Yahgan tongue). Tierra del Fuego.

Oncoy. The Pleiades. Supreme Being of Chavín.

Oniquguë. Ruler of Upper Amazon. Orellana's time.

Orejón ("Big Ear"). Group of Witoto. Seen by Orellana.

Ortiga brava. A fiber plant.

Osca. Chibcha narcotic.

Oyapoc. Orinoco people.

Pacaca curaca (Quechua). Headman of 100 persons.

Pacanamaru. Prehistoric Moche city.

Paca-Onaucoc (Quechua). Stone piles for determining time, such as when to begin planting.

Pacha. The Cara (Ecuador) wife of Huayna Capac. Mother of Atahualpa.

Pachacamac. Quechua coast religious center. Below present Lima, Peru.

Pachacuti. Ninth Inca.

Pachiuyrhizis. Quechua edible root.

Paguano. Indian ruler on Amazon. Orellana's time.

Paleocene. Earliest period of the Cenozoic Era and the Tertiary Age of Mammals. 17,000,000 years.

Pallar (Quechua). Kind of bean.

Palle (Auraucanian). Soul.

Palta (Quechua). Avocado.

Panche. "Wild" Colombian people near Chibcha.

Pantanel, El. Paraguay River swamp.

Paracona. Tupí tribe on the Pacuya River, Brazil.

Para paraiba. Tree, light wood.

Páramo. High bleak Andean plateau.

Parati. River fish prized by Tupinamba.

Parica. Stimulant made from various plants.

Patagón ("Big Foot"). Name given to Patagonian people by Magellan.

Patasho. Brazil backlanders. Warlike hunters.

Pato. Brazilian Indian group.

Patrilineal. Tracing descent through male line.

Patúa. Useful palm. Pãu Santo. Perfumed "Holy Wood."

Paxiuba. Useful palm. Various spellings.

Payagá. Chaco people.

Payni-quén. Northern Tehuelche in Patagonia.

Pehuelche (Auraucanian). "East People"; Andean and Patagonian and Pampan Indians.

Pehuenche ("Pine people"). Auraucanian highlanders on both slopes of Andes.

Peixi-poi. Manatee or sea cow.

Pemacameca. Eastern Amazon people.

Penche (Auraucanian). Squash.

Pencóa. Dolichocephalic Indian group of central South America.

Petrograph. Rock painting or carving.

Piassaba. Palm. Bark used for cordage.

Pichucavi. Small Auraucanian political division.

Picunchi. Central Chile Indians.

Pifulca. Auraucanian flute.

Pihuayo. Quechua plant food.

Pilagá. Chaco people.

Pilcomayo. Indians of Pilcomayo and Chaco region.

Pillán. Auraucanian Supreme Being.

Pima Pincí. Tiahuanaco platform construction.

Pincullo (Quechua). A whistle.

Pingo pingo. Quechua food and medicinal plant.

Pinquilhuë. Auraucanian vertical flute.

Pintado. Small transparent Amazon fish.

Piperi (Tupí). Raft.

Piqué, piquihuí, piquía. Amazon tree, edible oily nuts.

Piracuí (Guaraní). Powdered meat or fish.

Pirajá. 100-pound Amazon fish.

Piranha. Amazon cannibal fish.

Pirarucú. Huge fresh water fish. Much eaten.

Piruna Manco. Mythical 1300 B.C. Inca ruler.

Pirú. The molle or false pepper tree of Peru.

Pithecanthropus. Prehistoric hominid.

Pitheculitus. Mythical ape-type (Ameghino).

Plangi. Large-leafed plant.

Pleistocene Period. Prior to Holocene or recent period. 1,000,000 years.

Pliocene Period. First period of Age of Mammals. 11,000,000 years. Possible first appearance of man.

Pocra. Unruly people near Cuzco.

Poroto del Monte. Chaco bean.

Potiquara. Tupinamba tribe on Paranahyaba River.

Poto (Quechua). Small box with lid.

Poya. North Patagonian hill Indians.

Ppirí tacta (Quechua). Biscuits of quinóa flour.

Proboscideans. The elephants.

Proterozoic. Early geological age. *See* Geology.

Protosaura. Ancient reptiles.

Puca. Rough stones set in clay for walls.

Puelche. Central and north Chile Indians.

Puma chipiana. Animal zoo in Cuzco.

Puma curú. Animal zoo in Cuzco.

Puna. Chaco fruit.

Puna. Ecuadorian coast people.

Puré. Sister-wife of early Inca.

Purí. Chaco Indians.

Purí-Coroado. Chaco peoples.

Pyramidal. Designating pointed skull.

Pyrotheria. Prehistoric animals of the Pampas, some horselike in appearance, though not in reality.

Quanyp. Ona folk hero.

Quari (Quechua). Man, when mentioned as "not woman."

Quaternary Age. "Age of Man." Last 1,000,000 years.

Quechua. Leading people of Inca empire. Language widely diffused from Argentina to Colombia and in western trans-Andean jungles.

Quellán (Araucanian). Strawberry.

Quenos. Ona gods.

Quenque. Ona devil.

Quenyuco. Indian chief on middle Amazon, Orellana's time.

Quepán (Araucanian). Long dress, worn over one shoulder.

Querandí, Querendí. "People who have grease." Northern Patagonian and Pampan Indians. Now largely extinct.

Quezado. White-lipped peccary.

Quilquil (Culcul) (Araucanian). Musical animal horn.

Quimbaya. Colombian people near Chibcha.

Quinaquina (Quechua). Quinine.

Quinúa, Quinóa (Quechua). Edible pigweed. A grass grain.

Quipú (Quechua). Knotted varicolored cords for recording statistics, dates, and other data.

Rahua. Sister-wife of one of first four Inca brothers.

Ramu. Brazilian plant providing strychnine.

Raymi (Quechua). Fiesta. Chief Raymi was in December.

Recuay. Post-Chavín, pre-Inca culture, north Peru.

Repoussé. High-relief metal designs formed by pressure from the back or casting.

Rhea. Small South American ostrich.

Rhipalide. Parasite in Brazil.

Ricara. Quechua measurement, about 64 meters.

284

Rocana ("Finger"). Quechua length.
Ruca. Araucanian dwelling.
Rucana ("Finger Folk"). Provided the Inca's litter bearers.

Sábalo. Large Amazon fish.
Sabiá. Brazilian songbird.
Sachacandía. Chaco fruit.
Sachalimonas. Chaco mountain orange.
Sacsahuamán. Colossal Inca fortress above Cuzco.
Sairo. Collared peccary.
Saliva. Guiana people. Also called Macua.
Sambaquí. Brazilian river and shore shell mounds.
Sanapapa. Chaco people.
Sanguimán. Straits of Magellan flower.
Sano sano. Quechua food plant.
Saparinda. A genus of Sapotacea.
Sapauí. Chaco people.
Sapindos, Sapindus. Soap tree. Soap and fruits.
Sapodilla. A Sapotacea genus. Delicious fruits. Scores of species. One, the chico sapote, provides chicle for chewing gum.
Sapotacea. Enormous family of tropical fruits and trees (355 genera, 600 species).
Sapote, Zapote. See Sapodilla. Often called nispera.
Saya. Political division, Inca empire.
Sayahua. Boundary stones.
Seri. Tiburon Island Indian.
Sericora. Bird of Brazil.
Seriema. Brazilian and Chaco bird, large and graceful.

Setebós. The devil among Patagóns. Also called Cheleule.
Shabióa. Amazon Indians.
Shacaima (Jívaro). Husband of the Earth Goddess.
Shaman. Indian medicine man or priest.
Shavante, Chavante. Bolivian jungle Indians.
Sherente. Bolivian plateau Indians.
Sibú. Tree. Resin for lamps or light.
Sicama, Sicana. Vines. Bright flowers. Delicious fruit.
Sicya. Quechua measurement, about a yard.
Sincha Roca. Second Inca.
Sinchi (Quechua). A noble.
Siriono. Eastern Bolivian Indians.
Siriono. Guiana people. Also called Guaharibo.
Stratification. Geological level of archaeological data.
Sucurrí, sicurrú. Anaconda.
Surihualla ("Plain of the Ostriches"). Aviary south of Cuzco.

Taclla (Quechua). Metal-tipped digging tool.
Taihui. Araucanian hair fillet.
Taino. Indians of Caribbean. Arawak.
Tanajura. Fat ant eaten by Tupinamba.
Tanca. A Brazilian sea-mullet.
Tantarrh (Araucanian). Spear.
Tapadera. Stinging ray.
Tapaniu. S.W. Brazilian people.
Tapirage. Altering color of growing feathers on birds with various chemicais.
Tapirape, Tapurapi. Amazon tribe.

Tapuya. Southeast Brazilian people.

Tarahumara. North Mexican mountain Indians.

Tasca. Edible Chaco seed pods.

Tasi. Chaco food plant.

Tatú. Brazilian armadillo.

Teca (Auraucanian). Barleylike grain.

Tecoma conspicua (bigonia). Flexible wood used for bows.

Tehué. Patagonian people.

Tehuelche. Patagonian Indians, probably Auraucanian.

Tenetehará. Tupí Brazilian people.

Teosintle. Wild cereal; possibly either ancestor of maize or a retrogression.

Tepexpán Man. Skeleton found in Mexico. May date 11,000 years ago.

Terena. Chaco people.

Tertiary Age. "Age of Mammals." *See* Geologic periods. 74,000,000 years.

Tiahuanaco. Bolivian highland culture. When it flourished has not been satisfactorily settled. Tiahuanaco I may have been very early. Tiahuanaco II, a later flourishing, may have occurred thousands of years ago, though some archaeologists place it A.D. Inca culture not derived from it. Tiahuanaco II is also known as "Classical Tiahuanaco."

Tica, tika. Amazon game.

Timbíra. Amazon Indians.

Timbú. Parana delta Indians.

Tipití. Arawak device for preparing manioc mush.

Tobó. Chaco people.

Tocarú. Brazilian nut tree.

Tocoyricoco (Quechua). "He who sees well." Royal Inca inspector.

Toldo. Tent house.

Tomaquil Ona. Supreme Being.

Topa Inca. Tenth Inca.

Topo (Quechua). Standard lot or farm-size.

Topuí (Tupí). White-haired thunder and lightning God.

Toquí (Auraucanian). Political-military district headman. Also the battle-axe, symbol of his authority.

Toxodont. Prehistoric rhinoceros-sized mammal.

Triassic Period. First period of Age of Reptiles. Some of earliest land emerged.

Triprothomo plantensis. Theoretical monkey-man link in America (Ameghino).

Tsantsa (Jívaro). Shrunken head.

Tsén. Mythological Auraucanian serpent, who lifted up the mountains at the time of the Great Flood.

Tsón Con. Patagonian and Fireland language group.

Tsuca, tsucoc (Quechua). Gambling game.

Tucana, Tucano. Witoto or Arawak people of inner Ecuador and Colombia.

Tuco, tuco tuco (Guaraní). Gopher-type animal, Tierra del Fuego, Chaco.

Tucuma. Palm. Fiber used for hammocks.

Tuob. Gold in Hispaniola.

Tupí (Mycengatú-Tupí). Vast race stock. Usually considered first cousins of Guaraní.

Tupí-Cawahib. Branch tribe on upper Madeira.

Tupina. Guaraní coastal group, Brazil.

Tupinamba. Brazilian coast people (Guaraní).

Tupu (Arawak). Pin or brooch.

Turi. Useful palm (Bacaba).

Tuyuca ("Clay people"). A Tucano tribe, inner Ecuador.

Tyhyqui. Chibcha narcotic.

Uaca. Useful palm. Paddles made from it.

Uaupé, Vaupé. People on Uaupés River.

Ubigara, Ubiragara (Tupí). Light wood, used for ear plugs, boats, etc.

Ulluco (Quechua). Squashlike vegetable. Olluco.

Uma (Aimara). Water.

Umbaube, umbaubera. Light wood. Leaves used to polish wood.

Uranium daughter process. Process of dating materials by radiation from uranium by-products.

Urú. Earliest peoples of highland Bolivia. Perhaps Arawak.

Urucurú, urucú. Very useful palm. Provides dye.

Utiapa (Jívaro). Wrap-around sheet.

Vacaa ("People of the Excrements"). Chaco tribe.

Verruga. Andean disease. Huge brown warts burst and bleed. Usually fatal. Carried by night-flying insect. Now largely eliminated thanks to DDT.

Viehuela (Quechua). Guitar or harp.

Vilela. Chaco people.

Vinhatico. Yellow or red wood timber tree, Brazil (Plathymenia, Pethecolombium).

Viracocha. Eighth Inca.

Viracocha. Quechua Sun God.

Viscacha. Fur-bearing edible rodent.

Vitanmapú (Auraucanian). Folk country, nation.

Wishinu, Huizinú (Jívaro). Medicine man, shaman.

Witoto, Huitoto. Northwest Amazon tribe. Parana and upper Caquito Rivers.

Xosheoque-xamni (Ona). Twig bundles used for snowshoes.

Xue (Chibcha). Lord.

Yacón. Edible tuber.

Yacumama. Anaconda.

Yahgan. Indians of extreme southwest, Tierra del Fuego.

Yahima (Arawak?). People of northern South America.

Yahuar Capac. Seventh Inca.

Yamanadidi. Western Amazon Indians.

Yanacón (Quechua). Serf, servitor.

Yaro. Argentine coast and delta Indians.

Yatai-Quazú. Coconut.

Yefachel. Yahgan guardian spirit.

Yopa. Chibcha narcotic.

Ypa ("Hole Dwellers"). Chaco people.

Yucay (Quechua). Hard gray sandstone.

Yucú. Quechua measurement. Forefinger-thumb span.

Yungas. Bolivian eastern valleys leading down to jungle: people who lived there.

Yurema. Carire drink inducing visions.

Zamuco. Large Chaco race-stock. Four sublanguages.

Zaque. North Chibcha empire and ruler.

Zea Mays (Auraucanian). Maize.

Zipe. South Chibcha kingdom and ruler.

Abridged Bibliography

ACOSTA, JOSÉ DE. *Historia natural y moral de las Indias.* Sevilla, 1590. London, 1880.

AGUIRRE MORALES, AUGUSTO. *El pueblo del sol.* Lima, 1927.

ALARCÓN Y CANEDO, JOSÉ DE, and PITTINI, RICCARDO. *El Chaco Paraguayo y sus tribus.* Turin, 1924.

ALBO, FRANCISCO. *Diario . . . del viaje de Magallanes.* In Navarette Colección. Vol. 4. Madrid, 1837.

ALVAREZ, GERVASSO. *Guia . . . del departamento de Ayacucho.* Ayacucho, 1944.

AMBROSETTI, JUAN BATISTA. *Arqueología Argentina.* Anales del Museo Nacional de Buenos Aires. Vol. 9. Buenos Aires, 1902.

AMEGHINO, CARLOS. *Vocabulario Tehuelche, Tehues, Pampa, Auraucano.* Revista del Museo de la Plata. Vol. 22. Buenos Aires, 1913.

AMEGHINO, FLORENTINO. *La antiguedad del hombre en la Plata.* Paris, 1880.

AMERLAN, ALBERT. *Die Indiane des Gran Chaco.* Globus, Vol. 4. Braunschweig, 1882.

ANGELES, PEDRO. *Colección de obras y documentos . . . provincias del Rio Plata.* 6 vols. Buenos Aires, 1836-7. 5 vols. Buenos Aires, 1910.

APARICIO, FRANCISCO. *Investigaciones arqueológicos en . . . San Luis.* Congreso Internacional de Americanistas. Vol. 21. Göteborg, 1925.

ARNOTT, JOHN. *La Vida amorosa y conjugal de los indios del Chaco.* Revista Geográphica Américana. Vol. 4. Buenos Aires, 1935.

ARRIAGA, PABLO JOSÉ DE. *La extirpación de la idolatría en el Perú.* Colección de libros y documentos referentes a la historia de América. Madrid, 1920.

AZARA, FÉLIX DE. *Voyages dans l'Amérique Meridional.* 4 vols. Paris, 1809.

BACHMAN, CARLOS J. *Departamento de Lambayeque.* Lima, 1921.

BAESSLER, ARTHUR. *Ancient Peruvian Art* . . . 4 vols. Berlin, 1912–3.

BALDUS, HERBERT. *Indianerstudien im nordoestlichen Chaco.* Leipzig, 1931.

BALLIVIÁN, MANUEL VICENTE. *Monumentos prehistóricos de Tiahuanaco.* La Paz, 1910.

—— and CEVALLOS TOVAR, WALTER. *Noticias historicas . . . de la pampa de Bolivia.* La Paz, 1914.

BALLOU LANDA, ALBERTO. *Hombres de la selva.* Lima, 1916.

BANDELIER, ADOLF FRANCIS. *The Aboriginal Ruins at Sillustani, Perú.* American Anthropologist. Vol. 7, New York, 1905.

——. *The Indians and Aboriginal Ruins near Chachapoyos.* New York, 1907. (In Spanish, Lima, 1921.)

——. *The Islands of Titicaca and Koati.* New York, 1910.

——. *The Ruins of Tiahuanaco.* American Antiquarian Society Proceedings. Vol. 21. Worcester, 1911.

BARANDARIÁN, A. LEÓN. *Mitos, leyendas y tradiciones lambayocenas.* Lima, n.d.

BARRETT, S. A. *The Cayapa Indians of Ecuador.* 2 vols. New York, 1925.

BARTONONIO, LUDOVICO. *Vocabulario de la lengua Aymara.* 2 vols. Leipzig, 1879.

BAUDIN, LUIS. *L'Empire socialiste des Inka.* Instituto de Etnología. Vol. V. Paris, 1928. (In Spanish, Santiago de Chile, 1943.)

BEALS, RALPH L., and HOIJER, HARRY. *Introduction to Anthropology.* 2nd ed. New York, 1959.

BEAUVOIR, JOSÉ MARÍA. *Los Shelknam . . . de la Tierra del Fuego . . .* Buenos Aires, 1915.

BELAUNDE, VICTOR ANDRÉS. *El Perú antigua y los modernos sociólogos.* Lima, 1908.

BENNETT, W. C. CHIMÚ. *Archaeology.* Science Monthly. Vol. 45. Washington, D.C.

BETANZOS, JUAN DE. *Suma y narración de los Ingas. . . .* Ms. 1551. Escorial, Spain. Madrid, 1880.

BINGHAM, HIRAM. *The Story of Machu Picchu.* National Geographic Magazine. Washington, Feb. 1915.

——. *Inca Land.* Boston, 1922.

——. *Lost City of the Incas.* New York, 1948.

——. *Machu Picchu. . . .* New Haven, 1930.

BIRD, JUNIUS. *Antiquity and Migrations of the Early Inhabitants of Patagonia.* Geographic Review. Vol. 28. New York, 1938.

BOAS, FRANZ. *Handbook of American Indian Languages.* New York, 1911.

——. *Primitive Art.* Oslo, 1927.

BOMAN, ERIC. *Antiquités de la région andine de la republique de l'Argentine et du désert d'Atacama.* 2 vols. Paris, 1908.

Borgatello, Maggiorno. *Nella terra del fuoco.* 2 vols. Turin, 1921, 1924.

Borja, L. F. *El Indio ecuatoriano.* . . . Quito, 1923.

Bowman, Isaiah. *The Andes of Southern Peru.* New York, 1916.

———. *A Buried Wall at Cuzco . . . a Pre-Incan Race.* American Journal of Science. Vol. 34. New Haven, 1912.

———. *The Canyon of the Urubamba.* American Geographic Society, New York, 1912.

———. *Desert Trails of Atacama.* New York, 1924.

Boyd, William C. *Blood Groups of South American Indians.* Handbook of South American Studies. Vol. 6. Washington, 1950.

Bridges, Thomas. *La Tierra del Fuego y sus habitantes.* Boletín del Instituto Geográfico Argentino. Vol. 14. Buenos Aires, 1893.

———. *Yamaná-Ingles.* A dictionary. . . . Moedling, 1933.

Brüning, E. *Estudios ./. . del departamento de Lambayeque.* Chiclayo, 1922.

Buchwald, Otto von. *Das Reich des Chimus.* Globus, Vol. 95. Braunschweig, 1909.

———. *Tiahuanaco y Cuzco.* Boletín de la Sociedad Ecuatoriana de Estudios Históricos americanos. Quito, 1918.

———. *Migraciones sud-americanas.* Boletín de la Sociedad Ecuatoriana. . . . Quito, 1918.

———. *Los primeros Incas.* Boletín de la Sociedad Ecuatoriana. . . . Quito, 1919.

Bukasor, S. M. *The Potatoes of South America.* Leningrad, 1933.

Cabello de Balboa. *Histoire du Pérou.* Paris, 1840.

Cabeza de Vaca, Alvar Núñez. *Comentario.* Biblioteca de autores españoles (Hernández, Vol. 1). Madrid, 1852.

Caboto, Sebastián. *Confesion.* (In Medina, Vol. II). Madrid, 1908.

Cabrera, Angel, and Yepes, José. *Historia natural ediar: mamíferos sudamericanos.* Buenos Aires, 1940.

Cabrera, Pablo. *Córdoba del Tucumán.* Córdoba, 1932.

———. *Ensayos sobre etnología argentina.* . . . Córdoba, 1911.

———. *Los aborigenes . . . de Cuyo.* Córdoba, 1921.

Caldenius, Carl. . . . *Las glaciaciones cuarternarias en la Patagonia y Tierra del Fuego.* Geografiska Annalar. Stockholm, 1932.

Caldes Aferes, José Augusta. *Vocabulario . . . los Bororos coroados.* Cuiabá, 1899.

Calixto, Benedicto. . . . *Dos Sambaquis de Itanhaen e de Santos.* Revista del Museo Paulista. Vol. 6. São Paulo, 1904.

Camacho, José María. *Urus, Chayos y Atacamas.* Boletín de la Sociedad Geográfica. Num. 66. La Paz, 1943.

Carrera, Fernando de la. *Arte de la Lengua Ynga.* Lima, 1644.

CARRIÓN CACHOT, REBECCA. *La Cultura Chavín*. Lima, 1948.
——. *Paracas*. Lima, 1949.
CASAS, BARTOLOMÉ DE LAS. *De las antiguas gentes del Perú*. 3 vols. México, 1851. Madrid, 1892.
CASTELLANOS, JUAN DE. *Historia del nuevo reino de Granada*. 2 vols. Madrid, 1886.
CHAMBERLAIN, A. F. *Sur quelques families linguisticos*. . . . Journal de la Société Américaniste. Vol. 7. Paris, 1910.
CHARLEVOUX, PIERRE FRANÇOIS XAVIER DE. *Histoire du Paraguay*. 6 vols. Paris, 1757.
CHÁVEZ, OSCAR O. *Huancayo*. Huancayo, 1926.
CIEZA DE LEÓN, PEDRO. *Crónica del Peru*. Sevilla, 1553. Antwerp, 1554. 2 vols. Madrid, 1853, 1862, 1880, 1922.
CLEROT, LEON F. *Os sambaquis de Bahia de Macacú*. Congreso de Americanistas, Rio de Janeiro, Vol. 2. Rio de Janeiro, 1928.
COBO, BERNABÉ. *Historia del neuvo mundo*. 4 vols. Sevilla, 1898-93.
COLLIER, DONALD, and MURRA, JOHN. *Survey and Excavations in Southern Ecuador*. Field Museum of Natural History. Chicago, 1943.
COLÓN, CRISTÓBAL. *Las Relaciones*.
CONTRERAS Y VALVERDE, VASCO DE. *Relaciones de la ciudad de Cuzco*. Madrid, 1855.
COOPER, JOHN M. . . . *Bibliography of the Tribes of Tierra del Fuego and Adjacent Territory*. Bureau of American Ethnology. Bulletin 63. Washington, 1917.
CORNEJO BOURONCLE, JORGE. *Las comunidades indígenas*. Cuzco, 1935.
COTTOW, LEWIS. *Amazon Headhunters*. New York, 1954.
COUDREAUX, HENRI ANATOLE. *Voyage au Xingú* . . . Paris, 1897.
——. *Voyage au Tocatins-Araguaya*. Paris, 1897.
CREQUI-MONTFORT, G. DE. *Fouilles de la mision scientifique française à Tiahuanaco*. Congress of Americanistas. Stuttgart, 1904.
CUERVO MÁRQUEZ, CARLOS. *Estudios arqueológicos y etnográficos americanos*. 2 vols. Madrid, 1920.
DABBENE, ROBERT. *Los Indígenas de la Tierra del Fuego*. Boletín de la Institución Geográfico Argentina. Vol. 25. Buenos Aires, 1911.
DEBENEDETTI, SALVADOR. *Investigacions sobre arqueología de Jujuy*. Jujuy, 1909.
DELGADO, JULIO M. *Follore y apuntes para la sociología indígena*. Lima, 1931.
DEMERSAY, L. ALFRED. *Histoire du Paraguay*. 2 vols. Paris, 1860-64.
DÍAZ DE GUZMÁN, RUL. *Historia argentina*. Rio de Janeiro, 1835-37.
DOERING, HEINRICH. *Old Peruvian Art*. London, 1936.
DOMEYKA, IGNACIO. *Araucania i sus inhabitantes*. Santiago de Chile, 1845.

Domínguez, Manuel. *El Chaco boreal.* Asunción, 1925.

D'Orbigny, Alcides. *L'homme américain.* 2 vols. Paris, 1839.

Douay, Leon. *Contribution à la américaniseme du Cauca.* Berlin, 1890.

——. *Études etnologiques sur l'antiquité américaine.* Paris, 1891.

Eaton, George Francis. . . . *Osteological Material from Machu Picchu.* Connecticut Academy of Arts and Sciences. Vol. 5. New Haven, 1916.

Egiguren, Luís A. *El Ayllu peruano.* Lima, 1914.

Egurende, Larrea, D. F. *El Cusco.* Lima, 1929.

Ehrenreich, Paul Max Alexander. *Über die Puris Ostbrasiliens.* Zeitschrift für Ethnologie. Vol. 18. Berlin, 1886.

——. *Anthropologische Studien* . . . Braunschweig, 1897.

Eichstedt, Egon, Freiherr von. *Rassenkunde und Rosengeschichte der Menschheit.* Stuttgart, 1934.

Ercilla y Zúñiga, Alonso de. *La Araucana.* Madrid, 1569–89. Santiago de Chile, 1910.

Eschwege, Wilhelm Ludwig von. *Journal von Brasilien* . . . 2 vols. Weimar, 1818.

Estete, Miguel de. *La relación del viaje que hizo el señor Hernando Pizarro a Xauxa.* Sevilla, 1534.

——. *El descubrimiento y conquista del Perú, 1535.* Quito, 1918.

——. *Notica del Perú.* Quito, 1916, 1924.

Falcón, Francisco. *Relación sobre el gobierno de los Incas.* Lima, 1918.

Falkner, Thomas A. *A Description of Patagonia.* . . . Hereford, 1774. Chicago, 1935.

Farfan, J. M. B. *Clave de la lengua Quechua.* Lima, 1941–42.

Fasulo, Antonio. *Missioni Salesiani del Patagonia.* Turin, 1923.

Feijóo, Miguel. *Relación descriptiva de* . . . *Trujillo* . . . Trujillo, 1763.

Fernández Cornejo, Juan Adrián. *Expedición al Chaco.* (In Pedro de Angeles, Vol. 16) Buenos Aires, 1836, 1837, 1851–55.

Fernández de Oviedo y Valdés, Gonzalo. *Historia general y natural de las Indias.* 4 vols. Madrid, 1851–55.

Ferreira Penna, D. S. . . . *Os sambaquís do Pará.* Archivo del Museo Nacional. Vol. 1. Rio de Janeiro, 1876.

Figuera, José H. *Los primitivos habitantes del Uruguay.* Montevideo, 1892.

Fitzroy, Robert. . . . *Voyages of* . . . *"Adventure" and "Beagle."* 3 vols. London, 1839.

Flornoy, Bertrand. *The World of the Inca.* New York, 1958.

Fontana, Luís Jorge. *El Gran Chaco.* Buenos Aires, 1881.

Forbes, David. *On the Aymara Indians* . . . Journal of the Ethnological Society of London. Vol. 2. London, 1870.

FORD, JAMES A. *Excavations . . . Cali, Colombia.* Yale University Publications on Anthropology, Num. 31. New Haven, 1944.

FRANCO INOJOSA, JOSÁ MARÍA, and GONZÁLEZ, ALEJANDRO. *Exploraciones arqueológicas en el Perú.* Revista del Museo Nacional de Lima. Vol. 5. Lima, 1936.

FRENGUILLI, JOAQUÍN. *El ambiente geográfico . . . Santiago del Estero.* Relaciones de la Sociedad Argentina de Antropolgía. Vol. 2. Buenos Aires, 1940.

FRIČ, VOJTĚCH A. *Eine Pilcomayo-Reise in den Chaco Central.* Globus, Vol. 89. Braunschweig, 1906.

———. *Die unbekannten Stämme des Chaco Boreal.* Globus, Vol. 96. Braunschweig, 1909.

FRÓES DE ARBEU, SYLVIO. *Sambaquis de Imbituba e Laguna* (Santa Catarina). Revista de la sociedad geografica. Rio de Janeiro, 1928.

GALLARDO, CARLOS R. *Tierra del Fuego.* Los Onas. Buenos Aires, 1910.

GANDIA, ENRIQUE DE. *Historia del Gran Chaco.* Buenos Aires, 1929.

GARCÍA BORERRO, JOAQUÍN. *El Huila ys sus aspectos . . .* Bogotá, 1935.

GARCÍA ROSSELL, CÉSAR. *Los monumentos arqueológicos del Perú.* Lima, 1912.

GARCILASO DE LA VEGA. *El Inca. Comentarios reales de los Incas* (Under various titles). Lisbon, 1609. Madrid, 1722, 1723. Lima, 5 vols. 1918–20.

GARDNER, G. A. *Rock Paintings of Northwest Cordoba.* Oxford, 1931.

GILLEN, JOHN. *Moche. A Peruvian Coastal Community.* Washington, 1945.

GONZÁLEZ DE AGÜEROS, PEDRO. *Descripción de . . . Chiloé.* Madrid, 1791.

GONZÁLEZ HOLGUÍN, DIEGO. *Arte y diccionario qquechua-español.* Lima, 1608, 1901.

GONZÁLEZ SUÁREZ, FEDERICO. *Historia general de la República del Ecuador.* 9 vols. Quito, 1890–93.

———. *Los aborigenes de Imbabura y del Carchi. . . .* Quito, 1908–10.

GUEVARA SILVA, TOMÁS. *Historia de Chile: Chile prehispano.* 2 vols. Santiago, 1925–27, 1929.

GUSINDE, MARTIN. *Die Feuerland-Indianier.* 3 vols. Mödling bei Wien, 1931–37.

GUZMÁN, ARZE, HUMBERTO. *Selva* (fiction). 2nd ed. Cochabamba (n.d.).

GUZMÁN, AUGUSTO. *La Sima fecunda* (fiction). 3d ed. La Paz, 1946.

HARCOURT, RAUL D'. *Le Amérique avant Colomb.* Paris, 1923.

———. *Le Ceramique ancien du Pérou.* Paris, 1924.

HARRINGTON, MARK RAYMOND. *Cuba Before Columbus Came.*

HENRY, JULES. *Jungle People: A Kaingang tribe.* New York, 1941.

HERNÁNDEZ DE ALBA, GREGORIO. *Colombian Archeology.* Bogotá, 1941.

HERNDON, LEWIS, and GIBBON, LARDNER. *Exploration of the Valley of the Amazon.* Washington, 1853.

HERRERA, FORTUNATO L. *Etnobotánico. Plantas tropicales cultivadas por los antiguos peruanos.* Revista del Museo Nacional. Vol. 9. Lima, 1942.

HEWETT, EDGAR L. *Ancient Andean Life.* New York, 1939.

HOLSTEIN, OTTO. *Chan-Chan.* Geographical Review. Vol. 27. New York, 1927.

EL HOMBRE Y EL PAISAJE DE BOLIVIA. (Anthology of leading world writers.) La Paz, 1941.

HRDLIČKA, ALEŠ. *Early Man in South America.* Bulletin Bureau American Ethnology. Vol. 52, Washington, 1912.

———. *Genesis of the American Indian.* International Congress of Americanistas. Vol. 19. 1917.

———. *Skeletal Remains of Man.* New York, 1912.

HUMBOLDT, ALEXANDER VON. *Vues des cordilleras et monuments des peopls indigenes de l'Amérique.* Paris, 1816.

IBAÑEZ, VICTOR M. *Chachapuma (El Hombre León). Imperio Aymara* (Fiction). La Paz, 1919.

IHERING, HERNANN VON. *The Anthropology of the State of São Paolo.* San Paulo, 1906.

IHERING, RODOLPH VON. *Diccionario de animais do Brasil.* São Paulo, 1940.

IMBELLONI, JOSE. *Fuégidos y Láguidos. . . . Lagoa Santa.* Anales del Museo Argentino de Ciencias Naturales. Vol. 39. Buenos Aires, 1937.

IRVING, WASHINGTON. *History of the Life and Voyages of Christopher Columbus.* New York, 1824.

IZIKOWITZ, KARL GUSTAV. *Musical and Other Sound Instruments of the South American Indians.* Göteborg, 1935.

JARAMILLO, ALVARADO PÍO. *El Indio ecuatoriano.* Quito, 1936.

JEREZ, FRANCISCO DE. *La Conquista.* Paris, 1938.

JIJÓN Y CAAMAÑO, JACINTO. *El Ecuador interandino y occidental antes de la conquista castellano.* 2 vols. Quito, 1940–41.

———. *Puraka . . . Provincia del Chimborazo.* 2 vols. Quito, 1927

———. *La religión del imperio de las Incas.* Quito, 1919.

JIMÉNEZ BORJA, ARTURO. *Moche.* Lima, 1937.

JIMÉNEZ DE QUESADO. *Epitome of the Conquest of New Granada.* In Oviedo.

JOYCE, THOMAS A. *South American Archaeology.* London, 1912.

KARSTEIN, RALPH. *La civilisation de l'empire Inca.* Paris, 1952.

KING, PHILIP PARKER. *. . . Voyages of Adventure and Beagle . . . First expedition, 1821–3.* London, 1839.

KOPPERS, WILHELM VON. *Unter Feirland-Indianern*. Stuttgart, 1924.

——. . . . *Yagan und Alakaluf*. Congress of Americanistas. Session 21. Göteborg, 1925.

——. *Mythologie und Weltanschauung der Yagan*. Congress of Inter-americanistas. Göteborg, 1925.

——. *Gottesglaube und Gebete der Yamana auf Feirland*. Religiöse Quellenschriften. Vol. 17. Düsseldorf, 1926.

KROEBER, A. A. *Coast and Highland in Prehistoric Peru*. American Anthropologist Collection. Vol. 29. New York, 1927.

——. *Peruvian Archaeology*. New York, 1944.

LACERDA, FIHLO, and RODRIGUES PEXIOTO . . . *Estudo anthropologico das raças indigenas do Brasil*. Archivos do Museo Nacional. Vol. 1. Rio de Janeiro, 1876.

LACERDA, J. B. DE . . . *Os Sambaquis*. Boletín Comissão Geographco e geologica do estado do São Paulo. São Paulo, 1885.

LAFONE-QUEVADO, SAMUEL A. *Etnografía Argentina*. Ciencias Naturales Antropológicas y e etnológicas. Vol. 2. Santiago de Chile, 1911.

LARCA HOYLE, RAFAEL. *Los Cupisniques*. Lima, 1941. *Los Mochicas*. 2 vols. Lima, 1938–9.

LATCHAM, RICARDO E. *La agricultura preColombiano en Chile*. . . . Santiago, 1936.

——. *La alfería indigena chilena*. Santiago, 1928.

——. *La prehistoria chilena*. Santiago, 1928.

LA VAUX, HENRI. *Voyage a Patagonia*. Paris, 1901.

LEGUIZAMÁN, MARTINIANO. *La cuna del gaucho*. Buenos Aires, 1935.

LEHMAN, WALLER, and DOERING, HEINRICH. *The Art of Old Peru*. New York, 1924.

LEHMANN-NITSCHE, ROBERT. *Mitologia sud americana*. Revista del museo de la Plata. Vol. 24. Buenos Aires, 1918.

LEVI-STRAUSS, CLAUDE. *The Tribes of the Upper Xingu*. Handbook of South American Studies (Steward). Vol. 3. Washington, 1948.

LIMA, PEDRO E. DE. *Grupos Sanguneses dos indios do Xingu*. Boletín do Museu Nacional de antropologia. Num. 11. Rio de Janeiro, 1950.

LISTA, RAMON. *Viaje al pais de los Tehuelches*. Buenos Aires, 1879.

——. *Patagonia*. Buenos Aires, 1880.

——. *Territorio de los misiones*. Buenos Aires, 1883.

LOCKE, L. *The Ancient Quipú*. New York, 1923.

LÖFGREN, ALBERT. . . . *Os samaquis*. Boletín comissianao Geografico y Geologico de São Paulo. São Paulo, 1893.

LOOR WILFREDO. *Los indios de Manabi*. Quito. Saragosa, 1552.

LOPES GOMARA, FRANCISCO. *Historia de las Indias*. n.d. Madrid, 1749, 1849.

LOTHROP, S. R. *Indians of Parana Delta.* Annals of the New York Academy of Science. Vol. 33. New York, 1932.

———. *Indians of Tierra del Fuego.* New York, 1928.

LOUKOTKA, ČESTMIR. *A Grammar and Vocabulary of the Tupi Language.* Revista Trimestral de historia, geografia e ethnografia do Brasil. Vol. 43. Rio de Janeiro, 1880–81.

LOWIE, ROBERT H. *The Bororo.* Handbook of American Studies (Steward). Washington, 1946.

LOZANO, PEDRO. *Historia de la conquista de Paraguay* . . . Biblioteca del Rio de la Plata. Buenos Aires, 1873–74.

LUNARDI, FEDERICO. *El macizo colombiano en la prehistoria de Sur America.* Rio de Janeiro, 1934.

MANGLESDORF, P. C., and REEVES, R. G. *The Origin of Indian Corn and Its Relatives.* Texas Agricultural Experiment Station Bulletin. No. 574. 1939.

MANIZER, HENRI HENRIHOVITCH. *Los Kaingangs de São Paulo.* Congress of Americanistas. New York, 1928.

MARKHAM, CLEMENT ROBERT. *The Inca of Peru.* London, 1910.

MARTIN, RUDOLF. *Altpatagonische Schädel.* Vierteljahrschrift Naturforschenden Gesellschaft. Vol. 41. Zurich, 1896.

MARTIN DE MOUSSY, JEAN ANTOINE VICTOR. *Description géographique et statistique de* . . . *Argentine.* 3 vols. Paris, 1860–64.

McCOWN, THEODORE D. *Incaic Huamachuco* . . . University of California Publications, American Archaeology and Ethnology. Vol. 39. Berkeley, n.d.

MEAD, CHARLES. *Prehistoric Mining in Western South America.* American Museum of Natural History. New York, 1921.

MEANS, PHILIP AINSWORTH. *Ancient Civilizations of the Andes.* New York, 1931. (In Spanish.) Quito, 1919.

MEDINA, JOSÉ TORIBIO. *Descubrimiento del Rio de las Amazonas.* (Including Carbajal's account.) Sevilla, 1894. (In English.) New York, 1934.

———. *Los aborígenes de Chile.* Santiago de Chile, 1882.

———. *El veneciano Sebastián Caboto* . . . 2 vols. Santiago de Chile, 1908.

MÉTRAUX, ALFRED. *La civilisation matérielle des tribus Tupi-Guarani.* Paris, 1928.

MIDDENDORF, E. W. *Peru.* 3 vols. Berlin, 1893–5.

MILANESIO, DOMENICO. *La Patagonia.* Buenos Aires, 1898.

MIÑANO, G. JOSÉ ANGEL. *Las brujas y shapingos de Chicama.* La Nación, June 12–21. Lima, 1942.

MINNAERT, E. *La symbolique des cases des Nazca.* Brussels, 1932.

MOLINA (DE CUZCO), CRISTÓBAL DE. *Fables and Rites of the Incas (1585).* London, 1873.

Monografía de la Diocés de Trujillo. 3 vols. Trujillo, 1930–31.

Montell, Gösta. *Dress and Ornaments in Ancient Peru.* Göteborg, 1929.

Montesinos, Fernando. *Memorias antiquarias historiales del Perú.* (re 1640.) Madrid, 1882. London, 1920.

Morales, Emilio B. *Canals Fueginos.* Buenos Aires, n.d.

Moreno, Francisco P. *El origin del hombre sudamericano.* Anales de la Sociedad Científica de Argentina. Buenos Aires, 1882.

Morillo, Francisco. *Diario del viaje al Rio Bermejo.* Colección de documentos del río de la Plata. Vol. 6. Buenos Aires, 1837.

Morrúa, Martín de. (re 1595) *Historia de los Incas* . . . Lima, 1922–25.

Mortimer, W. Golden. *Peru; History of Coca.* New York, 1901.

Moure, Amédé. *Les indiens* . . . *de Mato-Grosso.* Paris, 1867.

Mualle, Jorge C. *Los valles de Trujillo.* Lima, 1936.

Navarette, Martín Fernández de. *Colecciones de los viajes* . . . *españoles.* 5 vols. Madrid, 1931.

Nimuendajú, Curt. . . . *Religion des Apapocúva-Guaraní.* Zeitschrift dur Ethnologie. Vol. 46. Berlin, 1914.

Nino, Barnardino de. *Ethografía chiriguana.* La Paz, 1912.

Nordenskiöld, Erland. *Copper and Bronze Ages in South America.* Göteborg, 1921.

———. *The Secret of the Peruvian Quipús.* Göteborg, 1925.

Nuñez de Pineda y Basunán, Francisco. *Cautivero Félix.* Santiago, 1673, 1863.

O'Bigny, Alcide d'. *Voyage dans l'Amérique meridionale.* 9 vols. Paris, 1835–47.

Oliva, Juan Anello. (re 1630) *Historia del* . . . *Perú.* Lima, 1895.

Olivas Escudero, Fidel. *Apuntes para la historia de Huamanga.* Ayacucho, 1924.

Olivera, Cézar F. *Datos arqueológicos* . . . Boletín del Instituto de Geografía. Vol. 16. Buenos Aires, 1895.

Ollanta. *Drama Incaica.* Revista del Archivo Nacional. Lima, 1936.

Olmos, G. Leonard. *El Chaco* . . . La Paz, 1929.

Orchard, William C. *Peruvian Gold and Gold Plating.* Museum of the American Indian. New York, 1930.

Ortiz, Fernando. *Cuba primitiva: las razas Indias.* Habana, n.d.

———. *Historia de la arqulogía indocubana.* Habana, 1923.

Outes, Felix F. *Los Querandies.* Buenos Aires, 1897.

———. *Estudios etnográficos.* Buenos Aires, 1899.

Outes, Felix F., and Bruch, Carlos. *Los aborígines de la República Argentina.* Buenos Aires, 1910.

Oyarzún, Aureliano. *Los indios Alacalufes.* Museo de etnología y antropología. Vol. 2. Santiago de Chile, 1922.

PALAVICINO, ENRIQUE. *Artes, juegos y deportes de los indios del Chaco.* Revista Geográfica Americana. Vol. 1. Buenos Aires, 1933.

PARDAL, RAMÓN. *Medicina aborígena americana.* Buenos Aires, 1937.

PAULA SOUZA, GERALDO DE. . . . *Caingangs.* Revista del Museo Paulista. Vol. 10. São Paulo, 1918.

PAULOTTE, OSVALDO. *La Toba . . . del Chaco.* Runa Vol. 1. Buenos Aires, 1948.

PAZ SOLDÁN, JOSÉ. *Geografía del Perú.* Lima, 1943.

PAZ SOLDÁN, MARIANO FELIPE. *Diccionario geográfico estadístico del Perú.* 1877.

PELLESCHI, JUAN. *Eight months in the Gran Chaco . . .* London, 1886.

PETRULLO, V. M. *Primitive peoples of Mato Grosso.* University Museum Journal. Vol. 23. Philadelphia, 1932.

PIGAFETTA. *Magellan's Voyage.* 2 vols. Cleveland, 1906.

PIZARRO, PEDRO. *Relación de descubrimiento y conquista. . . .* Lima, 1917.

POHL, JOHANN EMANUEL. *Reise im innern von Brasilien.* 2 vols. Vienna, 1832–7.

POMPEU SOBRINHO, TH. *Os Tapuias do nordeste.* Revista do Instituto do Ceará. Vol. 49. Ceará, 1935.

POSNANSKY, ARTHUR. *Ein prähistorische metropol in Sud Amerika.* Berlin, 1914.

———. *Tiahuanaco.* La Paz, 1912.

PREUSS, KONRAD THEODOR. *Arte monumental prehistórico.* 2 vols. Bogotá, 1931.

PRICE, WILLARD. *The Amazing Amazon.* New York, 1952.

QUATREFAGES, A. DE. *L'homme fossile de Lagoa Santa . . .* Compte-Rendu de l'Académie des Sciencies de Paris. Vol. 93. Paris, 1879.

QUEVEDO, RAFAEL. *El indio en la región interandina del Ecuador.* Quito, 1938.

RADIN, PAUL. *Indians of South America.* New York, 1942.

RAIMUNDO, ANTONIO. *El Perú.* 6 vols. Lima, 1874–1913.

RANKE, KARL ERNST. *Anthropologische beobachtungen aus Zentralbrasilien.* Munich, 1910

RECLUS, ELISÉE. *Colombia.* Bogotá, 1893.

REGAL, ALBERTO. *Los caminos del Inca en el antiguo Perú.* Lima, 1936.

RESTREPO, VICENTE. *Los Chibchas antes de la conquista española.* Bogotá, 1895.

REYNOLDS (no first name). *Versiones incaicos.* Vol. 1. Santiago de Chile, 1930.

RIVERO, MARIANO E., and TSCUDI, J. D. *Antiquidades Peruanas.* 2 vols. Vienna, 1851.

RIVET, PAUL. *Languas américaines.* (In Meillet et Cohen Les lengues du monde, Vol. 16.) Paris, 1924.

———. *Los elements constitutifs des civilizacions de nordouest e d l'ouest sudaméricain.* Göteborg, 1924.

———. *Los orígenes del hombre americano.* México, 1943.

———. *La race de Lagoa-Santa chez les populations précolumbiennes de l'Équateur.* Paris, 1908.

ROMERO, EMILIO. *El Departamento de Puno.* Lima, 1928.

ROSEN, ERIC VON. *Archaeological Researches on the Frontier of Argentina and Bolivia.* Stockholm, 1904.

ROWE, JOHN HOWLAND. *Absolute Chronology in the Andean Area.* American Antiquity. Vol. 10. New York, 1945.

RYDEN, STIG . . . *Archaeology of the Rio Loa Region.* Göteborg, 1944.

SAAVEDRA, BAUTISTA. *El Ayllu.* La Paz, 1903.

SAENZ, MOISÉS. *Sobre el indio ecuatoriano.* México, 1933.

———. *Sobre el indio Peruano.* México, 1933.

SALMÓN BALLIVÁN, JOSÉ. *Ideario aimara.* 2nd ed. La Paz, 1926.

———. *Por tierras calientes.* La Paz, n.d.

SÁNCHEZ, LUÍS ALBERTO. *Garcilaso: Inca de la Vega.* Santiago de Chile, 1939.

SANCHO DE LA HOZ, PEDRO. *Conquest of Peru* (re 1545). New York, 1917.

SANTA CRUZ PACHACUTI-YANQUI SALCAMAYGUA, JUAN DE. *Relación de antiguedades del Peru.* (Ms. National Library Madrid) Madrid, 1879.

SANTILLÁN, FERNANDO. *Relación del origin . . . de los Incas.* Madrid, 1879.

SANTO TOMÁS, DOMINGO DE. *Arte de la lengua quechua.* Leipzig, 1891.

SARMIENTO DE GAMBOA, PEDRO. *Geschichte des Inkareichs.* Berlin, 1906.

SAVILLE, MARSHALL H. *The Gold Treasure of Sisig, Ecuador.* New York, 1921.

SCHMIDT, MAX. *Indianerstudien en Zentralbrasilien.* Berlin, 1905.

———. *Kunst und Kultur Vom Peru.* Berlin, 1929.

SCOTT, WILLIAM BERRYMAN. *Estudio de etnología brasileira . . . 1900 e 1901.* São Paulo, 1942.

SERRANO, ANTONIO. *Los primitivos habitantes del territorio argentino.* Buenos Aires, 1930.

SERRANO, GLORIA. *Tierras del Kosko.* La Paz, 1939.

SEVER, JACQUES. *Chullpas. . . .* Jornal de la Société des americanistes de Paris. Paris, 1902.

SILVA, E. M. DA. *Blood Groups. . . . Mato Grosso.* American Journal of Physical Anthropology. Vol. 7. Washington, 1949.

SMITH, HERBERT H. *Brazil. The Amazons and the Coast.* New York, 1879.

SQUIER, E. GEORGE. *Peru . . . 1877.*

STADEN, HANS. *Warhaftige Historia . . . Neuenvelt America . . .* Frankfurt am Main, 1925.

STEINEN, KARL CON DEN. *Entre os aborigines do Brasil Central.* São Paulo, 1940.

STEWARD, JULIAN H. (Ed.). *Handbook of South American Indians.* 6 vols. 1946–1950.

STIGLICH, GERMÁN. *Diccionario geográfico del Perú.* Lima, 1922.

STUDART, CARLOS FIHLIO. *Notas historicas sobre os indígenas cearenses.* Revista Trimestre do Instituto do Ceará. Vol. 45. Ceará, 1931.

SWAN, MICHAEL. *The Marches of El Dorado.* Boston, 1958.

TAUNAY, ALFREDO DE ESCRANOGLLE DE. *Entre os nossos indios.* . . . São Paulo, 1913.

———. *Os indios Kaingangs.* Revista do Museo Paulista. Vol. 10. São Paulo, 1918.

TELLO, DEVOTTO RICARDO. *Historia abreviado de Huancayo.* Huancayo, 1944.

TELLO, JULIO. *Antigua Perú.* Lima, 1929.

———. *Arte antiguo peruano.* 2 vols. Lima, 1938.

———. *Introducción a la historia antigua del Perú.* Lima, 1921.

———. *Orígin y desarollo de las civilizaciones prehistóricas andinas.* Lima, 1942.

———. *Wira Kocha Inca I.* Lima, 1923.

TEN KATE, HERMAN F. C. *Sur les cránes de Lagoa-Santa.* Bulletin de la société Royal d'Anthropologie . . . de Paris. Vol. 8. Paris, 1885.

TESCHAUER, CARLOS. *Die Caingang.* Anthropos, Vol. 9, 1914.

TOOR, FRANCES. *Three Worlds of Peru.* New York, 1949.

TRIANA, MIGUEL. *Civilización Chibcha.* Bogotá, 1922.

TSCHOPIK, JR. *Highland Communities of Central Peru.* Washington, 1947.

TSCHUDI, JOHAN JACOB VON. *Travels in Peru, 1838–42.* London, 1847. (In Spanish, Lima, 1922.)

UHLE, MAX. *El Ayllu peruano.* Lima, 1911.

———. *El Reino de Quito.* Boletín del Academia Nacional de Historia. Quito, 1930.

———. *Die Ruine von Moche.* Journal of the Society of Americanistas. Vol. 10. Paris, 1913.

URIEL, GRACÍA J. *Guía Histórica artística del Cuzco.* Lima, 1925.

———. *La Cuestión agraria en el Cuzco.* Cuzco, 1914.

VALCÁRCEL, LUIS. *El Cuzco precolombiano.* Cuzco, 1924.

———. *Historia de la cultura antigua del Perú.* Lima, 1942.

———. *Mirador Indio.* Lima, 1937.

———. *Tempestad en los Andes.* Lima, 1927.

VALDEZ DE LA TORRE, CARLOS. *Evolución de las comunidades indígenas.* Lima, 1921.

VIGNATI, MELCIADES ALEJO. *Las culturas indigenas de Patagonia.* (In Historia de . . . Argentina.) Buenos Aires, 1936.

———. *La pictografía* . . . *de San Luis.* Relaciones de la Sociedad Argentina de Antropología. Vol. 1. Buenos Aires, 1937.

VILLAR CÓRDOBA, PEDRO EDUARDO. *Arqueología Peruana.* Lima, 1935.

VILLARD, GEHAN. *Etuds sur le lac Titicaca et les Indiens Uru.* Lima, 1950–51.

VIRREYRA, ABREÇU. *Origen de la palabra "Patagonia."* Buenos Aires, 1944.

VITORIA, FRANCISCO. *Reelecciones de Indios.* Madrid, 1526–46.

VOIGT, P. F. *Los Guayaquies.* Revista de la Universidad de Buenos Aires. Vol. 15. Buenos Aires, 1911.

WASSEN, HENRY. *The Ancient Peruvian Abacus.* Comparative Ethnographical Studies. Vol. 19. Göteborg, 1931.

WIENER, CHARLES. *Pérou et Bolivie.* Paris, 1888.

WIENER, CHARLES. . . . *Os sambaquis* . . . Archivo del museo Nacional. Rio de Janeiro, 1876.

WIESSE, CARLOS. *Las civilizaciones primitivas del Perú.* Lima, 1913.

WOLF, THEODOR. *Geografía y geología del Ecuador.* Leipzig, 1892.

WORMINGTON, H. M. *Ancient Man in North America.* 4th ed. Denver, 1957

XEREZ, FRANCISCO DE. *Narrative of the Conquest of Peru.* London, 1872.

YABAR PALACIO, LUIS. *El Ayllu de Qquerues.* Revista Universitaria. Cuzco, 1922.

YACOVLEFF, EUGENIO. *Arte primitiva entre los antiguos peruanos.* Revista del Museo Nacional de Lima. Vol. 2. Lima, 1933.

ZAHL, PAUL A. *To the Lost World.* New York, 1939.

ZÁRATE, AGUSTÍN DE. *Historia del descubrimiento y conquista del Perú.* Antwerp, 1555, Madrid, 1853.

ZELADA, M. ALBERTO. *El Kollasuyo.* Sucre, 1937.

Index

Kingsborough, Lord, 68
Kitchen implements, 98
Knoche, Walter, 146
Koch-Grünberg, Theodor, 125, 182, 184, 188–189
Koreans, blood type of, 77
Kroeber, A. L., 200
Kuntur Huasi, 207, 211

Labor forces, Inca, 248
Labrador, José Sánchez, 139
Labrets, 127, 134, 161, 182
Lacandón, 106
Lacerda, J. B. de, 145
Ladrillos, Juan, 119
Lagoa Santa, 48, 81, 82, 83, 144, 145
Láguidos, 84
Lambayeque, 34
Lancón, 208
Languages, 57–60, 66, 75, 77, 80, 126–127, 180
    Araucanian, 120
    Quechua, 103, 233, 238, 247, 254, 257
Lapa de Confins cave, 145
Lapa Vermehla cave, 145
Larco Hoyle, Rafael, 208, 209
Larsen, Helge, 76
Last Hope inlet, 107
Last Hope Island, 41
Latcham, Ricardo, 120
Lautaro, 103
Lebzelter, Viktor, 79
Ledesma expedition, 127
Lehman, Walter, 79
Lehmann, Henry, 196
Lehmann-Nitsche, Robert, 125
Lengua, 127, 129, 130, 134, 137, 138, 140, 141, 142
Lepe, Diego de, 7, 9
Levellier, Roberto, 8
Levo (clan), 123
Lima, road from, 38, 242
Linaloas, 3
Linguistic patterns (see Languages)
Lipán, 74
Lisa, 51
Literature, 102–105, 256–259
Llahuén (strawberry), 121
Llamas, 21, 26, 44, 145, 243, 251, 260
Llanca necklaces, 120
Llautu headdress, 23, 26, 45, 229, 237, 254
Lloque Yupanqui, 223
Lobo de Almada, Manuel da Gama, 184
Locke, Leland, 244
Löfgren, Albert, 145
Loma Alta, 198
Lopes de Souza, 104
Lowrie, Robert H., 148

Lozano, Pedro, 104, 118
Lú palm, 56
Lucumos, 57
Lulé, 127, 129, 136, 140
Lund, Pedro Wilhelm, 71, 145
Luquí (potato), 89, 90

Macacauba, 56
Macambia, 48
Macán, 127
Macanas, 55, 200
Machacalí, 146, 147
Machicuya, 126
Machipero, Lord, 17
Machoni, Antonio, 127
Machu Picchu, 45, 95, 96, 97, 101, 235–237
Maciel, Benito, 159
Macnú, 51
Macrebop, 148
Macú, 190
Macuá, 190
Macuehahua bird eggs, 164
Macuña (poncho), 120
Macundú people, 53
Macushi, 191, 192
Madeira River, 31, 53
Madi oil seeds, 121
Madre de Díos River, 49, 55, 181
Magalhães, Fernando (see Magellan, Fernando)
Magalhaes, Pedro de, 152
Magdalena languages, 180
Magdalena River, 7, 29, 30, 31, 197, 199, 202
Magellan, Fernando, 7, 12–21, 33, 104, 106, 114, 116
Magellan Straits, 30, 33, 36, 41, 107, 112, 114, 115, 119
Magnaghi, 8
Magú, 121
Maguey, 48
Maigará, 160
Maize, 87–88, 121
Malalvigo, 154
Malbalá, 127
Maldonado, Angel, 88, 255
Mama (mother), 223, 238
Mamacona, 252
Mamés (yams), 3
Mamona, 57
Mamoré tributary, 31
Manabí, 97, 99
Manacá, 56
Manão, 181, 182
Manáos, 18, 31, 168
Manchurians, blood type of, 77
Manco Capac, 222, 223, 224, 230
Mancol palm, 56

315